God, Morality, and Beauty

The Trinitarian Shape of Christian Ethics, Aesthetics, and the Problem of Evil

Randall B. Bush

LEXINGTON BOOKS/FORTRESS ACADEMIC
Lanham • Boulder • New York • London

Published by Lexington Books/Fortress Academic
Lexington Books is an imprint of The Rowman & Littlefield Publishing Group, Inc.
4501 Forbes Boulevard, Suite 200, Lanham, Maryland 20706
www.rowman.com

6 Tinworth Street, London SE11 5AL

British Library Cataloguing in Publication Information Available

Library of Congress Cataloging-in-Publication Data

Names: Bush, Randall B., author.
Title: God, morality, and beauty : the Trinitarian shape of Christian ethics, aesthetics, and the
    problem of evil / Randall B. Bush.
Description: Lanham, MD : Fortress Academic, 2019. | Includes bibliographical references and
    index.
Identifiers: LCCN 2019013440 (print) | LCCN 2019013691 (ebook) | ISBN 9781978704756 (Elec-
    tronic) | ISBN 9781978704749 (cloth : alk. paper) | ISBN 9781978704763 (pbk. : alk. paper)
Subjects: LCSH: Values—Religious aspects—Christianity. | Trinity. | Christian ethics.
Classification: LCC BJ1275 (ebook) | LCC BJ1275 .B87 2019 (print) | DDC 241—dc23
LC record available at https://lccn.loc.gov/2019013440

Printed in the United States of America

For Kimberly, Caleb, Casey, and Avery

Contents

Figures

Acknowledgments

Undertaking the present work and bringing it to completion would not have been possible apart from family members, my university, colleagues, and friends who afforded me needed time, resources, encouragement, and constructive feedback throughout the book-writing process. To my wife Cindy, I owe the greatest debt for her confidence in my abilities, her support, her inspiration, and her constant encouragement. My good friend and colleague, Harry S. Poe, has held me accountable and encouraged me in my pursuits. I am grateful to Union University for awarding me a Pew research study grant to help make my project economically feasible. To another Union colleague, C. Ben Mitchell, I want to express appreciation for his positive encouragement after reading my manuscript. I am indebted as well to students in an upper-level course I taught on God, morality, and beauty in the spring of 2016. These students provided valuable feedback on the earliest version of the manuscript. I am grateful to my friend Jason Crowder for reading and reviewing one of my manuscript revisions. His interactions and editorial suggestions were extremely helpful. Also, over the past year, my friend Dennis Murphy carefully and thoroughly read my entire manuscript, interacted with it, gave me lengthy verbal feedback in our weekly meetings, and posed questions that compelled me to expand and to tighten some of my arguments as to make them more comprehensible. Finally, I am grateful to the valuable suggestions and recommendations that the external reviewer for Lexington Books/Fortress Academic made regarding sources that needed to be included in this book.

Preface

The title of this book, *God, Morality, and Beauty: The Trinitarian Shape of Christian Ethics, Aesthetics, and the Problem of Evil*, may suggest that I have tried to "bite off more than I can chew." This indictment would be true if my intention were to give a comprehensive account of all these areas of investigation. Such a task, however, would prove infeasible; and there are already many books currently available that accomplish this task much better than I could hope to do here. The strength of this work thus lies not so much in its offering of totally new and groundbreaking insights into particular axiological, ethical, and aesthetic theories. Nor is it concerned to provide radically new insights concerning the problem of evil. Rather, what it does seek to do is to consider carefully the many interdisciplinary connections that exist *across* these subject areas. Often, paradigms of thinking that are too discipline-specific hamper persons from being able to investigate interdisciplinary connections or to appreciate their significance with any degree of profundity. I therefore intend to undertake an investigation of these connections with a view toward fostering a greater appreciation of how they cohere within a vision of reality that is more holistic than atomistic.

The scope of this book is thus wide-ranging. It attempts to bridge the philosophy of religion with philosophical theology in ways that are inclusive of other areas of existence that human beings consider to be of importance. What are the bridges that connect the physical, chemical, biochemical, psychological, social, political, economic, historical, philosophical, and theological perspectives on the whole of reality that human beings seek to grasp by employing axiological categories? One must move step by step over each of these bridges in order to gain a perspective on the whole. In the philosophical-theological vision I wish to present here, I thus shall attempt to investigate the nature of these bridges and to cross them in order to reveal how an understanding of God as Trinity can provide the most comprehensive vision of value from which all areas of existence and the bridges between them can be contextualized and appreciated.

Abbreviations

Apollod. Epit.	Apollodorus, *Epitome of the Library*
Aristot. Met.	Aristotle, *Metaphysics*
Aristot. Nich. Eth.	Aristotle, *Nicomachean Ethics*
Aristot. Phys.	Aristotle, *Physics*
Aristot. Poet.	Aristotle, *Poetics*
Aristot. Pol.	Aristotle, *Politics*
b. B. Bat. 16a	*Babylonian Talmud, Baba Bathra*
b. Šabb.	*Babylonian Talmud, Šabbat*
b. Sanh.	*Babylonian Talmud, Sanhedrin*
b. Yoma	*Babylonian Talmud, Yoma*
BNW	Aldous Huxley, *Brave New World*
CJ	Immanuel Kant, *Critique of the Power of Judgment*
CW	Carl Jung, *Collected Works*
E/O	Søren Kierkegaard, *Either/Or*
Fre	French
Ger	German
GMM	Immanuel Kant, *Groundwork of the Metaphysics of Morals*
Grk	Greek
Heb	Hebrew

LFA	G. W. F. Hegel, *Lectures on Fine Art*
Midr. Cant	*Midrash Canticles*
Midr. Deut	*Midrash Deuteronomy*
Midr. Exod	*Midrash Exodus*
Midr. Gen	*Midrash Genesis*
Midr. Lev	*Midrash Leviticus*
Midr. Num	*Midrash Numbers*
Midr. Ps	*Midrash Psalms*
Midr. Qoh	*Midrash Qoheleth*
Midr. Ruth	*Midrash Ruth*
MM	Immanuel Kant, *The Metaphysics of Morals*
NA	Francis Bacon, *The New Atlantis*
Ov. Met.	Ovid, *Metamorphoses*
PA	F. W. J. Schelling, *Philosophy of Art*
Plat. Gorg.	Plato, *Gorgias*
Plat. Meno	Plato, *Meno*
Plat. Phaedo	Plato, *Phaedo*
Plat. Phaedrus	Plato, *Phaedrus*
Plat. Rep.	Plato, *Republic*
Plat. Tim.	Plato, *Timaeus*
Ps.–J. Gen	*Targum Pseudo-Jonathan Genesis*
Tg. Neof. Gen	*Targum Neofiti Genesis*
Skt	Sanskrit
ST	Aquinas, *Summa Theologica*

Chapter One

Questions of Value

We assume there is such a thing as value, but we do not often ask *why* it exists or *how we can know* it exists. The fact that we *are* valuing creatures makes us unique among known lifeforms, for no other living thing possesses the human's ability for reflecting on the *meaning* and *purpose* of their existence. How do we account for our capacity to care about existence in some or all of its aspects? Are our perceptions of value *real*, or are they *illusory*? Are our values grounded solely in subjective opinions and tastes, or do they have some basis in objective reality?

Suppose we claim that our ability to value does have an objective basis. Then other questions will likely arise that will complicate our efforts to arrive at satisfactory answers. How do we explain, for instance, such wide fluctuations across the distances of time and space in the world's value systems? Can reasons be found for why people value different aspects of their existence in dissimilar ways? Why do people's opinions vary when it comes to *what* aspects of existence they value most? Why do they place greater value on some aspects but lesser value on other aspects? Should we let the sheer diversity of the ways that we value eclipse the question of *why* we value, or *can* value, anything at all? These questions present us with a compelling mystery worth investigating.

The interrogative "why" drives us to a deeper level of probing that points to a dimension of profundity not easily ignored. Answers to "why" questions are often wide-ranging and are anything but uniform. If, on the one hand, we claim that all values originate solely from the brute facts of tangible existence, then we might be unable to speak of value in any kind of *universal* sense. In this case, one might acknowledge the existence of *values*, but to make the claim that such a thing as *universal value* exists might be considered a step too far. Would it have to be true, then, that all values originate

1

from the kind of brute facts we can ascertain through scientific inquiry? If so, then are we to be left finally with a plurality of conflicting values?

On the other hand, if we make the claim that value originates from God, then we could speak of value as something universal. Still, speaking of value in this way really does little to help us account for why there is a diversity of values in the world—unless, perhaps, we were to blame this diversity on the problem of evil. What is our basis for believing there is such a thing as evil? How do we know what it is? What defines it? How do we distinguish it from good? How do we know we have distinguished it from good correctly? Furthermore, how does the problem of evil and our understanding of it shape our understanding of *who* or *what* God, as the ultimate source of value, might be like?

The above dilemma reveals that value, as a topic of inquiry, can be approached from several angles. Philosophers embark on one angle of approach when they pose the *axiological question*, which is a technical way of asking, "What is important?" The term "axiology" derives from two Greek words: "*axios*" (ἄξιος), meaning "value" or "worth"; and "*logos*" (λόγος), meaning "reasoning about" or "the study of." Axiology, simply defined, refers to the *study of values*. So, how might we even begin to undertake such a study? Should we remain content simply to *describe* the wide array of value-systems that currently exist, or have existed, across our planet? Some thinkers will answer this question affirmatively. Those who do, more than likely, will hesitate to probe further. Nevertheless, answers to the question, "What is important?" can typically lie almost anywhere across the map of existence, and this proves that the axiological question is more easily asked than answered. Answers will vary because philosophers will usually want to argue for the priority of one important thing over another.

Still other theorists, who find a purely *descriptive* approach insufficient, will feel pressed to advance beyond merely descriptive categories to offer *prescriptive* ones. In embarking on this second step, the prescriptive theorist will typically argue that human beings *ought* to value various aspects of existence—some aspects maybe more than others—or that they *should* do so in certain normative ways. Moral philosophers may try to provide valid arguments for advancing to this second step by constructing a reliable bridge. They hope thereby to span the distance between what *is* and what *ought to be*. Similar efforts to bridge the "*is*" with the "*ought*" occur among philosophers of aesthetics who seek to underpin their theories of beauty with theoretical insights that evoke at least some convincing degree of gravitas.

Others, who become discontented with merely descriptive or even prescriptive approaches, may embark on an even more difficult *third* step. This step begins with the profounder question, "Why is there such a thing as value or importance at all?" This question cannot settle for an answer that merely *describes* the values we accord to aspects of the world of particulars—such as persons, places, and things; relationships and associations; or specific goals and ideals toward which we might aspire. The question also probes beyond various attempts of philosophers to *prescribe* value systems that they believe are binding upon their fellow humans. Because this third step invites us to consider value's *ultimate* origin, it compels us to investigate what is *ultimately important* both as a reality that exists and as an object we can know.

"Why is there value?" as an ultimate question will therefore challenge answers that disregard the element of profundity that the question seeks to disclose to human intuition. Nontheists and theists alike, for instance, will sometimes resort to shallow answers; but in doing so, they will have only succeeded in demonstrating how alike they are and what the common ground is that they share. The common ground, I maintain, is their incapacity to tolerate any element of *mystery* that might be mediated through, or identified with, the various value-laden phenomena we experience in our transactions with the tangible world.[1] A more careful investigation, however, suggests reasons why we should not cease struggling with sorts of questions that launch us beyond the tangible into the dimension of the transcendental. "Why is there such a thing as value?" is thus the sort of question that one could label "meta-axiological." The intent of this type of question is to fathom "value itself" or "importance itself." It is this kind of question that I intend to explore in this book.

BEING AND KNOWING AS VALUING

As a field of philosophical inquiry, axiology should remain tied to the two other major branches of philosophy; namely, *ontology* (the study of being) and *epistemology* (the study of how we can know anything). Often, philosophers have viewed axiology through either an ontological lens or an epistemological one, but these manners of viewing have not always held dominance. With the arrival of the Enlightenment in the late seventeenth century—to cite one example—philosophers shifted to viewing *ontology* through the lens of *epistemology*. René Descartes (1596–1650) initiated this shift when, in his famous "*cogito ergo sum*" dictum, he assumed that the category of "knowing" should be promoted to a place prior in importance to the category of "being."[2] This switch in priorities significantly altered the direction of philosophy from that time forward and led increasingly to efforts to approach philosophy in a totally *objective* way. This so-called "objective" approach unfortunately discouraged the use of axiology as a lens for examining ontology and epistemology. Instead, Enlightenment thinkers spun "the myth of value-neutrality."

A quick survey of the history of philosophy reveals, notwithstanding, that axiology has always played an undeniably critical role in shaping philosophers' opinions about ontology and its relation to epistemology. For example, the two-world ontology of Plato (428/427–348/347 BCE) became linked to an epistemological perspective that birthed *skepticism*, for it was the New Academy of Plato that gave impetus to the Skeptical school in the first place.[3] Likewise, the pantheistic views of the ancient Stoics fitted hand-in-glove with the *dogmatic* epistemological approach they advocated.[4] The differences between the Stoics and the skeptics can thus be understood more easily by considering their *axiological* predilections than by assuming that they advanced their respective approaches to ontology and epistemology in a *value-neutral* way. Indeed, the Stoics and Skeptics *valued* the world quite differently; in doing so, they shared one criterion—they did value *something*. But despite sharing this "valuing criterion," the different ways they expressed value in relation to their ontological and their epistemological perspectives profoundly divided them into opposing schools of thought. The same can be said of the axiological presuppositions undergirding the scientific worldviews of the ancient Ionians and the pluralist philosophers.[5] These philosophers were, metaphysically speaking, *materialists* whose predilection for materialism accounts for the scientific type of epistemological approach they favored. Certainly, materialism both supported and was supported by the scientific approach they embraced.

An even broader investigation reveals that philosophers, by espousing their ontological and epistemological positions, have been guilty of smuggling unacknowledged axiological presuppositions through the back doors of their philosophical systems. Only recently have some postmodern approaches begun to tear off the "fig leaves" and uncover the nakedness of these hidden biases as to expose them.[6] Therefore, I believe that using axiology as one lens (among others) through which one can view the whole of philosophy would be a deeply desirable turn. Using an axiological lens does not necessarily require a jettisoning of ontological or epistemological lenses entirely; for we need not adopt a lens of philosophical inquiry that relies exclusively on any one branch of philosophy. What do seem unwarranted, however, are attempts to privilege one lens above all others without justification, or to insist that philosophy must be approached by using *one* lens while excluding all others.

To balance this discussion, I should perhaps cite one example of how the ontological lens was privileged above other epistemological and axiological lenses. One finds this example in medieval philosophy, which became entrapped in dogmatic scholasticism because it had not yet adequately come to terms with challenges that epistemological questions posed to their speculations. Unfortunately, however, the same sort of privileging occurred in modernist philosophy where ontology and axiology were subordinated to *episte-*

mology. Consequently, modernism trapped (perhaps even imprisoned) philosophy in the Cartesian stove. Now, however, we must entertain the new prospect of employing an axiological lens. Using such a lens can help us break free from suffocating ontological and epistemological biases and breathe some fresh philosophical air. An *axiological* approach to philosophical methodology might also help facilitate such an escape. But how do we manage it?

First, adopting an axiological approach to philosophy—or at least tentatively doing so—could reveal ways that dogmatism and bias infect all attempts to privilege one approach over competing approaches. Unacknowledged prejudice can prove formidable when it imprisons and oppresses the mind. *The tyranny of unacknowledged prejudice* perhaps concisely characterizes the condition that such an oppressive imprisonment imposes. The plight of the troglodytes in Plato's cave readily comes to mind. Cavernous ignorance epitomizes the worst kind of imprisonment because those chained to the back wall of the cave are wont to believe they are maintaining objectivity in their methodological approaches when in fact they are basing their approaches wholly on illusory and fleeting shadows. The sort of tyranny of which I speak rears its ugly head everywhere in modern society—in culture, in education, and in politics. The Freudian cure would naturally involve casting those in a state of denial onto the psychiatric couch and wringing their repressed biases from their minds. Not that this action alone would guarantee deliverance from prejudice, but it could at least be a good first start.

We who acknowledge our prejudices up front, on the other hand, may appear very much like the fools Desiderius Erasmus of Rotterdam (1466–1536) speaks of in his satire *In Praise of Folly.* The greatest of all fools in his estimation are those who freely admit they are fools.[7] Erasmus nonetheless intelligently argues that the one who admits he is a fool is a fool of the best sort. If Erasmus is right in his assessment, then perhaps freely acknowledging one's own folly will signal a meaningful first step down the path of wisdom. At least then, one might become more tolerant of the foolishness one detects in others.

Second, an axiological approach to philosophy could help us sort out our prejudices, acknowledge them, and test them. In testing them, we could then ascertain which of them might be justified and which ones might not. There is, after all, no proof that *all* prejudices necessarily require a negative appraisal. No prejudice should be dismissed simply *because* it is a prejudice. Prejudices concomitant with a predilection for the good, for instance, should, if anything, be lauded and encouraged. Related words such as "bias" and "discriminate" could thus stand to be rehabilitated as well and thereby be rescued from their present pejorative status. Indeed, if a person were said to be biased toward the *good*, then to excoriate that person would clearly show wrongheadedness. We surely would not think someone bad who discriminated at a salad bar between bacon bits and *arsenic sprinkles*!

Nevertheless, if the words we employ have happened to acquire too pejorative a meaning so that they fail to communicate as well as they might; then we might search for more value-neutral, alternative terms. For example, in his famous debate with Oxford philosopher Antony Flew (1923–2010), R. M. Hare (1919–2002) spoke, for example, of "bliks." Hare invented the term to classify certain predispositions that could be tested to see whether they were reasonable or not. Everyone obviously has "bliks," Hare maintained— *even atheists have them*. Consequently, any attempt on our part to hide our "bliks" from others will reek of dishonesty. On the other hand, we would not consider the "blik" of an insane individual to be as valid as the "blik" of someone who over time had proved himself to be trustworthy and sane.[8] Not all "bliks," therefore, can be deemed equally acceptable, and this means that we must judge convincingly between acceptable and unacceptable ones before we arrive at a reasonable verdict. What applies to our assessment of "bliks" would then need to be extended to prejudices, biases, and discriminations as well.

THE PERSISTENT VALUE-QUESTION

Most of us go through life believing there is such a thing as reality, so we may not be hard pressed to ask the *ontological question*, "What is?" We think, too, that we can *know* things, though we may not often ask the *epistemological question*, "*How* can we know?" The same oblivious attitude, however, cannot long be maintained regarding the *axiological* question, for this question lies only barely submerged beneath our conscious minds in a way that questions about being and knowing are not. The axiological question also tends to be pushed to the surface of consciousness more by our gut than by our cerebrum. Indeed, numerous physical and psychological states related to the gut have the power to push the question up to the surface of consciousness without warning. For instance, when we get hungry, the question "Where can I find food?" hits us almost automatically. Hunger appears as the most basic need of any life-form for nourishment, though hunger is by no means the *only* need living things experience. The so-called hierarchy of human needs is well known to any student of psychology. Abraham Maslow (1908–1970) identified these as our needs for food, clothing, shelter, social acceptance, sexual fulfillment, and self-actualization.[9]

Maslow assumed that the most basic human needs had to be satisfied before the higher ones. Others, however, have disagreed with the way he ordered the needs—and for good reasons.[10] The value one places on *how*, *when*, *where*, and in *what order* to meet one's needs varies from person to person and from culture to culture. Are higher needs more important than lower ones, or can the reverse be true? Marxist sociologist Ernst Bloch (1885–1977) identified hunger as the most basic of human needs, and he took "bourgeois psychotherapy" to task for being more concerned with persons' mental states than with their physical necessities.[11] What basis, then, did Bloch have for claiming that the human need to satiate hunger should be accorded any greater urgency than the process of self-actualization?

Persons' experiences of deprivation in a specific area of life can shape how they weigh the value of other aspects of their existence. One who has known hunger and homelessness will, predictably, lay greater stress on the importance of acquiring food and shelter. On the other hand, one who has never had to worry about such basic life requirements might show a greater preoccupation with issues of psychological health or social acceptance. Despite these differences, one truth concerning the human condition continually arises; namely, that we rarely find full satisfaction in our present state of existing, whatever that state may happen to be at any given time. In the heat of summer, we long for the cold of winter; when we feel winter's chill, we desire summer's warmth. If for too long we are hard at work, we seek leisure; if we have been too long at leisure, boredom will propel us to look for some diversion.

Common experiences of deprivation therefore always incentivize us to ask, "What is important?" However, as I have already indicated, not as many proceed to ask the meta-axiological question, "Why do we believe that there is such a thing as *value* at all?" When asked, for example, "Why is there hunger?" persons will typically respond with immediate or proximate kinds of answers. Such answers usually concern hunger's physical causes. "Why is there hunger?" for instance, might garner the answer that hunger as a phenomenon is purely a matter of chemistry and biology. While this may be partly true, biochemistry fails sufficiently to explain *why* physical hunger is experienced as something *more* than biochemical. An additional ingredient appears; namely, that we *value* a biochemical process in a way that this process cannot value itself. Our ability to value a biochemical process thus adds a further *context* that is missing from *mere* biochemical reactions.

Another proximate kind of answer to the question, "Why is there hunger?" may underscore causes that are socio-economic or political. These causes, of course, often do block people from obtaining food. Socio-economic and political causes are nonetheless *not ultimate*. They merely reveal ways that human failures of a social and political nature *exacerbate* the problem of hunger. Such causes do not yet account for why humans can experience hunger as a value-negating phenomenon in the first place. Few, it seems, venture beyond immediate or proximate kinds of answers to ponder ultimate reasons for why hunger as a reality gnaws at the under-timbers of our existence. Usually, questions of an ultimate nature do not occur to us unless we just happen to be confronted by *unexplained evil.*

When evil touches us—especially irrational or radical evil—satisfactory answers will typically elude our grasp. Indeed, a failure to explain the existence of radical evil impelled certain twentieth-century Existentialists to accept *the absurd* as the normative state of things. Thinkers such as Jean-Paul Sartre (1905–1980) and Albert Camus (1913–1960) experienced the numerous horrific evils that attended the two world wars and the Holocaust.[12] Their experiences of absurd evil produced in them both resignation and protest, while the proposition "God exists" became for them a *non sequitur.* Why, then, does atheism seem to some a more viable option than theism? Atheistic protest arises, after all, out of the conviction that such phenomena as good and evil do, in fact, exist.

Still, despite the attraction some feel toward protest atheism, religion will persist in playing a central role in humanity's effort to process the problem of good and evil. Most world religions and philosophical paradigms have at their core these central axiological concerns. Nevertheless, nontheists will no doubt continue as well to challenge religiously based perspectives, for the solutions and strategies these perspectives offer for actualizing good and diminishing evil have not only varied greatly, but sometimes they have also been contradictory. Such variations and contradictions that are of a theoretical nature only make the requirement that we further explore the subject of axiology more compelling.

Concerns of an existential and practical nature also require a further exploration of the subject of axiology. Most people are disconcerted, for instance, when they are forced to choose between the "lesser of two evils" or the "greater of two goods." In fact, to think that only *two* evils or *two* goods exist for us to choose between at any given time is itself incorrect, for goods are multiple just as evils are multiple. Indeed, the many ways we are bounded by finitude as we endeavor to actualize good and minimize evil further confounds our attempts to grapple with the axiological question. Obstacles such as our physical and intellectual abilities and skills, our prior obligations, and our present commitments and duties are enumerative of the ways that finitude restricts us from doing good. External obstacles can deter us, such as great distances between geographical locations, natural catastrophes, and limited material resources. Time constraints also limit the number of goods we can achieve. Because these and other kinds of obstacles restrict us in multiple ways, we constantly must strategize to determine what is the best course of action for exercising an effective stewardship of our talents, gifts, abilities, and resources.

THE MORAL AND THE BEAUTIFUL AS
SUBDIVISIONS OF AXIOLOGY

Traditionally, the fields of *ethics* and *aesthetics* have combined to form the broader discipline of philosophy known as *axiology*. Ethics engages in the study of and rationalization for human morality. Morality is concerned with restrictions that govern human behavior in relation to various aspects or dimensions of life. Ethics is tasked, as well, with the fostering of positive virtues and imperatives that regulate how we ought to live and act in relationship to all of life's aspects or dimensions. We can think of ways that ethical concerns govern the whole range of existence—from personal motivations, to human relationships, to the larger world, and ultimately to God.

Environmental ethics, for example, aims at upholding proper human stewardship of the earth's physical resources. Bioethics seeks warrants for how human beings should or should not treat and use biological life. Controversial bioethical topics today include the practice of abortion, embryonic stem-cell research, cloning, gene editing, and euthanasia; while future technological possibilities such as transhumanism and neural lacing even now have become topics of bioethical concern. Ethics touches, as well, on the psychological dimension of human existence. How should we treat other people and properly relate to them? Ethics, moreover, provides direction for the field of economics. On the smaller scale is the field of business ethics. On the larger scale, ethicists seek to ascertain what is the proper role of governments in facilitating certain types of human economic activity that advance humanity's greater good while restricting those activities that fail to do so. As it relates to broader cultures, ethics evaluates and seeks to justify rationales for war and peace as well as policies governing international relations. Ethics also informs the religious dimension. All the major world religions promote ethics, though they may disagree on what types of human behavior are or are not permissible, and why.

Ethics, as a branch of philosophy, therefore cuts across all these dimensions of human life and the relation of human beings to the total reality of the world and ultimately to God. By contrast, the field of aesthetics, which serves as a counterbalance to the field of ethics, engages in the exploration of the dimensions of the beautiful and the sublime. This branch of axiology is, perhaps, not as clear-cut in its *raison d'être* as ethics, but it is just as important because it entails the human quest for happiness. In aesthetics, we often face the question, "What is the *point* of the beautiful?" Beauty to some can seem pointless, but this opinion does not lessen its importance or suggest that we can jettison it without suffering deleterious consequences to our ultimate well-being. Aesthetics raises the question of the beautiful, not only regarding *what* is beautiful, but also regarding *why* we believe there is such a thing as beauty. Furthermore, as ethics intersects all areas of life, so does aesthetics.

A sunset, a butterfly, or glittering crystals inside a geode may strike us as beautiful, but why? Mathematicians speak of mathematical proofs as "beautiful,"[13] but what basis do they have for saying so? Biologists observe the beauty of something as simple as a cell under the microscope, but how are they able to recognize beauty in a cell? In attempts to explain why beauty exists, some biologists have theorized that plants and animals, in their interrelation to one another, apprehend beauty to some extent; but is the function of beauty in such cases purely *utilitarian*? Certain evolutionary biologists, for instance, may theorize that a flower evolved as it did because pollinating insects preferred it to other less attractive flowers. But pollinating insects are not the only creatures capable of recognizing beauty in a flower, if indeed they do at all. People in the flower business are glad that human beings also recognize the beauty of flowers because their livelihood depends on it! Likewise, one may attempt to explain the function of beauty in the development of various animal species. The feathers of the male peacock seem to have the utilitarian function of attracting a female; but human beings can recognize the beauty of peacock feathers as well. Why is this possible?

Architects like to build beautiful buildings and homes. Of course, one may imagine the motivation again to be purely utilitarian—they do this for the money! This does not explain, however, why their clientele prefers beautiful buildings to ugly ones. We decorate our homes with paintings and flower arrangements. Not only do these have no obvious utilitarian purpose, but they also collect dust. We use spices to make our food more palatable, we use spices; but these may be unnecessary from a nutritional standpoint (though some spices have been shown to have a medicinal advantage). We adorn sexual activity with beauty through the accoutrements of romance like St. Valentine's Day or wedding anniversary cards, flowers, perfume, music, candlelight, moonlight, cruises, etc. Why, then, are these accoutrements considered desirable?

For the most part, we are at a loss to give a reason for the desirability of any of the above phenomena aside from the fact that they are in themselves pleasurable to experience. The world is filled with beautiful things,[14] and human beings are capable of apprehending and appreciating them. Because we can appreciate beauty, the question of the beautiful relates to the greater axiological question that is concerned with the meaning of everything. Why are we here in this world? What meaning can our being here possibly have?

THE MORAL AND THE BEAUTIFUL:
INTERSECTIONS AND CONFLICTS

Sadly, the treatment of axiology, in the American academy at least, tends at present to be one-sidedly focused on ethics.[15] This phenomenon is doubtless cultural and can be traced back to the Reformation in its Calvinist phase. In Puritanism, the aesthetic dimension was sacrificed in favor of the ethical dimension. Puritanism exerted an enormous influence on the initial formation of American culture, and its residual effects can be observed even up to the present day. Hans Urs von Balthasar traces the Protestant version of "the elimination of aesthetics from Theology" ranging from Martin Luther (1483–1546) in the sixteenth century to Rudolf Bultmann (1884–1976) in the twentieth century. There are, of course, other examples of the conflict between those who emphasize ethics and those who emphasize aesthetics. What often is not considered, however, is the way that these two branches of axiology do and should intersect. Through the pages that follow, I will thus try to rediscover these points of intersection as well as to uncover reasons for the conflicts between them.

What clearly is needed is an approach that does not segregate ethics and aesthetics into airtight categories but seeks to understand how they are, and should be, interconnected. Throughout my investigation, I intend to consider as many of the dimensions of human existence as possible by considering tangible reality, transcendental reality, and all that lies between the two. Because I later will employ a theistic perspective to contextualize my findings, I want to demonstrate how ethics and aesthetics can be linked most effectively by a theologically-informed philosophical approach. In trying to achieve this aim, I also want to try to bridge the philosophy of religion with philosophical theology. The work is, therefore, not intended to be one that takes *either* a purely philosophical approach *or* a purely theological one. What I hope to do is to bridge these two approaches so that the reader may gain a more comprehensive picture of how the realities of God, value, morality, and beauty can and should be interrelated. As I do this, I hope to elucidate further the question of "value itself" with the hope that the reader may gain from my investigations a profounder appreciation of the topic.

NOTES

1. Philosopher Dale Tuggy, for instance, uses his analytic method to cut away all mystery and incomprehensibility regarding the doctrine of the Trinity. He coins the unfortunate and somewhat pejorative term "mysterian" to refer to anyone who allows mystery to creep into Trinitarian doctrine. Unfortunately, his elevation of the analytic method lands him in unitarianism, which causes him to stand well outside the mainstream of Christian orthodoxy. Tuggy, *What Is the Trinity: Thinking about the Father, Son, and Holy Spirit* (n.p., 2017), 95–111.

2. René Descartes, *Meditations on First Philosophy*, trans. Ronald Rubin, in *A Guided Tour of René Descartes' Meditations on First Philosophy* (Mountain View, CA: Mayfield, 1989), 24–25. James Sire has made this point in, "Preface to the Fifth Edition," *The Universe Next Door* (Downers Grove, IL: IVP Academic, 2009), 9–10.

3. Karsten Friis Johansen, *A History of Ancient Philosophy: From the Beginning to Augustine*, trans. Henrik Rosenmeier (London: Routledge, 1998), 471–83.

4. David Sedley, "The Protagonists," in *Doubt and Dogmatism: Studies in Hellenistic Epistemology,* ed. Malcolm Schofield, Myles Burnyeat, and Jonathan Barnes (Oxford: Oxford University Press, 1980), 1–17.

5. Daniel W. Graham, *Explaining the Cosmos: The Ionian Tradition of Scientific Philosophy* (Princeton, NJ: Princeton University Press, 2006), 260, 302–3. Ionians used the Greek word "*historia*" (ἱστορία) for "science."

6. See, for example, Frederick Ferré, *Being and Value: Toward a Constructive Postmodern Metaphysics* (Albany: State University of New York Press, 1996); Ferré, *Knowing and Value: Toward a Constructive Postmodern Epistemology* (Albany: State University of New York Press, 1998); Ferré, *Living and Value: Toward a Constructive Postmodern Ethics* (Albany: State University of New York Press, 2001).

7. Desiderius Erasmus, *In Praise of Folly* (London: Reeves & Turner, 1876), 184–87.

8. R. M. Hare, *Essays on Religion and Education* (Oxford: Clarendon, 1998), 37–38.

9. Abraham Maslow, *Motivation and Personality* (New York: Harper, 1954), 97–104.

10. Mahmoud A. Wahba and Lawrence G. Bridwell, "Maslow reconsidered: A review of research on the need hierarchy theory," in *Organizational Behavior and Human Performance* 15, no. 2 (1976): 212–40.

11. Ernst Bloch, "Hunger, 'Something in a Dream', God of Hope, Thing-For-Us," in *The Frankfurt School on Religion: Key Writings by the Major Thinkers*, ed. Eduardo Mendieta (New York: Routledge, 2004), 62; see also Bloch, "Marx and the End of Alienation," in *The Frankfurt School*, 78.

12. Robert Solomon, *Dark Feelings, Grim Thoughts: Experience and Reflection in Camus and Sartre* (Oxford: Oxford University Press, 2006), 5.

13. Bertrand Russell, "The Study of Mathematics," in *Mysticism and Logic and Other Essays* (London: Longman, 1919), 60.

14. See, for example, Thomas Dubay, *The Evidential Power of Beauty: Science and Theology Meet* (San Francisco, CA: Ignatius Press, 1999). Dubay speaks of "macromarvels, midmarvels, and micromarvels" in his discussion of the ranges of beauty (129–80).

15. As Jerrold Levinson states, "Recent developments aside, for the past thirty years or so in Anglo-American philosophy, ethics and aesthetics have been pursued in relative isolation, with aesthetics being generally regarded as the poorer, if flashier, cousin" (*Aesthetics and Ethics: Essays at the Intersection*, ed. Jerrold Levinson [Cambridge, UK: Cambridge University Press, 1998], 1).

Chapter Two

An All-Encompassing Compass of Value

"FROM DAWN TO DECADENCE": ACKNOWLEDGING THE PROBLEM OF CULTURAL DECLINE

Plato related the Form of "the Good" to the *ethical* and distinguished it from the Form of the "Beautiful." He nonetheless perceived the Good, the True, and the Beautiful as fundamentally linked.[1] St. Augustine (354–430 CE), taking his cue from Neoplatonism, also alluded to these three Transcendentals but never viewed them in isolation from each other.[2] From the period of late classical antiquity until the early modern period, belief in a transcendental basis that could both support and unite ethical and aesthetic truth remained high. However, as this belief faded in the West with the advent of modernity, the unifying basis for the dimensions of the ethical and the aesthetic became increasingly centered in human reason. Colin Gunton, in his 1992 Bampton Lectures, states,

> God was no longer needed to account for the coherence and meaning of the world, so that the seat of rationality and meaning became not the world, but the human reason and will, which thus *displace* God or the world. When the unifying will of God becomes redundant, or is rejected for a variety of moral, rational and scientific reasons, the focus of the unity of things becomes the unifying rational mind.[3]

Modern philosophers have not seemed terribly alarmed over the jettisoning of God and the Transcendentals despite its having resulted in an impoverishment of the human spirit, cultural bankruptcy, moral confusion, ideological deception, and the triumph of ugliness. Jacques Barzun (1907–2012), in his book *From Dawn to Decadence*, traces the cultural history of the West from 1500 to the present and described at length the phenomenon of the West's cultural decline.[4] Sadly, Western culture has for some time now stood at a critical juncture. Some philosophers, instead of owning as their calling the task of providing wisdom to escape the malaise, continue guiding us down pathways that portend even further decay.[5] They champion nihilism as an end to be "hoped" for; and in doing so, they have not come up short in suggesting new ways to achieve this end.[6] With regard to the dimension of the ethical, Dallas Willard observes the role played by nihilism in what he calls "the disappearance of moral knowledge."[7] The abandonment of transcendence in favor of nihilism has adversely affected the field of aesthetics as well, as Alejandro García-Rivera comments,

> A world that knows the Holocaust has little use of the transcendentals. What is Truth under the gallows of Auschwitz? Indeed, what is Good? Only now are we experiencing the full force of the nihilism unleashed in the misery of two world wars. Our contemporary nihilism, more importantly, is already at work in destroying a belief in Beauty itself.[8]

The loss of our culture's link with the Transcendent has led not only to ethical and aesthetic impoverishment; but it has, as well, resulted in a *cleavage* between the ethical and aesthetic dimensions of human existence that has only widened over the past several centuries. Even now a gaping nihilistic chasm is further deepening as resistance to a recovery of a Transcendent basis for the dimensions of the moral and the beautiful persists. Regrettably, as this chasm widens its jaws, too many seem mindlessly poised on its brink, ready with almost gleeful abandon to dive in and be devoured by it. The future prospect for our culture thus appears increasingly grim, especially if we remain content to continue along our current trajectory.

Reversing this ethical and aesthetic impoverishment, and bridging the cleavage between the ethical and aesthetic dimensions, should therefore concern us in a major way; but how shall we accomplish these objectives? A number of avenues have been suggested. As pertains to ethics, Robert Adams advocates a Platonic framework in which he seeks to recover a concept of the *transcendence* of the *infinite Good*.[9] In describing his project, he favorably speaks of his approach as theistic.[10] He nonetheless also calls his approach *economic*, which unfortunately renders his theism more minimalistic than may be necessary. Emmanuel Levinas is another who suggests a way to restore transcendence to the dimension of the ethical in his book *Totality and Infinity*.[11] Levinas rejects efforts of metaphysicians such as G. W. F. Hegel (1770–1831), who allowed transcendence to be "reabsorbed into the unity of the system, destroying the radical alterity of the other."[12]

Not everyone, however, has been satisfied with the one-sidedness of Levinas's focus on ethics. Does transcendence and infinity have anything to do with the dimension of the beautiful as well? Failure to include the category of the beautiful in the modern search for transcendence has led increasing numbers of scholars to suggest ways forward that seek to restore the transcendent dimension to *aesthetics*. For instance, Hans Urs von Balthasar, in his pioneering aesthetic theological work *The Glory of the Lord*, developed an impressive Christian theology in the light of the third transcendental—viz., the *Beautiful*.[13] David Bentley Hart, coming from an Eastern Orthodox perspective, has impressively investigated the topic of transcendent beauty in his work *The Beauty of the Infinite*.[14] Stephen John Wright has recently explored a theology of beauty in his dialogue with Lutheran and ecumenical theologian Robert Jenson.[15] Even more recently, Jeremy Begbie has taken up the topic as well in his work *Redeeming Transcendence in the Arts*;[16] and Jonathan King, coming from a Reformed theological perspective, has investigated the concept of beauty in relation to the doctrine of the Holy Trinity in the thought of Anselm of Canterbury, Thomas Aquinas, Herman Bavinck, and Karl Barth.[17] These works, along with others referred to within their pages, provide valuable insights into why the topic of transcendent beauty is receiving renewed attention.[18]

Clearly, there is a need to recover the transcendent basis of both ethics and aesthetics and to do so in a way that joins them rather than dividing them into separate airtight categories. My aim in this book is thus to find ways to *reconnect* the dimension of the transcendent with *both* the dimensions of the *moral* and the *beautiful*. By so doing, I hope also to suggest ways that these two dimensions can be brought into a relationship with one another that overcomes conflict and aims at achieving harmony and equilibrium. To accomplish these objectives, however, I must identify places where cultural values have deteriorated. Next, I shall try to expose the causes of their deterioration. Finally, I shall try to chart a way forward that will foster a reversal of their deterioration and bring about their restoration. I shall try to accomplish these objectives, first, by using a tool that I here will call "the value-compass."

THE NEED FOR A VALUE-COMPASS

If we happen to be lost in a dense wood, then using a geographical compass can help us find our way. Similarly, what may be called an "axiological compass" or an "all-encompassing compass of value" can help us orient ourselves with regard to the "forest" of values. What, then, would comprise the features of a "value-compass"? I suggest that the face of such a compass would include, first of all, four clearly marked cardinal *axiological* directions. We could label these directions *the transcendental, the tangible, the liberating,* and *the limiting.* Second, the needle on a value-compass would require "magnetic alignment" to the "true north of value," but what axiological point on this compass would best represent this "true north"?

COMPONENTS OF THE VALUE-COMPASS

The cardinal directions of a value-compass may be proposed as follows:

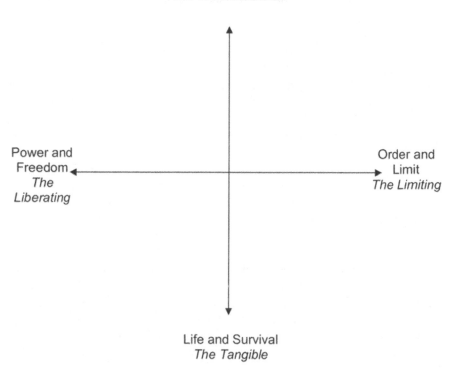

Meaning and Purpose
The Transcendental

Power and Freedom
The Liberating

Order and Limit
The Limiting

Life and Survival
The Tangible

Figure 2.1.   The Value-Compass.

The *transcendental* direction, which points to the dimension of the Divine, entails *meaning* and *purpose* as two interrelated categories. At the opposite point of the compass stand two other interrelated classifications—*life* and *survival.* These represent ways that we navigate the concrete dimension of existence by either affirming *positive* tangible values or by seeking to overcome *negative obstacles* that threaten tangible values. The left and right points of the compass represent two other opposing directions that humans always consider to be of value; viz., the *liberating* and *limiting* directions, respectively. These, in turn, correlate with two sets—one *individual* and the other *collective*. With respect to the *individual* set, the liberating direction entails *self-affirmation*; and the limiting direction entails *self-restraint*. I will refer to these as *freedom* and *limit*, respectively. The other set, which pertains to the liberating and limiting points in their *collective* aspect, correlates with ideas of collective *affirmation* and collective *restraint*. Collective affirmation corresponds to *power* and collective restraint to *order*.[19]

To elaborate further, I propose that *power* and *freedom* both operate as modes of *affirmation*. I shall simply call these "*yes*" values. Opposite these modes are *order* and *limit*. As modes of *restraint*, they can be called "*no*" values. Understanding the dialectical relationship between the *individual* and the *collective* is also crucially important; because within the individual-collective dialectic, the left and right points of the compass also come into play. We thus expect to find dialectics operating within dialectics as well as in tandem with one another. I suggest that we cannot, for this reason, take any of the four compass points in isolation from any of the others.

Tangible Values—Life and Survival

The tangible point of the compass represents the dimension where we experience the *fragility* and *vulnerability* of life, as Paul Ricoeur (1913–2005) has described so well in his discussion of "fragility" and "the flaw" in his work *Fallible Man*.[20] In the presence of this vulnerability and juxtaposed to it is life's *tenacity* with its drive to *survive* and to *flourish*. Again, "no" and "yes" values appear in the way we relate to the tangible dimension. Though they seem opposite, these values are not mutually exclusive. Children, for example, will usually experience the word "no" as *disagreeable*; and the word "yes" as *agreeable*. Life experiences, however, eventually teach us that negatives sometimes have a beneficial purpose, while positives sometimes harbor evils that we would do best to avoid.

Our fragility and vulnerability make us all too aware of the "no" values. Negative threats to our physical existence include scarcity of food, lack of protection from the elements, disease, old age, and the certainty of death. Tenacity, on the other hand, furnishes evidence of our persistence in affirming the "yes" values despite and even because of these threats. Human beings are inexplicably driven to thrive and to flourish. In so doing, we aim to achieve what Aristotle termed "happiness" or *eudaimonia*.[21] Because our physical bodies are composed not of titanium but of flesh and blood, we experience fragility; but the sheer fact of fragility alone does not suffice to make us aware of the *value* our fragile existence holds, or the *negation* of value that the threats to our existence portend. Computers, as fragile pieces of equipment, prove vastly superior to humans in memory capacity and computational ability, but no convincing evidence is there to prove that computers are capable of *valuing* their abilities in the ways humans do. Computers certainly cannot experience grief or a sense of loss when their hard drives crash! Philosophers John Searle (1932–) and Richard Swinburne (1934–) have argued in this vein that computers can *simulate* experiences, but they cannot *duplicate* them. There is simply no proof that they can have *private experiences* like the ones of which human beings are capable.[22]

Our capacity to be aware of our fragility both mentally and emotionally makes us different from computers; for while computers remain unaware of their fragility, humans are keenly aware of theirs. Humans possess a unique ability to experience vulnerability and know it *as such*. *Pain* especially makes us cognizant of our vulnerability by serving as a rudimentary *value-indicator*.[23] Pain functions as an indicator of negative values such as *need* and *injury*, but pain also begs for the *alleviation* of need and a *recovery* from injury. Our ability to experience pain proves that we think of need and injury not as value-neutral phenomena but as value-laden threats that we must surmount.

Pain hurls into our mental and emotional awareness our experiences of need and injury. Through it, we become conscious of a condition that Ricoeur calls the "*pathétique* of misery."[24] Pain, at the biological level, serves to warn us of the negation of a value—in this case, pain warns of an impending negation that threatens the *survival* of ourselves as *biological* organisms. *Survival*, as one side in the "survival-life" pair on our compass of value, also has as its objective the *alleviation* of pain and the *restoration* of the balance of *life* (with *life* comprising the other member belonging to this pair). However, in affirming the importance of *life*, we are usually dissatisfied with staying in a holding pattern or maintaining a state of *mere* equilibrium for very long. The absence of pain alone may entail a temporarily satisfactory state; but when boredom sets in, the absence of pain no longer proves gratifying enough. For this reason, our affirmation of *life* usually aims at a *telos* entailing *something more* than just our experience of the *absence* of pain; this *telos* normally entails, as well, our desire to experience *pleasure* and *enjoyment*. *Pleasure*, as the other rudimentary value-indicator, contains a *positive* affirmation of the value of life. In this respect, pleasure stands as the counterbalance to the *negative* rudimentary value-indicator, *pain*. Following our earlier recognition of the "no" and "yes" values that concern tangible existence, we thus find that the "no" value is conveyed by pain and the "yes" value by pleasure.

To clarify further, I suggest that we now try to correlate *pain* and *pleasure* with a revision that turns the Platonic doctrine of the Innate Ideas on its head. The insights of utilitarian philosopher Jeremy Bentham (1748–1832)regarding pleasure and pain as elements of his "happiness calculus" helps us achieve this clarification.[25] Though Plato spoke of the Innate Ideas,[26] and Augustine of the Eternal Objects,[27] both assumed that these were situated in the *mind* rather than in the *senses*. The situated-ness of the Innate Ideas in the mind, however, means that they are dislocated to too high a degree from the dimension of tangible existence. This dislocation is evidenced by Platonic dualism, which persistently views the dimension of the tangible in a less than favorable light. Pain and pleasure, on the contrary, are more innately, intimately, and immanently ingrained in the human senses than the Platonic Ideas are in the mind. Pain and pleasure are already present *before* the more reflective capacities of the human mind ever engage. Bentham understood this to be true of pleasure and pain. However, to avoid taking the empiricist-utilitarian doctrine of the mind as a blank tablet (tabula rasa) too far by applying it too exclusively to sense experience, I must clarify that pain and pleasure *are not learned* but are *givens* ingrained within the very fabric of biological life *before* any philosophical reflection upon our experience of them can be undertaken. No one needs to *teach* the baby *how* to cry or to coo: These responses, being innate, arise *naturally*.

Transcendental Values—Purpose and Meaning

Moving on to the *transcendental* direction of the compass, I suggest *purpose* and *meaning* as a second pair of related concepts. These stand at the opposite end of the spectrum from the tangible categories of *survival* and *life*. Purpose and meaning, however, need not exclude the survival-life point of the compass, for these transcendent categories can already be detected in specific ways in which our tangible experiences become open to the Infinite. Consequently, pain and pleasure, as rudimentary value-indicators, may be rooted in our experience of the tangible dimension of experience, but they need not be restricted to this dimension. Indeed, they already link up with our pursuit of purpose and our quest for meaning to the extent that we can, even in very tangible ways, find *meaning* in pleasure and *purpose* in pain. Of course, finding purpose in pleasure and meaning in pain is not entirely off the table. Otherwise, there would be neither hedonists nor masochists. Accordingly, not all pleasure is *necessarily* meaningful, and not all pain is *necessarily* purposive. Too many counterexamples exist for these claims to hold true. In particular, *libertarian freedom*, as a human capacity, runs counter to necessity and accounts for why purpose and meaning often appear ambiguous in the ways they relate to pain and pleasure as rudimentary value-indicators.

While *survival* and *life* constitute our responses to negative and positive values embedded in tangible experience (i.e., pain and pleasure), *purpose* and *meaning* link respectively to what I shall call the "no" and the "yes" in our experiences of the *Transcendent*. Rudolf Otto (1869–1937) famously expresses this double aspect of the Transcendent in his classic work, *The Idea of the Holy*. He uses the Latin phrase *mysterium tremendum et fascinans* to characterize the double mystery of the Holy that *incites fear* and *elicits fascination* in the human being.[28] With the *tremendum*, the Holy evokes a negative emotion; with the *fascinans*, it evokes a *positive* one.[29]

Ethical and *aesthetic* concerns also run the gamut of our experiences of value ranging between the dimensions of the transcendental and the tangible. Plato was wrong for this reason to locate the Good and the Beautiful *solely* in the world of the Forms.[30] Aristotle and Plotinus (203–270 CE) instead relate these concerns to the *sensible* as well as to the *intelligible* capacities.[31] At least these two philosophers relate the moral and the beautiful to *sensibility* insofar as the senses function as the vehicles through which we initially apprehend the dimension of the tangible as a dimension containing value.

To elucidate more precisely how ethics and aesthetics relate to the transcendental direction of the compass, I suggest here 1) that the aspect of the *ethical* relates more to a *transcendental purpose* as it impinges upon the tangible dimension of existence, and 2) that the aspect of the *aesthetic* relates more to a *transcendental meaning* that draws the human spirit out of its experience of the merely tangible and elevates it so that it participates in that meaning.

I must also elucidate further my claim that purpose is linked fundamentally to the transcendental "no," while meaning is linked to the transcendental "yes." *Transcendental purpose* is mediated through a mode that appears more *definite* than *indefinite*; while *transcendental meaning*, in a reverse way, is mediated through a mode that seems more *indefinite* than *definite*.[32] I do not intend to limit meaning to a quest for *absolute precision* like proponents of linguistic analysis attempted to achieve.[33] I intend, rather, to reveal a kind of significance that carries with it a *residue of ineffable mystery*—or what Ricoeur called "a surplus of meaning."[34]

With regard to the *mysterium tremendum* or the transcendental "no," we can experience the Transcendent impinging upon our existence in terms of *divine direction and determination*. This experience constitutes, as well, our experience of the divine purpose, which, in turn, seems preoccupied more with the dimension of the *ethical* than with the *aesthetic*. The ancient Hebrews, for instance, became especially focused on the ethical dimension during their forty-year period of wilderness wandering. The Hebrew Scriptures repeatedly assert that God *directs* his people Israel and *determines* their destiny. Indeed, the *divine purpose* becomes writ large in the Israelites' ongoing experiences of God's providential *direction* and *determination*. Evidence, too, that God's *direction* and *determination* of his people issues from an ethical motivation appears in the way law codes figure so prominently in the Hebrew Scriptures. The "thou shalt nots" of the Decalogue further reveal that the element of the *negative* dominated Hebrew experiences of the Transcendent during their wilderness period.[35] However, at the same time, one would be wrong not to detect traces of a *positive* divine mystery—i.e., the *mysterium fascinans*—emanating from these ethical commands as well;

only that this positive aspect seems subordinate here to the element of the *negative* divine mystery—i.e., the *mysterium tremendum*.

With regard to the *mysterium fascinans* or the transcendental "yes," on the other hand, *meaning*, as opposed to *purpose*, links up more clearly with the God who *inspires* and *persuades*. This God is, of course, the same who *directs* and *determines*, so that only the *focus* has shifted. But now that the focus turns to the *positive* side of the mystery, an openness to what is more *indefinite* than *definite* comes to the fore in the human experience of the Transcendent. Parallel to this shift is the transition from an *ethical* to an *aesthetic* perspective. Citing the ancient Hebrews again, one ascertains how the Hebrew Temple and the priestly rituals associated with it incorporated the aesthetic dimension of human experience and wedded it to the ethical. The Hebrew festivals comprehensively linked the rhythms of nature with dramatic events in Hebrew history. In the festivals and other aspects of Hebrew worship, the beauty of nature pointed not just to itself, but it also functioned as a mirror that reflected the beauty of the entire historical drama of Israel. Nature was thus elevated and brought into the service of a drama that mediated divine *meaning* to the worshiper. The Psalms, as the worship literature of the Second Hebrew Temple, are replete with descriptions of nature being suffused with the divine glory.[36] The element of the dramatic is conveyed well by the Hebrew concept of glory (*kabod* [כָּבֹד]), for it is a dynamic category that points to God's weighty reputation as Israel's deliverer, vindicator, protector, and provider.[37]

While the element of the *aesthetic* dominates the *ethical* in priestly Judaism, it nonetheless upholds the central importance of the ethical. Priestly Judaism at the same time adds the dimension of the *sublime* to the dimension of the beautiful. The *locus classicus* for this conception appears in Isaiah 6:1–8. The sublimity of the divine mystery is mediated through Isaiah's vision, wherein Yahweh appears as "high and lifted up." Yahweh's immense majesty lies beyond the gaze of the prophet, so that only the fringes of the garments of the Heavenly King appear visible. Yahweh's attending seraphim possess six wings but use only two of them to fly. Wings are, in themselves, symbolic of heavenly grandeur and loftiness. Two additional wings cover the seraphim's faces, while another two cover their feet. The association of wings with feet and faces may seem odd to the modern mind, but the symbolism is crucial for gaining a fuller understanding of the depth of Isaiah's aesthetic experience. The wing-covered feet point to the unfathomable distance between the lowest extremities of these holy creatures and the holy God. Since feet symbolize that part of human anatomy that comes into direct contact with the dimension of the profane and the earthy, the seraphim—whose feet are presumably holier than human feet—must not dare, any more than would human feet, to venture uncovered into God's holy presence.[38] The holy God is antithetical to the profane, and this means that the appearance of *feet* in his presence, even *angelic* feet, cannot be tolerated. The seraphim's feet must therefore be covered by wings, which again symbolizes transcendence. Furthermore, since these angelic creatures are reluctant to uncover their feet in the presence of the divine holiness, what does this say of human feet by contrast? The contrast serves to stretch even further the sense of awful distance between the Holy and the profane. Wings cover the faces of the seraphim as well. This symbolism reveals that even sublime beings must hide their *faces* from the face of the holy God, for they dare not look upon the One who, to an infinite degree, is more sublime than they.[39] If angels dare not show their faces in the presence of the holy God, then what does this say about human faces by comparison?

The chilling cry of seraphim's Trisagion, their startling announcement that "the whole world is filling up with the divine glory," the feel and sound of the rumbling and shaking of the Temple's doorposts and its thresholds, the sight and smell of the Temple filling up with smoke—all these phenomena dramatically combine the aesthetics of sight, sound, touch, and smell to rivet the prophet's senses and pierce his soul through with an experience of the holy God. Isaiah, a lowly and unclean man, stands in the presence of the God who is sublimely pure. The sense of drama further builds as coals of fire mix the aesthetics of pain and pleasure. The pleasure, however, is mixed with remorse that the soul experiences when it is simultaneously confronted by the ethical demands of the Holy and captivated by the divine grace and forgiveness. As the coals caress the prophet's lips, his entire being is enveloped and enraptured by the beauty of the sublime. Simultaneously, the prophet's unclean and ugly state is purged so that he is rendered clean. The sublime vision has the effect of transforming the prophet from a pitiful, trembling sinner into a mouthpiece for God.

Certainly, the *mysterium tremendum* appears here coupled with the *mysterium fascinans*; but in this case, the element of the *fascinans* comes to the fore as the *tremendum* recedes slightly into the background. The prophetic response to the divine calling is not so much motivated out of the prophet's profound sense of his *fear* as by his sense of irresistible *attraction* to God's sublime beauty. Hence, the prophet responds, "Woe is me, I am a man of unclean lips." He then adds, "Here am I, send me." The fluidity between the *tremendum* and the *fascinans* thus guarantees that this receding of the ethical into the background can be only temporary, for the ethical must return at its proper time to remind the erring human being of his moral deficiency.

Although prophetic and priestly Judaism continued along two distinct, yet interrelated, trajectories—viz., the ethical and the aesthetic—the tendency to divorce the two and to go to an extreme in one direction or the other seems to have posed a perennial danger for ancient Israel. The tendency to go to the aesthetic extreme may help explain why prophets like Hosea delivered Yahweh's pronouncement, "I desire mercy, not sacrifice."[40] God decries rituals emptied of ethical content. On the other hand, the tendency to go to the ethical extreme may explain why Jesus, upon encountering the hypermoralism of the Pharisees, shifted his focus away from the ethical and back in the direction of the aesthetic.[41] More must be said about these opposing tendencies at a later time. I suggest now, however, that we examine various problems that occur with this aesthetic-ethical link when the Transcendent is either no longer properly understood or else fails to be related adequately to the dimension of the tangible.

First Problem — The Transcendent Lost to the Tangible, and the Tangible Lost to the Transcendent

The loss of transcendence as a category of significance occurs in one way when the *life-survival* pair becomes cut off from it. Naturalism, secularism, atheism, and pantheism represent philosophical positions that reject the idea that the Transcendent truly exists outside of, and apart from, the dimension of the tangible. If there is a Transcendent, it is one with a lowercase "t." Thus, it is a "transcendent" that is collapsed into, and always fully contained within, the dimension of the tangible.[42] As Gunton notes, "God is displaced as the focus of the unity of all things."[43] Gunton further observes that the function God performs does not disappear. Rather, some other source of unity replaces God. Yet this source of unity turns out to be a false universal that operates deceptively or oppressively.[44]

Moreover, when belief in the Transcendent as an ultimate dimension is jettisoned and human activity becomes linked solely to the dimension of the tangible, one's experiences of existence will invariably start to loop in upon themselves.[45] For instance, the survival instinct, when disengaged from the transcendental divine purpose, may compel people to react to threats in ways that resemble the behavior of cornered animals. A loss of connection with the true Transcendent may also lead to an amplified sense of one's *vulnerability* that, in turn, can produce an exaggerated perception of one's victimhood that appears quite disproportionate to reality as it exists. As one's sense of victimhood increases, one feels compelled to rectify in tandem the "injustices" that one believes one has suffered. Predictably, the means of redress employed will turn out to be ever more extreme and excessive. However, when the survival instinct becomes purposively linked to the Transcendent, the assurance of ultimate vindication can help to moderate such extreme responses and make them more measured.

Tenacity, too, can loop in upon itself when disengaged from the dimension of the divine meaning. One of the starkest descriptions of tenacity turning into a vicious circle appears in the writings of Existentialist philosopher Albert Camus. The futility of a meaningless expenditure of tenacity appears in his rendition of the "myth of Sisyphus."[46] Camus describes how the gods condemned Sisyphus to roll a boulder up a mountain only to have it tumble down the other side. Sisyphus was charged with endlessly repeating this task throughout eternity. The Sisyphus myth clearly illustrates the futility of exercises in tenacity where the search for real meaning in life has been entirely abandoned in exchange for one's cheerful acceptance of life's meaningless plight. Such lopsided exercises in futility are always doomed to descend into tedious repetition and monotony.

Camus nevertheless says, "One must imagine Sisyphus to be happy"; and so, Camus extols Sisyphus as someone to be admired rather than pitied.[47] Is Camus' judgment, however, truly acceptable? Can one really find happiness by buying in to the Stoic delusion that a dismal fate can be something about which to be joyous? Though Camus extols Sisyphus' effort, his claim that one should be happy to embrace the "virtues" of a mundane and monotonous materialism seems an enormous stretch. If anything, the mountain in the myth appears to be little more than an enormous ash heap upon which the gods of modern ideology have condemned persons endlessly to roll up and down their stones of pointless temporal accomplishments. Yet why should anyone waste one's time perfecting science and technology so that such mountains will become simpler to scale or the stones easier to roll? Why bother if there is neither meaning in the mountain nor significance in the drudgery of stone-rolling?

While a loss of connection with the Transcendent can lead to situations in which the dimension of the tangible loops in upon itself, an opposite danger becomes observable when the Transcendent becomes so disconnected from the tangible that it altogether diminishes the importance of the tangible. If taken to an extreme, human reliance upon the Transcendent as a principle of vindication, or as a mode of escape, can admittedly cause the Transcendent to become "an opiate of the people," as Karl Marx (1818–1883) famously said of religion.[48] If, on the other hand, the reality of the tangible dimension is kept fully in view, then religion need not sink to the level of an opioid. Thus, at one extreme, an exclusive focus on the tangible dimension can produce in people animalist behavior; and/or an underdeveloped, truncated, or distorted sense of justice. At the other extreme, an exclusive focus on the Transcendent can potentially anesthetize people to the demands of ordinary life that they need courageously to face and/or to real injustices that need rectification.

Second Problem—Incomplete Visions of the Transcendent

Earlier, I appealed to the Hebrew prophetic and priestly traditions to reveal a paradigm that can link the concept of divine transcendence to *both* purpose *and* meaning, and not to one or the other exclusively. However, exploring notions of divine transcendence in other world religions also helps provide a clearer sense of how to approach the topic. Unfortunately, ideas of the Transcendent in some religious traditions appear incomplete when compared to what the Judeo-Christian tradition offers. They tend to focus too exclusively either on an inscrutable divine purpose *or* an incomprehensible divine meaning instead of emphasizing both together. The vastly different ideas of the Transcendent in Islam and Hinduism will help illustrate my point.

First Incomplete Vision—The Inscrutability of the Divine Purpose in Islam: Islam interprets the absolute supremacy of the *will* of Allah in terms of *arbitrary omnipotence.*[49] In Islam, no *singular* divine purpose can be identified that fully contextualizes Allah's omnipotence; rather, the opposite is true—Allah's omnipotence obscures any sense of a unified divine purpose that might otherwise be ascertainable. Consequently, while it may be clear that Allah has *purposes*, it is not clear that he has *a singular, comprehensive,* and *overarching purpose*. What, then, are the lenses through which the purposes of Allah in the world might be examined? First, Islam's *predestinarian* belief that Allah *directs* and *determines* all that happens in the world serves as a lens through which his purposes might be construed.[50] All that happens, happens according to the will of Allah. Second, an emphasis on *ethics* and *justice* constitute another lens through which Allah's purposes may be viewed.[51] Laws, commands, rules, and regulations must be obeyed without question. Third, a lens that clarifies Allah's purposes is the requirement that Muslims obey Allah's commands concerning *worship*. Obedience to Allah's commands, in turn, entails strict adherence to, and performance of, the requirements of Islam's Five Pillars.

The doctrine of predestination, the focus on ethics and justice, and adherence to the Five Pillars thus constitute the most important lenses through which Muslim believers can clearly know the *content* of Allah's purposes. Upon closer examination, however, this content appears truncated and lacking in both consistency of focus and comprehensiveness. Knowledge of any overarching divine purpose remains instead more indefinite than definite, and more ambiguous than clear. Muslim believers are thus precluded from seeing the big picture of what the divine purpose consists of or what it looks like over the *long term*. Indeed, if Allah does have a singular purpose, it appears from a human perspective at least to be *inscrutable*. Allah thus seems to hide his overall purpose from human view only to reveal snippets of it on a need-to-know basis.

Islamic conceptions of what the divine *purpose* entails also appear less clear than what conceptions of his *purposes* entail. This lack of clarity becomes apparent despite the Qur'an's insistence that its words contain the *clear* words of Allah,[52] and clarity only seems to diminish further as Allah's purposes proliferate. The conflict arising out of the resulting plurality of purposes then makes it appear as though Allah at times is even at *cross*-purposes. In some instances, Allah's purposes may also seem so *arbitrary*, *ambiguous*, and *contradictory* that it becomes hard to separate them out from the diverse array of human purposes with which Allah's purposes have become identified or confused. This confusion leads to practical consequences such as the power struggles that invariably ensue over differences of interpretation concerning what Allah's purposes may consist of at any given time.[53] This confusion is manifested most deleteriously today in the differing, and even conflicting, interpretations of what the practice of *jihad* should entail.

In addition to the conflicts that arise from its incomplete vision of a divine purpose, Islam also devotes too little attention to the *divine-meaning* aspect as a counterbalance to the *divine-purpose* aspect. If anything, the Islamic emphasis on Allah's *will* eclipses the role divine meaning should play in inspiring individual human souls to embrace the Good.[54] Contributing to this eclipse is Islam's aesthetics deficit, for Islamic prohibitions against the use of visual images that might serve to mediate *divine meaning* guarantees that the role of the aesthetic visual sense will be downplayed. Islam is thus left with a focus that almost entirely concentrates on the *mysterium tremendum*, thus guaranteeing that religious devotion and practice will be motivated more negatively by fear than positively by love. The *mysterium fascinans* is, on the whole, left behind.

Second Incomplete Vision—The Incomprehensibility of the Divine Meaning in Hinduism: By contrast with Islam, Hinduism (especially the *Shankara* school) engages its adherents in the pursuit of an incomprehensible *divine meaning*; for Brahman, the highest dimension of the Divine, epitomizes a kind of transcendental meaning that inspires the souls of individuals to seek reunification with the Infinite from which they have become separated. The individual soul thus becomes open to a divine meaning that lies hidden behind the visible, tangible world of *māyā*, or the *veil of illusion*. Once the soul is liberated from this illusion and achieves meaningful reunion with the Transcendent, it experiences freedom and positive release (*moksha*). The Transcendent, therefore, does not make itself known in *Shankara* Hinduism so much through *clear ethical commands* that link with some *divine purpose* as it does through an *inspiring ideal* that remains veiled by the tangible dimension until its meaning is apprehended by the eye of the soul. What the soul experiences comes as a surprise, and the meaning it beholds is universal and comprehensive. Through this vision of the Transcendent, the soul is elevated beyond the world of particularity and grasps intuitively the universal reality of the *divine meaning* that lies hidden within the tangible world. Again, the human spirit experiences this revelation in terms of surprise, novelty, and ecstasy.

Despite its strong emphasis upon divine meaning, however, *Shankara* Hinduism appears deficient with regards to an understanding of any *divine purpose* and the role of *ethics* in bringing that purpose to bear upon tangible existence. In the first place, it questions the essential goodness of the tangible world. Brahman creates the world for no apparent purpose but merely creates it to "sport with" (Skt=*līlā*).[55] There is no conception of *history* as involving a *purposive* movement of time from a definite beginning to a definite end. The *Shankara* vision is, rather, that of a cyclical world; and salvation ultimately requires the soul's *escape* from the physical dimension with its endless cycles of rebirth.

In the second place, Hinduism's view of *māyā* (except perhaps in the teachings of *Madhvacharya*) considers the world of particularity to be *illusory*. *Shankara* Hinduism especially denies that the tangible world can really intersect with anything resembling a *divine purpose*. Rather, the tangible world exists merely as the place where the law of *karma* holds sway, and karmic law operates impersonally and exactingly. The principle of *karma* provides justification, in fact, for accepting social inequality like that existing in the caste system. The doctrine of caste, which is logically consistent with Hindu beliefs in karmic law, the transmigration of souls, and reincarnation, therefore accepts human inequalities as givens that need no rectification. For this reason, Hinduism does not consider the problem of human inequality to be a product of *systemic social injustice*.

Just as there is no clear *purpose* to physical existence, questions of *morality* and *ethics* that so occupy the thought of human beings appear to be of little consequence to Brahman. The eminent Hindu scholar and political figure Sarvepalli Radhakrishnan (1888–1975)acknowledged this subordinate importance of morality when he compared his native *Shankara* Hinduism with Christianity's moral emphasis.[56] *Jñāna* or *knowledge* gives one the ability to peer through the veil of *māyā*, but *jñana* by its very aim transcends ethical goodness. The moral man is inferior to the spiritual man, for he must battle the illusion of his individual ego in a way that the one possessing *jñana* need not do. Only the spiritual man—the saint—can overcome selfishness by covering himself with the truth of the Universal Self. Becoming one with the Infinite thus entails what Albert Schweitzer (1875–1965) called "a pure act of the spirit which has nothing to do with ethics."[57] The soul's perfection is achieved through the ceaseless straining of the human soul to pierce through the crushing body, the distracting intellect, and the selfish will by apprehending and becoming one with the Universal Spirit.[58]

The ethical dimension is downplayed as well in Hindu conceptions of the incarnation of Vishnu as Krishna, as described in the *Mahabharata*.[59] Although the avatar doctrine of Vishnu's incarnation as Krishna may superficially resemble the Christian understanding of the incarnation of God in Jesus, the Hindu doctrine is not as radically ethical in its implications as the Christian understanding. There is no evidence that Vishnu's incarnation *embraces* the world of particularity or *suffers* because of it. Krishna's main objective is to restore religion in the world; not to "proclaim the year of jubilee."[60] Again, this form of Hinduism leaves the world of particularity behind as it opts for the total reabsorption of the soul into the reality of the Divine. By contrast, Christianity, through its vision of *the resurrection of the body and the life everlasting*, teaches that God embraces the world of particularity and redeems it.

To summarize then, Islam focuses more on Allah's transcendental *will*, his inscrutable purpose, and the role of *ethics* in religion, while neglecting the full importance of the *divine meaning* and the role of *aesthetics* in mediating that meaning. Hinduism, on the other hand, stresses the *divine meaning* and the *aesthetic* sense to the neglect of a clear doctrine of the *divine purpose* and the role of *ethics* in accomplishing that purpose. Again, overall ideas of the Transcendent in both religions seem only partially developed.

Liberating and Restricting Directions—Power and Freedom, versus Order and Limit

Intersecting the vertical line of the value-compass is the horizontal line with its extremes of left and right (see figure 2.1). *Power* and *freedom* stand at the left side of this line and correlate with the "yes" value we have discussed previously, while *order* and *limit* stand at the right side and correspond to the "no" value. The relation of the "yes" and the "no" to the horizontal line of the compass therefore differs from the way they correlate with the vertical line. On the vertical line, one finds *meaning* (the transcendental) and *life* (the tangible) related to the "yes." *Purpose* (the transcendental) and *survival* (the tangible), on the other hand, are related to the "no" value on the vertical line. One can, however, discern the transcendental-tangible polarities reflected in the pairs at the opposite points of the horizontal line. *Freedom* (the "yes") and *limit* (the "no") are *one* way of conceiving the dialectic that operates between *individual* expressions of liberty and sanctions that restrict individual liberty as well as *collective* expressions of *power* and the need to restrain power by promoting *order*.

Individual Liberation and Restriction—The Freedom-Limit Dialectic

Are we then to privilege *freedom* as the constant while making *limit* a subservient variable that must revolve around it, even if this means the variable must from time to time suffer eclipse by this constant? Or do we privilege *limit* as the constant and make *freedom* the variable that must revolve around and be subservient to *that* constant? Western and Eastern cultures vary significantly in their answers to these questions.

Western culture overall now privileges freedom as the constant and makes limit a subservient variable, but this view of the freedom-limit relationship has not always been the dominant one. A quick look at the Western tradition reveals that philosophical ideas derived from Plato and Aristotle stressed the principle of *limit*, whereas the principle of *freedom* was relegated to a place of secondary importance. Plato certainly privileged the role of the Forms in the scheme of things, stressing their superiority to all *dynamic* phenomena. He related dynamic phenomena, on the other hand, to his doctrine of relative nonbeing (Grk=*mē on* [μὴ ὄν]). In his description of the soul in the *Phaedrus*, for instance, virtue is tied to *reason*, not to the passions.[61] The passions must therefore become the slaves of reason. Aristotle, too, in his *Nicomachean Ethics* appealed to the Pythagorean concept of *limit* in his exposition of his doctrine of the *golden mean.*[62] This privileging of limit over freedom is found in the Western tradition from Augustine to Aquinas, and it only began to be weakened in the thought of Duns Scotus and William of Ockham during the transition from the High to the Late Middle Ages. With the move from medieval scholasticism to the Renaissance and Reformation, the emphasis upon limit waned and was gradually replaced by an emphasis on freedom—but *what kind* of freedom was it that was stressed?

During the seventeenth century, *enlightened freedom* was the view championed. This sort of freedom is one that comes as a *consequence* of the Enlightenment that education produces. Therefore, the chief enemy of enlightened freedom was *ignorance.* Frederick the Great of Prussia (1712–1786), who understood this well, thus instituted a program of universal compulsory education by which he hoped to achieve his goal of an enlightened populace.[63] The instituting of compulsory public education in England and the United States followed along the lines of this Prussian model.[64]

However, as Romanticism began to displace certain tenets of the Age of Reason, the concept of enlightened freedom gradually transitioned to a concept of *libertarian freedom.* Unlike enlightened freedom, freedom of the libertarian kind is one that precedes all choice and decision-making. The libertarian-freedom idea seems to have been championed first in the nineteenth century by F. W. J. Schelling (1775–1854) in his work, *Philosophical Inquiries into the Nature of Human Freedom.*[65] Søren Kierkegaard (1813–1855), who was influenced by Schelling, held to a doctrine of libertarian freedom,[66] as did Friedrich Nietzsche (1844–1900) in his concept of the "will to power."[67] In the twentieth century, one of the chief representatives of the libertarian-freedom concept was Jean-Paul Sartre who spoke of *absolute freedom.*[68] Such notions of libertarian freedom became ever more exaggerated as the twentieth century gave way to the twenty-first century. We now find ourselves in the West at an opposite point of the compass from where we began, for now the principle of freedom has virtually eclipsed the principle of limit.

As the West shifted its emphasis from *limit* to *freedom*, it began simultaneously to favor individualism over collectivism, which eventually resulted in the dominance of the philosophy of *radical* individualism. Marxist philosopher Marshall Berman (1940–2013) located the origins of radical individualism in the thought of some of the French *philosophes*, particularly Montes-

quieu (1689–1755) and Jean-Jacques Rousseau (1712–1778).[69] The privileging of libertarian freedom, together with radical individualism, occasioned an
imbalance between freedom and limit that has produced mixed consequences. Societies that embrace radical individualism but link it to a strong
emphasis on the competitive drive (e.g., United States, Great Britain, Austra-
lia, New Zealand, and Canada)[70] have demonstrated ingenuity, creativity,
and the ability to increase material wealth. Other Western societies (e.g.,
Sweden, Norway, France, Denmark, and the Netherlands) have coupled radical individualism with an emphasis on the cooperative drive. Economically,
these societies tend to fluctuate between capitalism and socialism.[71]

If the importance of the individual is stressed and the importance of the
collective is de-emphasized, or if the competitive drive is elevated above the
cooperative; then destructive consequences will invariably ensue. Among
these are high rates of drug abuse; widespread divorce; familial dysfunction;
delinquency; proliferating and conflicting sexual mores; increased rates of
crime and violence; failing educational systems; the coarsening of culture;
economic malaise; national indebtedness; and the general demise of the culture of respect. Radical individualism has also, unfortunately, demonstrated
in a variety of ways that it is inimical to and destructive of social contracts
that in previous eras proved strong enough to bind these societies together
and make them sufficiently cohesive to be governable. Increasingly, however, the ligaments that hold together the body politics of these societies are
growing weaker. Radical individualism, despite its advantages, is thus afflicted with an Achilles' heel; for societies that venture too far in embracing
extreme expressions of radical individualism face possible scenarios that
include, but are not limited to, the unraveling of society, anarchy, and civil
war.

In individualistic societies, *limit*, as the counterbalance to freedom, tends
to be achieved through arbitration rather than by following set rules.[72] In this
regard, freedom is upheld as the constant, and limit is made to revolve
around it. Such societies favor broad principles instead of specific rules that
have as their purpose the governing of every detail of life. Because the
principle of limit is arrived at arbitrarily, conflict invariably ensues between
individuals as they seek to forge mutually beneficial compromises. *Experimentation*, more than *tradition*, decides the grounds for ethics in individualistic societies.

By contrast with Western societies, societies of North Africa, the Middle
East (except for Israel), and the Far East privilege limit as the constant and
tether freedom to that constant.[73] Such societies have a high regard for authority and tend to be risk-averse. Being highly resistant to new ideas, they
favor the stability of tradition over novelty and experimentation. Life in these
societies appears highly ordered, and people are accustomed to obeying numerous rules and regulations that govern even the most specific details of

life. Decisions are often made at a pace that, to Westerners at least, appears painfully slow; for decisions are only arrived at after much care and deliberation.[74]

Collective Liberation and Restriction — The Power-Order Dialectic

While *freedom* and *limit* have more to do with how *individual* persons function within the greater society, society as a *collective* must also be taken into consideration in deliberations concerning questions of value. *Power* and *order*, as collective modes of liberation and restriction, have more to do with political and economic realities and the way these realities benefit some people while disadvantaging others. As with the limit-freedom dialectic, some societies elevate the principle of order while relegating the power principle to a secondary status. Others prefer power as the constant and relegate order to second place.

The transition in the West from an emphasis on order to an emphasis on power runs parallel to this transition from an emphasis on limit to an emphasis on freedom. Plato's and Aristotle's perspectives on legitimate and illegitimate forms of government reveal that they understood *power* to be subservient to *order*.[75] As concerns my value-compass, they allowed the principle of order to regulate the principle of power. Because freedom is restricted in this type of approach, what often is missing is an adequate emphasis upon those tangible human values with which the principles of life and survival are concerned.

Plato favored the given order of the status quo in his positive valuation of meritocracy;[76] though, to his credit, he was not encumbered with the notion of caste such as one finds in traditional Indian society. Plato held instead that one born among slaves could better oneself through hard effort and could even rise upward through the hierarchy to assume a higher status.[77] Although restricted in its capacity to offer persons "equal opportunity," the notion of meritocracy served—theoretically at least—as an escape hatch from the kind of stricter codes found in the Indian caste system, where persons' stations in life are entirely fixed from birth.

Aristotle, too, favors the given order of the status quo when he rejects the principle of revolution as a possible means toward a good end. Revolution comes instead as a negative effect that surfaces when badly governed civil society unravels.[78] The principle of order also prevails in Aristotle's list of the good forms of government, for these serve as correctives to social maladies that can lead to revolution. Wisdom thus dictates that society should practice these superior forms of government to avoid deteriorating into revolution. Therefore, both Plato and Aristotle favor *established* order over any prospect that might promote *arbitrary* or *radical* change. They clearly favor the principle of *order* as a constant and make the principle of *power* subservient to that constant. Their systems emphasize the role *justice* plays in imposing the principle of order on everyone. Still, their systems allow for minimal flexibility, and the principle of freedom happens to be constrained as a result.

A change in direction, however, occurred during the Italian Renaissance, when Niccolò Machiavelli (1469–1527), in his work *The Prince*, seriously challenged these earlier traditional ways of construing the power-order dialectic.[79] Machiavelli grounds his political views in the harsh realities of Italian politics, observing firsthand how questionable means of achieving good government could in certain cases prove beneficial, especially when practiced by an astute and shrewd politician. Machiavelli advocates that the principle of the *coup d'état,* or overthrow of the state, be put into action when warranted. In backing the application of this principle, he departs from Aristotle's negative assessment of revolution. Instead, Machiavelli promotes controversial and non-virtuous activities such as subterfuge, misinformation, propaganda, torture, and assassination as appropriate means for achieving the overthrow or disestablishment of entrenched malevolent political power. Thus, for him, the "good" as a goal to be achieved need not depend on *means* that are deemed good; rather, *the end could justify the means*, regardless of how terrible the means happen to be.

Machiavelli's political breakthrough would eventually foster the West's wholesale embrace of the principle of revolution as a means of achieving worthy political ends. In Britain, John Locke (1632–1704) advocated the principle of revolution in his *Second Treatise of Government* (1689).[80] Unlike Aristotle, who rejected revolution as a justifiable means of achieving a good end, Locke championed the human right to revolt as fundamental and unalienable. Revolution could thus serve as a means of achieving a worthy end.

Locke forged his theory of government with the English Civil War (1642–1651), the Cromwellian Dynasty (1649–1660), the Restoration of the Monarchy in 1660, and the Glorious Revolution of 1688 in mind. His theory was, therefore, steeped in an experience-based observation that systems of checks and balances needed to be formally instituted in government to limit the power of those who govern. Locke thus achieved a workable "elitist-populist" dialectic that transformed the solutions proposed by Plato and Aristotle. In America, prior to the 1960s, this dialectic functioned in such a way that the elitist element was still prominent and generally respected. However, this dialectic has since swung in the direction of a rather uncritical acceptance of crass populism, with an increasingly out-of-touch elitism being vigorously challenged from many quarters.

While the history of the *power order* dialectic in Western society has been one of transition, the same has not been true of civilizations of the Far East. The privileging of the principle of *order* over that of *power* remains a dominant feature of traditional societies in China, Korea, India, and Japan.

Power distribution in these societies is not egalitarian, for the power distance between those in authority and those under authority is wide.[81] A wide power distance between social classes is, in fact, indicative of societies where order is privileged over power. The structure of these societies is hierarchical.[82] In keeping with an emphasis on order, Eastern societies have also traditionally stressed the ideal of *collectivity*.[83] As a result, they see the need to curtail and even sacrifice individual freedoms to maintain those kinds of ordered relationships that bind their societies together and allow them to function as cohesive units. In places where power is held for the sake of maintaining order, power tends to be strongly established and entrenched.

In a similar way, people living in collectivist societies are predisposed to accept limit as nonnegotiable and binding. This predisposition requires that they exercise whatever freedom they have within the confines of these limits. In keeping with the emphasis upon order and limit, we find an elevated sense of appreciation for tradition in such societies. Respectfulness and politeness characterize the way individuals treat one another. The worst thing that can befall a member of the social unit is to lose face or to bring shame upon one's family, group, or nation.

Collectivist societies do not, however, always integrate the competitive and cooperative drives in the same way. Japan, for instance, remains a highly competitive society, though the competition tends to happen between groups of individuals or "teams" and not between individuals themselves.[84] Loyalty to one's group overrides one's self-interest in Japanese society. By contrast, Chinese society prizes the element of *cooperation* more highly than Japan; though it, like Japan, also stresses *collective competition*.

In societies of the Far East, *order* is favored as a regulating principle. Order is the constant that regulates power, and power revolves around this constant. The opposite is true in modern Western societies where egalitarianism serves to lessen the power distance between individuals.[85] Because power distance is low, egalitarian societies tend to privilege the principle of *power* over that of *order*. Hence, order serves not as a *cause* but as an *effect* that emerges out of negotiations between power players. Power thus serves as the constant around which order revolves. Consequently, power is also more easily disestablished in individualistic societies than in collectivist ones where the power principle is made to serve the principle of order.

By encouraging conformity to the pre-established rules of a fixed order, collectivist societies also disincline individuals to take the risks necessary to generate creative breakthroughs. Western societies, by contrast, maintain a greater edge in creativity, ingenuity, and inventiveness.[86] They do so by recognizing and rewarding individual incentive, risk, and accomplishment. Individuals in traditional Asian societies, on the other hand, prize accomplishments that bring recognition to the collective. Maintaining face within the group is thus esteemed more highly than achieving individual recognition. As a result, these societies tend to be risk averse and less creative, though they often do enjoy a reputation for sustaining greater quality in their workmanship.

The diverse ways of configuring the power-order dialectic thus produce political and economic ramifications that can prove either an asset or liability. Societies that privilege order over power tend to have greater political stability, though they may lag behind entrepreneurially. On the other hand, societies that privilege power over order may generate greater entrepreneurship, but they may also exhibit more political volatility and changeability. It seems in both cases that strength in one area can be cause for weakness in another. Strengths and weaknesses thus appear to be tied together.

"Gods" of Freedom, Power, Order, and Limit

Theologian Paul Tillich (1886–1965) suggests a way of linking our concepts of God with what he calls our "*ultimate concern*." Though Tillich acknowledges that God *should* be the object of our ultimate concern, he nevertheless is cognizant of the fact that *any object* toward which we address our ultimate concern becomes, in effect, "god" for us.[87] Our ability to direct our ultimate concern toward objects other than God thus opens up the possibility of our fashioning other gods and worshiping them instead. Tillich recognizes that this misdirection of our ultimate concern toward objects other than God constitutes *idolatry*.[88]

Tillich thinks that idolatry has a peculiarly close connection to the problem of the *demonic*, which he considers at length in his *Interpretation of History*.[89] In his *Systematic Theology*, he further discusses the problem in connection with Rudolf Otto's conception of the *mysterium tremendum et fascinans*. In his *Systematic*, Tillich highlights how we tend to relocate the Holy in tangible or proximate realities rather than in the dimension of the Transcendent where it rightly belongs.[90] This relocation of the Holy within the dimension of the tangible runs parallel to the way that we transform aspects of proximate reality into objects of our ultimate concern. Consequently, the proximate ceases to point beyond itself to a higher reality and fails to participate in that to which it points.[91] Once the proximate dimension has ceased to mediate a transcendence *beyond* itself, it starts pointing to itself alone. I have already referred above to our tendency to allow *life* and *survival* to loop in upon themselves. Clearly, the looping effect also happens when we elevate any of those *non-ultimate* elements represented by the liberating and limiting directions of the compass to a status of *ultimacy*.

In Western culture, for instance, certain individuals and special-interest groups have elevated the principle of *freedom* to a status of ultimacy. As freedom becomes an object of ultimate concern, it no longer functions as a vehicle that can mediate a transcendence higher than itself. *Freedom itself* instead becomes identical with the Transcendent. Various philosophies of freedom and liberation harbor the danger that those espousing them may venture too far in allowing their philosophical perspectives to become for them the Absolute. Championing ideas of freedom and human rights is, of course, not wrongful as long as these ideas are moderated by other concerns. A problem arises only when the preoccupation and obsession with these ideas *exclude* the importance of other points of the value-compass. When this exclusion occurs, demonic manifestations are invariably unleashed.[92] Freedom and liberation cease then to be the *means* toward a higher end and instead become *ends* in themselves. As ends, they function as "gods" despite the protestations of those who refuse to acknowledge that their ideas have now, for all practical purposes, become *religious doctrines*.

The obsession with freedom may qualify as one form of idolatry, but the obsession with limit can develop into something equally idolatrous. In many Western societies, this obsession has produced the various canons of *political correctness*. Certain groups appear to be obsessed with imposing their versions of political correctness—sometimes quite eccentric—upon others with whom they disagree. Since power politics is usually the means they use to privilege their dogmas of political correctness, they often will resort to an excessive employment of arbitrary means that are almost certain to violate common sense. Through these means, their peculiar doctrines of political correctness are reified into *gods* of limit as well. Accordingly, their ideal of what should be entailed in the principle of limit no longer functions as a way of mediating a higher transcendental purpose beyond their arbitrarily determined laws and moral codes; rather, it becomes *the purpose itself*. The West, of course, is not the only culture that manifests these forms of idolatry. The phenomenon manifests itself worldwide and can, for instance, be identified in the Islamic preoccupation with establishing a world caliphate where sharia law would be imposed. It also appears in Asian societies where the state severely restricts personal freedoms, particularly the freedoms of those existing at the bottom of the social order. Interestingly, in the West, people may worship the gods of freedom and limit simultaneously by maximizing *freedom* for themselves and invoking *limit* to constrain or punish those whom they oppose.

In addition to freedom and limit, *power* and *order* can just as easily function as gods if they become objects of ultimate concern. The extent to which politicians will grasp for power and try to hold on to it once it is obtained creates in Western democracies a state of endless conflict that spills over into the greater society and poisons the culture with cynicism, hatred, disrespect, and despair. At the same time, power is used to impose and to maintain a *kind* of *order* that is often corrupt and rife with injustice. Despite the corruption that results, *order* becomes for those who happen to be its beneficiaries identical to the Transcendent itself; but for those who are oppressed by it, all hope might as well be abandoned. If order is everything, then Machiavellian politics becomes fully justified as the means of maintaining it. All these demonic sorts of manifestations—which result from making *power* and *order* objects of ultimate concern—introduce into human experience, both individually and collectively, manifestations of hyper-conflict on the one hand and paralysis on the other.

Because modern Western culture has lost its sense of the Transcendent, freedom and limit, and power and order have become turned against one another and have become engaged in destructive conflict. However, if the Transcendent is recognized as the Archimedean point from which the hanging pendulum of human culture swings dialectically between the liberating and limiting directions of its individual and social experience, then the pendulum's becoming disconnected from its fulcrum can only signal the end of a smoothly operating dialectic with its promise of equilibrium. Instead, freedom, limit, order, and power become stagnant principles that endlessly loop in upon themselves. As this looping occurs, civilization has nowhere to go except to plummet into a downward spiral. Freedom, limit, order, and power as the means of mediating the true Transcendent now become wholly transformed into "ends in themselves." Freedom for the sake of freedom, limit for the sake of limit, power for the sake of power, and order for the sake of order become the new deities that promise something better but never deliver anything but cultural conflict, stagnation, and decline. To make matters worse, these new deities, like the gods of Greek polytheism, either set themselves at odds against one another, or they form unholy alliances that inveigle people with deceptive promises and subject them to gross injustice.

FINDING "TRUE NORTH" ON THE VALUE-COMPASS

It thus appears that the loss of the Transcendent becomes to the value-compass what the loss of true north is to the geographical compass. Unfortunately, this loss of true north invariably causes the value-compass to spin out of control. The liberating and restricting directions, which belong to the horizontal directions of the compass, also become unreliable as the compass needle spins irrationally. Indeed, the more the dimension of the tangible interferes with the "magnetic field" exerted by the dimension of the Transcendent, the more these dilemmas seem to increase in tandem. Human existence becomes ever more confused and disoriented as a result. An ever-greater sense of disorientation becomes evident as directions must constantly be corrected in our futile attempts to orient ourselves. The compass meanwhile goes on spinning without indicating any clear direction of how we should proceed.

Sadly, the catastrophic situation brought on by the inability of the value-compass to find true north still contains something infinitely more valuable than a morass of confusion, for caught in the confusion are disoriented and misdirected human beings who no longer can connect with the Good, the True, and the Beautiful. In response to this cultural catastrophe, one can only hope to discover those places where the balance and equilibrium among the dialectics working in the compass of value are still being maintained and fostered. The task then becomes the difficult one of extending the balance and equilibrium from those places to the broader culture.

Reorienting the needle on the value-compass toward the true north of transcendence can also help our culture achieve an amicable reconciliation between ethics and aesthetics. The cleavage between these two branches of axiology, which is apparent everywhere, is also responsible for precipitating cultural and spiritual decline as well as moral and aesthetic degradation. As a result, the survival of Western culture and civilization is at stake. Because ethics has become emptied of aesthetic content and aesthetics has become devoid of morality, the resulting cultural and spiritual vacuum has sucked the purpose and the meaning out of existence. Moralism without aesthetics has, on the one hand, proved deficient in its capacity to compel participation in the sense of wonder and the kind of inspiration that can facilitate one's encounter with *divine meaning*. On the other hand, aestheticism devoid of morality has proved deficient in its ability to connect people with *divine purpose*.

NOTES

1. Plat. Phaedrus 246e–247e. See Robert Merrihew Adams's discussion in *Finite and Infinite Goods: A Framework for Ethics* (Oxford: Oxford University Press, 1999), 13–14.

2. Augustine of Hippo, *Confessions*, trans. Carolyn J.-B. Hammond, in *Loeb Classical Library* 26 (Cambridge, MA: Harvard University Press, 2014), bk. 3.

3. Colin E. Gunton, *The One, the Three and the Many: God, Creation and the Culture of Modernity* (Cambridge, UK: Cambridge University Press, 1993), 28.

4. Jacques Barzun, *From Dawn to Decadence: 1500 to the Present, 500 Years of Western Cultural Life* (New York: HarperCollins [Perennial edition], 2001), xv–xviii.

5. See, for example, Allan Bloom, *The Closing of the American Mind: How Higher Education Has Failed Democracy and Impoverished the Souls of Today's Students* (New York: Simon & Schuster, 1987), 196.

6. As, e.g., Mark C. Taylor, *Erring: A Postmodern A/theology* (Chicago, IL: University of Chicago Press, 1984), 29–33.

7. Dallas Willard, *The Disappearance of Moral Knowledge*, ed. and compl. Steven Porter, Aaron Preston, and Gregg A. Tens Elshof (New York: Routledge, 2018), 344. Willard observes that the phenomenon of this disappearance has occurred in four overlapping stages: (1) From the late 1700s to the mid-1800s, the prevailing ethical understandings of Christian European society did not provide an adequate basis for individual and social existence in the Modern world; (2) "professional" ethical theorists, who saw the effort to meet the need for this basis, sought the basis for moral understanding and practice in secular knowledge and "science"; (3) "Noncognitivism" in the form of emotivism ruled out both naturalistic and nonnaturalistic interpretations of moral distinctions, signaling the outright rejection of the very possibility of

moral knowledge and bleeding over into "postmodernism"; and (4) roughly from about 1950 to the present, attempts were made to pull back from noncognitivism (emotivism) and nihilism by basing moral thought and practice in a "rationality" without truth and without the standards of logic that previously were associated with truth (345–48).

8. Alejandro García-Rivera, *The Community of the Beautiful: A Theological Aesthetics* (Collegeville, MN: Liturgical Press, 1999), 63.

9. Adams, *Finite and Infinite Goods*, 1.

10. Adams, *Finite and Infinite Goods*, 5–6. His version of theism has thus sometimes been referred to as "thin theism."

11. Emmanuel Levinas, *Totality and Infinity: An Essay on Exteriority*, trans. Alphonso Lingis (Pittsburgh, PA: Duquesne University Press, 1969), 33–52, 82–101, 220–47.

12. Levinas, *Totality and Infinity*, 35, 37.

13. Hans Urs von Balthasar, *The Glory of the Lord: A Theological Aesthetics*, vol. 1, trans. Erasmo Leiva-Merikakis, ed. Joseph Fessio and John Riches (San Francisco, CA: Ignatius Press, 2009), 9. See also the discussion of Frederick Christian Bauerschmidt, who has suggested this possibility by bringing Jean-François Lyotard's idea of the transcendent sublime into rapprochement with the insights of von Balthasar on the "theological sublime." Bauerschmidt, "Aesthetics: The Theological Sublime," in *Radical Orthodoxy*, ed. John Milbank, Catherine Pickstock, and Graham Ward (London: Routledge, 1999), 201–9.

14. David Bentley Hart, *The Beauty of the Infinite: The Aesthetics of Christian Truth* (Grand Rapids, MI: Willaim B. Eerdmans, 2003), 1–4. See, however, Hart's critique of the Kantian perspective of Levinas (14–15). Hart writes, "'Infinity', as Levinas uses the word, indicates a kind of purely ethical sublime, recognizably Kantian in its joyless rigor, and so jealously preserved against the idolatrous proclivities of human minds as to take on the characteristics of gnostic myth. . . ."

15. Stephen John Wright, *Dogmatic Aesthetics: A Theology of Beauty in Dialogue with Robert W. Jenson* (Minneapolis, MN: Fortress Press, 2014).

16. Jeremy Begbie, *Redeeming Transcendence in the Arts: Bearing Witness to the Triune God* (Grand Rapids, MI: William B. Eerdmans, 2018), 16–34.

17. Jonathan King, *The Beauty of the Lord: Theology as Aesthetics* (Bellingham, WA: Lexam Press, 2018), loc. 645–828 of 18389, Kindle.

18. E. g., Paul Fiddes, "The Sublime and the Beautiful: Intersections between Theology and Literature," in *Literature and Theology: New Interdisciplinary Spaces*, ed. Heather Walton (Farnham, UK: Ashgate, 2011), 127–41. Fiddes investigates Iris Murdoch's dialogue with Kant and suggests that Murdoch's emphasis on particularity, which sees the "sublime *in* the beautiful" evokes a sense of the "positive sublime" as contrasted with Kant's negative emphasis. See also John D. Caputo and Michael J. Scanlon, eds., *Transcendence and Beyond: A Postmodern Inquiry* (Bloomington: Indiana University Press, 2007).

19. Some categories of the value-compass I am developing here were originally suggested to me by my friend and mentor the late F. W. Dillistone, Canon Emeritus of Liverpool Cathedral and Fellow and Chaplain of Oriel College, Oxford. He did not use the terminology "value-compass," but he referred to four categories that he called, "security (life), meaning, freedom, and order." See discussion in Dillistone, *The Christian Faith* (Philadelphia, PA: J. B. Lippincott, 1964), 29–39.

20. Paul Ricoeur, *Fallible Man*, trans. Charles A. Kelbley (New York: Fordham University Press, 1986), 81–132, 133–46.

21. Aristot. Nich. Eth. 1.4.2.

22. John Searle, "Minds, Brains, and Programs," in *Philosophy of Mind: Contemporary Readings*, ed. Timothy O'Connor and David Robb (London: Routledge, 2003), 349; Richard Swinburne, "The Soul," in *Philosophy of Mind*, 38. Computers do not possess *incorrigibility*, which was the doctrine Descartes established by means of his famous *cogito*.

23. Pain and pleasure, as rudimentary value-indicators, can also be classified as *qualia*, which is a term coined by Clarence Irving Lewis in his book *The Mind and the World-Order: Outline of a Theory of Knowledge* (New York: Charles Scribner's Sons, 1929), 61.

24. Ricoeur, *Fallible Man*, 5.

25. Jeremy Bentham, *Principles of Morals and Legislation* (Oxford: Clarendon, 1907), ch. 3, sec. 1; ch. 4, sec. 16 and 18; and ch. 5.

26. Plat. Meno 81c, 86a; Plat. Phaedo 74c–76e.

27. Augustine, *On Christian Doctrine*, trans. unkn. (Radford, VA; SMK Books, 2013), 38.42, 34–35.

28. Rudolf Otto, *The Idea of the Holy: An Inquiry into the Non-Rational Factor in the Idea of the Divine and Its Relation to the Rational*, trans. John W. Harvey (Oxford: Oxford University Press, 1923), 22–41.

29. Otto devotes an entire chapter to "the holy as a category of value" (*The Idea of the Holy*, 51–61).

30. See Plat. Rep. 476b, 493e, 507b.

31. Aristot. Poet. 3.1448b4–10. Plotinus, *On Beauty*, in *Ennead*, trans. A. H. Armstrong, in *Loeb Classical Library* (Cambridge, MA: Harvard University Press, 1966–1988), 1.6.

32. See Jerry Gill's concept of mediated transcendence in Gill, *Mediated Transcendence: A Postmodern Reflection* (Macon, GA: Mercer University Press, 1989).

33. For example, Alfred J. Ayer, *Language, Truth, and Logic* (London: Victor Gollancz, 1936).

34. Ricoeur, *Interpretation Theory: Discourse and the Surplus of Meaning* (Fort Worth: Texas Christian University Press, 1976), 12, 19–22, 45–46, 57.

35. Otto, *Idea of the Holy*, 13–14. See especially chapter 10.

36. Pss 8:1; 19:1; 24:7–10; 29:3, 9; 57:5, 11; 72:19; 96:3; 97:6; 108:5; 145:11.

37. This observation is not meant to deflect from von Balthasar's emphasis upon the aspect of "form" with regard to the concept of *glory* (see *Glory of the Lord*, 114–15). I do, however, think that von Balthasar, in his effort to distance himself from Protestant suspicions toward the aesthetic dimension, does not place enough of an emphasis on the *dynamic* aspect of glory. Still, he is not averse to speaking of the *unfolding* of the Form (470–78) with regard to Christ and the inherent *power* (*dynamis*) of the Form (478–83) with regard to the Holy Spirit.

38. See Gen 18:4; 19:2; 24:32; 43:24; Exod 3:5; 30:19, 21; 40:32.

39. Gen 17:3, 17; 19:1; 32:30; 33:10; 38:15; 42:6; 43:3, 5; 44:23, 26; 48:12; Exod 3:6; 10:28; 33:11, 20, 23; 34:29, 30, 33; Lev 9:24; 17:10; 20:3, 5–6; 26:17; Num 6:25–26; 12:8; 14:5, 14; 16:4, 22, 45; 10:6; 22:31; Deut 5:4; 7:10; 31:17, 18; 32:20; 34:10.

40. Hos 6:6.

41. For example, Jesus' forgiveness of sins (Mark 2:1–12; Luke 7:48; Matt 9:1–8) and his Sabbath healings (Mark 3:1–6; Luke 13:10–17; Matt 12:10; John 9:14–16).

42. Begbie refers to this kind of "transcendent" as entailing *horizontal* transcendence (*Redeeming Transcendence*, 6).

43. Gunton, *The One, the Three and the Many*, 31.

44. Gunton, *The One, the Three and the Many*, 31.

45. This resembles the doctrine of *homo incurvatus in se* (man curved in upon himself) discussed by Augustine, Martin Luther, Karl Barth, and Jürgen Moltmann among others. See Matt Jenson, *Augustine, Barth, and Luther on 'Homo Incurvatus in Se'* (Edinburgh: T & T Clark, 2006).

46. Albert Camus, *The Myth of Sisyphus and Other Essays*, trans. Justin O'Brien (New York: Alfred A. Knopf, 1967), 119–23.

47. Camus, *The Myth of Sisyphus and Other Essays*, 123.

48. Karl Marx, *A Contribution to the Critique of Hegel's Philosophy of Right* (1843), in *Deutsch-Französische Jahrbücher*, trans. unknown, ed. Andy Blunden and Matthew Carmody (Paris: February 7 and 10, 1844), Introduction.

49. *Qur'an* 8:59.

50. For example, the doctrine of *qadar*, meaning "fate," or "fore-ordainment." See Qur'an 9:51. On surrendering the human purpose to Allah's purpose, see Qur'an 2:112; 3:20; 4:125; 10:105; 30:30; 30:43; 31:22; 72:14; 92:20.

51. See Qur'an 4; 17.

52. Qur'an 98; 2:99, 118, 159, 185, 209, 211, 213, 253; 3:7, 86, 103, 105; 4:153, 174; 5:35; 6:57, 105, 157; 7:85, 101; 10:15, 61, 74; 11:6; 14:52; 16:44; 24:58–59, 61; 27:75; 28:49; 34:3; 37:117. The *Qur'an* speaks of clear proofs being given to the prophets prior to Mohammad,

such as Moses and Jesus, but the claim that the Scriptures of Christians and Jews are corrupt (the doctrine of *taḥrīf*) makes it impossible to know what those clear proofs were, or in what respect the Hebrew and Christian Scriptures corrupted them.

53. The purpose of Allah was unclear regarding Mohammad's successor. The succession question caused the rift between Sunni and Shi'a Islam. One wonders why Allah did not reveal his clear purpose to Mohammad regarding this extremely important matter.

54. For example, Shi'a and Sunni Muslims vigorously resist Sufi Islam, where mystical experience is allowed.

55. William Sturman Sax, ed., *The Gods at Play: Līlā in South Asia* (Oxford: Oxford University Press, 1995).

56. Sarvepalli Radhakrishnan, *Eastern Philosophy and Western Thought* (Oxford: Oxford University Press, 1969), 58–114. Radhakrishnan tried defending Hinduism against what he perceived were erroneous Western misinterpretations, especially the charge that Vedanta Hinduism allows little room for ethics. He thus wrote his MA thesis on *The Ethics of the Vedanta and its Metaphysical Presuppositions* (Madras: The Guardian Press, 1908).

57. Albert Schweitzer, *Indian Thought and Its Development*, trans. Charles E. B. Russell (Redditch, Worcestershire: Read Books Ltd.), loc. 605 of 3852, Kindle. Radhakrishnan frequently cites Schweitzer in *Eastern Philosophy*, 95.

58. Radhakrishnan, *Eastern Philosophy*, 96–102.

59. *The Mahabharata of Krishna-Dwaipayana Vyasa*, trans. Pratap Chandra Roy, 12 vols. (Calcutta: Oriental Publishing, 1962), vol. 10 (*Santi Parva*), 617–19; vol. 11 (*Anusasana Parva*), 378–79.

60. Isa 61:2; Luke 4:19.

61. For example, Socrates says in Plato's *Phaedrus* (237e–238a), "Now when opinion leads through reason toward the best and is more powerful, its power is called self-restraint, but when desire irrationally drags us toward pleasures and rules within us, its rule is called excess." Socrates then mentions various vices that arise from excess. Plato, *Phaedrus*, trans. Harold N. Fowler, ed. W. R. M. Lamb, in *Loeb Classical Library* 36, vol. 1, ed. Jeffrey Henderson (Cambridge, MA: Harvard University Press, 1914), 445.

62. Aristotle writes, "Virtue, therefore, is a mean state in the sense that it is able to hit the mean. Again, error is multiform (for evil is a form of the unlimited, as in the old Pythagorean imagery, and good of the limited), whereas success is possible in one way only (which is why it is easy to fail and difficult to succeed—easy to miss the target and difficult to hit it); so this is another reason why excess and deficiency are a mark of vice, and observance of the mean a mark of virtue: Goodness is simple, badness manifold." Aristotle, *Nicomachean Ethics* 2.6.13–14, trans. R. Rackham, in *The Loeb Classical Library* 73, vol. 19 (Cambridge, UK: Harvard University Press, [1934] 2003), 95.

63. Gerhard Ritter, *Frederick the Great*, trans. Peter Paret (Berkeley: University of California Press, 1968), 169.

64. In other words, through Thomas Carlyle. See W. H. G. Armytage, *German Influence on English Education* (London: Routledge, 2012), 47–54.

65. Friedrich Wilhelm Joseph von Schelling, *Philosophical Inquiries into the Nature of Human Freedom*, trans. J. Gutmann (Chicago, IL: Open Court, 1977), 17–18.

66. Søren Kierkegaard, *The Concept of Anxiety: A Simple Psychologically Oriented Deliberation in View of the Dogmatic Problem of Hereditary Sin*, ed. and trans. Alastair Hannay (New York: Liveright Publishing, 2015), 132–49.

67. Friedrich Nietzsche, *The Will to Power*, trans. Walter Kaufmann and R. J. Hollingdale (New York: Vintage Books, 1968), 403–13.

68. Jean-Paul Sartre, *Being and Nothingness*, trans. Hazel E. Barnes (New York: Philosophical Library, 1956), 484, 526.

69. Marshall Berman, *The Politics of Authenticity: Radical Individualism and the Emergence of Modern Society* (London: Verso, [1970] 2009), 32–44.

70. Geert Hofstede, *Culture's Consequences: Comparing Values, Behaviors, Institutions, and Organizations Across Nations*, 2nd ed. (Thousand Oaks, CA: Sage Publications, 2001), 292–93. I rely heavily upon Hofstede's cultural dimensions while trying to assimilate them to my own categories. These dimensions are as follows: (1) Power distance (high versus low), (2)

uncertainty avoidance (risk amenable as opposed to risk averse), (3) individualism (as opposed to collectivism), (4) masculinity (as opposed to femininity), (5) long-term orientation (as opposed to short term), and (6) indulgence (versus restraint).

71. Hofstede, *Culture's Consequences*, 292–93.

72. Hofstede, *Culture's Consequences*, 174–75, 180–81.

73. Hofstede, *Culture's Consequences*, 187.

74. Hofstede, *Culture's Consequences*, 180–81.

75. Plat. Rep., bk. 8. Aristot. Pol., bk. 6.

76. Plat. Rep. 415a–417b.

77. Plat. Rep. 473c–d, 540d–541b.

78. Aristot. Pol., bk. 5.

79. Niccolò Machiavelli, *The Prince*, trans. N. H. Thompson (New York: Cosimo Classics, 2008), 4. 5.

80. John Locke, *The Second Treatise of Government* (Project Gutenberg e-book, 2010), ch. 19, secs. 223–25, www.gutenberg.org/files/7370/7370-h/7370-h.htm.

81. Hofstede, *Culture's Consequences*, 127 (Exhibit 3.13).

82. Hofstede, *Culture's Consequences*, 107–8 (Exhibit 3.8).

83. Hofstede, *Culture's Consequences*, 209–14. Hofstede mentions that cultures with wide power distance ratios correlate with collectivism, while cultures with low power distance ratios correlate with individualism (*Culture's Consequences*, 216).

84. Hofstede, *Culture's Consequences*, 294 (Exhibit 6.8).

85. Hofstede, *Culture's Consequences*, 100.

86. Gerard A. Puccio and David W. Gonzáles, "Nurturing Creative Thinking: Western Approaches and Eastern Issues," in *Creativity: When East Meets West*, ed. Sing Lau, Ann N. N. Hui, and Grace Y. C. Ng (Singapore: World Scientific Publishing, 2004), 410–17.

87. Paul Tillich, *Systematic Theology*, 3 vols. (Chicago: University of Chicago Press, 1973), 1:118.

88. Exod 20:4.

89. Tillich, *Systematic Theology*, 1:211–12, 220–23. See also *The Interpretation of History*, trans. N. A. Rasetzki and Elsa L. Talmey (New York: Charles Scribner's Sons, 1936), 82–85.

90. Tillich, *Systematic Theology*, 1:216.

91. Tillich, *Systematic Theology*, 1:216.

92. David E. Bernstein provides a libertarian critique of the present focus of the American Civil Liberties Union in chapter 12 of his book, "The ACLU and the Abandonment of Civil Liberties," *You Can't Say That! The Growing Threat to Civil Liberties from Antidiscrimination Laws* (Washington, DC: Cato Institute, 2003), 145–53.

Chapter Three

Identifying Value-Indicators

The geographical compass serves as a useful analogue to the value-compass paradigm that I offered in the previous chapter. However, whereas a geographical compass depends on the *physical law* of magnetism to operate properly, the value-compass does not. Consequently, between physical laws and axiological principles an incongruity appears that has the capacity to render applications of the value-compass analogy ineffectual beyond a certain point. *Libertarian freedom* factors into the way axiological principles operate *voluntarily* in the context of the value-compass, while physical laws cause the geographical compass to operate *involuntarily* and according to strict *necessity*. Persons exercising libertarian freedom thus have the power to act in voluntary ways that *may not accord* with the laws of nature and, in fact, may *disrupt* them. In these respects, the dimension of the *voluntary* often transcends, and sometimes even defies, the dimension of the *involuntary*. To understand the nature of the relationship between these dimensions, I must therefore explore in greater depth what I referred to in the previous chapter as "value-indicators."

INSTINCTS, IMPULSES, DRIVES, AND ASPIRATIONS

Common experiences guide us in discerning the differences between instincts, impulses, drives, and aspirations. Instincts are the most biologically ingrained and innate of the factors that motivate biological life. The most obvious among these is the *survival* instinct, which, as an unlearned behavior, manifests itself biologically and psychologically both in *positive* and *negative* ways. One observes its positive manifestation in the baby's biological dependence upon its mother for milk and in its grasping reflex. The baby instinctively coos in response to *pleasure*, or cries in response to *pain*. Pain automatically evokes the baby's cry, for no one needs to teach the baby how to cry when it experiences discomfort. This innate cry response, being innate, is unlearned. Instinctual responses are therefore the most immediate kinds of responses to experiences of those rudimentary value-indicators that we call *pleasure* and *pain*.

Though pleasure and pain function as positive and negative value-indicators, respectively, these designations must not at this level be interpreted *dualistically*. More specifically, they must not be assessed from the standpoint of highly developed categories in which good and evil appear starkly opposed. If anything, the positive and negative values retain an element of *ambiguity* at this level; for while the baby reacts to pain as something negative, from the mother's standpoint, the cry of her baby plays a positive role in alerting her to her baby's need.

Like other members of the animal kingdom, the earliest human responses to stimuli causing pleasure and pain seem nonreflective and immediate, much like the purring of a cat or the yelping of a dog indicate the animal's pleasure or distress. Nevertheless, between these psychophysiological factors that we identify as *pleasure* and *pain*—and our responses to these factors—a gap begins to appear; though admittedly this gap is initially quite minuscule and short in duration. In the lower species, this gap tends to remain minuscule; but as one ascends the scale to the higher vertebrates, through the reptilian and up to the mammalian, the gap expands proportionally. It is this gap that allows predators with higher intelligence to strategize as they hunt their prey. It also allows the prey space to develop evasive skills wherewith to escape their predators. In human beings, this gap can become even more expansive. Indeed, it can expand to the degree that it allows space for *mental reflection* and for the possible interruption of *volition* that can alter and channel behavioral responses that are otherwise instinctually rooted.[1]

Impulses are closely related to instincts and contain within themselves a *residue* of what is instinctual. Most human beings agree, however, that impulses can be reflected upon, evaluated, suppressed, repressed, curbed, and channeled. Types of human behavior aimed at seeking immediate gratification when pleasurable objects are presented to the senses are usually labeled "impulsive." So are avoidance behaviors that enable one to steer clear of obstacles that may be perceived to inflict pain in the short term but promise higher fulfillment over the long haul. Societies across the world have discouraged their young from giving in to impulsive behaviors. At the same time, they have also encouraged their young to subdue their appetites, passions, and immediate desires, and to channel their drives constructively toward life's higher pursuits and aspirations.

Moving from impulses to drives, we observe ways that the drives carry within them a residue of the impulsive, just as impulses carry within them a residue of the instinctual. Drives, however, are most easily recognized at the place where the psychological dimension of human experience begins to connect in purposive and meaningful ways to socio-historical and transcendental dimensions of reality. The two psychological drives that become manifested socially are the *competitive* and *cooperative*. The desire to *win* arouses the *competitive* drive; the desire to *belong*, the *cooperative*. Though sometimes at cross-purposes, and though not always balanced in the same way across the world's cultures, these drives appear universally in the human species. In the drives, we observe more clearly the intrusion of the dimension of the voluntary into what hitherto has been only instinctual and impulsive. Because the intrusion of the voluntary becomes a factor, the competitive and cooperative drives are able to *free* themselves from merely instinctual and impulsive sorts of behavior by connecting with life's higher pursuits.

Competitive and cooperative drives can thus function at a social level of expression, but they can also be directed toward and taken up into our aspirations. Two aspirations can, in fact, be identified. One of these I will call *the quest for height* and the other, *the search for centeredness*. *The quest for height*, on the one hand, entails the human quest for *status* and *recognition*. In this regard, it is focused more on the good of *individuals* of the species, while the good of the species as a *collective* remains a secondary concern. *The search for centeredness*, on the other hand, is preoccupied with the human search for *belonging* and *relatedness* to others of the species. The search for centeredness in these regards focuses on the good of the *collective* reality of the human species and secondarily on the good of *individuals* within that species.

Because the quest for height and the search for centeredness entail the greatest possible expressions of freedom, these two aspirations have the capacity to be thrown into greater disequilibrium than the competitive and cooperative drives ordinarily do when they are exercised at less complex social levels. At these less complex levels, the competitive and cooperative drives may appear to be more *playful* and *game-like* in the ways they overlap. However, when they become connected to the *aspirations*, they have the potential to become *serious*. The degree of seriousness attained happens to link proportionally to the degree of risk that the aspiration requires from the aspirant. The greater the aspiration, the greater the risk; and the greater the risk, the greater the gravity of the consequences that could befall one if one fails to fulfill the aspiration toward which a drive is aimed.

EVALUATIVE LENSES AND THE
CONFLICT OF INTERPRETATIONS

Philosophers, scientists, psychologists, sociologists, and theologians have, however, been unable to reach agreement on how to evaluate and distinguish between instincts, impulses, drives, and aspirations. Their disagreement stems from the fact that they make assumptions that in themselves are *axiologically* driven. They may nonetheless be unaware that they even harbor such value-laden presuppositions. They may simply assume that the philosophical lens they use to evaluate the phenomenon of human life *happens* to be the right one simply because it *feels* right to them. On the one hand, they may randomly choose a lens that tries to view human life solely from the dimension of the *tangible*. On the other hand, they may try to view life purely from a *transcendental* dimension. They will then proceed to explain human instincts, impulses, drives, and aspirations either from one or the other of these opposing vantage points.

Unfortunately, extremes in outlooks usually lead to a conflating and confusing of categories on both sides, albeit in differing ways. One is often forced then to choose between mutually exclusive paradigms. The choice then becomes one of a strict *either/or*. A materialist explanation, on the one hand, moors the instincts, impulses, drives, and aspirations entirely to the dimension of the *tangible*. An uncompromising focus on *particularity* eliminates the need for any focus on *transcendent universals* that might be mediated through the tangible dimension. An *idealist* explanation, on the other hand, might attempt to dissolve these distinctions into some universal spiritual substance. When this is done, particularity seems either to evaporate or to be dissolved into the Universal. The conflict of such extreme methodological approaches then leaves us with what seems an irresolvable conflict of interpretations. Such a choice, I argue, not only commits the fallacy of false dichotomy, but in both cases, a *fuzzy blur* results that precludes intellectually satisfactory answers.

The Fuzzy Blur of Materialism

This fuzzy blur is already detectable in ideas of the earliest Greek materialist philosophers. Anaximander of Miletus (c. 610–c. 545 BCE) claimed that the four elements—earth, fire, air, and water—caused *injustice* (Grk=*adikia* [ἀδικία]) toward one another after they had arisen out of the quintessential element that he called the *apeiron* (i.e., the "boundless" or the "unlimited"). To satisfy the demands of justice (Grk=*dikē* [δίκη]), Anaximander contended that the elements would have *to pass sentence* upon one another. Only by receiving their just condemnation could the four elements make reparation for the "crimes" they committed against their competing elements. [2]

Though Anaximander is usually classified as a materialist, this classification seems partly contraindicated by the fact that he freely employs *moral* terminologies to describe *physical* kinds of processes. He uses the terms "injustice," "reparation," and "crime" to describe what occurs when the four elements separate out from the *apeiron* and return to it. His usage of such terms might seem innocuous enough at first glance, but a closer examination reveals that he blurred the distinction between *purely physical* and *moral* categories. A *fuzzy blur* thus appears because the terminologies he uses are much too value-laden in their connotation to describe what truly is going on between the "warring" elements.

The fuzziness problem persists in the speculations of other pre-Socratics as well. Heraclitus of Ephesus (c. 535–c. 475 BCE) contradicted Anaximander's verdict when he asseverated that the principle of *"justice"* (Grk=*dikē* [δίκη]) governs the types of relationships that exist between the four elements.[3] "Justice," of course, is quite as much ethically value-laden a term as "injustice." Empedocles (c. 495–c. 444 BCE) it seems, tried to have it both ways when he famously spoke of the *love* (Grk=*philia* [φιλία]) and *hate* (Grk=*neikos* [νεῖκος]) of the elements.[4] He used these categories in a manner resembling the Taoist concepts of *yin* and *yang*. Like *yin* and *yang*, the principles of love and hate govern the ebb-and-flow cycle that regulates how the elements relate to one another. But in what respect can love and hate be construed as merely *physical* forces, especially if we think of them as *ethically* value-laden principles that resemble the *human* qualities of *love* and *hate*?

The pre-Socratics' projection of value-laden conceptions onto natural phenomena might very well have resulted from older traditions derived from Greek polytheism where aspects of nature were routinely personified. The so-called "scientific" explanations of the Ionian philosophers are thus not as far removed from belief in the Hellenistic nature gods as what might first appear. Nor does the pre-Socratics' tendency to *confuse* the categories of the *personal* and *mechanistic* end with them. Aristotle, who inherited their philosophical traditions, adjusted them in ways that comported with his own paradigm. But in doing so, he perpetuated their error despite his usually keen ability to make categorical distinctions. He follows Empedocles' cue, for instance, when he accommodates the latter's *principle of love* to his own philosophical system. Aristotle speaks of *love* as the *force of attraction* that the Unmoved Mover elicits from the entire universe (though he does not, like Empedocles, locate the love principle *within* the physical universe).[5]

Aristotle's understanding of the divine power of attraction is, however, still far removed from the Judeo-Christian understanding of divine love; for in Aristotle's view, God is *impersonal* rather than *personal*. Indeed, Aristotle favors an impersonal God when he contends that the power of attraction extending from the Unmoved Mover over the entire universe is a *necessary* rather than a *voluntary* force.[6] His emphasis on divine necessity, in turn, raises a question: In what sense would it be appropriate to accord to a necessary principle of attraction the *same degree* of value as that accorded to a voluntary act of love? To accord them *equal* value seems problematic insofar as Aristotle's conception of God as the Unmoved Mover bears a striking resemblance to such necessary, mechanical, and impersonal laws or forces as gravity and magnetism.

Judeo-Christian biblical perspectives, by contrast, conceive of divine love as having originated from a *personal* Deity. There is simply no comparison between this view and that of Aristotle, and to demonstrate the absurdity of the comparison, one only needs to compare the statement, "My spouse loves me," with the statement, "Earth's gravity loves me." An impersonal, mechanical principle can in no way allow for the same level of freedom, flexibility, give-and-take, and reciprocity that the dimension of the personal affords. The dimension of the impersonal, for this reason, simply fails to supply the same degree of *ethical* and *aesthetic* justification that the dimension of the personal provides. Indeed, if love were a necessary force originating from an ultimate *impersonal* principle, then what is the basis for claiming that such a principle is fully capable of operating as the ultimate ground or goal of any *ethical purpose* or *aesthetic significance*?[7]

While the Greek "materialist" traditions tend to project value-*laden* categories onto value-*neutral* phenomena, other materialist theories advocate a *reduction* of value-laden categories to "value-neutral" ones. This kind of reduction is achieved when a necessary, impersonal, and mechanistic principle is assumed to function as the ultimate ground and goal of the *good*. The following illustration reveals the fallacy of this way of thinking. Most people would agree that having a car with a running motor is always *good*, and in many circumstances, this judgment would hold true. However, a running motor rarely appears as an end in itself. The *purpose* of a car's running motor is to get passengers from point A to point B, but the *full value* of that running motor can only be gauged by what A, B, and the relation between the two consist of context-wise. Here, a *mechanical* kind of apparatus only takes on *moral* or *aesthetic* significance when it becomes related to a context of significance *beyond* itself.

Take, for example, the scenario of Bonnie and Clyde's getaway car. Suppose that "A" happens to be the bank they are planning to rob, "B" is their hideout, and the relation between "A" and "B" is their escape route and the time needed to traverse that route successfully. From the standpoint of Bonnie and Clyde's victims, the failure of the car motor to run would clearly qualify as a favorable development, though it would not be so from Bonnie's and Clyde's perspectives. Suppose, however, that the scenario entails the approaching birth of a child where both child and mother are at risk? If "A" is home where the expectant mother is located; "B" is the hospital; and the relation between "A" and "B" is the distance and time the expectant mother must traverse for her and her child to be brought safely through the birth process, then a failure of the motor to run would clearly prove threatening. What constitutes the difference between these two hypotheticals *is not* the running motor itself, but the overall *context* in which that motor runs and the degree to which it serves a specialized purpose in bringing about a desirable end beyond itself.

We are therefore not talking about just *any* context, for some contexts appear quite mundane and routine when compared to others. In routine contexts, the failure of a car motor to run might at worst be an inconvenience. But what if the context is one involving *extraordinary risks*? Suppose, for example, that the risk entails the possibility of *life* or *death*. Then the running of the car's motor, or its not running, will appear either *very good* or *very bad*, depending on what outcomes the taking of such extraordinary risks actuate. The two examples given above reveal that the risk factor in extraordinary kinds of scenarios is never neutral: Risk is *always* value-laden.

Now if something like a running car motor provides a scenario of the way the universe runs, then it becomes easier to see where this scenario fails to explain phenomena such as bank robberies and successful childbirths. The Deists of the seventeenth and eighteenth centuries, for instance, used a mechanistic analogy to explain their conception of the relationship between God and the universe. They succeeded through their use of rhetoric in convincing many to relegate supernatural phenomena such as miracles and angelic beings to the status of mere superstition.[8] Still, the Deists could not account for the presence of that meaningful residue within humanity that philosophers such as René Descartes called the "soul" or the "mind." Descartes' solution was to modify the mechanistic view of the universe. He argued, on the one hand, that bodies, as "extended things," operate according to mechanistic laws. He insisted on the other hand that "the mind" or "the soul" could not be explained in terms of mechanism.[9]

Later, Gilbert Ryle (1900–1976) disparaged what he caricatured as Descartes' "ghost in the machine."[10] Ryle went on to classify Descartes' notion of a soul separate from the body as a "category mistake."[11] To disparage Cartesian dualism, Ryle attempted to compare the human body-soul phenomenon to the University of Oxford and its relation to the Oxford colleges.[12] Anyone who knows the University of Oxford also knows that it does not exist as a separate entity *apart from* the conglomeration and interrelationship of all the individual Oxford colleges that comprise it.

Roy Varghese (1957–), however, suggests an alternative to Ryle's University of Oxford analogy. Suppose a primitive person possessing absolutely no knowledge of modern technology were to find an abandoned radio playing on a deserted beach. That person might logically deduce that the station playing on the radio must indeed be somewhere *inside* the radio and therefore *identical* with the radio's components.[13] Clearly, this would not so much be a "category mistake" as it would be a failure to have *enough categories* to explain the phenomenon of the playing radio. This example can serve as a useful counter-analogy to Ryle's attempt to explain the phenomenon of the human soul as something *identical with* the reality of the physical organism.

Ryle was clearly a reductionist. Whereas most people tend to think of phenomena such as the soul as intrinsically value-laden, reductionists do not. Some unknown motivation drives them to account for such phenomenon by proposing that they originate in the lowest common denominator of physical existence. Scientific sorts of explanations often reveal this motivation, though the motivation itself does not always seem overtly hostile. The late physicist Stephen Hawking, for instance, did not appear hostile when he proposed his "theory of everything."[14] He was merely trying to identify a common basis that could explain the strong nuclear force, the weak nuclear force, electromagnetism, and gravity.[15] The problem only appeared with his ambitious use of the term "everything." His effort to provide credibility for his assumption is impressive. However, what remains unconvincing about his project is his attempt to *reduce* everything to a theory that, at its basis, is explicable solely in terms of his specialized field of interest and expertise; namely, *physics*. His "theory of everything" may prove satisfactory to physicists; however, artists, musicians, and poets will predictably remain unconvinced and unimpressed.

Still another common error in reductive sorts of theories appears in the way the role of some lower aspect of a greater whole tends to be exaggerated in an attempt to explain the whole. Sigmund Freud (1856–1939) uses this kind of exaggeration when he inflicted his famous "psychological wound" on the thought-world of his day.[16] Freud tries to explain the human soul (the whole) in terms of human sexual drives and impulses (a lower aspect of the whole). It may, of course, be true that the sexual drives function as *components* of the soul. Even Plato speaks of the appetites in this way.[17] However, Freud's insights do not need to imply that these components *alone* could explain what the soul is in its entirety. Freud's successor, Carl Jung (1875–1961), recognized his predecessor's fallacious thinking and rejected it outright.[18] My previous *motor-in-the-car* analogy may illuminate the role the sexual drives play in the context of the soul. Certain parts of the running motor (not all) could be taken to represent the sexual drives. However, the sexual drives by themselves can no more explain the soul than a running motor can explain a bank robbery or a childbirth. Car motors and sexual drives do not necessarily imply the inevitability of bank robberies or the existence of souls.

Unfortunately, reductive thinking post-Freud has led to interpretations of human sexuality that assume a doctrine of full-blown biological determinism to be self-evidently true. It is, of course, accurate to say that we are biologically determined to be what we are *in some respects*. For instance, the two possible combinations of the X and Y chromosomes biologically determine the sex of a child; though categories of gender are now being questioned by some who would turn a blind eye to the obvious biological evidence.[19] However, the claim that various types of sexual compulsions are *necessarily* determined in a manner that is equal to biologically determined male and female sexual characteristics does not logically follow when one considers them in the light of other human behaviors where voluntary and involuntary sorts of actions are observed to be in interplay. Breathing, for example, is most of the time an involuntary function of the human organism. Still, I can have a limited degree of voluntary control over this involuntary activity when I decide to hold my breath or to hyperventilate. Granted, I can only exercise such voluntary ability over this involuntary action for a short time, for the point will come when I *must* take a breath or stop hyperventilating. Otherwise, I will pass out. Likewise, involuntary and voluntary actions govern the human need for water and food, but they do so in a manner that is proportionally less pressing than our need for air. I can go without water longer than I can go without air, and I can go without food longer than I can go without water. However, just as there is a limit to how long I can go without air, so there is a limit to how long I can go without water or food.

How then do we compare the impulses to breathe, drink, or eat, with the sexual drive? There is plenty of evidence to suggest that the sexual drive can be voluntarily suppressed longer than the need for air, water, or food. Indeed, some willingly choose to live in a state of lifelong celibacy, and they seem to live fulfilling lives despite their choice. There exists, however, no compelling evidence that the fuller contexts in which our sexuality comes to be expressed are themselves biologically *determined* or *necessary*. Just as one cannot prove that committing a bank robbery is necessarily caused by the reality of a running motor, choices of contexts in which we express our sexuality are not necessarily implied in the biological basis of our sexuality. Contexts in which our sexuality comes to be expressed therefore remain as separate a sphere from the biological realm as the car motor does from a bank robbery in which that car motor may happen to be used.

What I have been arguing against up to this point is the notion that everything human beings do that appears *voluntary* can somehow be reduced to and explained in terms of purely *involuntary* mechanistic causes. Human freedom may find itself in conflict with the aspect of the involuntary, true; and there are of course ways that necessity places boundaries upon human freedom.[20] But as I have tried to explain above, not all these boundaries impinge upon the exercise of our freedom equally. As we have seen in the case of our need for air, water, and food, nature enforces some of these more exactingly than others.[21]

Other boundaries, which are not imposed upon us by nature, are imposed on us by the societies in which we live. Some societies enforce these impositions upon its members more rigidly than others. There are also boundaries we voluntarily choose to abide within. Boundaries of this sort may be imposed by the social or religious traditions and mores of the cultures we inhabit. We may also engage in the arbitrary construction of boundaries for ourselves to assert a unique kind of identity, or we may seek to impose our arbitrarily constructed identities upon others by force or by shaming others into submission.

The nature-convention dialectic, which harks back to Socrates and his dialogue with the Sophists,[22] is a related topic worthy of mention at this juncture. Indeed, the nature-convention dialectic closely aligns with the limit-freedom dialectic discussed in the previous chapter. On the one hand, appealing to nature as the basis for ethics ordinarily requires one to adjust one's behavior to conform to the greatest possible degree to nature's demands and strictures (i.e., to *limit*). To conform to nature's limits, human free will must thus be restrained. Individuality must be subsumed beneath the collective, and freedom must be made to conform to the flow of nature.[23] An appeal to convention, on the other hand, maximizes the role of *freedom*. Free individuals establish their own rules and boundaries for life. These rules and boundaries tend, however, to be arbitrarily decided on, and they often disregard whatever boundaries nature tries to impose. Because individuality is preferable to conformity to the collective, convention becomes a useful tool 1) for mediating between individuals with all their disparate drives and ambitions, 2) for forging a common vision for life in a communal setting, and 3) for reaching consensus on what may constitute common cause.

Asserting the priority of nature over convention, or of convention over nature, is a topic of an ongoing dispute in moral and political philosophy.[24] A question arises as to whether it is best to base ethical behaviors on the observation of the principles of *nature* (as, e.g., in Stoicism or Taoism), or to appeal to the principles of *convention* (as do Francis Bacon [1561–1626], Thomas Hobbes [1588–1679], and John Locke). If nature and convention are both to play roles in the deciding of ethical theory, then how do we sort out these roles?

Often, philosophers try to justify their ethical theories by using *naturalism* as a basis. In so doing, they attempt to move from merely descriptive categories to prescriptive ethical ones. G. E. Moore (1873–1958) famously called the attempt to derive an "ought" from an "is" the "naturalistic fallacy."[25] Efforts to derive ethics from nature alone perhaps would be acceptable if ethical laws operated at the same level as the laws of chemistry and physics. Unfortunately, they do not. Experiments in the hard sciences are repeatable and, therefore, predictable, while "experiments" in the social sciences usually vary in their outcomes.[26] Nature is more definite in what it reveals about cause-and-effect relationships at the physical-chemical level, but it is not *as* definite in what it reveals about cause-and-effect relationships at the moral level. Indeed, nature may at times appear inconsistent in the way it comports with the moral law: For example, the sun shines on the just and the unjust, and the rain falls upon both.[27]

The laws of cause and effect in sciences such as physics and chemistry are clearer, more immediate, more easily observable, and more successfully repeatable in experiments than are the laws of cause and effect in the moral realm. One reason for the discrepancy is that the moral realm is more complex in its configuration than nature is at its organic level. As one ascends from the purely physical to the moral dimension, causes tend to proliferate instead of remaining singular. Indeed, in addition to being natural, causes may range from the social to the historical to the cultural to the religious.

Ongoing attempts have been made nonetheless to resolve the conflict between opposing categories, such as the *mechanistic* and the *moral*, or the *natural* and the *conventional*. One such attempt *conflates* the categories "fact" and "value." Atheists Sam Harris (1967–) and Richard Carrier (1969–) have argued separately, for instance, that values should be considered as facts like any other facts.[28] However, a comparison of moral causality to physical causality reveals that these two levels of causality are incongruent regardless of whether one is willing to acknowledge the incongruity.[29] One can only wonder what benefit Harris or Carrier derives from obfuscating this incongruity by relegating moral value to the level of fact. Recognizing and affirming the *distinction* between facts and values is still a more plausible position.[30] *Eliminating* the distinction seems to be an attempt to make *their* values immune from questioning, because one cannot argue with *facts* in the same way one might question values. Such efforts at obfuscation seem at best to hinge on semantic quibbling rather than real substance.

The approach that Harris and Carrier represent also suggests that it would truly be beneficial to move from a descriptive stance to a prescriptive one. Both believe that the gap between the "is" and the "ought" can be bridged by doing away with the fact-value distinction.[31] However, I argue that the only thing gained by such a move is the tenuous verdict that ethical relativism must somehow be true. Ethical relativism then leads to a proliferation of conflicting moralities that, to be fair, should all be deemed equally valid. At best, society is left not with a *beneficial verdict* at all but with a *free-for-all*. Anyone seeking to unify such divergent moral proliferations into a common vision or cause would be faced with something much worse than "herding cats." "Herding snakes" might serve as a more apt metaphor.[32]

Harris and Carrier, however, are confident that with "reason" as their guide they can accomplish this task cleanly and efficiently. To do so, however, they must somehow extract and distil from this quagmire of competing values what *their* reason convinces them are the only valid moral truths. *Their* reason also determines what is abhorrent and repugnant. This determination, incidentally, requires Carrier to do a "hatchet job" on the God of the Bible.[33] Carrier thus sets himself up as judge, jury, and executioner of this God without bothering to investigate all the facts about the cultural contexts that could shed light on and provide a rationale for God's commands within

the contexts in which they are given.[34] Instead, Carrier champions *his* morality as a superior alternative. However, what does not seem clear is any
factual basis he has for deciding what his superior morality should consist of
other than the "facts" of nature with all its ambiguities and *his* "reason" as
the tool he uses to sort through the muddle. He picks and chooses from
Taoism, Confucianism, and Buddhism to find ethical precepts that "ring
true" to *his* thinking,[35] but then he makes himself the final arbiter in determining which elements in these other traditions should be accepted and
which ones should be rejected. His claim to scientific objectivity turns out
then just to be another form of begging the question, and it just so happens
that his use of reason loops in upon itself.[36]

The option thus now appears to be between two choices—ethical relativism or what Carrier calls "metaphysical naturalism."[37] On the one hand, if
we are finally left with the option of embracing ethical relativism, the question arises, "How far will we be willing to go to allow ethical relativism to be
normative and ethically compelling?" The wide variance between the radical
Muslim jihadist terrorist and Saint Teresa of Calcutta[38] cannot be accounted
for by merely describing it. *My* reason may tell me that Saint Teresa stands at
the apex of virtue and that the radical Muslim jihadist has sunk to the nadir of
vice. The jihadist, however, will certainly reason otherwise. I can accuse him
of being irrational, but from his point of view he could say the same thing
about me.

On the other hand, if we embrace Carrier's metaphysical naturalism, then
we remain hard-pressed to find adequate justification for condemning the
terrorist for his viciousness or extolling Saint Teresa for her virtue. Indeed, if
we opt to privilege the ethical opinions of a Harris or a Carrier over those
whose opinions differ from theirs, then we still will not have effectively
argued for why we *should* accept theirs and not others. At best, we are finally
left with an approach in which "each man does what is right in his own
eyes."[39] No doubt, the metaphysical naturalist will use his best ammuni-
tion—namely, reason—to convince as many as possible that anyone who
does not agree with him/her is irrational, but there is very little difference
between this and the dogmatic fundamentalist's use of pejorative language in
calling the atheist an *infidel*. Again, one wonders how Harris or Carrier, who
so vehemently oppose religious perspectives while considering their own to
be correct, can have any real basis or justification for their opposition beyond
the ambiguity of nature and of their opinions on how to overcome that
ambiguity. Surely, we are not expected to believe that their opinions are valid
simply because they are theirs.

The Fuzzy Blur of Idealism

Up to now, I have been discussing the shortcomings of a variety of materialist views concerning impulses, drives, and aspirations; but idealist vantage
points appear equally flawed when they try to explain physical and chemical
laws by using higher value-laden kinds of phenomena such as the soul. The
fuzzy blur thus appears again, albeit in a different manner from the way it
appears in materialism. A dominant analogy can be traced back to Plato, who
used the human mind-body connection to describe the very nature of the
physical universe. Plato's use of the mind-body analogy in his *Timaeus*
formed the basis of his idea of the World Soul.[40] However, his use of this
analogy caused him to take an unfortunate misstep: He endowed physical
laws and principles with the mystical qualities one normally associates with
the *human* soul. Plato thus committed an opposite fallacy from that the
materialists committed when he attempted to project mystical categories onto
the physical dimension. Instead of collapsing the higher dimensions into the
sheer materiality of the lower ones, he elevated the lower dimensions by
projecting the higher ones onto them.

Still, Plato was baffled by the obstinacy that the lowest dimension of
reality exhibited; namely, *matter*. Matter, instead of conforming to the
Forms, always resisted union with them. Plato was thus confronted with a
kind of residue very different from the type that the Deists confronted. Where
the Deists were challenged with the residue of the supernatural called the
soul, which simply could not be explained as a mechanistic process, Plato
was challenged by the incomprehensible and irrational residue often referred
to as the "dark weight of matter."

Platonic idealism has had numerous resurgences and augmentations
throughout history. Indeed, in modern times, these have often been advanced
in response to mechanistic and deterministic philosophies. From the seventeenth to the nineteenth centuries, for instance, various attempts to envision
the physical universe by relying on divine categories gained ground. Against
deism, atheism, and the reductive materialism of Hobbes's view that everything, including God and the human soul, consisted of *matter in motion*,[41]
there appeared the contributions of the Cambridge Platonists, Nicolas Malebranche (1638–1715), and Bishop George Berkeley (1685–1753).[42] Berkeley
is particularly interesting because he proposes the notion that the physical
universe exists only as *an idea in the divine mind*.[43] By suggesting this line
of reasoning, he dismisses the idea that the *material* universe exists at all. He
thus departs significantly from the empiricist approach laid out by his predecessor John Locke, who had cleverly adapted Aristotle's distinction between
"substance" and "accidents" to the corpuscular theory that he (Locke) had
borrowed from his friend and colleague Robert Boyle (1627–1691).[44] More
specifically, Locke's assumption that things possess *primary qualities* corre-

sponds to Aristotle's idea of *substance*, while the former's assumption that things possess *secondary qualities* corresponds to the latter's idea of *accidents*.[45] Primary qualities thus referred to the material reality that things were composed of, whereas secondary qualities referred to the way things are perceived under varying conditions. Locke, who was nonetheless skeptical about going too far with the Aristotelian understanding of substance, also said, "substance is something I know not what."[46] Motivated by this skepticism regarding "physical" substance, Berkeley proceeded to reject Locke's view that such things as primary qualities could, in fact, exist at all. Instead, Berkeley believed that only *secondary* qualities could exist.[47] Berkeley's peculiar brand of empiricism thus led him to deny that the universe was *physically real*.

Meanwhile, on the European continent, Baruch Spinoza (1632–1677) found an alternative way of rejecting both deism and Cartesian dualism. Spinoza adopted *pantheism* when he affirmed that the physical universe and all things and persons contained in it were attributes or modes of God's (or Nature's) being.[48] Spinoza's "God or Nature" (*Deus sive Natura*) is, however, entirely impersonal; and in this, Spinoza significantly parts ways with Berkeley, who at least still held to a belief in a *personal* God.[49]

The subjective idealism of Berkeley and the impersonal pantheism of Spinoza would figure prominently in influencing the wide array of ideas that the German idealist tradition advanced. J. G. Fichte (1762–1814), F. D. E. Schleiermacher (1768–1834), Arthur Schopenhauer (1788–1860), Immanuel Kant, G. W. F. Hegel, and F. W. J. Schelling would explore various ways of interrelating and reconciling the objective and subjective dimensions of reality.[50] Kant and Schopenhauer, for instance, would keep the objective and subjective—and the personal and impersonal—dimensions absolutely separate.[51] Fichte and Hegel would ultimately subsume the objective dimension of reality under the auspices of the Absolute Subjectivity of God.[52] Schelling would maintain that the subjective dimension would, somehow, emerge magically or evolve mysteriously out of a kind of fructifying, unconscious, and indefinable principle of nonbeing (i.e., the *Urgrund*).[53] More will be said of these thinkers later.

Nineteenth-century idealism would, however, die its death as confidence in the "Titanic" of inevitable progress came crashing headlong into the twentieth-century "iceberg" of the World War I. To use another analogy from the World War II era, that philosophical spark called existentialism quickly exploded the hydrogen-filled dirigible of lofty aspirations and sent its intellectual world plunging in a fiery, downward spiral into absurdity. But despite the death of idealism in some of its forms, a version of it emerged again in the early twentieth century in the thought of Alfred North Whitehead (1861–1947), who projected voluntary kinds of cause-and-effect relationships onto what he should have understood as the dimension of the involuntary.[54] In this way, Whitehead promoted a form of what I would call "atomistic voluntarism," in which he imagined his version of the atoms—viz., the "actual entities" or "actual occasions"—to be endowed with real libertarian freedom.[55]

In conclusion, the fuzzy blurs of idealism seem equally as problematic as the fuzzy blurs of materialism. Indeed, both vantage points suffer from perspectives that are too reductive or too abstractive to see the whole picture. Either one cannot see the forest for the trees (materialism), or one cannot see the trees for the forest (idealism).

Bringing the Fuzzy Blurs into Focus

I must thus conclude at this juncture that either/or answers to the question, "Do differences exist between instincts, impulses, drives, and aspirations?" have proved insufficient in their explanatory capability. Materialist theories fail to account sufficiently for value-laden phenomena because they try to trace the cause of higher values back to facts that, in comparison with these higher values, are either *valueless* or, at best, *rudimentary* in value. Even nonreductive expressions of ethical naturalism fail to provide an adequate explanation of how one gets from the point A of value-*deficient* facts to the point B of value-*laden* facts.[56] It fails to explain how the transition from mechanistic causes to voluntaristic causes is at all possible.

One would be wise, therefore, to uphold the distinctions between facts and values, and between involuntary and voluntary causes, and not try to collapse voluntary causes into involuntary causes that are more mechanistic than personal. To do so fails to provide an adequate explanation for why our drives can be taken up into and transformed by our aspirations. Aspirations are therefore not identical to instincts, impulses, and drives. Though impulses and drives may work in tandem with aspirations, these value-indicators should never be conflated or confused.

On the other hand, projecting higher categories of value onto impersonal, mechanistic, physical categories and principles is just as erroneous a misstep. Elaborate metaphysical systems end up being developed that resemble fiction more than they do reality. Such developments may be acceptable in poetry and fantasy literature, but when we blur the distinction between subjective imagination and objective fact in our scientific perspectives, we risk promulgating superstition.

The best way to get rid of fuzzy blurs would be to use two lenses together at the same time rather than just one or the other separately. I suspect here that the problem with using one lens only is that we are trying to view a three dimensional picture without using the proper spectacles. The blur appears because we are trying to view a picture in 2D that was shot in 3D. We may thus need to put the materialist lens and the idealist lens together to form a more comprehensive viewing apparatus if we are to ascertain the value of human existence more clearly. How then might this 3D viewing apparatus effectively combine the materialist and idealist lenses, and what, exactly would this apparatus look like? This is a question that I will continue to explore in the chapters that follow.

NOTES

1. This gap resonates with what has been called "Hume's fork"; namely, the cleavage between "matters of fact" and "relations of ideas." Gottfried Leibniz's principle of sufficient reason failed to recognize this cleavage. See David Hume, "An Enquiry Concerning Human Understanding," in *Collected Writings* (Oxford: Benediction Classics, 2013), sec. 4, pt. 1, 498–502.

2. Simplicius, *Comments on Aristotle's Physics*, trans. J. O. Urmson (Ithaca, NY: Cornell University Press, 1997), 24.13.

3. Heraclitus, *The Cosmic Fragments*, trans. G. S. Kirk (Cambridge, UK: Cambridge University Press, 1954), 59–62.

4. Empedocles, *The Extant Fragments*, trans. M. R. Wright (New Haven, CT: Yale University Press, 1981), 6.

5. Aristot. Met. 1.4.985a2; 12.7.1072b4–5; 12.10.1075b7–10.

6. Aristot. Met. 12.7.1072b6–10.

7. The proposition "God is Necessary Being" need not entail that his volition be bounded by necessity. God is necessary as the *cause* of all that is in the sense that all contingent reality depends upon God as its ultimate cause.

8. James A. Herrick, for example, examined the English Deists' use of "radical rhetoric" to sway popular opinion. See Herrick, *The Radical Rhetoric of the English Deists: The Discourse of Skepticism, 1680–1750* (Columbia: University of South Carolina Press, 1997), 51–75.

9. René Descartes, *Meditations on First Philosophy* 2.13, 6.17.

10. Gilbert Ryle, *The Concept of Mind* (London: Routledge, 2009), 5–6.

11. Ryle, *The Concept of Mind*, 6.

12. Ryle, *The Concept of Mind*, 6.

13. Roy Abraham Varghese, *The Wonder of the World: A Journey from Modern Science to the Mind of God* (Fountain Hills, AZ: Tyr Publishing 2003), 57.

14. Or "grand unification theory." See Stephen Hawking, *A Brief History of Time* (New York: Bantam Books, 1996), 76–77.

15. Hawking, *A Brief History of Time*, 72–76.

16. Sigmund Freud, "A Difficulty in the Path of Psycho-Analysis [1917]," in *The Standard Edition of the Complete Psychological Works of Sigmund Freud*, 24 vols., ed. James Strachey (New York: W. W. Norton, 1976), vol. 17.

17. Plat. Phaedrus 246A–248A.

18. Carl Gustav Jung, *Modern Man in Search of a Soul*, trans. W. S. Dell and Cary F. Baynes (North American e-book, 2011), 116–17.

19. See Elof Axel Carlson, *The Seven Sexes: Biology of Sex Determination* (Bloomington: Indiana University Press, 2013), 126–27. The phenomenon of androgyny in true hermaphroditism is a biological anomaly—an abnormal chimeric phenomenon that occurs when fraternal-twin embryos fuse. As such, this fusion represents an aberration of nature that should not be extended into a general rule.

20. I refer here to *libertarian* freedom.

21. For example, Peter van Inwagen presents "incompatibilism" as an alternative to "compatibilism" in the freedom and determinism debate. *An Essay on Free Will* (Oxford: Clarendon Press, 1983), 1, 2. Compatibilism views freedom as being compatible with necessity. Van Inwagen identifies and rejects a presupposition that lies at the heart of the compatibilist view;

namely, that free will is compatible with a *strict causal determinism* or that free will *entails* determinism.

22. Plat. Gorg. 488e–499e.

23. A good example of this can be found in Taoism (see the *Tao Te Ching*, trans. James Legge, in ed. Max Müller, *Sacred Books of the East* (Oxford: Oxford University Press, 1891), chs. 28 and 34).

24. See, for example, the discussion in Richard Norman, *The Moral Philosophers: An Introduction to Ethics*, 2nd ed. (Oxford: Oxford University Press, 1998), 12–15.

25. G[eorge] E[dward] Moore, *Principia Ethica* (Mineola, NY: Dover Publications, [1903] 2004), 13, 18, 38; ch. 1, sec. 10.

26. See, for example, the insights of Alasdair MacIntyre, *After Virtue: A Study in Moral Theory* (Notre Dame, IN: University of Notre Dame Press, 1984), 88–108.

27. Matt 5:54.

28. Richard Carrier, *Sense and Goodness Without God: A Defense of Metaphysical Naturalism* (Bloomington, IN: AuthorHouse, 2005), 40–42; Sam Harris, *The Moral Landscape: How Science Can Determine Human Values* (New York: Free Press, 2010), 4–14.

29. Medieval scholastic Duns Scotus, who was aware of this incongruity, thus disagreed with Thomas Aquinas over the nature of the divine will. Scotus argued that Aquinas, by subordinating the divine will to the divine intellect, had made it impossible for God to be free to choose between two distinct possibilities. Scotus, *Philosophical Writings*, trans. Allan Wolter (Indianapolis, IN: Hackett, 1987), 80–81.

30. See Arthur Holmes, *Fact, Value, and God* (Grand Rapids, MI: William B. Eerdmans, 1997), 173–80.

31. See, for example, where Carrier attempts to evade the charge that his ethical theory commits the "naturalistic fallacy" (Carrier, *Sense and Goodness Without God*, 231–33). See also Harris, *The Moral Landscape*, 10–11. Harris observes that the "firewall" erected between fact-value has its origins in David Hume, but I hold that Hume was correct to erect this "firewall" because it challenged the causal determinism of Gottfried Leibniz at its very heart. Hume allows libertarian freedom to be real in his view that habit and belief are causal agents that operate independently of Leibniz's "principle of sufficient reason." *Habit* and *belief* are looser, freer, and more arbitrary than Leibniz's views of strict causal determinism. *Habit* also allows for the possibility that errors may occur in *human belief* when humans imagine cause-and-effect relationships to exist that are, in fact, purely imaginary.

32. Jean-Jacques Rousseau encountered this problem when he tried to extract the *general will* from the *will of all*. See *The Social Contract and Emile*, trans. G. D. H. Cole and Barbara Foxley (E-artnow, 2018), loc. 2149 of 12592, Kindle. The only way this could be done, he suggested, was to eliminate the egoistic element inherent in the *will of all*. The means of achieving this elimination would be the political process. Power politics would thus inevitably have to come into play.

33. Carrier, *Sense and Goodness Without God*, 9–19.

34. Atheists of the persuasion of Carrier, Harris, Richard Dawkins, Christopher Hitchens, and Daniel Dennett seem oblivious to the harsh cultural realities of the Ancient Near East where rites such as human sacrifice were commonplace and holy war was universally practiced. For a refutation of their position, see Paul Copan, *Is God a Moral Monster? Making Sense of the Old Testament God* (Grand Rapids, MI: Baker Books, 2011), 15–19.

35. See Carrier, *Sense and Goodness Without God*, 12–13.

36. This, of course, is what it means to be caught in the "hermeneutic circle." See Paul Ricoeur, *Time and Narrative*, Vol. 1, trans. Kathleen McLaughlin and David Pellauer (Chicago: University of Chicago Press, 1990), 76.

37. Carrier, *Sense and Goodness Without God*, 65–70.

38. Canonized September 4, 2016.

39. Judg 21:25.

40. Plat. Tim. 69C–70E.

41. Thomas Hobbes, *Leviathan*, produced by Edward White and David Widger (Project Gutenberg e-book, [1651] 2009), locs. 2143, 5698, 8733, 8772, and 9147 of 9789.

42. For example, Ralph Cudworth, *The True Intellectual System of the Universe: Wherein All the Reason and Philosophy of Atheism is Confuted and Its Impossibility Demonstrated*, ed. Thomas Birch (New York: Gould & Newman, 1837), 34, 73–74, 119; George Berkeley, "A Treatise Concerning the Principles of Human Knowledge" (1710), in *The English Philosophers from Bacon to Mill*, ed. Edwin Burtt (New York: Random House, 1939), 510–79. The philosophy attributed to Malebranche and Berkeley is called "occasionalism," which suggests that the connection between all mental and bodily events are "occasioned" by God *directly*. Minds and bodies cannot, therefore, function as *efficient* causes. See Nicolas Malebranche, *Dialogues on Metaphysics and Religions*, trans. David Scott, ed. Nicholas Jolley (Cambridge, UK: Cambridge University Press, 1997), 83–94.

43. Berkeley, *Principles of Human Knowledge*, 54, 61, 75–76

44. John Locke, "An Essay Concerning Human Understanding" (1689), in *The English Philosophers from Bacon to Mill*, bk. 4, ch. 4, sec. 7.

45. Michael Ayers, *Locke: Epistemology and Ontology* (London: Routledge, 1991), 18–20.

46. Locke, *Essay Concerning Human Understanding*, bk. 2, ch. 23, sec. 3.

47. Berkeley, *Principles of Human Knowledge*, sec. 9.

48. Baruch Spinoza, *The Ethics*, trans. R. H. M. Elwes (B & R Samizdat Express, 2014), propositions 5, 14, and 29.

49. Spinoza, *Theological-Political Treatise*, 2nd ed., trans. Samuel Shirley (Indianapolis, IN: Hackett Publishing, 2001), 71–77.

50. Julia A. Lamm, *The Living God: Schleiermacher's Theological Appropriation of Spinoza* (University Park: Pennsylvania State University Press, 2010), 55–56; "Introduction," to G. W. F. Hegel, *The Difference between Fichte's and Schelling's System of Philosophy*, trans. H. S. Harris and Walter Cerf (Albany: State Uuniversity of New York Press, 1977), 1–78; Ashley Underwood Vaught, "The Specter of Spinoza in Schelling's '*Freiheitscrift*,'" PhD diss., Villanova University, 2008, 1–23, ProQuest.

51. Dale Jacquette, *The Philosophy of Schopenhauer* (London: Routledge, 2014), 27–28.

52. See Johann Gottlieb Fichte, *Fichte: Early Philosophical Writings*, trans. and ed. Daniel Breazeale (Ithaca, NY: Cornell University Press, 1988), 133–34; pt. III, sec. 8. 64–66. See also Fichte, *Foundations of Transcendental Philosophy (Wissenschaftslehre) Nova Methodo*, trans. and ed. Daniel Breazeale (Ithaca, NY: Cornell University Press, [1796/99] 1992), 144–46. Hegel, *Phenomenology of Spirit*, trans. A. V. Miller (Oxford: Oxford University Press, 1977), 62–63.

53. F. W. J. Schelling, *Of Human Freedom*, 360–62, 374–75.

54. Alfred North Whitehead, *The Adventure of Ideas* (New York: Simon & Schuster, 1967).

55. Whitehead, *The Adventure of Ideas*, 177, 195–97.

56. See argument against materialism in Varghese, *Wonder of the World*, 43–54.

Chapter Four

The Function of Value-Indicators within Frameworks of Contextualization

Materialistic and idealistic frameworks of contextualization are needlessly restrictive because they are either *too reductive* or *too abstractive*. A more comprehensive viewing apparatus would, therefore, need to allow room for maximal interplay between the physical and ideal dimensions of reality rather than allowing one dimension to be derived entirely from the other or to be elevated above the other. Thus, to comprehend adequately how instincts, impulses, drives, and aspirations interrelate to and oppose one another, we need to pay close attention to the way higher layers of contextualization *purposively* and *meaningfully* take up lower layers into themselves.

HOW INSTINCTS, IMPULSES, DRIVES, AND ASPIRATIONS DIFFER AND INTERRELATE

From a physical standpoint, we can, just by observing nature, identify two basic kinds of behaviors many species exhibit. In the human species, these are *competitive* and *cooperative* types of behaviors, but similar behaviors appear innate and instinctual in other species as well. Various species vie with members of their own and other species to ensure their basic survival and the survival of their progeny. This type of animal behavior is analogous to *competitive* human behavior. But there is, too, a kind of animal behavior that runs parallel to human *cooperative* behavior: Avian species exhibit flocking behavior, while some of mammalian species form packs, prides, and herds. These sorts of group behaviors make possible the procreation, survival, and care of the progeny of these species.[1]

We thus find analogues in nature to the competitive and cooperative drives that human beings exhibit. Such analogues from the animal kingdom should not, however, be forced into univocal correspondences with human drives. The human species also stands apart from others in the following important regards: (1) The competitive and cooperative drives are interwoven into both the fabric of individual human personality and the organization of human society as a collective in more highly complex and profoundly unified ways than ways occurring in other species. (2) The human species reflects upon the significance of these drives and expresses its understanding of them through *language* and *action*. Other species lack these reflective and expressive capabilities.

CONTEXTUALIZING THE DRIVES: COMPETITION AND COOPERATION

Irrespective of cultural background, human beings recognize the role that the competitive and cooperative drives play in their pursuit of value. Various cultures affirm these drives as important even though they have not always used the same terminologies to describe them. Beginning with Auguste Comte (1798–1857), moral philosophers have used the terms *egoism* and *altruism*.[2] *Egoism* refers to the tendency of human beings to act in their self-interest, while *altruism* refers to their desire to act in others' interests.

The *psychological fact* that competitive and cooperative drives exist in the human species universally is undeniable. However, as I have pointed out, difficulties arise when one tries to derive moral categories from the mere facts of nature alone. Even if we allow the facts of nature to include facts concerning *human* nature as well, establishing moral categories based on these facts can prove difficult. Nature by itself cannot provide a fully adequate basis for morality. Indeed, nature is too *ambiguous* and *unclear* to offer clues about *how* the drives should be prioritized in the human species specifically.

Social Darwinists in the vein of Herbert Spencer (1820–1903), for instance, tried to prioritize the *survival* instinct. In doing so, they elevated the *competitive* drive over the *cooperative*.[3] Their interpretation of nature also allowed them to justify their beliefs about racial superiority, beliefs that in turn (1) fostered the ultra-nationalist fervor so characteristic of the shape of world politics during the nineteenth and twentieth centuries, (2) justified the practice of war and its concomitant atrocities, and (3) provided fodder for the eugenics movement, which, in its extreme expression, contributed to the blight of genocide and encouraged biological experimentation and extermination policies such as those implemented by Nazi Germany.

Feminist thinkers such as Josephine Donovan (1941–), on the other hand, have dismissed the perspectives of Social Darwinists. Donovan, who is equally as indebted to naturalism as they, preferred instead to elevate the *cooperative* drive over the competitive.[4] Donovan's research revealed how easily interpretations of nature could be mistaken when *all* the facts failed to be given equal consideration. Modern feminist critiques of Darwinism have, perhaps justifiably, placed Darwinism under the umbrella term "patriarchy." However, by moving in an opposite direction without sufficient cause or justification, feminist critiques raise the very same question that Social Darwinism raised; viz., what basis is there for preferring the cooperative drive over the competitive one? Is preferring one of these drives over another merely an arbitrary judgment based upon subjective preference?

The Restrictiveness and Ambiguity of Naturalistic Contexts

How to prioritize drives is indeed one problem ethical naturalists have not been able adequately to resolve simply by observing nature and appealing to it as a standard. Their inability to prioritize drives perhaps explains why their theories have ended up being scattered all over the philosophical map. For instance, John Rawls (1921–2002) developed his theory of *ethical altruism* based on his understanding of "justice as fairness."[5] He believes that we should set aside all our previous knowledge about our history and our privileged social status by assuming what he called a "veil of ignorance."[6] By assuming this veil, he contends that human beings would become better equipped to ensure the impartiality of their judgments. On the other hand, persons enjoying an advantaged socio-economic status would be biased in their judgments by not assuming this veil.[7] On the other hand, Ayn Rand (1905–1982), in her "objectivist ethics," excoriates all theories that promoted altruism in any form and opted instead for a doctrine of *ethical egoism*. She argues that human beings would benefit society to a greater degree if they acted rationally in their own self-interest.[8]

Both Rawls and Rand appeal to *reason* as a basis for their theories. Rand, in particular, argues against the intrusions of subjectivism and feeling into ethical doctrine. However, merely *appealing* to the principle of reason does not guarantee that those using it will truly remain immune from prejudice and passion. There is always a danger that reason will allow itself to become enslaved to rhetoric; for rhetoric, to be effective, must appeal not only to *logos*, but to *pathos* and *ethos* as well. The balance of these three elements, of course, will differ from philosopher to philosopher. Rawls, for instance, avoids the sort of inflammatory rhetoric that appears in the works of Karl Marx and Friedrich Engels (1820–1895), and he makes clear that his call for justice as fairness does not go so far as to advocate anything as extreme as the total abolition of private property in the interest of redistributing wealth. [9] Rand, too, manages to distance herself from the ethical egoism of Friedrich Nietzsche, who exaggerated his principle of the "Will to Power" to excess while virtually condoning the victimization of the weak. [10] Rand's call for people to cultivate the *"virtue of selfishness"* is certainly not *as* rhetorically charged as Nietzsche's, though it does seem *more* rhetorically charged than Rawls's writings.

The use of extreme rhetoric can signify, however, that a theory suffers from imbalance, for imbalanced theories are more easily susceptible to extremism and rigidification than balanced ones. Indeed, the degree of extremism and rigidity can often be gauged by the extent to which excessive rhetoric is used to cover up theoretical deficiencies or to dissuade potential detractors from zeroing in on what may turn out to be a theory's Achilles' heel. The use of excessive rhetoric might, in this regard, end up being nothing more than an attempt to *overcompensate* for the fact that the foundation of one's ethical theory is inadequate from the start.

The use of excessive rhetoric may have the advantage of producing dramatic short-term results, but its use may also influence people to begin sliding down the proverbial *slippery slope*. Logicians and moral philosophers alike, of course, will point out that slippery-slope arguments are *logical* fallacies; but I maintain that logical cause-and-effect sequences do not always hold true in cases where human emotions—especially extreme emotions—come into play. When excessive emotion outweighs reason, cause-and-effect scenarios that defy logic can easily develop. The phenomenon of the slippery slope does not, of course, prove that *moral* outcomes are *necessary* or *inevitable*. To make this claim would be to reduce morality to the level of mechanism. If, on the other hand, libertarian freedom is introduced into the equation, a slippery slope becomes *possible*, if not *probable*. Indeed, the probability may increase in contexts that provide a "climate" in which "a perfect storm" may develop.

The use of rhetoric aside, I believe it is correct to say that the writings of Rawls and Rand lack adequate safeguards. The deficiency in Rawls's theory may allow practitioners of more extreme forms of ethical altruism the room they need to venture the "extra mile" in their over-practice of altruism. [11] Some Rawlsians, for instance, have attempted to battle the problem of poverty only by throwing monetary resources at it. However, attempts to address a problem that may have a moral as well as a monetary component with "money sans morality" will doubtless fall short of achieving a satisfactorily remediation. Instead of extinguishing the fires of need, desire, and greed, the over-appropriation, misdirection, and misuse of monetary resources can fuel those fires and cause them to rage out of control. The image of someone trying to use gasoline to extinguish a fire comes to mind. [12]

The lack of a safeguard in Rand's theory of ethical egoism, on the other hand, allows too much leeway for those who would extol selfishness as a virtue. Rand may, of course, be correct in certain regards when she asseverates that others are indirectly benefited when people pursue their own interests, but I argue that this is only partially true. Selfishness taken to an extreme can also promote vices such as pride and greed, and pride can deceive a person into embracing the notion of the "self-made man" as being unequivocally true. People who believe the *myth of the self-made man* will conveniently forget aspects of their own being and character that are *not* self-made. We certainly had nothing to do with our own conception, gestation, and birth. Following our organic dependence upon our mothers, we became socially dependent upon our parents to clothe us, feed us, and provide us with shelter. Teachers made sacrifices to teach us. Mentors graciously helped to guide us morally, intellectually, and vocationally.

It thus seems that even theories that purport to be rational can fail to have "all their bases covered." They fail because they do not anticipate the unintended consequences of ideas that are imbalanced to start with. Such lack of foresight permits vulnerabilities to surface that render a theory susceptible to distortions and extreme interpretations. The lack of a safeguard is certainly more evident in Nietzsche's theory than in Rand's (it appears more obfuscated in Rand's). Certainly, Nietzsche's lack of a safeguard allowed room for Adolf Hitler (1889–1945), himself a devotee of Nietzsche, to apply Nietzsche's philosophy in a manner that Nietzsche would likely never have countenanced.[13] Still, blame for the genocide committed by Nazi Germany can be laid, at least partially, at Nietzsche's feet; for Nietzsche's attempt to pass rhetoric off as sound philosophy fertilized the soil in which Nazi ideology would afterward germinate and flourish.[14] The same proneness to distortion can be detected in Marx's rhetoric more than in Rawl's writings (the proneness to distortion is subtler in Rawls than in Marx). Marx's rhetoric provided both the space that allowed and the impetus that drove Josef Stalin (1878–1953) to commit and justify his many atrocities against his own people in Marx's name.

No one, therefore, should be surprised when a philosopher's views are later distorted, if indeed their lack of adequate safeguards leave them open to being easily distorted from the start. Of course, the distance between the egoism of Nietzsche and Rand, like the distance between the altruism of Marx and Rawls, is a matter of degree. The problem, however, comes in justifying *to what degree* one is justified in going as one practices either forms of egoism without altruism or altruism without egoism. In fact, the problem of degree becomes especially problematic when a doctrine of ethical altruism leaves egoism completely off the table or when a doctrine of ethical egoism rejects all appeals to altruism. The divorce of egoism and altruism can then only signal the loss of those mutually imposed checks and balances that inhibit the gradual drift of these two impulses toward one extreme or the other.

To gain an adequate understanding of how to manage and direct our egoistic and altruistic tendencies, I suggest that we fully consider contexts and perspectives that are irreducibly *psychosocial* and touch upon the dimension of *transcendental purpose* and *transcendental meaning*. To elaborate on the first point, I hold that one should not, in the final analysis, speak *purposively* or *meaningfully* about psychological impulses apart from the way various societal matrixes contextualize them. Expanding upon the second point, I maintain that one ought to treat the belief systems of various societies regarding the transcendental dimension as *psychosocial facts* regardless of whether these belief systems can be proved as objectively and metaphysically *true*. The question then remains, "How does one sort these out when they happen to entail contradictions?"

The Drives Related to Social and Transcendental Contexts

The Hebrew rabbinic tradition that produced the Babylonian Talmud (c. 200–c. 500 CE) provides some of the earliest insights into how impulses are linked to social contexts and to the dimension of the Transcendent. These insights would not have been possible apart from a theological perspective belonging to an earlier strata of Hebraic tradition. Since the ancient Hebrews believed the covenant that God had made with Israel was inextricably bound up with an emphasis on *divine command*,[15] they also believed that the covenant *transcended* nature and, therefore, could not be *reduced* to nature.

The ongoing struggle between Hebrew monotheism and the nature religions of the Ancient Near East sheds light on how purely naturalistic interpretations of the human impulses and drives diverge from the Hebrew Bible's interpretation of them. By promoting the *covenantal* ideal, the Bible re-contextualized and thereby elevated human sexual relationships beyond the purely natural categories that characterized sexual practices belonging to the Canaanite fertility cults.[16] In this way, the Hebrew covenantal emphasis challenged, and ultimately succeeded in overturning, the Canaanites' worship of raw sexual power and fertility inherent in the male and female aspects. By linking the concept of covenant to the ideal of monogamous marriage, the Hebraic perspective limited the kinds of human sexual relationships and practices allowable. Furthermore, the ideal of covenantal marriage, by contextualizing human sexuality and sexual practices, provided a viable framework that would maximally benefit the larger society. Divine commandments belonging to the concept of the covenant, such as "Honor your father and your mother" and "You shall not commit adultery," reveal specific restrictions that protected covenantal marriage and reinforced the institution of the family.[17] Stable family structures, in turn, extended salient benefits to the larger economic and political realities as well.

The Rabbis, who inherited the traditions of the *Tanak*,[18] went on to identify within the human heart two competing impulses that they believed needed to be kept in proper equilibrium to achieve maximal ethical benefit both to individuals and to society. The Rabbis were keen, as well, to describe how these impulses should be contextualized in the light of social situations, demands, and obligations. They identified these as "the *good* impulse" (Heb=*yetzer hatob* [יֵצֶר הַטּוֹב]) and "the *evil* impulse" (Heb=*yetzer hara* [הָרַע יֵצֶר]). This latter designation, however, needs further explication, since the English word "evil" does not have exactly the same meaning as the Hebrew word *ra*. The English meaning of the word usually calls to mind the *destructive effects* of human moral choices rather than the *impulse* to commit evil acts. The Hebrew view, by contrast, views the evil impulse as a potentiality for evil that has not yet produced actual evil consequences, though it has the capacity to do so.[19]

The Hebrew rabbinic tradition did not, therefore, interpret these impulses dualistically but taught that *both* impulses—the *evil* as well as the *good*—were divinely created *tendencies* or *potentialities*.[20] Furthermore, since God created both impulses as *good*,[21] *both* were accordingly deemed *necessary* for the continuing survival and procreation of the human species. Indeed, the Rabbis believed that only an *imbalance* between these impulses would result in the kind of destructive manifestations that are identifiable as *actual* evil.

The rabbinic tradition further maintained that the impulses fall out of balance when persons actualize one of them continually without adequate regard for the other. This is stressed with respect to the evil impulse in Genesis 6:5, which reads, "The impulse of the thoughts of their hearts was only evil *continually*" (Heb=כָּל־הַיּוֹם). The emphasis here is on the word "*continually*." Some rabbis likewise testified that a *continual* abandonment of the evil impulse in favor of the good impulse could produce ill effects; for if humanity were to avoid all actions motivated by self-interest, persons would not procreate, establish families, build homes, or care for their young.[22] In short, if human beings entirely relinquished their survival impulse, the species would perish. For this reason, it would be more appropriate to translate the two impulses in terms we have already considered: the *good impulse* corresponds to the *altruistic* inclination and the *evil impulse* corresponds to the *egoistic* inclination.

The ways that the *good* and *evil impulses* are exercised are furthermore deemed righteous or sinful by the way they are assessed in relation to the *context* in which they are exercised. The Rabbis, for instance, recognized that obsessive obedience to the evil impulse was the origin of sin, particularly the sins of idolatry, unchastity, rebellion, pride, and murder.[23] Because of its power to deceive and lead one into sin, the evil impulse therefore had to be resisted, restrained, and properly channeled.[24] These modes of limitation could be accomplished in one way through sacrifice, confession, and repentance.[25] Hence, one's outward expression of repentance by performing the sin-offering sacrifice as prescribed by the Book of Leviticus could also symbolize one's inward sacrifice of the evil inclination.[26] Obedience to the Torah was another way that human beings could be guided and instructed on how to be good and righteous stewards of the two impulses.

Engaging in self-sacrifice and obeying the Torah thus restrained and guided the inclinations and insured one's proper stewardship of them. In return, these practices held as their promise a life of *blessedness*. The Hebrew words for "blessed" (*bārûk* [בָּרוּךְ] and *'ešer* [אֶשֶׁר]) denote a positively value-laden condition in life—not entirely unlike Aristotle's concept of "happiness" (Grk=*eudaimonia* [εὐδαιμονία]).[27] On the other hand, self-indulgence and disregard for the instruction of the Torah would bring disobedient souls under the misery of the curse, and this condition is just as negative in its value connotation as the concept of blessing is positive. To experience true blessedness, the Hebraic view of human behavior thus envisions that the impulses (i.e., the two *yetzers*) must be taken up in appropriate ways into the human competitive and cooperative drives.

CONTEXTUALIZING THE ASPIRATIONS: THE QUEST FOR HEIGHT AND THE SEARCH FOR CENTEREDNESS

How then do the human competitive and cooperative drives relate to the aspirations, and how do the aspirations contextualize the drives? Clearly, individuals aspire to many types of tangible goals, but I believe the aspirations themselves, like the drives, can be categorized under the two general rubrics that I introduced in the preceding chapter. These are the quest for height and the search for centeredness.

The quest for height alludes to the human preoccupation with conquering height, whether physical, personal, social, or spiritual. Humankind has tried to conquer height in physical ways by building towers, spires, and skyscrapers and by devising technologies that make flight possible. We have also imagined the conquest of outer space to be within our grasp, so we have built rockets that have enabled us to embark, if only in minuscule ways, upon space exploration.

Physical height is not, however, the only kind of height human beings feel compelled to attain. We also yearn to conquer height personally and socially by succeeding in life and by garnering affirmation, recognition, and praise from others. The attainment of social status comes by pursuing education, distinguishing oneself with professional accomplishments, and accumulating wealth and power. The psychological reward that accompanies the attainment of social status, however, is usually tied to our need for recognition and approval. This need does not have to be overt, for sometimes it is enough simply to know that we have benefited others through our achievements.

Besides the aspiration that I have labeled "the quest for height," humans yearn for a sense of belonging, association, relationship, and connectedness. I believe all these aspects can be summed up in what I call the search for centeredness. From the beginning of recorded history, human beings have searched, both in physical and spiritual ways, for a center of meaning in which to anchor their lives. Our species cannot remain content for this reason to achieve height only. We are social creatures who also desire to belong—to be loved and accepted despite our successes and failures.

Conflicting Aspirations and Human Psychological Experience

Human beings do not, however, always value the aspirations in ways that afford them equal emphasis. The harmonious integration of the aspirations is difficult to achieve psychologically, because doing so demands what psychologist Carl Jung called a "coincidence of opposites" (*coincidentia oppositorum*).[28] Just as the competitive and cooperative drives stand in opposition to one another, so do the quest for height and the search for centeredness represent movements running in opposite directions. People for this reason often experience the two aspirations as being in conflict. The quest for height can work against the search for centeredness, and the search for centeredness can stunt the quest for height.

One instance of how the quest for height eclipses the search for centeredness appears in the Greek myth of Daedalus and his son Icarus. When Icarus tried to soar to heaven on wings made of wax and feathers,[29] his aspiration deceived him into disregarding the wisdom of his father's warning not to fly too close to the sun. When Icarus did happen to get too close, the sun's heat melted his wings and sent him plummeting to his death. The young man's overreach, which was inspired by his quest for height, thus resulted in tragedy.

Without the centeredness of *love* to restrain and counterbalance the quest for height, individuals will often find themselves experiencing the uncanny feeling of isolation and loneliness that so often accompanies "life at the top." Their accomplishments may, in retrospect, appear to them hollow and meaningless. A devastating psychological crisis may then ensue that has the potential to supplant whatever importance one once attached to fame, power, and fortune. Inordinate efforts expended to achieve some imagined happiness then suddenly appear ludicrous as a void of engulfing disappointment, emptiness, loneliness, and meaninglessness swallows one's soul. Such a void always seems to loom ahead for persons who become so overwhelmingly preoccupied with their aspiration to climb to ever higher goals that they destroy their relationships with others along the way.

While the quest for height can become destructive and tragic for those who disregard the need for centeredness, the opposite can be true when the search for centeredness interferes with the quest for height. The search for centeredness can easily stagnate into a "slough of despond" whenever the quest for height is abandoned. The need that most clearly motivates the search for centeredness is the need for *love*; and interestingly, being *in love* is often perceived as the prelude to settling down, getting married, and starting a family. Our restlessness coupled with our sense of isolation ultimately sparks in us a desire to search for centeredness in life, for we are ill-equipped to endure for very long the dizzying hubbub of fame, the blinding limelight, and the interminable restlessness that drives us to pursue ever higher summits. As fatigue sets in, we ache to rest, to retire, and to find ourselves settled into more permanent and fulfilling relationships.

Yet, with the search for centeredness, a danger lurks that is opposite to the one that the quest for height without centeredness poses. The French Existentialist philosopher Jean-Paul Sartre expressed this danger in his play, *No Exit*. One of his characters, Garçin, makes the statement, "Hell is—other people."[30] In another work, *Being and Nothingness*, Sartre recognizes the danger of relationships in which persons have become mere objects of each other's sexual desires. He speaks disparagingly of *erotic love*, because this kind of love almost invariably drives one to try to possess another person completely without regard or respect for that person's *transcendence*.[31] *Transcendence*, we should note, is related to the idea of *height*; and centeredness without height is a centeredness that can be inimical to transcendence itself.

We may imagine ourselves to be in an ideal relationship with someone whom we love; or, more precisely, we may be in love with the idea of being in love. But ideal relationships rarely exist in real life. A gap invariably appears between the *ideal imagined* and the *reality lived*, and this gap can often breed resentment that can irreparably damage or even terminate a relationship. Two extremes usually become evident as we try to transform the *ideal* relationships of our imaginations into *real* relationships.

At one extreme lies the one-sided commitment where one person's undying allegiance is reciprocated by an unwilling partner's rejection or infidelity. The well-known disorder that psychologists call "codependency" often plagues this kind of relationship.[32] The codependent person fully believes his or her commitment to the unwilling partner will ultimately bring them around, resulting in a better, if not a perfect, relationship. Consequently, the codependent individual will often play the role of the dutiful servant who does not want "to ruffle feathers." This role usually aims at making the relationship perfect. However, instead of bringing about the intended effect, the codependent individual more often than not produces resentment in his or her partner that causes the relationship to deteriorate further. At the other extreme from codependency is the fear of long-term commitments or obligations. Someone who has had an unpleasant experience in a relationship may not want to risk getting emotionally "burned" again. Many individuals today suffer from one or the other of these two extremes. Nevertheless, at the heart of both these failures to achieve meaningful relatedness, connectedness, and centeredness is a common problem; namely, the loss of the element of mutual respectfulness in the relationship. Frequently, in these sorts of one-sided relationships, one person seeks to "devour" the transcendence—or the *height*—of another or to disregard it entirely. On the one hand, the codependent person may disallow a partner to retain his or her individuality. On the other hand, the person who wants to be free of obligations may show his or her partner a lack of respect. Both alternatives present themselves as equally undesirable.

We thus come to recognize that our compulsion to achieve height and our need to find centeredness often come into conflict with one another, thwart one another, and even cancel out one another. Our quest for success and height, on the one hand, often causes us to rupture the centeredness of wisdom and love, and to upset the balance of life. On the other hand, the magnetic lure of the center, where we hope to find acceptance and rest, can just as easily thwart our drive to achieve success in life. On both sides of the equation, the dark aspects of our personality have the potential to rise up against us and destroy us. The diabolical axe hacks asunder what is good in our psychological experience and turns one side against the other. Our quest for height and search for centeredness then frustrate one another, which leads to the destruction of individual personality. What happens in the individual psychological dimension then becomes extended to society.

The Aspirations and Society—Contrasting Utopian Visions

Not only do the quest for height and search for centeredness have a psychological application; they have social applications as well. Social applications of the aspirations appear beginning with the Renaissance and culminating in the nineteenth century when many Western intellectual elites abandoned traditional Christian doctrines of the Fall and otherworldly salvation. Jerry Gill observes that, since roughly the 1500s, "the natural and/or social aspects of the world increasingly have become the axis of human awareness and activity, while traditionally transcendent considerations have played an ever-diminishing role."[33] A horizontal understanding of reality thus gradually replaced a vertical understanding.

Consequently, in both theory and practice, forward-looking speculations about the real possibility of human progress in this world replaced traditional theological conceptions. More specifically, the otherworldly focus so typical of much traditional Christian theology gave way to this-worldly utopian visions. However, not all of these utopian visions were the same. In fact, two opposite utopian ideals seem perennially to crop up during the timeframe in question. I will call these "the utopia of simplicity" and "the utopia of complexity."

The Utopia of Simplicity and the Search for Centeredness

"Utopia" was a sixteenth-century construct that originated with the Renaissance focus upon Christian humanism. In 1516, Thomas More (1478–1535) explored the idea in his work by that name. Ironically, "utopia" means "no place" and hints that More's work is of a fantastical nature, though there can be little doubt that he intended its ideas to have concrete applications as well.

More's *Utopia* contains the fictitious account of one Raphael Hythloday, who was a traveler and companion of the Italian explorer Amerigo Vespucci. On one of his many journeys, Hythloday and his companions discover the island of Utopia.[34] The inhabitants of this imaginary island exemplify the virtues of simplicity, peacefulness, industry, courage, and intelligence. Exceedingly rare, however, are vices such as envy, avarice, pride, and laziness. All levels of society engage in work for the common good, except for the slaves who do all the hard labor. Utopia, like Plato's Republic, permits and justifies slavery. Slaves deserve subjugant status as rightful punishment for crimes committed against Utopian society.[35] Otherwise, all the island's inhabitants share in other work they do; for instance, everyone, without exception, engages in agriculture.

The inhabitants of Utopia place little value on material things. Since they have no need of money, they value neither silver nor gold.[36] Indeed, gold is of so little value that the Utopians fashion it into chamber pots and chains for their slaves. Even to wear gold or silver is considered shameful.[37] Utopians eschew fancy dress and instead wear plain and simple clothing. Indeed, anyone who wears fine and expensive clothes intending to impress others appears to them silly and ridiculous.[38]

In religious matters, the Utopians exhibit tolerance toward all. Among them, the highest expression of religion—and the one that most Utopians gravitate towards and ultimately embrace—is belief in the One Transcendent God, Father of all, and Creator and Governor of all things.[39] Though they are very much inclined to accept the Christian religion when they first hear of it, they do actually exile one Christian convert who shows intolerance toward others who have not accepted the Christian faith.[40]

At the end of his work, More opines, "I cannot perfectly agree to everything he [Hythloday] has related," but adds, ". . . there are many things in the commonwealth of Utopia that I rather wish, than hope, to see followed in our governments."[41] More's words—"I cannot perfectly agree"—reveals his apprehensiveness in advocating such radical views in a direct manner. Such an approach could have easily ignited the ire of the King of England. The work itself reveals, notwithstanding, that More approved of the principles practiced by the Utopians. His vision, of course, would fail to persuade King Henry VIII, who preferred instead the "playbook" of Niccolò Machiavelli. [42]

More's vision not only represents the "utopia of simplicity" theme, but he also clearly elevates the cooperative drive above the competitive. In this regard, his view is thematically related to collectivistic and communistic sorts of ideology, though his view differs from Marx's in that it allows room for divine transcendence. One can also see in More's great emphasis on cooperative endeavors his psychological unease with the extremely competitive and cutthroat court of Henry VIII, to which he, as time would tell, had the misfortune of belonging.

Still, one can only wonder whether More's emphasis on cooperation would truly produce the kind of incentive needed to stave off boredom in such a utopian society. Would their industry in agriculture alone be enough to keep monotony at bay? Perhaps More anticipated that it would not be enough, so he imagines that the Utopians have interests in learning and reading. However, their technological ability, which appears extremely limited, does not evidently arise out of their simplistic way of life. The technologies they do possess, such as the making of paper and printing presses, have been introduced from the outside. [43] The Utopians must therefore remain, at least to some degree, parasitic on external societies for their technology. Without adequate technological infrastructure, one also wonders how they could refine gold or silver or fashion it into the various commodities they consider worthless, or why they would even desire to do so.

The Utopia of Complexity and the Quest for Height

A second kind of utopian vision, and one diametrically opposed to More's vision, is the "utopia of complexity." The first example of a utopian ideal of this sort occurs in Francis Bacon's work, *The New Atlantis*. While the title suggests that Bacon used Plato's allusion to the ancient civilization of Atlantis, the word "new" signals a significant departure from Plato. For the first time in the history of Western culture, what some modern philosophers have referred to as the "category of the new" began to cast its spell over the human imagination. [44]

The New Atlantis describes how a group of nautical travelers providentially land on the island of Bensalem after a storm throws their ship off course. [45] The island is home to an unknown but highly advanced civilization where learning is "cutting edge" and where scientific experiments of all kinds are constantly being carried out. Centrally important to Bacon's portrayal of the civilization of Bensalem in *The New Atlantis* is the scientific method that Bacon himself advocates. Bensalem, in every regard, epitomizes the "utopia-of-complexity" ideal.

In Bensalem, an institution known as "Salomon's House" (*Solomon's House*) or "The College of the Six Days' Work" holds preeminent status. Not only do the fellows of Solomon's House boast of an ancient history going back to King Solomon himself,[46] but they also claim to possess the ancient Hebrew monarch's lost works on natural history in which everything is described "from the cedars of Lebanon to the hyssop that grows in the wall."[47] Because the inhabitants of Bensalem have imbibed the ancient Solomonic wisdom, theoretical and practical science flourish among them. To keep its knowledge up to date, their society also secretly sends out Fellows or Brethren to collect and bring back knowledge of advancements from other countries. These investigators are chiefly concerned about the kinds of knowledge that will aid their own technological advancement.[48]

Bensalem is also a society highly tolerant of religion. Oddly, they are Christian after having received the faith through their discovery of an ark floating on the waters, mysteriously illuminated by a cross, and containing the canonical gospels. The Bensalemites are, however, also tolerant of Jews, who reciprocate with an equal tolerance toward Christians. What seems to matter most for Bacon is how the denizens of Bensalem have put aside all religious differences to embark on the common quest for scientific and technological knowledge. Thus, in a manner foreshadowing deism, Bacon relegates religion to a secondary level of importance at the same time that he promotes science and technology to a place of primary status.

In time, a Jewish merchant named Joabin befriends one of the visitors and helps him gain an audience with the "Father" of Solomon's House.[49] The Father proceeds to reveal to his guest the purpose of their foundation, the preparations and instruments they use for their work, the various employments and functions their fellows are assigned to, and the ordinances and rites they observe. At this point in Bacon's treatise, the extent to which his utopia qualifies as a utopia of complexity becomes fully evident. Scientific observation and experiments of all sorts are being carried out everywhere in Bensalem from the earth's deep caverns to artificial towers that reach high into the clouds.[50] The scientific expertise of Solomon's House is wide-ranging and extensive. It includes knowledge of physics, chemistry, mineralogy, meteorology, biology, and astronomy. Through their technologies, they have unraveled many of the secrets of nature. They have found cures for a variety of diseases and have tested the health benefits of pharmaceuticals. They have learned how to desalinate water, purify it, and artificially pump it. They excel in horticulture, agriculture, and food production. Their machinery and manufacturing capabilities are exceptionally advanced. Indeed, the list is too lengthy to delineate further.[51]

I earlier pointed out that More's *Utopia* stresses the role of the *cooperative* drive more than the *competitive*. Interestingly, Bacon does not overtly stress the role of competition as much as one might expect,[52] though he does stress the importance of productive work and industry that leads to the continual advancement of science and technology. Bacon views the vices of sloth and indolence with disapproval, and he disparages those who try to take shortcuts in solving difficult problems.[53]

If Bacon stresses the role of competition at all, it is what one might call "healthy competition," for he is all too aware of the dangers of envy and pride (or vain-glory) that often attend those engaged in competitive endeavors.[54] On the other hand, the competitive aspect of Bensalemite society may be reflected to some degree in the fact that they keep a number of their discoveries secret.[55] Some secrets they keep even from the State. The purpose of secrecy can only be to restrict knowledge to those deemed trustworthy to receive it and to prohibit it from falling into the hands of would-be competitors. In this way, those privy to such secrets will maintain a competitive edge against those not in the know.

Utopian Beliefs Tested in the Crucible of Human Experience

Powerful utopian beliefs like those of More and Bacon would eventually foster concrete *social experiments*. Vasco de Quiroga, the first Bishop of Michoacán, Mexico, enacted one experimental application of More's utopian vision.[56] Quiroga, who aided in the conversion of many Chichimec Indians to Christianity, organized the Indians according to the principles set forth in More's *Utopia* with impressive results, and the legacy of this utopian experiment has continued beneficially to the present day. More's *Utopia* was also influential on some aspects of the radical phase of the Protestant Reformation, influencing such groups as the Mennonites, the Amish, and the Quakers.[57]

However, most groups that embraced the utopia-of-simplicity ideal have fallen short of bringing about its full and lasting embodiment within tangible human existence. The ideal remains to a high degree incongruous with tangible reality. However, the relative success of the tangible embodiment of the ideal within limited contexts—like with the Amish—does at least demonstrate that the ideal can exert some positive influence upon human existence. Nevertheless, what works well in small-scale contexts does not necessarily work well in contexts of larger scale and greater complexity. Naturally, *some* complexity is necessary for the proper functioning of human society; but *how much*? The Amish continue to ask this question, and it remains one that the broader human society should continue to ask as well.

What, then, of the alternative vision of utopia—namely, the vision that seeks the tangible embodiment of the "utopia of complexity"? The first at-

tempted tangible embodiment of the Baconian vision came with the formation of the Royal Society in Britain in November of 1660. This institution, in
turn, provided the impetus to carry Bacon's vision forward to materialization.
His vision did, in fact, inspire the scientific and technological revolutions
that transformed England into the most advanced society of Europe by the
end of the eighteenth century.[58]

The first Industrial Revolution (1760–1820), which owed much to the
Baconian vision, succeeded in that it saw the standard of living increase
dramatically among members of Britain's middle and upper classes. Eighteenth-century scientific and technological revolutions unleashed competition
that created enormous wealth. However, while the middle and upper classes
fared better than ever, the working classes saw their standard of living plummet as people migrated from rural to urban settings in search of employment.[59] Squalor, disease, and malnutrition accompanied this migration and
became rife in England's larger cities. At the same time, the invention of the
spinning jenny and the mechanical loom made cottage industries such as
spinning and weaving redundant.[60] The English Midlands or Cotswolds,
which earlier had prospered in wool production and weaving, was driven
down into irreversible economic hardship and impoverishment. The breed of
sheep that the ancient Romans had introduced into Britain, commonly known
as the "Cotswold lion," once dotted the landscape by the millions; but these
eventually dwindled to the verge of extinction as their wool was found too
brittle for use on the mechanical loom.[61]

Bacon may have downplayed the role competition played in realizing his
utopian vision, but to propel forward Britain's scientific and technological
advancements, his successors would have to become increasingly ruthless in
their competition than seems to have been the case with the imaginary denizens of Bacon's Bensalem. The ugly side of this competitiveness can already
be seen in Isaac Newton's (1642–1726/27) famous controversy with Gottfried Leibniz (1646–1716) over the question of who invented calculus. Newton, who at one point served as president of the Royal Society, managed to
get the support politically to take the credit.[62]

In order to advance, the field of science would have to become ever more
fiercely competitive. The extreme competition in the fields of science and
technology would inevitably widen the divide between the "haves" and the
"have-nots." Each new technological development seemed to widen the gulf
between those fortunate enough to possess the technology and those for
whom the cost of it lay beyond their reach. In the late eighteenth century and
early decades of the nineteenth century, the militant Luddite movement,
whose proponents tried in various ways to sabotage the technology that had
robbed them of their livelihoods, revolted.[63] Many who had formerly worked
in the woolen and textile industries found themselves being replaced by
machines, so machines became the objects of their scorn.

While the Luddites were ruthlessly suppressed because of their attacks upon industry, they also garnered sympathy from many of England's intellectual elite who became identified with the Romantic movement. One early exponent of more idyllic utopian themes that echoed Luddite concerns and went contrary to the Baconian "utopia of complexity" was the Romantic poet and engraver William Blake (1757–1827). He opposed the Enlightenment's elevation of autonomous reason and viewed the split between reason and imagination that result from this elevation as evidence of the fall of Albion, the primordial man whom he also identified with universal humanity and with England itself.[64] The severing of reason from imagination had produced among other things the one whom Blake called "Urizen," and perhaps more jestingly, "Nobodaddy."[65] Blake used these titles to refer to the Father God who lords his authority over others by passing laws merely for the purpose of limiting, constraining, and ultimately subjugating them. Blake identifies Urizen as a mixture of the God of Moses, the God of Francis Bacon, the God of Isaac Newton, and the God of deism.[66] Though Blake acknowledges Urizen as the Creator, especially of science, Urizen's role in the scheme of things resembles that of the Gnostic demiurge who created the evil material world.[67] Urizen in this respect is also cast in a *satanic* role.[68]

Blake understood that reason divorced from imagination was largely responsible for fostering the very industrial revolution that had blighted certain English cities with dirty factories. These ugly eyesores enslaved their workers, impoverished them, and plunged their lives into every kind of misery imaginable. Blake disparagingly referred to these factories as the "Dark Satanic Mills," and their increasing presence caused him to question whether the ancient English legend of Christ's visit to Glastonbury with Joseph of Arimathea could ever have truly happened. Was it even remotely possible that Jerusalem could once have been built in Albion, a land now so fallen and blighted by the products of Urizen's machinations?

In his poem "Jerusalem," Blake assumes his prophetic battle stance against this demiurge and pledges not to cease his fight against him. The arsenal of weapons with which he must wage battle will include his bow of burning gold by which he will shoot arrows, not of reason, but of desire. Like Eros (Cupid), Blake must launch his arrows, piercing his hearers' hearts and awakening them to become warmed by their passions and ruled by their imaginations instead of being governed by cold, unfeeling reason. Armed with his spear, as well, he asks for his chariot of fire to be brought to him. Presumably, he is alluding to the chariot that once carried away the prophet Elijah. But now that chariot must return so that prophecy, too, may return. Blake, assuming the mantel of an unrelenting prophet, then pledges, "I will not cease from mental fight, nor shall my sword sleep in my hand, till we have built Jerusalem in England's green and pleasant land."[69]

We can observe from the foregoing discussion how the pendulum swings back and forth between the ideals of simplicity and complexity. As Blake and other Romantic figures sought to rectify the extremes brought on by the Baconian vision, conflict between these opposite utopian ideals inevitably erupted. Under the influence of Romanticism, nineteenth-century social reformers, literary figures, and philanthropists such as William Wilberforce (1759–1833), Charles Dickens (1812–1870), and Angela Burdett-Coutts (1814–1906) impacted society by bringing social inequities to the attention of the British populace and offering tangible solutions.[70] The series of reforms passed by the British Parliament,[71] coupled with efforts to raise awareness of poverty and encourage philanthropic efforts, served to lift up those, who—like Dickens's character Stephen Blackpool—had "fallen through the cracks" of British society.[72]

However, by far the most extreme nineteenth-century reaction against the destructive consequences of competition and the economic system of capitalism that was largely responsible for these consequences appeared in the writings of Marx and Engels. Marx's and Engels's grand vision of how to bring about a communist utopia through revolution enticed the working masses. Ironically, the destruction of the simpler, rural way of life was blamed on *mechanization*; and Marx agreed that the concept of the machine, when imported into politics, had created the monstrous political devices that capitalists used to subjugate and control disadvantaged people.[73] Marx nonetheless seems himself to have adapted a political version of the machine to his own program as a means of "speeding up the inevitable."[74] On the one hand, Marx, through his dialectical-materialist doctrine, confidently teaches that capitalist economic systems are doomed to fall, while communist systems are destined to replace them. On the other hand, revolution and the dictatorship of the proletariat could now be viewed as political "mechanisms" that could speed up this dialectical process. Ironically, the same Marx who was so concerned about alienation when it concerned the oppressed and downtrodden of earth was also willing to treat those whom he perceived to be oppressors as mere objects or commodities to be exploited and processed through the "machinery" of revolution and proletarian rule. He thus advocates the confiscation of all private property,[75] regardless of whether that property has been justifiably obtained or not. However, the Marxist utopian philosophy was tested in the crucible of human history and found wanting as well. The abolition of private property in the former Soviet Union, for instance, had the unintended consequence of stifling the competitive drive. Soviet leadership thus inadvertently destroyed the incentive necessary for the creation of wealth; and once there was no longer enough wealth left to redistribute, the bankruptcy of the Soviet state became a *fait accompli*.[76]

We can certainly see from these historical instances how easily conflict between utopian ideals arises due to an excessive emphasis on one or the other utopian ideal. Ironically, the remedy for this conflict is not to become *more* excessive, but *less* so. If a smaller dose of medicine will cure an ailment, it does not follow that a larger dose will prove more effective.

The Specters of Dystopia

There are thus darker aspects to our "better angels" than what might initially appear. These are the "specters of dystopia" that haunt human society. They belong to the shadow side of the ideals of simplicity and complexity that we have discussed. In one respect, the shadow side of an ideal may be compared to the "genie" that appears when we rub the proverbial *Aladdin's lamp*. At first, the genie seems good and full of promise—indeed, almost angelic. However, as we allow it ever greater control over our lives, it also has a way of enslaving us.

Some writers have displayed adeptness at ripping the "angelic masks" off these genies to reveal the true faces of the malignant spirits that lie behind. Blake's portrayal of "Urizen" is one example, but others would follow. Echoing Blake's line of thought was Aldous Huxley (1894–1963), who produced the dystopian novel *Brave New World*. George Orwell (1903–1950), on the other hand, would reveal in such works as *Animal Farm* and *Nineteen Eighty-Four* the shadow side of the aspiration related to the search for centeredness.

Brave New World and *Nineteen Eighty-Four* thus convey two versions of *dystopia*. The former, I maintain, reveals the shadow side of the "utopia of complexity," while the latter reveals the shadow side of the "utopia of simplicity." These two novels reveal the consequences incurred when one or the other of the two utopian visions is taken too far. What the novels agree on, however, is the issue of what happens to individual human beings in a society whose members willingly relinquish control over their own lives for the sake of attainting to some imagined "higher ideal."

The Dystopia of Complexity

In *Brave New World*, Huxley reveals a society where technology has invaded every aspect of life and led to the loss both of individual control and meaningful human relationships.[77] No aspect of life in Huxley's World State is immune from technological interference. Because natural human reproduction is outlawed, sex no longer is tied to procreation. Sexual activities are, rather, pursued solely for physical pleasure and for no other purpose. Babies are no longer gestated in their mothers' wombs but are engineered in test tubes and gestated in hatcheries.[78] Cloning has become common practice, and technological manipulation at the embryonic stage guarantees that children will be tailor-made to function as members of one of the five castes necessary for society to run smoothly.[79] A technological means called the "hypnopaedia" (sleep-teaching) method is used to educate these children.[80]

To counteract any psychological discontentment that the citizens of the World State may experience or manifest, they are freely prescribed a pharmaceutical called "Soma," which has no side effects but produces a euphoric psychological state. Since the consequences of natural sexual relationships have been eliminated, sexual experimentation is allowed and even encouraged—though the formation of lasting relationships is forbidden.[81] There is thus no danger that adulterous sexual relationships will prove damaging to families because families have become obsolete social constructs. The State has eliminated and outlawed the societal roles of mother, father, and family.[82] Indeed, the citizens of the World State view the notion of the family as absurd, ridiculous, and even humorous.[83] Since the consequences of sex have been eliminated, sexual taboos have become a thing of the past as well. This means that children, too, are sexualized from an early age.[84]

Huxley introduces characters into his story line who nonetheless prove to be discontented with the World State. One of these, Bernard Marx, suffers anxiety and discontentment because his physical stature seems to him too small for the place he occupies in society. At the other extreme is Helmholtz Watson, who suffers boredom because his mental acuity exceeds the demands of work that he finds unchallenging and unfulfilling.[85] Most interesting of all the characters, however, is John, also known as "the Savage." John's very existence reveals hypocrisy and scandal that reach to the highest levels of the World State. His mother, Linda, a member of the Beta caste, had become pregnant by a chief member of the Alpha caste—namely, the "Director" of the "Central London Hatchery and Conditioning Centre."[86] This happened many years previously during a visit to the "Savage Reservation" in New Mexico. After Linda gets lost in a storm and is presumed dead, the Director returns home.[87] Unbeknownst to him, members of the reservation rescue Linda and bring her to live there. She gives birth to John; but later, the members of the reservation exile her because they think she is too sexually promiscuous.[88]

John and his mother live as outcastes from the World State until Bernard Marx and his coworker, Lenina Crowne, discover his true identity during a visit to the reservation. John and Linda are thereafter permitted to come to live in the World State. Initially, John is excited about this prospect because he thinks the place will be like the "Brave New World" that Shakespeare referenced in his play, *The Tempest*.[89] However, Shakespeare's works are virtually unknown in the World State, and John's love of them proves the catalyst of his undoing. Because the human qualities conveyed by Shakespeare's plays stand in such stark opposition to the dehumanizing World State, what John had initially imagined to be a "Brave New World" increasingly proves to be a place of utter emptiness and meaninglessness.

The more John observes the World State, the more conflicted he becomes. His very presence upends its status quo, and the revelations about his true origin prompts its Director to resign in shame. John's inner conflict reaches critical mass, however, when his mother dies. No one shows the least concern, sadness, or sympathy over her death or John's loss. Instead, they ridicule him for making his grief such a spectacle. John reacts by lashing out against the insensitivity of the State and tries to incite a riot at a Soma-dispensing facility. Once the riot is quelled, however, Mustapha Mond, the World State's chief spokesman and apologist, threatens John, Helmholtz Watson, and Bernard Marx with exile to a faraway island of their own choosing. John, however, decides not to go into exile with the others. Instead, he bids them goodbye and retreats to a lighthouse in the countryside where he gardens and practices self-flagellation to purify himself from "civilization's filthy contamination."[90]

Eventually, news of John's practices become public, and citizens of the World State descend upon him *en masse*, intent on making a spectacle of him.[91] To deter them, he brandishes the whip he uses for his self-flagellations; however, instead of fighting them off, his actions only inflame their passions to the point that they engage in an orgy. To his shame, John, too, is drawn in. When he comes to his senses the following morning, he is so overcome with anger and outrage at submitting to the ways of the World State, he hangs himself.[92]

The Dystopia of Simplicity

By contrast with Huxley's *Brave New World*, Orwell's dystopian society represents the shadow side of the "utopia of simplicity." In *Nineteen Eighty-Four*, all individuals relinquish control to "Big Brother" because they are under the illusion that he knows what is best for them.[93] The regime of Big Brother, also known as the World State or Ingsoc,[94] utilizes every possible vehicle of manipulation, propaganda, and control to ensure that its citizens will not deviate in the least from the official Party doctrine.

Conformity to the Party's version of "Truth" is expected of all citizens. Books considered subversive are banned, and all literature is constantly purged or altered to support the ideology of Ingsoc.[95] Free thought is forbidden. The State redefines truth in patently absurd ways, which is evidenced by the Party's three slogans: "War Is Peace," "Freedom Is Slavery," and "Ignorance Is Strength."[96] Even if the Party insists that two plus two equals five, the citizen must believe it without question. Ingsoc's three principles are "newspeak," "doublethink," and "the mutability of the past."[97] With "newspeak," Ingsoc controls the language used in all discourse and thought and aspires to make the language perfect by "cutting it to the bone."[98] Ingsoc boasts that "newspeak" is the only language in the world whose vocabulary gets smaller every year.[99] "Newspeak" is the standard that governs people's ideas, and ideas that are perceived to threaten this dogma are labeled criminal.[100] "Doublethink" is the word Ingsoc uses to refer to a state of mind in which one is "conscious of complete truthfulness while telling carefully constructed lies, to hold simultaneously two opinions which cancelled out, knowing them to be contradictory and believing in both of them."[101]

The organization of the World State includes four "Ministries" whose names belie their real purpose. "The Ministry of Peace concerns itself with war, the Ministry of Truth with lies, the Ministry of Love with torture, and the Ministry of Plenty with starvation."[102] At regular mandatory mass assemblies, propaganda videos are aired that whip up the citizens to hate fabricated enemies.[103] Examples of "hate events" are the "Two Minutes Hate" and "Hate Week."[104]

Using ubiquitous electronic surveillance systems, the State spies on every detail of the private lives of its citizens and employs maximally invasive forms of micromanagement to control them. Fear of torture and death deter most who would even dare *think* wrong thoughts about the World State and Big Brother, much less actively *rebel*. To keep its citizens thinking straight, the State employs "Thought Police" who are granted carte blanche authority to arrest anyone whom they even suspect of entertaining unorthodox opinions.

The novel's protagonist, Winston Smith, happens to work in the Records Department of the Party's Ministry of Truth (referred to in "newspeak" as "Minitrue").[105] His job is to revise history by altering historical facts so that they will comport with the "official version" of history that Minitrue endorses. His job also entails eliminating references to so-called "un-persons" whose ideas or actions are inconsistent with the Party's official doctrine.[106]

As the novel progresses, Winston begins harboring doubts about the Ministry's intentional omission and manipulation of facts to fabricate their own slanted version of the "Truth." Not only does *he* hold doubts about Ingsoc, but he also imagines that one of the Inner Party's officials, O'Brien, secretly opposes Big Brother and belongs to a renegade organization called the "Brotherhood."[107] Though Winston has no substantial evidence to support his feelings about O'Brien's "unorthodoxy," he nonetheless becomes convinced in his mind that O'Brien is a renegade whom he may be able to trust at some point.

Later, Winston becomes sexually involved with a woman named Julia, who happens to be, like himself, a member of the "Outer Party."[108] As they meet regularly for trysts, he experiences a modicum of happiness for the first time in his life.[109] However, the State views sexual relationships as dangerous and threatening to its ideals. On this ground, the State forbids sex, except for the purpose of procreation.[110] Indeed, the State's goal is ultimately to eradicate the sexual instinct along with sexual pleasure, because these encourage bonds of spousal and familial loyalty that are inimical to the State's view that the citizen's loyalty to society should be paramount.[111] Winston and Julia must therefore hide their affair by meeting in a place where they think the State's surveillance capabilities are deficient.[112]

Winston's tragic fate is set into motion when he is deceived and betrayed by one Mr. Charrington, whom he initially trusts but who is eventually revealed to be a member of the Thought Police.[113] Winston and Julia are found together naked when a loud voice blares out the startling announcement, "Clasp your hands behind your heads!"[114] Surrounded, and with no hope of escape, they comply. Through the window and the door, the police crash in upon them in their vulnerable, unclothed state; arrest them; subdue them; and haul them away separately to be interrogated and reprogrammed.[115]

From this point forward, Winston's world unravels. He is imprisoned and subjected to round after round of excruciating torture.[116] O'Brien, whom Winston had taken for a renegade and eventually made the mistake of trusting, turns out to be the very one in charge of administering the torture.[117] As Winston undergoes interrogation on a device that delivers increasingly intense bouts of piercing pain, he is coerced into accepting only the State's version of the "Truth." O'Brien's criterion for success in reprograming Winston demands nothing short of achieving complete mind control over him. O'Brien holds up four fingers and asks Winston, "How many fingers do you see?" If Winston replies with "four" instead of "five," the torture continues. O'Brien must eradicate Winston's belief that "two plus two make four" because earlier in the novel, Winston had set forth as his axiom,

> Freedom is the freedom to say that two plus two make four. If that is granted, all else follows.[118]

To end his torture, Winston must therefore agree with O'Brien's blatant contradiction of this obvious factual truth. Finally, Winston, having been totally broken down by O'Brien's relentless assaults, admits that he sees five fingers when O'Brien is really holding up only four.[119] Winston finally confesses that he *truly believes* two plus two equals five.[120] O'Brien and the State thus succeed in wresting from Winston his last remaining shred of freedom.

The Two Dystopias: Contrasts and Connections

In summary, what we find in these two dystopian novels are extreme attempts to relocate the Transcendent in humanly contrived structures of *power* and *order*. To motivate and control people, the most rudimentary value-indicators, pleasure and pain, must therefore be coopted and maximally exploited. In Huxley's novel, pleasure and the love of pleasure become the chief means of motivating persons; while in Orwell's novel, the chief instruments of control are pain and the fear of pain. The goal, however, happens to be very much the same in Orwell's dystopia as in Huxley's. One of the State's major objectives in both novels is to *eradicate human individuality* and to achieve what C. S. Lewis famously called "the abolition of man."[121] To achieve this aim, the State must stoop to using any means necessary, no matter how immoral or cruel. The State's other major objective is to eliminate all meaningful and purposive human interpersonal relationships and to replace them with an impersonal collective.[122] In Huxley's dystopia, this impersonal collective becomes identical with *meaning itself.* In Orwell's dystopia, on the other hand, the impersonal collective becomes identical with *purpose itself.* However, because both dystopias cut themselves off from the *Transcendent, power* and *order* now only loop in upon themselves, which results in a destruction of *meaning* and *purpose.*

Utopian Ideologies and the Shadow

The "genie in Aladdin's lamp" analogy illustrates how ideals, which at first seem *angelic*, can, in fact, have a *demonic* core. Blake understood this when he spoke of *angels in hell* and *devils in heaven.*[123] Poetic images like these help us visualize the fluid relationship between *good* and *evil* in human experience. Depth psychologist Carl Jung offers a penetrating analysis of various psychological mechanisms that explain how utopian and dystopian visions belong to the two edges of the "double-edged sword" that is the human psyche. What, then, are these mechanisms that help explain why utopian visions can morph into dystopian nightmares?

In discussing how certain psychological mechanisms function, Jung interjects his concept of "the self," which refers to the encompassing center of human personality.[124] *The self* is also sort of a clearing house where the forces of unconsciousness and consciousness intersect and conflict. One of these forces is "the shadow," which represents certain weaknesses, inhibitions, and inferiorities that the self refuses to acknowledge or accept. The shadow thus belongs to the dimension of the *personal unconscious*, and, as such, the self prefers to repress it.[125] Despite attempts to keep the shadow repressed, Jung thinks that one can become aware of it without too much difficulty, though bringing it to the level of consciousness can prove a fearful and frightening experience.[126] The fear and fright results from the powerful influence of another unconscious force within human personality; namely, what he terms the "*anima*" or the "*animus.*" He uses the term *anima* to refer to this unconscious force in the masculine psyche and *animus* to refer to this same force in the feminine psyche.[127]

Although the *anima/animus* can have a *creative* influence when it inspires the masculine and feminine personalities, respectively, to transcend their limitations, it can also exert itself in *deceptive* ways that harbor damaging consequences. These consequences occur when the *anima/animus* produces an idealized picture of *the self* that refuses to come to terms with *the shadow*. Because the self can allow no place for the shadow, the *anima/animus* drives *the shadow* out of *the self* and justifies a projection of it onto other individuals or groups exterior to the self.[128] Such demonized individuals or groups are then viewed by those engaged in projecting as objects to be loathed, as mere things to be hated, and as worthy only of castigation and ill treatment.[129] The self is consequently *deceived* when it perceives itself as righteous and the other as demonic.

Whenever this phenomenon of shadow projection occurs, the individuals or groups of persons upon whom the shadow is projected are usually demonized as scapegoats and are subsequently victimized. Jung believes, in fact, that the Nazis' widespread projection of the shadow onto Jews during the Third Reich explained why they persecuted the Jews. This shadow projection phenomenon was not, however, limited to Germany.[130] It occurred in the United States as well during the days of segregation and Jim Crow, and during the "Red Scare" of the McCarthy Era.

Jung's discussion of the interactions between these psychological mechanisms reveals the important link that exists between evil as *deception* and evil as *injustice*. His idea of shadow projection helps elucidate *why* deception allows personal relationships to be transformed into impersonal ones. Certainly, when the transition from the personal to the impersonal occurs in a relationship, the element of *impersonal distance* is exaggerated while the element of *personal affinity* is diminished or even eradicated. When this deceptive phenomenon becomes writ large upon the greater society, we see how deception invariably gives birth to injustice. The specters of dystopia begin to rear their ugly heads. Widespread shadow projection is certainly a feature of both dystopias I have discussed.

Because of shadow projection, the ideologies initially perceived to be angelic and filled with hopeful promise turn into demonic traps where despair reigns supreme and all hope of escape has vanished. The Baconian "utopia of complexity" morphs into the Huxleyan dystopia as the emotional entanglements of life are discarded and *pleasure* and *self-gratification* at their most basic level are promoted as "the highest goods." In an opposite way that turns out to be just as demonic, More's "utopia of simplicity" morphs into the Orwellian dystopia where *pain* and torture, both physical and mental, are liberally employed as a means of forcing people to accept total uniformity as "the highest good."

Aspirations and the Context of the Transcendent

A broad look at the current cultural situation existing in the West confirms that we are living at least partially in both the Huxleyan and Orwellian dystopian nightmares at once. Indeed, one cannot help but wonder if certain instigators of current social and cultural change have read these dystopian novels and mistaken them as guidebooks for the improvement of society! Are the current proponents of political correctness, who are intent on micromanaging our language, merely advancing their own peculiar version of newspeak? Have the modern news media become vehicles of various Minitrue propaganda machines? Have our universities succeeded in teaching their students how to achieve adeptness and facility in the art of doublethink? And what of the current disintegration of the family and the push to legalize drugs? Has our sexually liberated society forced procreative sex and the institutions of marriage and family into becoming the new taboos? Is marijuana the closest approximation we can find to the drug Soma? To the extent that all these questions can be answered affirmatively, they reveal how much Orwellian and Huxleyan kinds of methods are being adopted and employed by some for the purpose of achieving maximal social influence and control.

What, then, do dystopian nightmares ultimately reveal about human nature? As I continue to sort out how the competitive and cooperative drives relate to the two aspirations, I believe it is of paramount importance to consider ways that the aspirations can be redirected toward a transcendence that lies beyond the dimension of the purely tangible. This cannot happen, however, as long as we make the mistake of reducing the transcendental "Good Itself" to some tangible good and invest our life energies in the procurement of that tangible good as though it were, in fact, ultimate. And once a tangible good is obtained, what happens next? Is it then and only then that the incongruity between this good as an imagined "ultimate" and "the Good Itself" is starkly revealed? Such often seems to be the case. Unfortunately, the revelation this incongruity conveys becomes a source not of satisfaction, but only of disappointment. The "Good" turns out neither to be definable nor to align perfectly with whatever our own mental constructs of it once happened to be. The transcendental and ineffable dimension of "the Good Itself" thus continues to elude our grasp.

Utopian Beliefs as Examples of Misplaced Transcendence

Our tendency to confuse tangible goods with "the Good Itself" helps explain, too, why so many of the utopian beliefs I have discussed successfully cast their deceptive spell upon human minds but end up disappointing those who invest in them. Sociologist Ernst Bloch, in his own utopian speculations, conjectured that a sense of boredom would predictably ensue once utopia was reached, and this caused him to rethink whether utopia should best be conceived of as "a state arrived at" or as a "continual process of arriving." Indeed, in the aftermath of the obtainment, we often experience what Bloch called "the melancholy of fulfillment."[131]

Bloch's insight concerning the elusiveness of meaning and the transitory nature of happiness is, of course, nothing new. In the biblical book of Ecclesiastes, Qoheleth (a.k.a. "the Preacher") expresses how the meaning of life had eluded him. Most people would agree that the range and scope of Qoheleth's "rich experiences" were nothing short of utopian, but his attitude toward them all is rife with unmitigated pessimism. His verdict, "vanity of vanities, all is vanity,"[132] reveals the condition of someone who had searched for happiness in all the wrong places yet had failed to obtain it. Each successive disappointment only reinforces this verdict; and no forthcoming experience, it seems, will suffice to overturn it. The Preacher insists that he has searched for "the all" or "the whole" (Heb=הַכֹּל) of the matter, but this whole always remains elusive and beyond his reach.[133] His attempt to find it in the realm of human existence that lies "under the sun"[134] is "vain" or "empty" (Heb=הֶבֶל).[135] At the end of the book, the commentator concludes with such phrases as "Remember now your Creator in the days of your youth, before the evil days come," and "Fear God and keep his commandments, for this is the whole duty of man."[136] Still, even these statements seem to beg for something more than what they can offer. One is left instead with a sense of melancholy and nagging emptiness at not having reached the most important of intrinsic ends—i.e., true happiness, blessedness, or fulfillment.

Perhaps it is significant that the Book of Ecclesiastes, which in time was accepted as one of the five scrolls of the Jewish Megilloth associated with the Hebrew festivals, became specifically attached to the Feast of Tabernacles (*Sukkot*). This association is significant because Tabernacles was the Hebrew festival that pointed forward to the end of time and anticipated God's final judgment upon the world and its inhabitants. The Tabernacles festival is replete with symbols of transcendence such as the "everlasting light" and the "life-giving waters" that would flow from Jerusalem into the world at the end of time.[137] Indeed, one finds veiled within biblical descriptions that appear to be tangible, intimations toward a meaning that is, in fact, intangible, transcendent, and eternal. The Apocalypse of St. John the Divine borrows imagery from the Festival of Tabernacles, as well, in the book's final chapters; but the New Jerusalem presented there transcends all earthly situated utopias. The imagery of the everlasting light and the life-giving stream belongs instead to the "new heavens and the new earth."[138]

The juxtaposing of Ecclesiastes with the Feast of Tabernacles in Judaism thus suggests a stark contrast between the dimensions of the temporal and the eternal, as well as between the dimensions of the tangible and the Transcendent. This contrast assumes the existence of a barrier between dimensions. The barrier must somehow be traversed if one is to transition from this present world that lies under the sun to the world to come that is situated above it—and indeed above all the luminaries that shall dwindle before the coming of the day of the Lord.[139] Ecclesiastes, with its pessimistic qualities, belongs to the biblical theme of the final judgment and corresponds to what is commonly referred to as "the life review" that some people claim to have had during near-death experiences. The transitory quality of temporal life and its emptiness is emphasized; but what is this an emptiness of, exactly? The answer is, "Of the fullness of the divine transcendence." This is the "whole" or the "all" that the Preacher sought to grasp as he engaged in life's trivial pursuits. The whole, however, continues to elude him because it belongs to the transcendent dimension of the Creator and not to the created dimension; thus, the advice, "Remember now thy Creator in the days of thy youth, while the evil days come not, nor the years draw nigh, when thou shalt say, I have no pleasure in them."[140]

TOWARD A COMPREHENSIVE TRIADIC PATTERN AS THE ULTIMATE CONTEXT

Up to now, I have discussed the way that impulses are taken up into drives and how drives can become the means of fulfilling aspirations. At this point, it appears that the aspirations provide the context in which impulses and drives begin to be endowed with a greater value than what is made possible by their own more limited contexts. However, the very fact that the quest for height and the search for centeredness can be thrown into conflict and produce tragic results reveals our need to posit a context of value that transcends even the aspirations themselves. One thing we must acknowledge is that the two aspirations do not come into conflict merely because of factors such as necessity, randomness, or fate. Human free will, choice, and decision also appear as determinates that affect how the aspirations are, or are not, fulfilled.

The very fact that we can commiserate with tragic outcomes points to the fact that we recognize a value of which the tragic outcome falls short. What, then, is this value that precedes manifestations of the tragic? How is this value to be construed? We already detect triadic patterns recurring from the lowest to the highest of the value-indicators. The rudimentary value-indicators are *pain* and *pleasure*, but the *relation* between the two completes the triadic pattern. The triadic pattern is revealed again in the *cooperative* and *competitive* drives, and the *relation* between them. The *quest for height*, the *search for centeredness*, and the *relation* between these human aspirations reveal still another triad, while *transcendental purpose*, *transcendental meaning*, and the *relation* between *these* dimensions disclose yet another.

The value-compass reveals a series of triadic patterns as well. There is the dimension of the tangible, the dimension of the transcendental, and the relation between the two. There is *freedom, limit,* and their *relation* to one another. Finally, *power, order,* and their interrelationship form a further triadic pattern. Eventually, I shall endeavor to show how these recurring triadic patterns are reflections of an ultimate triadic reality—namely, the Trinitarian God as the *summum bonum* of Value Itself, and a *summum bonum* that encompasses both the Good Itself and the Beautiful Itself. But how are we to understand the element in the triadic pattern that I have identified as "relation"? I propose in the next two chapters to explore this question by investigating *two vehicles* human beings use to express value; namely, *language* and *action.* These are vehicles through which impulses, drives, and aspirations can be meaningfully interrelated and contextualized.

NOTES

1. See *Evolutionary Theory in the Social Sciences,* Vol. 2, ed. William M. Dugger and Howard J. Sherman (London and New York: Routledge, Taylor & Francis Group, 2003), 116–118; Jessica L. Barker, Pat Barclay, and H. Kern Reeve, "Within-Group Competition Reduces Cooperation and Payoff in Human Groups," *Behavioral Ecology* 23, no. 4 (July–August 2012): 735–41.

2. Auguste Comte, *Système de politique positive, ou traité de sociologie, instituant la religion de l'humanité,* Vol. 1 (Paris: Librairie Scientifique-Industrielle de L. Matthias, 1854).

3. Herbert Spencer, *Principles of Sociology,* 3 vols. (New York: D. Appleton, 1898), 3:608–12.

4. Josephine Donovan, *Feminist Theory: The Intellectual Traditions,* 4th ed. (New York: Continuum, 2012), 42–44.

5. John Rawls, *A Theory of Justice,* rev. ed. (Cambridge, MA: The Belknap Press of Harvard University Press, 1999), ch. 1. Rawls, for instance, speaks of "perfect altruism" (164–65) but more often of "mutual disinterestedness" (12, 110–12, 128–31).

6. Rawls, *A Theory of Justice,* 11, 118–23.

7. Rawls, *A Theory of Justice,* 11.

8. See, for example, Ayn Rand, *The Virtue of Selfishness: A New Concept of Egoism* (New York: Signet, 1961), 13–39.

9. Rawls, *Theory of Justice,* 234–39.

10. For example, Nietzsche's statement, "The weak and the botched shall perish: first principle of our charity. And one should help them to it." *The Antichrist,* trans. H. L. Mencken (Lexington, KY: Pantianos Classics, 2017), sect. 2.

11. See, for example, Alan Ryan, "Rawls," in *The Return of Grand Theory in the Human Sciences,* ed. Quentin Skinner (Cambridge: Cambridge University Press, 1990), 104–10.

12. See, for example, Robert Lupton, *Toxic Charity: How Churches and Charities Hurt Those They Help, and How to Reverse It* (New York: HarperOne, 2012).

13. Nietzsche, *Beyond Good and Evil: Prelude to a Philosophy of the Future,* trans. Judith Norman, ed. Rolf-Peter Horstmann and Judith Norman (Cambridge: Cambridge University Press, 2002), 8.250–51 (pp. 140–43). Indeed, the fact that Nietzsche's philosophy influenced Theodor Herzl and Jewish Zionism shows that Hitler did not derive his anti-Semitism expressly from Nietzsche. See Jacob Golomb, *Nietzsche and Zion* (Ithaca: Cornell University Press, 2004), 1–4, 23–24.

14. On Nietzsche's use of rhetoric, see ch. 2 of Alan Norman Watt, "Nietzsche and Rhetoric," PhD diss., University of Warwick, 1992, http://wrap.warwick.ac.uk/4327/1/

WRAP_THESIS_Watt_1992.pdf, p. 34. For Rand's use of rhetoric, see James Aune, *Selling the Free Market: The Rhetoric of Economic Correctness* (New York: Guilford Press, 2001), 61.

15. For a treatment of "divine command theory" as related to other ethical theories, see John E. Hare, *God and Morality: A Philosophical History* (Oxford: Blackwell, 2007), 260–73.

16. See Frank Moore Cross, *Canaanite Myth and Hebrew Epic* (Cambridge, MA: Harvard University Press, 1997), 66, 173.

17. Exod 20:12, 14; Deut 5:16, 18.

18. The word "*Tanak*" is an acronym derived from the first letters of the three Hebrew words, *Torah*, *Nebi'im*, and *Kethubim*. These refer respectively to the *Law*, the *Prophets*, and the *Writings*.

19. See discussion in Norman Powell Williams, *Ideas of the Fall and Original Sin: A Historical and Critical Study* (London: Longmans, Green, and Co., 1927), 60–61, 114; W. D. Davies, *Paul and Rabbinic Judaism: Some Rabbinic Elements in Pauline Theology* (London: S.P.C.K, 1958), 20–27.

20. God is sometimes viewed as the author of evil in the Old Testament (e.g., Job 2:10; Isa 45:7; and Amos 3:6). The Talmud shares this opinion regarding the evil impulse: "If God created the evil inclination, he also created the Torah as its remedy" (*b. B. Bat.* 16a).

21. See *Midr. Exod* 46:4: "Thou hast created in us an Evil Inclination from our youth." See also *Midr. Ps* 32:4.

22. *Midr. Qoh* 3:2:3. In this passage, Rabbi Nehemiah (c. 150 CE) affirms that the creation of the evil inclination by God is "very good." See also *Midr. Ps* 9:1.

23. *Midr. Cant* 7:8:1.

24. *Midr. Lev* 29:7. See also *Midr. Deut* 2:33; *Midr. Cant* 4:4:1; 4:3:4; *Midr. Ruth* 8:1; *b. Sanh.* 111a; *Midr. Ps* 86:5.

25. *Midr. Lev* 9:1; *Midr. Num* 13:15, 16; *b. Sanh.* 43b.

26. *Midr. Lev* 7:2.

27. Aristot. Nic. Eth. 1.4.

28. Carl G. Jung, *The Collected Works* [hereafter abbreviated as *CW*], 20 vols., ed. H. Read, M. Fordham, and G. Adler, trans. R. F. C. Hull (Princeton, NJ: Princeton University Press, 1953–79), 8:679.

29. Ov. Met. 8.183–220; Apollod. Epit. 1. 11–13.

30. Jean-Paul Sartre, *No Exit and Three Other Plays* (New York: Vintage Books, 1949), 47.

31. Sartre, *Being and Nothingness*, 342–59.

32. For a detailed list of references, see Charles L. Whitfield, *Co-Dependence: Healing the Human Condition* (Deerfield Beach, FL: Health Communications, Inc., 1991), 281–317.

33. Gill, *Mediated Transcendence*, 7.

34. Thomas More, *Utopia* (London: Cassell, 1901), 6.

35. More, *Utopia*, 16–17, 40.

36. More, *Utopia*, 43.

37. More, *Utopia*, 44.

38. More, *Utopia*, 44–45.

39. More, *Utopia*, 70–72.

40. More, *Utopia*, 71–72.

41. More, *Utopia*, 83.

42. See Machiavelli's *The Prince*.

43. More, *Utopia*, 56.

44. Examples include Walter Benjamin's idea of the *Angelus Novus* or the Angel of the New in *Über den Begriff der Geschichte*, in *Gesammelten Schriften* I:2 (Frankfurt am Main: Suhrkamp Verlag, 1974), IX; and Ernst Bloch in *The Principle of Hope, 3 Vols.*, trans. Neville Plaice, Stephen Plaice, and Paul Knight (Oxford, UK: Basil Blackwell, 1986), 1:200–205.

45. Bacon, *The New Atlantis* [hereafter cited as *NA*], in *Great Books of the Western World*, vol. 30, ed. Robert Maynard Hutchins and Mortimer Adler (Chicago: William Benton/Encyclopædia Britannica, 1952), 199.

46. Bacon, *NA*, 206. The "six-days' work" being an allusion to Bacon's program set forth in his "Great Renewal," in *The New Organon*, ed. Lisa Jardine and Michael Silverthorne (Cambridge, UK: Cambridge University Press, 2000), 2–5.

47. Bacon, *NA*, 206.

48. Bacon, *NA*, 214.

49. Bacon, *NA*, 209.

50. Bacon, *NA*, 211.

51. Bacon, *NA*, 210–14.

52. As Susan Bruce notes, "intense competition" is at the heart of power politics and the enlargement of empire in the context of the race between European powers during the seventeenth century. "Introduction," in *Three Early Modern Utopias: Utopia, New Atlantis, and The Isle of the Pines*, ed. Susan Bruce (Oxford: Oxford University Press, 1999), xxxv.

53. Bacon, "Great Renewal," in *New Organon*, 2–5; *Advancement of Learning*, ed. Robern Maynard Hutchins and Mortimer Adler (Chicago: William Benton/Encyclopædia Britannica, 1952), 2.15.1 (p. 62).

54. Bacon, "Of Envy," in *The Essays* (New York: Cosimo Classics, 2007), 23–28. See also "Of Vain-Glory," in *The Essays,* 134–35.

55. Bacon, *NA*, 214.

56. J. Benedict Warren, s.v. "Quiroga, Vasco de," *Encyclopedia of Mexico: History, Society, and Culture*, Vol. 2, ed. Michael S. Werner (Chicago & London: Fitzroy Dearborn, 1997), 1215.

57. David Weil Baker, *Divulging Utopia: Radical Humanism in Sixteenth-Century England* (Amherst: University of Massachusetts Press, 1999), 15–16.

58. Benjamin Farrrington, *Francis Bacon: Philosopher of Industrial Science* (New York: Henry Schuman, 1949), 15–25.

59. Joel Mokyr, *The British Industrial Revolution: An Economic Perspective*, 2nd ed. (Boulder, CO: Westview Press, 1999), 105–7.

60. Mokyr, *British Industrial Revolution*, 21, 80.

61. Jane Bingham, *The Cotswolds: A Cultural History* (Oxford: Oxford University Press, 2010), 34, 82–86.

62. J. B. Shank, *The Newton Wars and the Beginning of the French Enlightenment* (Chicago, IL: University of Chicago Press, 2008), 178–93.

63. George Beaumont, "The Beggars Complaint," in *Factory Production in Nineteenth-Century Britain*, ed. Elaine Freedgood (New York: Oxford University Press, [1812] 2003), 123.

64. William Blake, "Jerusalem, The Emanation of the Giant Albion," plate 71, stanzas 50–60 in *The Complete Writings of William Blake*, ed. Geoffrey Keynes (London: Nonesuch Press, 1957), 480–81.

65. Blake, "Poems and Fragments from the Notebook" (1793), plate 61, in *The Complete Writings of William Blake*, 186–87. "Urizen" sounds like "your reason"—in other words, "autonomous reason."

66. Blake, "The First Book of Urizen," plate 15, in "Complete Writings of William Blake," 635; see also, *Jerusalem, The Emanation of the Giant Albion*, plate 52, in *Complete Writings*, 682–83.

67. Blake, "The First Book of Urizen," ch. 1, in *Complete Writings*, 222–23.

68. Northrup Fry writes, "This solitary super-ego, or old man of the sky, Newton's *Pantocrator* (M. 4:11), Blake calls 'Nobodaddy' in the Rossetti MS, 'Urizen' (fallen) in the earlier prophecies, and 'Satan' in 'Milton' and 'Jerusalem.' The essential attribute of Blake's Satan is death, and he works within man as what we should now call the death-impulse, the inner traitor of the soul who, like Judas Iscariot, eventually goes to his own place (M. 11:12; cf. M. 28:41)." Fry, "Notes for a Commentary on Milton," in *The Divine Vision: Studies in the Poetry and Art of William Blake, Born November 28th, 1757*, eds. Vivian de Sola Pinto, Kathleen Raine, and William Blake Bicentenary Committee (London: Victor Gollancz, 1957), 113.

69. Blake, *Jerusalem*, from "Preface to Milton: A Poem in 1 [2] Books," in *Complete Writings*, 480–81.

70. See Gertrude Himmelfarb, *Poverty and Compassion: The Moral Imagination of the Late Victorians* (New York: Vintage Books, 1991), ch. 13.

71. *The Health and Morals of Apprentices Act* of 1802, *The Cotton Mills Act* of 1819, *The Poor Law Amendment Act* of 1834, *The Chimney Sweepers' Act* of 1875, and *The Factory Acts*

of 1833, 1844, 1847, 1867, 1878, 1891, and 1895, *The Mines and Collieries Bills* of 1842 and 1850, *The Coal Mines Inspection Act* of 1859, and *The Coal Mines Regulation Act* of 1860.

72. Of Stephen, Dickens writes in his novel *Hard Times*, ". . .somebody else had become possessed of his roses, and he had become possessed of the same somebody else's thorns in addition to his own." Charles Dickens, *Hard Times* (Champaign, IL: Project Gutenberg e-book, 1997), 37.

73. Karl Marx and Friedrich Engels, *The Communist Manifesto* (Project Gutenberg e-text, 1993), 7–11, 20.

74. See, for example, Vladimir Lenin, "What is to Replace the Smashed State Machinery?" in *The State and Revolution* (New York: International Publishers, 1932, 1943), 35–39.

75. Marx and Engels, *Communist Manifesto*, 14–15.

76. John Bowman, *Socialism in America*, 2nd ed. (New York, Lincoln, and Shanghai: iUniverse, 2005), 241.

77. Aldous Huxley, *Brave New World* [hereafter abbreviated as *BNW*] (Cutchogue, NY: Buccaneer Books, 1932, 1946).

78. Huxley, *BNW*, 2–4.
79. Huxley, *BNW*, 2–3.
80. Huxley, *BNW*, 16–17.
81. Huxley, *BNW*, 26–30.
82. Huxley, *BNW*, 26.
83. Huxley, *BNW*, 124–25.
84. Huxley, *BNW*, 21.
85. Huxley, *BNW*, 42–47.
86. Huxley, *BNW*, 78–79.
87. Huxley, *BNW*, 64–65.
88. Huxley, *BNW*, 81–82.
89. Huxley, *BNW*, 95.
90. Huxley, *BNW*, 164–66.
91. Huxley, *BNW*, 173–75.
92. Huxley, *BNW*, 176–77.
93. George Orwell, *1984: A Novel* (New Delhi: Rupa Publications, 2013), 1–8.
94. Ingsoc, it is speculated in the novel, may be the "newspeak" version of the "oldspeak" term, "English socialism." Orwell, *1984*, 36.
95. Orwell, *1984*, 27–28.
96. Orwell, *1984*, 4.
97. Orwell, *1984*, 26.
98. Orwell, *1984*, 51.
99. Orwell, *1984*, 52.
100. Orwell, *1984*, 3.
101. Orwell, *1984*, 35.
102. Orwell, *1984*, 216.
103. Orwell, *1984*, 12.
104. Orwell, *1984*, 1, 9, 11–13, 180.
105. Orwell, *1984*, 3.
106. Orwell, *1984*, 43.
107. Orwell, *1984*, 152, 157.
108. Orwell, *1984*, 128.
109. Orwell, *1984*, 150.
110. Orwell, *1984*, 65.
111. Orwell, *1984*, 267.
112. Orwell, *1984*, 120, 124, 127.
113. Orwell, *1984*, 224.
114. Orwell, *1984*, 221.
115. Orwell, *1984*, 222.
116. Orwell, *1984*, 229–59.
117. Orwell, *1984*, 244.

118. Orwell, *1984*, 81.

119. Orwell, *1984*, 249–58.

120. Orwell, *1984*, 174–76.

121. C. S. Lewis, *The Abolition of Man* (Oxford: Oxford University Press, 1943), ch. 3. One should remember here, too, that Lewis himself wrote a dystopian novel. See C. S. Lewis, *That Hideous Strength* (London: The Bodley Head, 1945).

122. The eradication of the family, which is a theme in both novels, was first suggested by Yevgeny Zamyatin in his novel *We*. See Martin Seymour-Smith, *The 100 Most Influential Books Ever Written: The History of Thought from Ancient Times to Today* (Secaucus, NJ: Citadel Press/Carol Publishing, 1998), 445.

123. William Blake, "The Marriage of Heaven and Hell," plate 6, in *Complete Writings*. Blake, e.g., writes subversively of John Milton, "The reason Milton wrote in fetters when he wrote of Angels & God, and at liberty when of Devils & Hell, is because he was a true Poet and of the Devil's party without knowing it."

124. Jung, *CW*, 6:460; 9, 2:23–35.

125. Jung, *CW*, 9, 2:8–9.

126. Jung, *CW*, 9, 2:11.

127. Jung, *CW*, 9, 2:11–22.

128. Jung, *CW*, 9, 2:53.

129. Jung, *CW*, 6:425–26.

130. See Jung, *CW*, vol. 10, especially articles entitled "Wotan," "After the Catastrophe," and "The Fight with the Shadow."

131. Ernst Bloch, *The Principle of Hope*, 1:299.

132. Eccl 1:2, 14; 2:1, 11–26; 3:19; 4:4–8, 16; 5:7–10; 6:2–11; 7:6; 8:10, 14; 11:8–10; 12:8.

133. The Hebrew word is variously translated "all," "everything," and "the whole" in Eccl 1:2, 14; 2:11, 16, 17; 3:11, 19, 20; 6:6; 7:15; 9:1, 2; 10:19; 11:5; 12:8, 13. See Paul Fiddes, "Wisdom as a Search for the Sum of Things," in *Seeing the World and Knowing God: Hebrew Wisdom and Christian Doctrine in a Late Modern Context* (Oxford: Oxford University Press, 2013), 298–323.

134. The Hebrew for "under the sun" is תַּחַת־שֶׁמֶשׁ in Eccl 5:18; 8:15, 17; 9:3, 9, 11.

135. The Hebrew term for " the all" juxtaposed to the term for "empty" reveals an existential contradiction at the heart of *Qoheleth's* experience.

136. Eccl 12:1, 13.

137. Zech 14:6–10. Verse 16 of this chapter establishes the link of this imagery to the Feast of Tabernacles.

138. Rev 21:23; 22:1–5.

139. Joel 2:10; Isa 13:10. Cf. Matt 24:29; Mark 13:24.

140. Eccl 12:1. Buddhism shares with the Book of Ecclesiastes this view of the transitory nature of this existence, but instead of identifying the Transcendent with "the Whole" or "the All," Buddhism identifies it with "the Nothing," in other words, "Nirvana" meaning "no flame." The goal of transitory life is thus the extinguishing of life.

Chapter Five

Language as a Vehicle of Value

Impulses, drives, and aspirations are expressed and unified in significant ways through the vehicles of *language* and *action*. Through these vehicles, human beings carry out, participate in, and reflect upon the elaborate and complex interweaving of their competitive and cooperative drives as they relate to the two aspirations. I do not advocate separating these two vehicles into airtight categories; for the sake of discussion, chapter 5 will examine *language* as a vehicle that expresses value. The next chapter will then examine *action's* role as a vehicle of value mediation. First, however, I must briefly discuss the link between language and action.

LINKING LANGUAGE AND ACTION THROUGH "LANGUAGE GAMES"

Examining how the phenomena of human language and action are intrinsically linked provides one way of discovering how the competitive and cooperative drives become linked to human aspirations. Ludwig Wittgenstein's (1889–1951) insights into "language games" provide an inroad for understanding the nature of this linkage. By the time Wittgenstein, in his *Philosophical Investigations*, spoke of "language games," he had moved well beyond the methodology in his *Tractatus Logico-Philosophicus*, a work that inspired the Logical Positivists of the Vienna Circle.[1] Their methodology was too constrictive and reductive to reveal the inherently meaningful reciprocity that Wittgenstein observed in the link between language and meaningful human action.[2]

I believe Wittgenstein was headed in the right direction when he spoke of this link in terms of "language games" for two reasons: 1) Games do not slavishly follow logical rules, and 2) the actions that active participants express in games cannot be classified in terms of purely *mechanical* sorts of cause-and-effect relationships. Games do have rules; however, when they are *played*, too many variables emerge to warrant their being classified as *merely* logical or *purely* mechanical sorts of actions. When games are played, players and observers alike experience a *surplus of meaning* that transcends mere rules and basic mechanics. Players and fans know this in an immediate way, for when they experience this surplus of meaning, they will predictably respond with cheers of exuberance. They will otherwise boo and hiss when they perceive meaning being threatened.

In the playing of games, both the cooperative and competitive drives become contextualized within a larger and more meaningful framework that the participants believe will fulfill their aspirations. On the one hand, the ideal of what it means to be a *team* contextualizes the *cooperative* drive and *inspires* this drive in a meaningful way. The ideal of *winning*, on the other hand, contextualizes the *competitive* drive and *purposively* directs it. The ideal of a "winning team" thus represents the merging and continual inter-play of the competitive and cooperative drives, and winning teams will make efforts to maintain these drives in a state of balance and equilibrium. Though in competitive sports, the cooperative drive becomes subordinate to the com-petitive drive, this does not mean that competition will be allowed entirely to eclipse the element of cooperation. Talented individuals may perform well *separately*, but the real test of whether a team will succeed in winning will usually be gauged by their ability to *cooperate* and work together *as a team*.

Clearly, a team's *aspiration* to win stands apart from the competitive and cooperative drives that this aspiration evokes and organizes. In games, the competitive and cooperative drives cease to be purely instinctual when the aspiration to win recontextualizes these drives and charges them with a high-er purpose and meaning that they did not initially possess. It also happens to be true of language that the one who is adept at communication cannot be tied slavishly to linguistic mechanics; just as a talented basketball player will know how to play adeptly within the boundaries of the established rules. Occasionally, rules will be violated, and this means penalties will have to be imposed. Rules are therefore necessary to make any game meaningful, for without them the competitive and cooperative drives would have no signifi-cant function or aim. At the same time, playing passionately, skillfully, and creatively within the boundaries of the given rules is more desirable than "playing it safe." People do not attend football games to see grown men play patty-cake. On the other hand, no one would want to watch a team attempt to play a game where *no rules* were followed. In such a case, the expenditure of time and energy would be pointless.

BEYOND "LANGUAGE GAMES"

Wittgenstein's analogy, by linking the phenomenon of human language to games, provides insight into one level of *meaningful* and *purposive* human activity. The analogy, however, can itself be considered reductive if one insists on viewing all human expression and activity as being *merely* "game-like." While it is true that life itself has a *game-like quality*, this cannot be taken to imply that life is *merely* a game. Games do, of course, entail elements of chance and risk, but what degree of value does one attach to these elements? Certainly, the amount of risk taken against the vagaries of chance will vary between different individuals participating in a game, regardless of whether those participants are players or spectators. In playing a game, a professional athlete will risk losing more than a mere spectator will risk—unless, of course, the spectator happens also to own the team or has wagered a significant amount of money on a game's outcome. In such situations, mere frivolity at winning or mild disappointment at losing gives way to something much more serious and much weightier.

When one considers that participation even in common games has the capacity to place one in quite serious circumstances, it follows *a fortiori* that something as wide-ranging as the *whole of life* itself must transcend Wittgenstein's characterization of language as a "game." Blaise Pascal (1623–1662) understands this to be the case when he advances his celebrated wager in relation to two contexts with one being proximate and the other being ultimate. If the ultimate context happens to be true—namely, that God exists—then the wager one makes by choosing to believe or not to believe in God involves the greatest possible promise of reward, or the greatest possible risk of loss. One manner of choosing holds the promise that heaven will be gained. The other warns of eternal consequences in which nothing is gained but everything is forfeited. Pascal maintains, however, that even a more proximate context warranted that we wager by choosing to believe in God rather than to disbelieve.

The proximate context Pascal alludes to pertains to the living of this temporal life.[3] *All human beings desire happiness above all things*—this was Aristotle's insight.[4] Aristotle also maintains that we desire happiness for its own sake and for no other reason. However, the kind of faith Pascal speaks of goes far beyond mere assent to, or mental acknowledgment of, the proposition "God exists." It also goes well beyond the kind of "thought experiments" philosophers of religion engage in. Thought experiments have the capacity to shield the detached philosophical observer from suffering any truly life-threatening consequences. Pascal's wager is, on the contrary, much more akin to what Søren Kierkegaard calls "the leap to faith."[5]

It now becomes clear that the game analogy, while useful, cannot express well enough what the total scenario of life entails. Any contention that "life is but a game" trivializes the real meaning and purpose of life. For this reason, we must seek to grasp a meaning and discover a purpose that is higher and more profound than what mere games are capable of mediating. Wittgenstein, I believe, left room for this higher and more profound dimension when he said in his *Tractatus*, "whereof one cannot speak thereof one must be silent," but not everyone who read his statement reached this conclusion. Proponents who took the route of logical positivism and linguistic analysis interpreted Wittgenstein's statement as proof that language about metaphysics, ethics, and aesthetics could only amount to *nonsense*.[6] Consequently, logical positivists and linguistic analysts refused to wrestle with the element of mystery in language because their minds were too enslaved to empirical methodology even to try.

Kierkegaard's Johannes de Silentio could provide a more promising avenue of escape from such mental enslavement and a way forward.[7] With de Silentio, the human soul must wrestle with mystery before its quest to find ultimate meaning and purpose can even begin. The soul's quest must then traverse what St. John of the Cross called "the dark night of the soul."[8] The soul's dark night is not, however, a state of mere *agnosia* or ignorance from which one cannot hope to escape; for if it be true that God has set eternity in the hearts of men,[9] then the quest for transcendence cannot so easily be stifled. Nicholas of Cusa (1401–1464), in a similar vein, speaks of the *docta ignorantia* or "learned ignorance."[10] Augustine, expressing it in terms of the need of the heart to connect with God, writes, "My heart cannot find rest, O God, until it finds rest in Thee."[11] Also speaking of this phenomenon of the heart's restlessness, Martin Luther describes the soul's being in the condition he called "*Anfechtung*," which means "trial" or "testing."[12]

The restlessness of the human heart certainly appears active in what I have previously called "the quest for height" and "the search for centeredness"; viz., the two aspirations toward which the competitive and cooperative human drives are aimed. The quest for height can produce a kind of conflict that brings *alienation*, and this kind of conflict begs to be overcome by means of *reconciliation*. The search for centeredness, on the other hand, can produce a kind of conflict that entails *fragmentation* and *disordering*. This kind of conflict begs to be overcome through *integration*. Language possesses a "logos quality" that expresses how these two types of conflict may be resolved. What, then, is meant by "logos quality"? How does language relate to "logic" and to "logos"?

THE "LOGOS" QUALITY OF LANGUAGE AND THE
CHALLENGE OF DERRIDA'S *"DIFFÉRANCE"*

I maintain that language itself not only possesses a *logos quality*, but the concept of *logos* has the potential as well to integrate and reconcile aspirations that happen to be at cross-purposes. For *logos* to accomplish integration and reconciliation, however, it must be rescued from the constraints imposed upon it by *methods* of logic as they have been traditionally understood and practiced. The syllogistic logic of Aristotle, the inductive method of Francis Bacon, the modal logic of William of Ockham (1285–1347), and the logic of George Boole (1815–1864)—all, I maintain, are too restrictive to accomplish this task. Indeed, postmodernist philosophers such as Jacques Derrida (1930–2004) reject logocentrism for this reason; and, for better or for worse, Derrida's insights have even affected theological discourse concerning the use of the term *logos* by the writer of the Fourth Gospel. [13]

There are times when nailing categories down with logic resembles attempts to nail gelatin to a wall. Jacques Derrida alludes to this problem when he uses the French word *différance* [14] to describe a ghostly problem that haunts all attempts to impose logical constraints upon the reality we experience. *Différance*, as Derrida understands it, has both a spatial and temporal aspect and application. In its spatial sense, the term refers to the fact that everything we experience is haunted by the *absence* of *something*; whereas in its temporal sense, *différance* entails the problem of *deferral*. In this section, I have decided to employ Derrida's concept of *différance* in a way that may appear anachronistic; but I believe this term, because of its ability to encompass the above-mentioned spatial as well as temporal elements, can help us identify a long-standing difficulty that attaches to the Western philosophical tradition as a whole.

Returning to my previous discussion in chapter 3 of the ways that Anaximander and Heraclitus speak of "injustice" and "justice," I must cite Derrida's observation that an act of "violence" is always committed in the execution of *justice*, and not just of *injustice*. [15] There is little wonder, then, that confusion would arise over whether the four elements, in their relationship to one another, were in a state of injustice or justice. If an act of violence taints them both, then how does one decide which act of violence is *just* and which one is *unjust*? Since every attempt to execute justice is haunted by the very kind of violence it seeks to rectify, it appears that *justice* as an ideal always remains elusive and is something always deferred. Justice can therefore never become something we automatically dispense in the way machines dispense neatly packaged items. Indeed, the very ways that we dispense justice proliferate and become ever more manifold over time.

Logic itself is haunted by the problem of *différance*. Although Plato does not deal with formal logic in the way Aristotle does, the problem initially appears in the former's distinction between *thinking* and *sense experience*. For Plato, thinking, which is the chief vehicle through which we arrive at truth, contrasts with sense experience, which only provides us with an inferior level of understanding that he calls *opinion* (Grk=*doxa* [δόξα]).[16]

The gap between thinking and sense experience is wider in Plato than in Aristotle, but it nonetheless appears as the *difference* between the latter's *prior* and *posterior* analytics. Ideally, what is experienced *a posteriori* should be like the "hand" that fits perfectly inside the "glove" to which the *a priori* structure corresponds, but an absolutely perfect fit does not always result. Indeed, the problem of *différance* that lies between Aristotle's two analytics seems to have been the very anomaly that precipitated the transition from *deductive* to *inductive* thinking, which is a transition that Bacon initiated in the seventeenth century. Bacon reversed Aristotle's *prior* and *posterior* analytics and elevated the latter to a place of prominence over that of the former; and yet, he did not fully succeed in bridging the gap between Aristotle's two analytics.[17] The *incongruity* between *thought* and *experience* continued to persist in Bacon just as it had done in Aristotle.

The persistence of this incongruity is nowhere better epitomized than in the wide variance between the methodologies of the British empiricists and the continental rationalists. Whereas this variance manifested itself in one way as the incongruity *between* the methodologies these two traditions employed, it appeared in another way *within* each of methodological approaches themselves. For example, in using an *a posteriori* approach to reasoning, which proceeded by way of *synthesizing* the data that sense experience furnishes our minds, the British empiricists—John Locke, George Berkeley, and David Hume (1711–1776)—produced three widely varying perspectives. In a similar way, the continental rationalists—René Descartes, Baruch Spinoza, and Gottfried Leibniz—arrived at three disparate views using an *analytic* approach to reasoning that was based upon their acceptance of an *a priori* truth that existed prior to, and apart from, sense experience.

Of course, other philosophers have tried in varying ways to bridge the gap between *deductive* and *inductive* methods of reasoning by recognizing both to be valid in certain respects. Thomas Bayes (1701–1761) sought in one way to bridge this gap by offering his famous theorem.[18] In another way, Immanuel Kant tried to link the *analytic* approach of the continental rationalists to the *synthetic* approach of the British empiricists by means of his *"synthetic a priori."* Still, the gap between "sensation" and "thought," which recurred in the epistemological insights of Parmenides (c. 515–c. 450 BCE), Plato, and Descartes, remained unbridgeable in Kant as well. The problem of *différance* persisted.

Others attempted to bridge the gap between inductive and deductive thinking through abductive[19] or what Richard Swinburne calls "C-inductive" reasoning.[20] This type of reasoning looks at the probability of a conclusion in the light of all the evidence available. Like the theorem of Bayes, this approach has not, however, eradicated the problem of *différance*, for there remains a gap between conclusion and evidence that cannot be fully closed. Therefore, inductive sorts of reasoning cannot produce conclusions that are entirely certain but ones that are only probable to a greater or lesser degree.

However, the question does occur, "For the concept of *logos* to be valid, must the problem of *différance* be entirely eliminated from it?" It seems that an affirmative answer would be in order if we were to insist upon "enthroning the goddess reason" in the cathedrals of our minds.[21] Unfortunately, from at least the time of Plato and Aristotle onward, the element that Derrida identified as *différance* has presented to the faculties of reason an insurmountable obstacle. One may, for instance, decapitate one head of the hydra only to find two more subsequently sprouting from that wound where the violence to the first was inflicted.[22] For both Plato and Aristotle, *différance*, like the heads of the hydra, proliferates into further negative obstacles that are best eradicated as they crop up. Other images of violence come to mind, such as the bed of Procrustes where the "body" of facts is torturously stretched to fit a preconceived paradigm of truth; or, if that "body" is too large to fit, then parts of it are lopped off and handily eliminated.[23] The following conclusion, then, seems inevitably to follow: If the concept of *logos* is taken to be *identical* to what reason can discover, then we can perhaps understand why Deconstructionists have come to oppose logocentrism in virtually all its forms.

We nevertheless would do well to inquire here as to whether the Greek rationalist tradition has needlessly biased Western thought in a direction that misguided Derrida as well. Derrida, I think, gives tacit credence to the rationalist tradition in the way that he views *différance* as an element that is negative in quality. He describes *différance*, for instance, as being on the order of an infection that destroys health or of a corruption that contaminates purity. In these respects, he seems to adhere to an understanding of *différance* that shares affinities with what Robert Parker labeled *miasma*—namely, the element of contamination that perpetually antagonized the ancient Greeks and of which they went to great lengths to rid themselves.[24] Predecessors like Pythagoras and Plato would no doubt have agreed with Derrida's negative assessment of *différance*, even though they remained confident that reason could eventually purge away ignorance and falsehood. Reason, in this way, could act as a pharmaceutical that could eventually eliminate the infection of *différance*. Unlike them, however, Derrida completely lost confidence in the power of reason to overcome this negative. Even the pharmaceutical, which is the cure for what ails us, can poison us as well, Derrida observes.[25] We are thus doomed to remain stuck in our diseases and impurities. In this rather fatalistic assessment, Derrida anticipates the condition of the postmodern person: We are not only stuck in the *aporias* that life constantly throws up before us, but the "truth" will forever elude us as well.[26] The specter of Greek fatalism thus returns to haunt postmodern humans as their confidence in the all-encompassing power and guaranteed successfulness of logic to overturn *différance* flags and fails.

In my analysis of Derrida here, I argue that he did, in fact, substitute one form of reductive thought in place of another. The reductive tendencies of such philosophical schools of thought as logical positivism and French structuralism are abandoned in favor of what I would venture to call a "reduction to nihility."[27] Indeed, one can see this kind of reductive thinking at work in deconstructionist philosopher/theologian Mark C. Taylor's book *Erring: A Postmodern A/theology*.[28] Taylor, who applies Derrida's insights to theology, jettisons the *either/or* and the *both/and* because they pay homage to the Western predilection to express things in terms that are *binary*.[29] In place of these, Taylor advocates what he calls the *neither/nor*.[30] The implications of Taylor's move for moral philosophy are nothing short of devastating, and this is seen in his discussion of what he calls "mazing grace."[31] All moral components are jettisoned as Abraham's journey of faith and the peregrinations of the Prodigal Son into depravity are conflated to become virtually one and the same sort of journey![32]

Derrida has nonetheless broken important ground in his effort to rescue the idea of *différance* from the kind of routinely negative assessment it has received over the course of the entire Western tradition. This assessment derives from the way that the Western tradition has persistently categorized *différance* as a negative concept by forcing it into binary opposition to the principle of *identity*. Derrida, by resisting the tendency to force reality into binary oppositions, wishes instead to ascribe to *différance* a kind of neutrality that is *neither* positive *nor* negative. I maintain, however, that by doing this Derrida stops short of asking the question, "Are there 'different' sorts of *différance*?" By rejecting *logocentric* thinking, he is tacitly placing *negative* value on *logos* in a way that would have seemed inconceivable to previous generations of philosophers. This rejection, in fact, puts him in the position of not really being able to *reason* about *différance*. Indeed, in the face of *différance*, Derrida finds that he *cannot speak*, and this echoes Wittgenstein's aforementioned dictum. Derrida's failure to identify the different kinds of *différance* suggests that he, in the final analysis, cannot speak of anything and therefore must remain silent about everything.

Despite my critique here, I do not want to suggest that Derrida's insights into the problem of *différance* are entirely without validity. I do not want to be guilty here of demolishing straw-man arguments that fail to convey the subtleties of his views. I do think, however, that Derrida reacts to a peculiarly Western understanding of logocentric thinking that centers on *dialectical* reasoning and *logic*, but which demonstrates a marked aversion to *paradox*. From the time of Plato onward, the dialectic has involved attempts to reconcile opposites by means of a *formal synthesis*.³³ G. W. F. Hegel has routinely been credited with representing the latest of Western philosophers to utilize such an approach.³⁴ The idea of synthesis in both Plato and Hegel, however, represents limit and closure; and in Hegel's view, the final synthesis that would be reached at the "end of history" is also totalizing and all-encompassing.³⁵ Hegel's view of the state of Absolute Knowledge (or Knowing)³⁶ reached at the end of history thus appears to allow no room for any further breaking in of ultimate transcendence, or any surplus of meaning, beyond that *end*. One, therefore, also imagines that once this state of Absolute Knowledge is reached, there will be no further need for logic to be used as a tool for gaining understanding. Since logic will then have served its purpose, and since it can be expected to have no further use, it can be jettisoned.

Understood in another way, there is the suggestion in Hegel that what is important is the *end* of the logical-dialectical process, and this means that once the answer is arrived at, the whole *process of arriving* at it fades into insignificance. In this regard, the *destination* becomes more important than the *journey* and the *solution* becomes more significant than the *problem* needing to be solved. Now if a logical process governs history's movement and its direction, as Hegel believed it did, then it follows that the past is something that finally can be discarded, too, once progress has accomplished its goal. In this way, novelty begins to be accorded a higher value than tradition; and tradition, having served its purpose, starts resembling old clothes needing to be consigned to the ragbag.

What is obvious here is the way that negative and positive values are being assigned to *process* and *goal*. This way of assigning values harks back to Plato and Aristotle themselves. In Plato, negative value belongs to relative nonbeing (Grk=*mē on* [μὴ όν]), while positive value is ascribed to the world of Pure Being (Grk=*to ontōs on* [το ὄντως όν]) where the unchanging and eternal Forms reside.³⁷ Aristotle proceeds along this trajectory despite his not sharing Plato's pessimism regarding physical existence. Still, Aristotle's distinction between *potentiality* (Grk=*dunamis* [δύναμις]) and *actuality* (Grk=*energeia* [ἐνέργεια]) makes clear that the *telos* or end of the process is more axiologically *positive* than is the dynamic process that leads to actualization.³⁸ The principle of potentiality, on the other hand, is axiologically negative simply because it *lacks* actuality. Indeed, since potentiality already belongs to the phenomenon of *privation* (Grk=*sterēsis* [στέρησις]), it becomes improper to attribute *potentiality* to God. As Thomas Aquinas later claims, God as the Unmoved Mover is therefore claimed "without potential."³⁹

REASSESSING THE ROLE OF *DIFFÉRANCE* IN THE TRADITIONS

The examples from Plato and Aristotle I have just given are, in fact, the tip of an enormous iceberg. Certain axiological assumptions that run through the entire Western tradition are wide-ranging and systemic. For this reason, I want to provide a brief overview of the problem as I see it by reexamining some of the sources that lead to Derrida's recognition of the problem of *différance*. These sources include: (1) Parmenides, Plato, and the ontological-epistemological divide, (2) How does the infinite dyad proceed from the original monad?, (3) Hebraic perspectives on *différance*, and 4) Attempts to integrate Greek and Hebrew views concerning *différance*.

Parmenides, Plato, and the Ontological-Epistemological Divide

Parmenides is the first to recognize the problem of *différance* by making a distinction between what he calls the Way of Seeming and the Way of Being.[40] Being, in his estimation, is one continuous, indivisible, changeless, motionless reality. Without multiplicity or plurality, Being neither comes into existence nor passes away. Since multiplicity, plurality, change, motion, becoming, or perishing cannot be attributed to Being, all these attributes are illusory and therefore unreal.[41] Parmenides arrives at this conclusion by claiming that "it is impossible for nothing to be."[42] Reality therefore either *is* or it *is not*. There can be no middle ground between these options.[43]

Parmenides' whole approach to knowing, however, cannot be self-sustaining because it is haunted by the very problem of *différance* he has tried to exile from the dimension of Being. The element of *différance* nonetheless persists in the distinction he makes *between* the Way of Being and the Way of Seeming. His epistemology and ontology thus suffer from an incongruence that happens to be haunted by the very *différance* he tries to exorcise from his ontology.

Parmenides' conclusion seemed wrong to Plato as well; so, as a corrective, Plato substitutes his idea of *relative nonbeing* (Grk=*mē on* [μὴ όν]) in place of Parmenides' idea of *absolute nonbeing* (Grk=*ouk on* [οὐκ όν]). By invoking the idea of relative nonbeing and contrasting it with *Pure Being*, Plato finds a way to speak of another kind of being that lies midway between these two dimensions. He refers to this third dimension as the dimension of *Intermediate* reality.[44] This dimension does allow for the real existence of plurality, multiplicity, change, motion, becoming, and perishing.

Plato thus allows room for the principle of *différance* in his philosophy *ontologically* in a way Parmenides does not; though Plato, in the vein of Parmenides, refuses to allow this principle of nonbeing to play any real *positive* axiological role in his ontology. Because *différance* derives from nonbeing rather than from Pure Being, Plato has to exile both nonbeing and *différance* from *positive* into *negative* axiological territory. As a result, only Pure Being could have any positive ontological significance for Plato. Non-being, and by association, *différance*, could have only negative ontological standing. This negative assessment appears as well in Plato's understanding of how the many different Forms populate the world of Pure Being. He refers to the *communion* (Grk=*koinonia* [κοινωνία]) of the Forms.[45] Consequently, though they seem distinct from one another, they enjoy a kind of communion that cannot allow any shadow of *différance* to come between them.

How Does the Infinite Dyad Proceed from the Original Monad?

This second problem, which can be traced back to the Pythagoreans, was inherited by Plato and the Neoplatonists.[46] It entails the question, "How does the number one—the primordial monad—give rise to the infinite dyad—i.e., the principle of plurality that begins with the manifestation of the number two?" The Pythagoreans identify the Good with the principle of *limit*;[47] while Plato identifies it with the *Forms*.[48] They thus respectively view qualities such as *limit* and *form* in a positive light. On the other hand, the infinite dyad corresponds to the Pythagorean principle of the *void* (Grk=*kenon* [κενόν]) and to Plato's view of the *receptacle* (Grk=*hypodochē* [ὑποδοχή]). Plato, for instance, speaks of "the Mother" (Grk=*mētera* [μητέρα]), "the Receptacle of the generated world,"[49] and the "Nurse of all Becoming" (Grk=*yeneseōs tithēnēn* [γενέσεως τιθήνην]).[50] This principle, according to Plato, is the cause of all multiplicity and change in the world. The receptacle in Plato's philosophy obviously correlates with his concept of relative nonbe-ing (Grk=*mē on* [μὴ ὄν]).

The *kenon* of the Pythagoreans and the *hypodochē* of Plato are negative principles that are responsible for causing change, difference, multiplicity, and evil. How then does the principle of limit, which is associated with the number one, give rise to unlimit, which is associated with the number two? The Pythagoreans explain this theoretically by resorting to mathematics. Since the number one can be multiplied by itself or divided by itself and yet remain the number one, the Pythagoreans consider it to be both an *even* and an *odd* number. Still, despite this theoretical explanation, there is no practical explanation of how *one* gives rise to *two*. It simply *happens*. But does it happen accidentally, coincidentally, necessarily, voluntarily, or purposeful-ly?

The Pythagoreans and Plato provide no adequate answer to these questions but veer back and forth between various inadequate explanations. One of these is offered by Plato, who theorizes that a figure called the *demiurge* (Grk=δημιουργός) fashioned the tangible world.[51] Using the perfect Forms as his guide, the demiurge, as an intermediary between the world of the Forms and material reality, shapes already existing matter into the concrete particulars that populate the physical world. The demiurge does not create the physical world out of absolutely nothing but only gives form to it; and this means that the problem of how the primordial monad gives rise to the infinite dyad remains unresolved. The world of Pure Being and the world of matter are eternally coexistent, and there is no indication that one derives from the other.

During the period of Middle Platonic thought, the theological perspective called gnosticism did not fare any better in producing an adequate understanding of the origin of *différance*. On the contrary, the gnostics merely combined elements of polytheism with elements of dualism to describe how the evil physical world was produced.[52] Plato's demiurge is not, in his philosophy at least, the cause of evil. He is, rather, a *good* artisan who did his best to copy the world of the Forms in those things that he fashioned in the physical world. The gnostics, however, radically depart from Plato's idea of a "good" demiurge and debased this semi-mythological being into a sinister, even diabolical, figure whom they call Yaldabaoth, the offspring of the lower Sophia (wisdom) who is called *Achamoth*.[53] They view the physical world as evil because Yaldabaoth made it. Indeed, their opposition to any notion that the physical world might in some respect be good is revealed in the revisionism they engage in as they interpret the account of creation in the Book of Genesis. They conflat their idea of Yaldabaoth with the Hebrew Creator God. As a result, they denounce this Creator, identifying him as the villain in the story of creation; whereas the serpent, who opposedthe Creator, they applaude as the hero. Their reason for conflating their evil demiurge with the Hebrew Creator of the physical world of course logically follows if *différance* is only thought of as something purely negative, and if it can have no positive purpose or meaning to contribute to reality.

As one transitions from Middle Platonism to Neoplatonism, the question of how the infinite dyad arises from the primordial monad is still not convincingly answered. One way the Neoplatonist Plotinus does this is by elevating the monad (the One) to a dimension of incomprehensible transcendence beyond Pure Being (i.e., Pure Being as Plato had understood it), and thus beyond the categories of good and evil as well. He does not, however, resolve the problem of how the many derives from this transcendent One. Plotinus does not explain whether physical existence arises *accidentally* or *necessarily* from the One Beyond Being.[54] According to him, matter "drifts down" from the One through a process he calls "alienism,"[55] but there seems to be no positive reason why this process happens. On the one hand, emanation is responsible for what A. O. Lovejoy calls Plotinus' "principle of plenitude."[56] This may be viewed as a more *positive* way of assessing existence. On the other hand, emanation is due to the "principle of privation," and privation is the cause of evil. This is a more *negative* way of viewing existence. The relationship between the positive and the negative, however, is vague as well as ambiguous.

Hebraic Perspectives on *Différance*

Plotinus certainly would not have attributed the process of alienism to the will or purpose of some good Creator in the way the Hebrew tradition does. It is remarkable, though, that Derrida—who himself was Jewish—seems to have missed some of the important insights that the Hebraic tradition offers regarding his concept of *différance*; for an examination of the Hebraic tradition reveals answers to some of the unsolved questions raised by Platonic and Neoplatonic philosophy. Indeed, such an examination reveals that certain Hebraic ideas stand in diametrical opposition to some of the central views of Plato and the Pythagoreans.

One way that the Hebrew tradition significantly departs from the Platonic and Pythagorean traditions pertains to its axiological perspective on the phenomenon of *dynamism*. As I have tried to show, none of the Pythagorean, Platonic, or gnostic systems allow the dynamic principle in things to have its origin in *Being*, and even Aristotle finds dynamism or potentiality to derive from the material cause. These traditions variously relate their concepts of being to limit, form, and actuality. On the other hand, the dynamic principle, which is also the principle that explains multiplicity and plurality in the world, has its origin in the infinite dyad, nonbeing, or matter. Since the dynamic principle is always understood in terms of *deficiency* or *privation*, its *axiological* (as well as *ontological*) standing is rendered negative overall.

An assessment of the Hebrew tradition, on the other hand, reveals that Platonic, Pythagorean, and Aristotelian views concerning the dynamic principle are about as far removed from the Hebraic understanding of the nature of reality as is possible. When *YHWH* reveals his name to Moses as the "I will be who I will be" (Heb=*ehyeh asher ehyeh* [אֶהְיֶה אֲשֶׁר אֶהְיֶה]), he also reveals his ultimate reality to be, in fact, opposite from the way thinkers in the Hellenistic tradition perceived ultimate being *to be*.[57] Far from being identified with limit, the *ehyeh asher ehyeh* is identified with the principle of *unlimit*. In keeping with this emphasis, no *form* of the Deity could be placed on the Ark of the Covenant between the cherubim that overshadowed the Mercy Seat. Instead, there was only the empty *space* where *YHWH* made his name or reputation to dwell.[58] This absence of an image was based on the second commandment's prohibition against the making of graven images.[59]

Thus, the Hebrews view in a *negative* light principles such as limit, form, and actuality that the Pythagoreans and Platonists view in a *positive* light. On the other hand, the Hebrews view in a positive light the principles of unlimit and dynamism that the Pythagoreans, Platonists, and Aristotelians view as the source of *evil* in all things. Indeed, the Hebrews view these principles as *a* source—if not *the* source—of *good*.

The conflict between the Hebraic and Greek traditions perennially crops up in the history of Western theology and philosophy because they are heirs of these traditions. Augustine, to his credit, wrestles with the two traditions in his *City of God* when he attempts to graft a Hebraic understanding of the theology of history onto a Neoplatonic system. Neoplatonism speaks of the *exitus* (exit) and *reditus* (return)[60] of all things from the One, but Neoplatonism in its indigenous forms still owes much to Plato's notion of *anamnesis* (remembering, recollecting, or recovering from amnesia).[61] Plato's *anamnesis* idea, which is akin to what Mircea Eliade calls "the myth of the eternal return,"[62] involves not a *dis*covery *of new territory*, but merely a *recovery of lost territory*. All the knowledge that the soul possesses initially in its state of being as it dwells among the Forms is lost through a fall that produces *amnesia*, so it is only *this* knowledge that is regained through the process of *anamnesis*. There is, however, no radically *new* knowledge that can be gained via this process.

The Hebrew perspective on temporal and historical categories, by contrast with the Greek tradition, allows these categories to serve as vehicles by which God brought creation into existence and revealed himself to his chosen people. The Hebrews believe as well that history operated as the vehicle by which God would bring to fruition his projects of redemption and the new creation. The Hebrews view history as *purposive*, and therefore, as *axiologically positive*. This view, however, seems as foreign to the philosophical speculations of Plato and Plotinus as it does to those of *Shankara* Hinduism. The notable Hindu scholar Sarvepalli Radhakrishnan, whom I referred to earlier in this book, observes that Plotinus has much in common with the *Shankara* school of Hindu thought. I agree with his judgment. His comparison is interesting because the *Shankara* school holds to the view that the world is veiled by *māyā* or illusion, much like Plato's world of intermediate being is veiled in opinion or the realm of seeming (*doxa* [δόξα]).[63] Furthermore, since *Shankara* must also view time in an axiologically negative way, this means that history (if there even is such a thing) is purposeless and meaningless as well.

Though Augustine is influenced significantly by Plotinus, his Christian orientation helps him at least partially to break free from the confines of Neoplatonic thought. Whether he *fully* succeeds in doing so is another question that must be explored further. Still, however one decides this question, Augustine does at least *attempt* to graft into the Neoplatonic system a *Hebraic* understanding of history. By doing so, he manages at least in part to interject a *positive* reassessment of temporality into a system that tended to view temporality as a negative. It does, in fact, seem that the old wineskins of

Greek philosophy already had begun to show signs of bursting when they became filled with the new wine of the Judeo-Christian tradition.[64]

A more thoroughgoing attempt than Augustine's challenged the Platonic and Neoplatonic negative valuations of *différance* in the fourteenth century. This attempt was achieved through Jewish Neoplatonic philosophy, which produced the Jewish *Kabbalah*. Kabbalah offers a more positive assessment of the role of *matter* in the scheme of things than the more negative views advanced by Neoplatonism in its pagan and Christian forms. This Jewish form of Neoplatonism serves, for this reason, as a needed counterbalance to these other traditions. First, the Kabbalists integrate into their system the traditional Hebrew interpretation of the physical world as God's *good* creation. The Hebrew word for "good," *tob* (טוֹב), occurs repeatedly throughout the first chapter of Genesis.[65] I remind the reader here that the word *tob* does not mean "perfect" as a significant number of Christian theologians have interpreted it to mean. It means, rather, "good for something" or "for a good purpose."

The fact that Judaism does not interpret the Genesis account of the consequences of the sin of Adam and Eve as a Platonic type of "fall" is also significant, for without a Platonically influenced Fall doctrine, the creation still possesses a high degree of purposive goodness even *after* Adam committed the original sin and not merely *prior* to his having committed it. The Kabbalists also reject traditional Platonic and Neoplatonic views of matter as a principle that is alien to the divine world. Instead, they deem the material dimension of existence capable of functioning as an *instrument* that God could use to achieve positive outcomes. The principles of matter and darkness, and not just those of form and light, are thus brought under the auspices of the incomprehensible divine unity and the operations of the divine will.[66]

Kabbalists make a theoretical distinction between God above (Heb=*Ein-Sof* [אֵין סוֹף] or *Y HWH* [יהוה]) and God below (Heb=*Elohim* [אָתֶּם]).[67] This distinction has its basis in Genesis 1:28, where the image of God in man is identified as "male and female."[68] Because of its emphasis upon "God below," and in keeping with the scriptural affirmation that the feminine is an *aspect* of the image of God in man, Kabbalists alter Plato's rather negative view of the feminine principle in creation. I have already alluded to the fact that in Plato's cosmology the *receptacle* as the *feminine principle* is viewed in a negative light. Kabbalah, by contrast, offers a *positive* reassessment of the role of the feminine principle, not only in the world here below, but also in the very nature of God. While God above is viewed as *masculine*, God below is considered *feminine*. The principle of matter—i.e., the feminine principle—is thus no longer viewed as an *enemy* of God: It can now function as an *instrument* of the Divine as well.

Attempts to Integrate Greek and Hebrew Views concerning *Différance*

The above analyses lead me to conclude that *différance*, and its related concept of relative nonbeing, can be viewed as having a positive as well as a negative function. Indeed, some efforts have already been made over the past couple of centuries to attribute a positive role to relative nonbeing. These efforts were undertaken by such major figures as Nikolai Berdyaev (1874–1948), Sergei Bulgakov (1871–1944), Martin Heidegger (1889–1976), Paul Tillich, Carl Gustav Jung, F. W. J. Schelling, and Ernst Bloch. These thinkers attempted in various ways to speak of relative nonbeing in terms of "productive" nonbeing.

Schelling is the first to identify relative nonbeing (Grk=*mē on* [μὴ όν]) with what he calls "the *Urgrund*."[69] This is the German word he uses to describe the dark, primordial, abysmal, unconscious, and fructifying first principle present in both Nature and God. From this first principle, the principles of Form and *Logos* emerge much like a child emerges from the darkness of its mother's womb into the light of day.[70] Schelling believes that the negative potential of the *dark principle* latent in the *Urgrund* eventually comes into conflict with a *light principle*—i.e., Form or *Logos*—after this second principle becomes manifested out of the dark principle's depths. However, he also believes that the dark principle, at some future time, would reach a final synthesis with the light principle.[71] This synthesis is described in terms of *ekstasis*, a *coincidentia oppositorum*, or a synthesis in which the light and dark principles present in both God and Nature become mystically integrated.[72]

Following Schelling's lead, Russian philosopher Nikolai Berdyaev speaks of relative nonbeing in terms of "*meontic* freedom"; viz., the kind of libertarian freedom that human beings possess prior to all their decisions and choices.[73] Eastern Orthodox theologian Sergei Bulgakov also speaks of it in his "sophiology."[74] But it is the depth psychologist Carl Jung who writes so prolifically about this dark principle and relates it to his understanding of each of the three stages of the psychological process he calls "individuation."[75]

One way that Jung advocates for an inclusion of the *mē on* (μὴ όν) or relative nonbeing in the stages of psychological development is through his insistence that the human psyche must acknowledge and integrate this kind of nonbeing into itself at every stage.[76] Jung attributes to relative nonbeing the material-diabolical-feminine qualities of what he terms Plato's "missing fourth" element, which is the element that constantly resists union with the Forms.[77] Jung believes that the "missing fourth" needs to be integrated into the psyche at every stage of its development. Otherwise, the psyche will develop in destructive and malevolent ways.

Taking his cue from Schelling, Lutheran theologian Paul Tillich also seeks to integrate the principle of relative nonbeing into his understanding of the First Person of the Trinity.[78] He refers to this principle both as the "abysmal nature of God" as well as the element that made God "the living God." He has to admit, however, that God's abysmal nature had the potential of becoming demonic if not for the fact that it remained in eternal unity with the element of Form in the Divine Being.[79] In the vein of Schelling, Marxist sociologist Ernst Bloch, in his *Philosophy of Hope*, also adopts the concept of relative nonbeing into his understanding of "the Not in Origin," which is the principle that makes possible the dialectical movement of matter toward what he called "concrete utopia."[80]

All these thinkers followed the common tradition that originated with Schelling, who had tried to combine the insights of theosophist Jakob Boehme (1575–1624) with elements of the Platonic tradition. I do not think, however, that these attempts to identify the principle of will with Platonic notions of relative nonbeing have been successful. In the Schellingian tradition, what could, in fact, be construed as two principles, such as the principle of will and the principle of productive nonbeing, are conflated in such a way that they are conceived of as a *single* principle. The result of this conflation is a dynamic principle that resembles a blind, amoral, unconscious force with no clear sense of moral rectitude, direction, or purpose. Indeed, this principle of will only gains a consciousness of good and evil after it reflects back on the good and evil ways it has manifested itself over time. Through this process of "coming to consciousness," it gains a moral perspective that it did not originally possess. As a result, the dynamic principle of will in the Schellingian tradition is an *alogical* one. Indeed, this lack of a logical principle in Schelling's *Urgrund* is the very thing that impelled Hegel to refer to it as "the night in which all cows are black."[81]

To be sure, there is a close correlation between Schelling's concept of the *Urgrund* and what philosophers call "libertarian freedom." However, while it may be true that this kind of freedom in human beings initially possesses an unconscious and amoral quality, this does not mean that it remains so. Over time, experience from the outside world informs this freedom and guides it. Worse still are the ways that thinkers like Schelling, Tillich, and Jung conflate the element of will in nature with the element of will in God. By identifying the *mē on* (μὴ ὄν) or the *Urgrund* with the Divine Life, Greek tradition wins out over the Hebrew tradition and eclipses it. Suddenly, the God of the Hebrew tradition is reenvisioned in such a way that he appears amoral and almost animalistic. Nowhere is this more apparent than in the ruminations of Jung. All Hebraic notions of a God whose will is *purposive* are replaced by notions of a God whose power is *raw, capricious,* and *arbitrary,* not to mention *childish.*

IS A CONCEPT OF *LOGOS* THAT EMBRACES
DIFFÉRANCE POSSIBLE?

After examining the history of the meontic tradition, one sees clearly how the Platonic concept of relative nonbeing ends up introducing considerable ambiguity into philosophical views of what Derrida calls *différance*. For this reason, it is important to suggest ways that the concept of *logos* can be expanded to include aspects of *différance* rather than to exclude them. To accomplish this, the concept of *différance* must be reassessed from an axiological standpoint.

On the one hand, there are some kinds of *différance* that need to be rescued from the negative connotation that derives from its being associated with the Platonic concept of relative nonbeing. We may ask, for instance, whether it is proper to ascribe the quality of relative nonbeing to categories such as "will," "libertarian freedom," and "potentiality." If one restricts being to Form alone, then it is hard to imagine how the dynamic principle could ever be derived from anything other than from the negative erosion of positive kinds of being by relative nonbeing. On the other hand, if such categories as "will," "libertarian freedom," and "potentiality" are reenvisioned as modes of *being*, then there is at least some justification for why these categories may have to be moved from *negative* into *positive* axiological territory.

I have already discussed how the Hebrew tradition provides a positive assessment of dynamic phenomena such as will, libertarian freedom, and potentiality; so, it stands to reason that these categories may, with certain qualifications, be assessed positively. The concept of the *yetzer ha tob* (the good impulse) again comes to mind as an example of how "good" can be ascribed to a phenomenon that is potential and not just actual; however, one must qualify that a *good potential* does not necessarily guarantee that the *actualization* of that potential will also turn out to be *actually good* and not just *potentially good*. In other words, though libertarian freedom can be viewed as good in one regard, by its very nature any free agent possessing it can employ it to make evil choices as well as good ones. Thus, libertarian freedom, as it comes to be exercised on the human level, must imply at least the *possibility* of evil. Here, the gap between stimulus and response that exists to a greater degree in human beings than in other animals again appears as that place where the voluntary is capable of intruding into the dimension of the involuntary. Because of this gap, the relation between stimulus and response cannot be explained in terms of necessary or mechanistic kinds of cause and effect. What has occurred now between stimulus and response is a rupture made possible by the *transcendence* of the dimension of the *personal*.

The Hebrew conception of God as the "I will be who I will be" makes possible a positive assessment of potentiality and dynamism as well. This means that temporal categories, such as the element of deferral that Derrida ascribed to *différance*, can be accorded positive axiological value. One obstacle, however, needs to be surmounted; namely, the element of the arbitrary that appears to haunt the reputation of the God of Israel. The very idea of this element has caused atheists such as Richard Dawkins outright disgust and incited them to lash out with "righteous indignation" against theists who dare to advance an apologetic defending this God.[82] I shall have to wait until the final chapter of this book to address these sorts of challenges.

THE PRINCIPLE OF *DIFFÉRANCE* AND APOPHATIC THINKING

Derrida's thought on *différance* has sometimes been linked to the *apophatic* approach of Pseudo-Dionysius the Areopagite, which is an approach that attempts to grasp the super-essential reality of God by negating all affirmative language used to describe the Divine. Derrida, however, insists that his understanding of *différance* can not be correlated with the negative theology of Pseudo-Dionysius.[83] I cannot presume to guess Derrida's reasons for distancing himself from the apophatic tradition, but I suspect that one reason could be that the Dionysian paradigm fails to incorporate the principle of *différance* as it relates to the mystery associated with *dynamically destructive phenomena*; namely, the *mysterium tremendum*. Though it is called *negative theology*, the mystical experience to which negative theology leads correlates instead with the *mysterium fascinans*. This is a *positive* experience of the divine mystery, which is an experience of the mystery that fascinates, and it is not to be confused with the method of *affirmative* or *cataphatic theology*, which is an epistemological approach.[84]

The Greek philosophical tradition could not have provided Pseudo-Dionysius with a way of assessing the *mysterium tremendum* in any positive way. The *mysterium tremendum* in Greek theology is associated with the arbitrary and capricious actions of the gods at the same time that it is dissociated entirely from categories such as morality and purpose. The *tremendum* in Greek theology thus has the capacity to produce in people the emotions of fear and terror, but it does so to no good end. The *tremendum* instead produces the kind of emotion that led Epicurus to reject belief in the gods entirely; for if the gods incite fear, and if fear paralyzes the human spirit, then eliminating the gods would liberate human beings from fear of divine retribution.[85] This liberation, in turn, produces the state of *ataraxia* or tranquility that the skeptics Pyrrho and Sextus Empiricus adopted and bequeathed to Epicurus.

I do not think it advisable, however, for the *mysterium tremendum* of the Transcendent to be jettisoned simply because it was prone in Greek theology to produce in people *paralyzing fear*. The Hebrew understanding of the *tre-*

mendum must, instead, be brought to bear here. In this tradition, the fear the *tremendum* produces is aligned with ethics and the divine purpose. Fear thus can lead to a good end by motivating persons to turn from their immoral behaviors and seek moral rectification. This factor becomes especially true if the Transcendent who incites the fear has also given every indication of being trustworthy. In such a case, the Transcendent, though initially experienced from a human point of view as something *negative*, also has the capacity to produce a response in the end that is *positive*. The *mysterium tremendum* must not, however, be emphasized to the exclusion of the *mysterium fascinans*. Both, rather, can be taken together and related to a concept of *différance*.

THE ORIGIN AND GOAL OF THE *LOGOS* IN PARADOXICAL TRANSCENDENCE

At this point, I suggest that theological conceptions of *logos* can aid in expanding the overly rational and dialectical understandings of *logos* that are typified by the Greek tradition.[86] What I suggest is a thorough reorienting of the concept of *logos* by rooting it in a *paradoxical* understanding of God's transcendence. To carry this out, we must speak of the *logos* in terms of its eternal *origin* and its eternal *goal*. On the one hand, the eternal origin of the *logos* is one in its transcendental unity with the God of *purpose*, who is conceived of primarily in terms of a personal God of inexhaustible power, who directs, guides, protects, and provides for the creation that he has called out of nothing. In Trinitarian language, this refers to the Person of God the Father. On the other hand, the eternal goal of the *logos* is one in its transcendental unity with the God of *meaning*, who is experienced in terms of an *infinite meaning* that is mediated through *Wisdom*. This refers to the Person of the Holy Spirit. These two dimensions of God's transcendence cannot be encapsulated within a paradigm based upon dialectical reasoning alone. A paradoxical understanding of the *Logos* must therefore be offered that unites these two dimensions of God's transcendence.

Dialectic cannot, therefore, express the ultimate means by which the aspects of the Transcendent are connected because dialectic is worked out in the realm of *finitude* through a continuous process of conflict and resolution, as G. W. F. Hegel proposes. Dialectical realities that are rooted in the finite realities of human experience and the world should not, therefore, be projected onto the dimension of the Divine in *univocal ways*. The God whom we view through the lenses of dialectical reality must not be made to conform to the lenses themselves with the result that there remains no transcendent *surplus of meaning*. Viewed rightly, however, finitude, and the dialectical processes that hinge upon it, can serve as lenses through which we can view something much profounder; namely, the paradoxical nature of the Transcendent, which, unlike the dialectic, is implied in the Infinite who is God. Understanding the relationship between paradox and dialectic is therefore crucial; for just as the Infinite must, by definition, include the finite if it is to be Infinite, so must the paradoxical include within itself the dialectical while at the same time radically transcending it. The proposition "the paradoxical entails the dialectical" is therefore a nonconvertible proposition.

If the concept of *logos* is expanded to include *différance*, then space can be allowed for the intrusion into dialectical reality of transcendental elements that can only be expressed paradoxically. The Transcendent can be mediated dialectically, but this does not mean that the dialectical can be allowed to hem the Transcendent in with frameworks that are limiting and restricting. Such a concept of *logos* can then also provide a theological justification for how ideas of the incarnation and the atonement of Christ can *purposefully* and *meaningfully* embrace and transform the problem of absurd evil. I intend to investigate these themes in a later chapter.

THE TRANSCENDENT AS PROVIDING THE ULTIMATE CONTEXT FOR LANGUAGE AND ACTION

I have tried in this chapter to find ways to rescue language from attempts to *anchor* it entirely in some aspect of the dimension of the tangible. The very nature of language as a phenomenon that develops and grows reveals an opposition to attempts to anchor it solely within the tangible dimension. However, if language, like *logos*, has its ultimate origin and goal in the dimension of the Transcendent, then the metaphor of "anchoring" fails to allow an adequate context that can account for language's ability to convey *meaning* and *purpose*. A better metaphor might be that of an *artesian spring* continuously flowing with crystal-clear water. This metaphor points to the source of water as symbolizing the inexhaustible transcendent source or the ultimate origin from which all language flows. Language, when contextualized by this metaphor, appears not to be fixed but is free in its ability perpetually to replenish itself and flow beyond its present fixities. In this respect, one might think of this artesian spring as a source that continually replenishes a pond, which is replete with its own ecosystem. Language, in its more tangible respect, could be said to be symbolized by the life forms that flourish in and around this pond. Like the living network of life forms that inhabit the pond, language is represented by the living network of significances that flourish within the context of a Transcendent that is also ultimate. In this respect, all individual elements of language resemble creatures whose existences are sustained by the context of the spring-fed pond as well. If, then, this "linguistic pond" is continuously renewed by the artesian spring that flows into it from the ultimate transcendent Source, to cut this pond off from the dimension of the Transcendent would have the effect of reducing that pond to stagnation.

When the transcendental basis of language is recovered, language ceases to function as only the kind of tool that can be used only for achieving ever greater precision and clarity. It can become an *artistic* tool as well. Interestingly, the hatred of ambiguity and mystery often goes hand in hand with the insistence of some that achieving greater clarity and precision constitutes language's only valid purpose. Language in this sense functions as a *logical* (understood in its traditional sense) tool; not as an *artistic* one. Unfortunately, some linguistic philosophers use their "logical" tools to *cut away* the ambiguous and mysterious elements of language that they find abhorrent. In doing so, they kill living language and submit it to the art of taxidermy. Novelists, on the other hand, use language as an *artistic* tool to create their narratives and symbols. For them, ambiguity and mystery are the very things that breathe life into their stories and make them compelling.

Earlier in this chapter, I mentioned Wittgenstein's metaphor of "language games," which he uses to describe the relationship between language and action. Although I believe Wittgenstein took a step in the right direction, I pointed out that the "language-game" metaphor remained too restrictive in its ability to convey the full range of linguistic purpose and significance. In the chapters that follow, I thus intend to examine further the connections between language, action, and value. One way of investigating *action* as a vehicle that expresses value is to focus on what it means to *practice virtue*. The practice of virtue has a way not only of connecting meaningful and purposive language to meaningful and purposive action, but it can also aid in reunifying the dimensions of the moral and the beautiful that have become divorced from one another in the modern world. While virtue tends often to be connected more with the field of ethics than aesthetics, I shall endeavor to argue that virtue, when understood properly, can reunite the dimensions of the aesthetic and the ethical.

After exploring the role of virtue, I intend to appeal to more comprehensive analogies, or *clusters* of analogies, to describe how the interweaving of language and action can function as a vehicle that expresses even greater value. One *analogical cluster* would be comprised of varieties of linguistic expression such as *story, drama, narrative,* and *symbol*. These types of linguistic expression can connect language and action in ways that are more *purposive* and *meaningful* than any one of their component parts can be when taken alone. Such types of linguistic expression have the capability not only of mediating transcendence through the aspect of the tangible, but they also reveal ways that the integration and reconciliation of the dimensions of the ethical and the aesthetic have been achieved. These types of linguistic and practical expressions provide, as well, scenarios that reveal ways that persons have succeeded in maneuvering their way through the labyrinth of existence or have failed to do so. Finally, what does it mean for one *to live* one's story? The move from conceptualization to action implies that one cannot fully experience value by being a mere *spectator* of stories that are meaningful and purposive. One must also *live out* one's own story in ways that are intentional, inspirational, and connected to other persons and their stories.

NOTES

1. Ludwig Wittgenstein, *Philosophical Investigations*, trans. G. E. M. Anscombe (Oxford: Basil Blackwell, 1958), 1.3–7.

2. Wittgenstein was not alone in linking language to action. J. L. Austin, in his William James Lectures delivered at Harvard University in 1955, investigated this link as well by showing how ordinary language accomplishes certain tasks by means of performative utterances. Austin, *How to Do Things with Words*, ed. J. O. Urmson (Eastford, CT: Martino Fine Books, 2018), 4–9.

3. Blaise Pascal, *Pensées* (New York: E. P. Dutton, 1958), 68, Kindle.

4. Aristot. Nic. Eth. 1.7.1097a1–5.

5. Sometimes referred to as "the leap of faith," though Kierkegaard never explicitly used this terminology. See Søren Kierkegaard, *Concluding Unscientific Postscript to the Philosophical Crumbs*, ed. and trans. Alastair Hannay (Cambridge, UK: Cambridge University Press, 2009), 83–84.

6. Wittgenstein, *Tractatus Logico-Philosophicus*, trans. C. K. Ogden (London: Kegan Paul, Trench, Trubner, 1922), 90. A. J. Ayer certainly took his linguistic analysis in this direction.

7. The pseudonymous author of Kierkegaard's *Fear and Trembling*, trans. and ed. Howard V. Hong and Edna H. Hong (Princeton, NJ: Princeton University Press, 1983), 1.

8. St. John of the Cross, *The Dark Night of the Soul*, trans. and ed. E. Allison Peers (Los Angeles: Image Books, 1959), ch. 1.

9. Eccl 3:11.

10. Nicholas of Cusa, *On Learned Ignorance*, trans. Jasper Hopkins (Minneapolis, MN: Arthur J. Banning, 1981), 1.10.

11. Augustine, *Confessions*, trans. Carolyn J.-B. Hammond, in *Loeb Classical Library* (Cambridge, MA: Harvard University Press, 2014), 1.1.2.

12. Martin Luther, *Luther's Works*, vol. 16, ed. Jaroslav Pelikan and Helmut Lehmann (St. Louis and Philadelphia: Concordia, and Fortress, 1955–1972), 286.

13. See, for example, Werner Kelber, "In the Beginning Were the Words: The Apotheosis and Narrative Displacement of the Logos," *Journal of the American Academy of Religion* 58, no. 1 (Spring 1990): 69–98.

14. Jacques Derrida, *Writing and Difference*, trans. Alan Bass (Chicago, IL: University of Chicago Press, 1978), 161, 176, 192, 197, 198, 203.

15. Derrida, *Writing and Difference*, 107, 117. See also discussion of violence in David Bentley Hart, *The Beauty of the Infinite: The Aesthetics of Christian Truth* (Grand Rapids, MI: William B. Eerdman's, 2003), 2–5.

16. Plat. Rep. 509c–511e.

17. Francis Bacon, *The New Organon*, ed. Jardine and Silverthorne (Cambridge: Cambridge University Press, 2000), aphorisms 1:54 (p. 46) and 1:63 (pp. 51–52).

18. Thomas Bayes, "An Essay towards solving a Problem in the Doctrine of Chances," communicated by Mr. Price, in a letter to John Canton, M. A. and F. R. S., www.stat.ucla.edu/history/essay.pdf.

19. See Charles Sanders Peirce, "Perceptual Judgments," in *The Philosophical Writings of Peirce*, ed. Justus Buchler (New York: Dover Publications, 1955), loc. 5767 of 7992, Kindle.

20. Richard Swinburne, *The Existence of God* (Oxford: Clarendon, 2004), 6–22.

21. The analogy refers to the enthronement of the goddess reason in place of the Pietà, which occured in 1973 in the Cathedral of Notre Dame in Paris during "the Reign of Terror."

22. See Hesiod, *Theogony*, trans. Glenn W. Most, in *Loeb Classical Library* (Cambridge, MA: Harvard University Press, 2006), lines 306–32.

23. See Plutarch, *Life of Theseus*, trans. Bernadotte Perrin, in *Loeb Classical Library* (Cambridge, MA: Harvard University Press, 1914), 11.1.

24. Robert Parker, *Miasma: Pollution and Purification in Early Greek Religion* (Oxford: Clarendon, 1983), 18–31. Purification, according to Parker, involves a division or separation.

25. Derrida, *Dissemination*, trans. Barbara Johnson (Chicago, IL: University of Chicago Press, 1981), 24–25, 70, 94, 98, 118.

26. Derrida, *Dissemination*, 118, 160.

27. See, for example, George Pattison, *God and Being: An Inquiry* (Oxford: Oxford University Press, 2013), 308–9.

28. Mark C. Taylor, *Erring: A Postmodern A/theology* (Chicago, IL: University of Chicago Press, 1984).

29. Taylor, *Erring*, 8–9.

30. Taylor, *Erring*, 11, 112.

31. Taylor, *Erring*, 149–69.

32. Taylor, *Erring*, 159.

33. See, for example, Plat. Rep., bk. VII (532b and 533b–533e).

34. According to Gustav E. Mueller, the actual terms "thesis," "antithesis," and "synthesis," which appeared explicitly in Fichte's writings, were never used by Hegel. Mueller, "The Hegel Legend of 'Thesis, Antithesis, Synthesis,'" in *The Journal of the History of Ideas* (Philadelphia: University of Pennsylvania Press, 1958), 411–14.

35. G. W. F. Hegel, *Lectures on the Philosophy of World History*, trans. Hugh Barr Nisbet (Cambridge, UK: Cambridge University Press, 1975), 24, 74, 197.

36. Hegel, *Phenomenology of Spirit*, trans. A. V. Miller (Oxford: Oxford University Press, 1977), 479–93.

37. Plat. Phaedrus 248c. Plat. Tim. 28a.

38. For discussion of *potentiality* or *potency*, see Aristot. Met. 5.11.1019a9–5.12.1019b12. For discussion of *actuality*, see Aristot. Met. 9.3.1047a9–1047b10; 9.6.1048a1–1048b6.

39. See Aristot. Met. 5.22.1022b1–4. Aquinas, *ST* I.3.1 and I.3.4.

40. Parmenides, *Poem of Parmenides: on nature* VI, lines 1–4 Burnett.

41. Parmenides, *Poem of Parmenides*, VIII, lines 1–14 Burnett.

42. For "Way of Seeming," see Parmenides, frag. 8, lines 50–55 (*Simplicius, Phys.* 30.14) in *The Pre-Socratic Philosophers: A Critical History with a Selection of Texts*, ed. G. S. Kirk and J. E. Raven (Cambridge, UK: The University Press, 1962). For "Way of Truth" see Parmenides, frag. 2 (Proclus, in *Tim.* 1. 345).

43. Parmenides, *On Nature* VIII, lines 15–24 Burnett.

44. Plat. Rep. 478a–478e.

45. Plat. Rep. bk. 3 (416e); Plat. Tim. 18c.

46. See John Dillon, *The Middle Platonists: 80 B.C. to A.D 220*, rev. ed. (Ithaca, NY: Cornell University Press, 1977), 3–4.

47. Aristot. Met. 1.5.986a6–9.

48. Plat. Phaedrus 246e–247e.

49. Plat. Tim. 51a.

50. Plat. Tim. 52d.

51. Plat. Tim. 28c–29b.

52. Dillon, *The Middle Platonists*, 170, 173–74.

53. Dillon, *The Middle Platonists*, 170, 173–74. See also Elaine Pagels, *The Gnostic Gospels* (New York: Vintage Books, 1979), 35; "The (First) Apocalypse of James," trans. William R. Schoedel, in *The Nag Hammadi Library*, ed. James M. Robinson (San Francisco, CA: HarperCollins, 1990), Codex V.

54. Plotinus mentions that souls that fall into evil do so because of *audacity*. This word is from the Greek *tolma* [τόλμα], a Neo-Pythagorean term that refers to the *infinite dyad*. Plotinus, *On the Three Primary Hypostases* V.1.1.4–5.

55. Plotinus, *On Matter*, in *Ennead* 2.4.5.25–35 and 2.4.14.20–25.

56. Arthur O. Lovejoy, *The Great Chain of Being* (Cambridge, MA: Harvard University Press, 1964), 62–63.

57. Exod 3:14.

58. E.g., 1 Sam 4:4.

59. Exod 20:4–5.

60. Or withdrawal (Grk=*proödos* [πρόοδος]) and return (Grk=*epistrophē* [ἐπιστροφή]). See Giovanni Reale, *A History of Ancient Philosophy*, Vol. 4: *The Schools of the Imperial Age*, trans. and ed. John R. Catan (Albany: State University of New York Press, 1990), 322.

61. Plat. Meno 80d–e.

62. Mircea Eliade, *Cosmos and History* (New York: Harper Torchbooks, 1959), 34–48.

63. Sarvepalli Radhakrishnan, *Eastern Religions and Western Thought*, 50–51.

64. Something of an uneasiness appears, e.g., in the way Augustine tries to navigate between the opposing Hebrew and Neoplatonic paradigms. Though he attempted a philosophical synthesis, at places the synthesis seams break apart, which raises more questions than it answers.

65. Gen 1:4, 10, 12, 18, 21, 24, 31.

66. Moses de Leon, *The Zohar ha Sefiroth, Bereshith* 1:16a connects the *tohu* [Heb=תֹּהוּ] (i.e., without form) of Genesis 1:2 with formless Matter, and the *bohu* [Heb=בֹּהוּ] (i.e., void) of that same passage with the primordial principle of Form that remains latent until it is empowered by the Spirit (Heb=*ruach* [רוּחַ]) of God to emerge from the *tohu*, clothe creation, and bring creation into existence.

67. de Leon, *Zohar, Bereshith* 1:16b; 1:29a–b.

68. Gershom Scholem, *On the Kabbalah and Its Symbolism*, trans. Ralph Manheim (New York: Schocken Books, 1960), 103, 105, 107.

69. F. W. J. Schelling, *Philosophical Inquiries into the Nature of Human Freedom*, trans. J. Gutmann (Chicago, IL: Open Court Publishing), 360–62, 374–75.

70. Schelling, *Of Human Freedom*, 406–408.

71. Schelling, *Of Human Freedom*, 411–12.

72. Schelling, *Of Human Freedom*, 409.

73. Nikolai Berdyaev, *Freedom and the Spirit*, trans. Oliver F. Clark (San Rafael, CA: Semantron Press, 2009 [5th ed.]), 41–42, 165.

74. Sergei Bulgakov, *Sophia, The Wisdom of God: An Outline of Sophiology*, trans. Patrick Thompson, O. Fielding Clark, and Xenia Braikevikt (Hudson, NY: Lindisfarne, 1993), 6, 53, 62, 72.

75. Carl Jung, *The Collected Works* [*CW*], 8, eds. H. Read, M. Fordham, and G. Adler, trans. R. F. C. Hull (Princeton, NJ: Princeton University Press, 1953–79): 132–33, 157, 388; *CW*, 11:168–76.

76. See my discussion in Randall Bush, *Recent Ideas of Divine Conflict: The Influences of Psychological and Sociological Theories of Conflict upon the Trinitarian Theology of Paul Tillich and Jürgen Moltmann* (San Francisco, CA: Mellen Research University Press, 1991), 51–62.

77. Jung, *CW*, 11:197–98.

78. Paul Tillich, *Systematic Theology*, 1 (Chicago, IL: University of Chicago Press, 1973): 209, 281.

79. Tillich, *Systematic Theology*, 1:210–11.

80. Ernst Bloch, *The Principle of Hope*, 1:306. For discussion of Schelling's influence upon him, see Bloch, *Gesamtausgabe*, 16 vols. (Frankfort am Main: Suhrkamp Verlag, 1969–77), 7:74–75, 70–77, 261–62; 12:227–41, 306–19.

81. Hegel, "Preface," in *Phenomenology of Spirit*, 9.

82. See, for example, the oft-quoted diatribe of Richard Dawkins in *The God Delusion* (Boston: Houghton Mifflin, 2006), 8.

83. Harold Coward, Toby Foshay, and Jacques Derrida, *Derrida and Negative Theology* (Albany: State University of New York Press, 1992), 3.

84. *Apophatic* (negative) and *cataphatic* (positive or affirmative) are *epistemological* categories, while *tremendum* (negative) and *fascinans* (positive) mystery are *axiological* ones.

Because the *mysterium tremendum et fascinans* belongs to the category of mystery, however, it also belongs to *apophatic* rather than *cataphatic* thinking.

85. Epicurus, *Letter to Menoeceus*, trans. Robert Drew Hicks, accessed from classics.mit.edu/Epicurus/menoec.html.

86. In suggesting this redefinition of the *logos*, I am broadly sympathetic with the project of David Bentley Hart, *The Beauty of the Infinite: The Aesthetics of Christian Truth* (Grand Rapids, MI: William B. Eerdmans, 2003), 7–8.

Chapter Six

Action as a Vehicle of Value

ETHICAL AND AESTHETIC ACTION

While *language* is one vehicle that expresses value, *action* is another. The role that action plays in expressing value needs, however, to be expanded beyond an overly pragmatic kind of designation; namely, that action, to be valuable at all, must always be *practical* in its aims. In the realm of the ethical, practical application is, of course, crucially important. Still, not all action must be of the ethical type to convey value. In this respect, we should examine again Aristotle's consideration of the kind of action that serves the dimension of the *aesthetic*. He called this type of action *poesis*. Commonly translated using the English word *poetics*, the word *poesis* happens to be broader in its meaning than what the English word implies. *Poesis* means "to make," and Aristotle specifically employs this meaning in his discussions of aesthetics that appear in his work, *The Poetics*. His discussion of the *practice of virtue* thus does not focus exclusively on the dimension of the *moral*, but it includes, as well, the dimension of the *beautiful*.

In chapter 2, I suggested that the divorce between ethics and aesthetics lies at the heart of the West's present slide into societal confusion and cultural demise. Achieving a reunification of these two dimensions thus becomes paramount for reversing the slide and remedying the deleterious social and cultural consequences. How then are we to achieve such a reunification? To answer this question, I suggest that we return briefly to the value-compass idea that I explored in chapter 2 where I alluded to various efforts to privilege one of the points of the compass to the status of an *absolute* and to *anchor* value in that absolute. We can observe such efforts being made by investigating historically how philosophers have grappled with how to relate ethics to aesthetics.

The history of ethical and aesthetic theories is too long, detailed, and convoluted for me to embark upon a comprehensive overview here. Nevertheless, to provide at least some degree of context, I shall need to explore and evaluate some key paradigms where attempts have been made to interrelate ethical and aesthetic insights. A way forward might best be accomplished by attempting to answer a series of questions: "How should the virtues be *oriented*?" "How are the virtues to be *practiced*?" "Toward what *goal* should the practice of virtue be directed?" "Where does beauty find its true orientation?" "How can beauty become incarnate through action?" "What is the aim of the beautiful?" To begin answering these questions, I shall first explore the insights of Aristotle.

THE UNITY OF ETHICS AND AESTHETICS IN ARISTOTLE

For Aristotle, the overall *goal* of the practice of virtue is *eudaimonia* or happiness.[1] This goal is the *intrinsic end* that everyone desires for its own sake and for no other reason. Aristotle equates this pursuit of happiness with the pursuit of the *good* (Grk=*to kalon* [τὸ καλόν]).[2] The term *kalon*, however, entails not only the idea of *moral* goodness but also the idea of the *beautiful*. Virtue, for Aristotle, thus features an aesthetic component, and this suggests that his aesthetic theory ought to be considered together with his theory of ethics.[3]

The Orientation and Goal of the Virtues

To pursue happiness as an intrinsic end that is desired for its own sake, the four cardinal virtues—prudence, fortitude, temperance, and justice—must be rightly practiced.[4] Aristotle, like Plato, preferrs to orient the virtues in a *transcendental principle* that he envisages in terms of *limit*. This principle guides Aristotle in the way he "front-loads" the virtues before they are brought to bear upon the variety of circumstances human beings encounter that stand in need of moral rectification.

In Aristotle's *Nicomachean Ethics*, the principle of *limit* as a *Pythagorean ideal* informs his understanding of how virtue should be properly *oriented*.[5] A clear way of visualizing how he applies this ideal can be ascertained by imagining a right-angle triangle that situates the right angle above the hypotenuse. In Pythagorean symbolism, the right angle represents the principle of limit (good), while the hypotenuse opposite the right angle symbolizes the principle of unlimit (evil). The positioning of the right angle at the *apex* of the triangle places the right angle in a position that would normally be associated with the dimension of the *transcendental*; whereas the hypotenuse, which lies beneath the right angle, can be taken to represent the dimension of the *tangible*. As such, the right angle standing above and over against the hypotenuse may be viewed as a *transcendental principle of limit* that has the potential to *govern* tangible reality. As far as the virtues are concerned, prudence (Grk=*phronēsis* [φρόνησις]) or practical wisdom is symbolized by the right angle, for it is this virtue that steers the other virtues in much the same way that the charioteer of reason steers Plato's chariot of the soul.[6] Because prudence is linked to reason, Aristotle classifies it as an *intellectual* virtue. However, this intellectual virtue especially connects as well with the most significant of the *moral* virtues; namely, courage, temperance, and justice.[7]

The two angles opposite the right angle would then represent the principles of *excess* and *deficiency*.[8] (See figure 6.2.) If deficiency stands at the left side of the triangle's hypotenuse, then excess stands at the right side. As the right angle opposite the hypotenuse shifts rightward, the principle of deficiency thus decreases as the principle of excess increases. On the other hand, as the right angle opposite the hypotenuse shifts leftward, the principle of deficiency increases as the principle of excess decreases. How then would the virtue of fortitude or courage be brought to bear upon the hypotenuse? Courage, in Aristotle's estimation, veers in the direction of *excess* rather than *deficiency*. (See figure 6.3.) So, if the vices that attend the virtue of courage are *rashness* (excess) and *cowardice* (deficiency), then courage stands closer to *rashness* than it does to *cowardice*.[9] However, as compared to a rash response, the courageous response appears more measured and more reasonable. Rash responses, being evoked by emotion, disregard reason entirely. Courageous responses, by contrast, are rational. Accordingly, where rash responses are usually hasty and careless, courageous responses, insofar as they are governed by *prudence*, are more thoughtful and measured. The right angle, in the case of the virtue of courage, must therefore shift toward excess and away from deficiency. The line extending from the right angle down-

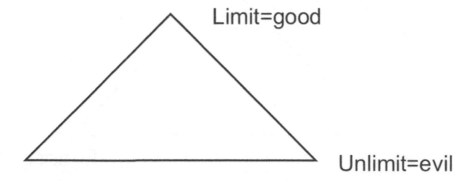

Figure 6.1. Aristotle's Pythagorean Formula.

ward and perpendicular to the hypotenuse thus forms a right angle with the hypotenuse. The resulting right angle then illustrates how the virtue of courage is brought to bear in a *right* way upon those concrete situations in life that this virtue needs to *rectify*. Expressed in another way, the virtue of courage as a *right* principle applied in a *right* way has the capacity to *rectify* a situation where vice is exhibited. Achieving *rectification* is thus the result of the *right application* of a *right principle*.

Unlike courage, the virtue of temperance veers in an opposing direction—i.e., toward *deficiency* instead of *excess*.[10] (See figure 6.4.) This differing direction, however, must consider characteristics of the vices related to the virtue of temperance. The vice of *profligacy*, *prodigality*, or *licentiousness* is characterized by *excess*, while the vice of *insensibility* is characterized by *deficiency*. The profligate or licentious person typically lives a life of unbridled hedonism. As such, he preoccupies himself solely with self-gratification and becomes unrestrained in the indulgence of his basic human pleasure-drives. Examples of insensitive persons, on the other hand, are rare. However, if one were to encounter an insensitive person, that person would presumably appear apathetic, unmoved, and detached in the face of pleasure stimuli that would induce most other persons to seek gratification. Thus, the proverbial "stick-in-the-mud" would most aptly characterize the insensitive individual. Temperance, like courage, must therefore depend upon *prudence* to limit the human tendency to veer in the direction of excess when pursuing what is pleasurable.

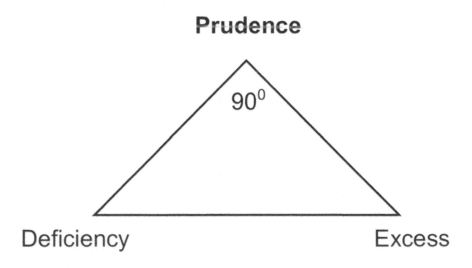

Figure 6.2.   Aristotle's Virtue of Prudence.

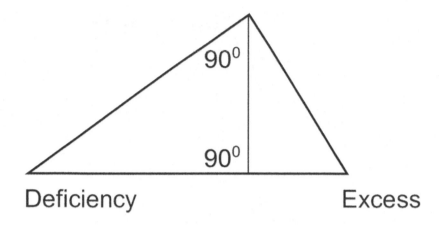

Figure 6.3.   Aristotle's Virtue of Courage.

In exercising the virtues of courage and temperance, Aristotle further notes that pain and pleasure are always attendant factors.[11] *Courage*, for instance, calls upon one to embrace pain *voluntarily*.[12] On the contrary, people *do not voluntarily choose cowardice*, for it is the natural default position that persons settle into to avoid pain. *Profligacy*, on the other hand, entails the willful *pursuit* of pleasure, and this willful element distinguishes it from the vice of *cowardice*.[13] Humans pursue pleasure to satiate their bodily appetites, which is a characteristic they share with the animals. Hence, the *unbridled* pursuit of pleasure makes humans *bestial*.[14] Moreover, whereas men who exercise the virtue of courage are *ennobled*, men who engage in the unbridled pursuit of pleasure become *debased* and *irrational*. The virtue of courage thus differs from that of temperance, for whereas courage calls upon one voluntarily *to endure pain* for a noble purpose, temperance calls upon one willfully *to restrict pleasure* for the same reason.[15] Aristotle thus views the vice of profligacy as being worse than cowardice, since profligacy is more willful in its aims.

Justice, in Aristotle's estimation, is the most comprehensive of all the moral virtues, for justice, more than any other virtue, seeks the "good of *others*."[16] (See figure 6.5.) Whereas prudence *guides* the exercise of the virtues, justice is the virtue that achieves through its *practice* the greatest degree of rectification in all situations where rectification is called for. Courage, on the one side, and temperance on the other, only bring limited kinds of rectification. Justice, however, represents the "whole of virtue" because it aims at the most comprehensive kind of rectification possible.[17] In a parallel way, injustice as the opposite of justice represents the *entirety of vice*.[18]

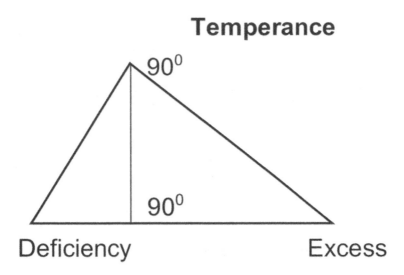

Figure 6.4.   Aristotle's Virtue of Temperance.

Justice in the *general* sense is the most perfect and sublime virtue.[19] There are, however, examples of justice and injustice in the *particular* sense as well. The existence of injustice in the particular sense is proved when individuals display vices such as cowardice and profligacy. Injustice manifests itself in particular ways under two aspects; viz., as *unlawfulness* and *unfairness*.[20] Likewise, justice in the particular sense, as the means of redressing injustice, aims to rectify particular instances of unfairness and unlawfulness. While *distributive* justice addresses the problem of *unfairness*, *corrective* justice addresses the problem of *unlawfulness*.[21] More specifically, distributive justice aims at achieving fairness where particular instances of unfairness are exposed, while the practice of corrective justice aims to rectify illegality that pertains to private transactions. Since *distributive* justice assigns goods based on what is *deserved*, it is *proportional*.[22] *Corrective* justice, by contrast, attempts to *equalize* what is unequal.[23] Here the law weighs the losses that a victim sustains against the gains that a perpetrator of injustice acquires. By applying corrective justice, the law then seeks to reinstate equality by removing the ill-gotten gains from the perpetrator and restoring what the victim has lost.

Aristotle's use of the golden mean formula works well when correlated with the cardinal virtues, but he clearly admits that there are certain vices for which no virtuous mean exists.[24] Hence, though the cultivation of virtue ordinarily depends upon practical wisdom (i.e., *phronēsis* or prudence), logic may prove inadequate in determining how virtue should be applied in *excep-*

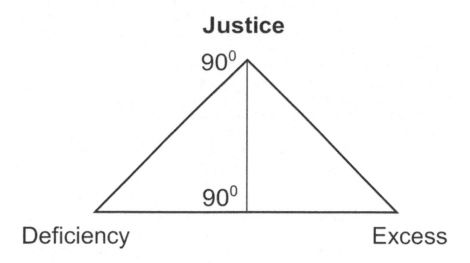

Figure 6.5.   Aristotle's Virtue of Justice.

tional situations. The person who has inculcated *phronēsis* through adequate experience—the *phronimos* (Grk=φρόνιμος)—would, in most cases, qualify as a guarantor of the proper practice of virtue, but this may not always hold true in situations beset by vagueness and ambiguity. *Dilemmas* often challenge the proper application of virtue and bring into question choices that can be deemed *clearly* right. The extreme complexity of some dilemmas can also make ethical decision-making seem impossible. Added to such complexity is the element of *timing*, which can create the demand for an ethical decision to be made hastily and without adequate forethought. When faced with making snap decisions, the decision maker may feel paralyzed. As he/she encounters and seeks to rectify impossible scenarios, the principle of limit may indeed fail to help identify the proper *boundary* that will determine a right application of the golden mean. Such situations precipitate the possibility of the *tragic*, for the tragic victim is often *too late smart*. The flaw in the tragic hero's character is one that anybody acting as a *phronimos* can have. Tragic outcomes consequently point to the inexorable power of the principle of limit to *destroy* and not just to guide. The question then arises, "Can there be such a thing as *tragic beauty?*" This is a question that we must now explore as we examine Aristotle's aesthetic insights.

How Aristotle's Aesthetics Correlates with His Ethics

Because Aristotle upheld a much more positive understanding of the role of sense experience in accumulating knowledge than did Plato, he exhibits a more positive attitude toward the role of aesthetics in his theory of beauty than Plato did. Plato's view that beauty is first and foremost a transcendent Form precludes him from thinking favorably about any *aesthetic* theory of beauty. All efforts at *imitation* of the perfect Form of beauty, Plato believes, *cannot themselves be beautiful.* By contrast, Aristotle's location of the Forms *inside* material existence made possible his espousal of an *aesthetic* theory of beauty. The elements of his theory can be gleaned from his *Poetics.*

The title of Aristotle's work comes from the Greek "*poesis*" (ποίησις), meaning "to make"; and *making* in the poetic sense involves a certain kind of *action.* Aristotle holds that *poesis* entails a kind of activity that is indicative of all types of artistic renderings.[25] Therefore, *poetics*, in the broad sense of the word, goes well beyond what modern people commonly call poetry. Where Plato wanted to *exclude* the reading of poetry from his *Republic*,[26] Aristotle fundamentally departed from his mentor's opinion and considered Homer to be the best example of the poetic genre available.

When answering the question, "What makes poetry, poetry?" Aristotle compares poetry to history to show poetry's superiority. The *creative* element involved in the making of poetry immediately becomes apparent in Aristotle's comparison of the two genres. *History* involves a statement of facts about events that *have happened in the past*; however, history does not speculate about the ramification of past events for *future actions*.[27] Herodotus's historical writings, for example, could be put into verse, but doing so would hardly qualify them as poetry. Poetry differs from history in one important respect: *While history describes what has happened, poetry describes what may happen.*[28] Poetry is thus concerned with *probabilities* in a way that history is not. Poetry, as well, opens the possibility of an experience of transcendental meaning in a way history cannot achieve. Poetry is also more *philosophical* in its aim than history; for history expresses the *particular*, while poetry expresses the *universal*.[29] By expressing the universal, poetry thus also aims to mediate *transcendental meaning*.

Aristotle's *Poetics* also maintains a more positive assessment of the role of *mimicry* in artistic enterprises than can be found in Plato's treatment of art. Plato's demiurge, for instance, is a "maker" or "artist" who endeavors to fashion something that *mimics* the world of the Forms. What the demiurge renders in this process of making, however, always falls short of perfectly representing the ideal world he tries to imitate. Aristotle rejects Plato's assessment here, arguing instead that mimicry is a fundamental human characteristic that can be found already in children.[30] Without mimicry, the learning of language would be impossible; and, of course, language forms the basis of everything meaningful about human society. For Aristotle, therefore, *all* art relies upon mimicry; and since mimicry must not be deemed a substandard kind of enterprise, neither should art as an enterprise be judged as inferior.

Aristotle's theory of beauty is thus less speculative than Plato's. Ever the scientist, Aristotle observes what human beings uphold as exemplary standards of beauty in epic poetry, tragedy, comedy, dithyrambic poetry, and music. Clearly, tragedy is the poetic form that Aristotle favors most highly because tragedy entails a kind of *action* that reveals *character*.[31] Other elements appealing to aesthetic experience are woven together as well to make a great tragedy, but out of all of these, *plot* qualifies as the most significant element. Plot, as "the soul of tragedy,"[32] serves as the unifying thread of the dramatic work of art. All other elements are, as it were, brought into the orbit of the plot and are contextualized by this one superior element.

Throughout Aristotle's discussion of the elements that comprise a great tragedy, we also detect his predilection for such qualities as excellence, skill, symmetry, balance, and believability. Extremes, such as *too much spectacle*, should be avoided.[33] He discusses at length what techniques should be employed and to what degree, as well as what excesses should be avoided in the writing of a tragedy. Clearly, we find throughout his discussion of poetic elements an emphasis on what I previously referred to as *transcendental limit*. This is the standard that governs Aristotle's poetics and not just his ethics.

Aristotle proceeds to discuss what the *ends* of a poetic work should be. In other words, "What is the aim of the beautiful?" In some cases, the end of a poetic work is *practical*, but often the end is *pure enjoyment*. Some beautiful things are not meant to *do* anything, they simply *are*. As such, they should be enjoyed. The idea of enjoyment links closely with Aristotle's ideal of "happiness" (*eudaimonia*) as the goal that we desire for its own sake and for nothing else. Tragedy, however, stands superior to all other art forms because it aims at producing *catharsis* (purgation or cleansing) as its ultimate end.[34] At the heart of tragedy lies the "sin" (Grk=*hamartia* [ἁμαρτία]) or fatal flaw of the hero's character. Indeed, it is this sin that finally overtakes him and brings about his undoing.[35] Working against the tragic figure are deficiencies such as ignorance, lack of time, and missed opportunities. The flaw overcomes and destroys the tragic victim because he learns too late that his fate has already entrapped him. The sin contaminates the victim, and the contamination must be eliminated. Cleansing from this contamination can only be accomplished through the untimely death of the tragic hero.

A comparison of Aristotle's ethics with his aesthetics reveals how *catharsis* or *purgation* stands as the goal of aesthetics in the same way that *eudaimonia* or happiness stands as the goal of ethics.[36] The life lived virtuously is the means of achieving the goal of *eudaimonia*, but "sin" or the fatal flaw in the tragic hero's character obstructs this goal and produces an opposite result; namely, *misery*.[37] Tragedy produces catharsis in the audience precisely because the tragic hero, as a superior exemplar, is finally overtaken by his flaws in a horrific and untimely manner. As the audience contrasts their own inferiorities and flaws with the hero's superior character, they cannot help but feel sympathy for the tragic victim and a sense of terror at his demise.[38]

Because the hero is of nobler character than the members of the audience, they experience the emotions of *fear* and *pity*.[39] *Fear* arises when they compare their own lack of virtue with the virtuous character of the tragic victim. Each person is made to think, "If such a tragic fate can happen to a person more virtuous than I, then how much worse might my own fate be if I fail to rid myself of the excessive emotions that are the basis of my own similar vices?" *Pity* arises when one compares one's own undeserved good fortune to the fate of the tragic hero who perhaps did not deserve the excessive misery entailed in the fate that overtook him. One cannot help but feel pity for the tragic hero as one compares the hero with oneself. The example of the tragic hero thus inspires members of the audience, through their experiences of fear and pity, to purge themselves of all vice and to rededicate themselves anew to the aim of living virtuously.[40]

In retrospect, how does Aristotle's view of aesthetics line up with our earlier discussions of the value-compass? Certainly his focus on the goal of tragedy as catharsis links up closely with the way that transcendental meaning is mediated through the tangible dimension of existence. The "sin" (*hamartia*) or "fatal flaw" that overtakes the tragic hero is a contamination of which he may be unaware.[41] Here, however, the principle of limit ceases to function as an *ethical guide* and instead looms over his head like the "*sword of Damocles*." In tragic cases, tangible reality always *veils* transcendental meaning. This veiling is akin to the way the world of *māyā* (illusion)—according to the Hindu *Shankara* theology—veils truth and produces *avidyā* (ignorance).[42] Karmic law, however, which inexorably operates despite this ignorance, requires the tragic hero to pay for his mistakes. As *wisdom* is finally revealed through the unraveling of the plot, transcendental meaning breaks through into the tangible dimension via the experience of *catharsis*. This is akin to the Hindu experience of *moksha* (salvation or release). Transcendental meaning is no longer veiled but is revealed in the experience of the one who experiences catharsis. The audience is inspired in this way to purge themselves of the contamination of sin and vice and to embrace virtue with a sense of renewed devotion.[43]

Because Aristotle chooses tragedy as an art form superior to comedy, we find him, despite his disagreements with Plato, still favoring the dimension of the *transcendental* over that of the tangible. The tangible dimension remains important for Aristotle to the degree that it retains the capacity to mediate transcendental reality. Aristotle believes, for this reason, that dramatists were wrong to use the "god in the car" (*Deus ex machina*) device to achieve the denouement of a plot.[44] The solution instead should be to bring the tangible into the service of the transcendental, which can best be achieved by striving for *poetic excellence*. Here, Aristotle's emphasis on the realm of particularity (i.e., the dimension of the tangible) surfaces in his aesthetic theory as it does in his ethics, and this makes possible a more "incarnate" view of beauty than what Plato espouses. Plato focuses too extensively on the way that the tangible dimension of reality *veils* the transcendental dimension rather than *revealing* it. For Plato, the tangible dimension is thus perceived mainly in terms of a negative that must be escaped. Aristotle, by contrast, demonstrates how tangible particularity can play a positive role in mediating transcendental meaning. Indeed, transcendental meaning is revealed when particularity is brought into connection with meaning's unity and universality.

One further comment about Aristotle's understanding of the function of tragedy must be made to complete this discussion. For Aristotle, tragedy's main purpose was *not* entertainment in the modern sense of the word. Rather, its main purpose was to contribute to the spiritual and moral health of the community. The overall participation of the audience and their collective experience of *catharsis* are *both necessary* for this communal function to be accomplished. Aristotle's emphasis upon the quality of the audience reveals how important for him this communal aspect is. [45] He certainly does not favor a "casting of pearls before swine" when it comes to performing a tragic play in front of an audience. Aristotle expects something of the *audience* just as he does from the *makers of tragedy*.

THE CHALLENGE OF ALTERNATIVE ETHICAL AND AESTHETIC THEORIES TO THE ARISTOTELIAN PARADIGM

Because of its emphasis upon transcendental limit, the Aristotelian paradigm was unable to deal adequately with a unique problem; namely, how does one deal with the various kinds of *dilemmas* that ambiguities arising out of the dimension of the tangible pose to the human experience of value? The dimension of the tangible generates dilemmas most notably in places where human vulnerabilities are susceptible to exploitation. In one way, the principle of limit guides persons toward discovering avenues of wisdom that help them regulate life. In this regard, the principle of limit can help render vulnerabilities less threatening. However, the principle of limit can also end up *overregulating* life. When this happens, the principle of limit can stifle *tenacity*, which is an indispensable precondition for the flourishing of life beyond efforts at mere survival.

As the West, from the time of the Enlightenment onward, began to focus increasingly on the tangible dimension of the value-compass, the freedom-limit dialectic shifted from an emphasis upon the *transcendental* to an emphasis on the *tangible*. At the same time, the emphasis upon *limit* shifted to an emphasis upon *freedom*. These related shifts transpired at a time when

Aristotle's philosophy also began falling into disfavor. Britain became the first European society to abandon Aristotle's deductive approach to learning as it succumbed to the allurement of Francis Bacon's new *inductive method*.[46] Others soon followed.

From the end of the eighteenth to the beginning of the nineteenth century, two new ethical theories vied to replace the ethics of Aristotle. One was the deontological or duty-based ethic of Immanuel Kant with its grounding in what he termed the *categorical imperative*. The other was utilitarian ethics. Often, commentators have stressed the ethical components in Kantian and utilitarian theories with little regard for the ways these ethical theories connect with the field of aesthetics. I shall thus try to remediate this one-sided focus by examining the ethical-aesthetic links in the thought Kant then the Utilitarians.

THE ROLE OF ETHICS AND AESTHETICS IN THE THOUGHT OF IMMANUEL KANT

Kant's ethical theory rests upon his principle of the categorical imperative, which is a principle that has often been likened to the Golden Rule, "Do unto others as you would have them do unto you."[47] Expressing it in two related ways, Kant says, "Act only according to that maxim through which you can at the same time will that it become a universal law," and "so act as if the maxim of your action were to become by your will a universal law of nature."[48] To achieve these related aims, Kant finds it necessary to move beyond mere *hypothetical* imperatives, for these are based on maxims that are purely *subjective* and *particular* rather than *objective* and *universal*. Maxims, as merely subjective and particular principles of action,[49] thus prove insufficient to provide a proper orientation for ethics. On this point, Kant parts ways with Jean Jacques Rousseau and David Hume,[50] for Rousseau chose to orient his ethical theory in *sentiment*,[51] while Hume oriented his in *sentiment, feeling*, or *sympathy*.[52]

Duty as the Basis for Ethical Action

Entailed in Kant's statement of the categorical imperative is the *principle of universalizability* by which he attempts to posit a *universally valid reason* that can both support and justify ethical action.[53] Thus, maxims by themselves cannot provide sufficient grounding for ethics unless they are *rationally universalizable*. Kant finds this rationally universalizable basis in the exercise of *duty*, which must, in turn, find its basis in *reason*; for duty transcends the inclinations in the same way that reason transcends sentiment. The *good* consequently becomes located not in a *telos* that lies *beyond* the human will[54] but in a *telos* that lies *inside* the human will itself. What Kant calls the *good will* thus ends up becoming its own *telos*.

The *good will* as *telos* forms the basis as well for Kant's contention that persons should always be treated as *ends*, and never as a *means* toward some other end. Hence, two other versions of categorical imperative read as follows: (1) Therefore, every rational being must so act as if he were through his maxim always a legislating member in the universal kingdom of ends; and (2) So act as to treat humanity, whether in your own person or in that of another, in every case as an end and never only as a means.[55]

Kant, by anchoring his ethical theory in *duty* performed by persons of *good will*, essentially roots ethics in a *transcendental conception of human freedom*.[56] However, though this freedom is transcendental, it is a transcendental embodied *particularly* in each individual self.[57] Kant thus finds a way to replace Aristotle's *transcendental limit* with his own concept of *individual human freedom* as the *transcendental* in which he anchors ethics. Despite what Kant tries to accomplish through this attempt, however, individual human freedom refuses to be as easily directed by reason as Kant would have desired. On the one hand, Kant speaks of the "perfect duties" one owes to oneself and to others. More specifically, one performs one's perfect duty to *oneself* by simply *refraining from committing suicide*,[58] while one performs one's perfect duty to *others* by *refraining from making false promises*. Perfect duties are *necessary*, *formal*, and *negative*.[59] As such, they are narrow and are *not* open-ended.[60] Thus, they can be performed perfectly as long as suicide is not attempted, and false promises are not made.[61]

The same, however, cannot be said of *imperfect* duties that one owes to oneself and to others. One's imperfect duty to *oneself* entails one's *cultivation of one's talents and abilities*,[62] whereas a person's imperfect duty to *others* involves *assisting others in need*.[63] By contrast with perfect duties, imperfect duties *are* broad duties that have to do with the cultivation of virtue.[64] They are *contingent* rather than necessary, *material* rather than formal, *positive* rather than negative, and *wide* rather than narrow.[65] As such, they are *open-ended*; and this means that their performance remains always incomplete. What is one to do, then, when one's duty to oneself conflicts with one's duty to others? The attempt to balance the two types of imperfect duties can in no way be helped by Kant's categorical imperative. Instead, the specter of the dilemma once again raises its ugly head.

As I have indicated, the problem of dilemmas arises out of the dimension of the *tangible* where the phenomenon of *vulnerability* tends to be laid bare. Kant addresses the tangible dimension in one way by emphasizing *individual human freedom* and the possibility of the *good will*. However, because he is wholly unconcerned about situations and circumstances on which the principle of duty should have a bearing, the application of duty appears to be rather hit-and-miss. By attempting to orient ethics in the good will of the individual self, Kant thus tries to embody the transcendental in the tangible dimension in a *particular* way. This embodiment ends up, in the final analysis, being only partial. The way the transcendental is embodied appears incomplete because it becomes detached from the various tangible kinds of scenarios wherein the one living the ethical life plays his part in relation to actual situations and circumstances. Ethics, it would appear, must then be practiced in something of a vacuum.

Relation of Kant's Aesthetic Theory to his Ethics

As we turn to Kant's discussion of aesthetics, we again find him attempting to orient aesthetics in a principle of *freedom* that originates from the will of the individual self and not from outside the self. As with his ethical theory, individual freedom entails the existence of a *transcendental* element that resides *within* each individual self. Now, however, the transcendental element within the self serves as the basis for Kant's understanding of *aesthetic taste*.

In his *Critique of the Power of Judgment*, Kant returns to the trajectory he began in his previous works, *The Critique of Pure Reason* and *The Critique of Practical Reason*. In the third and final of his critiques, Kant discusses how both *pure* reason and *practical* reason operate together in our making of judgments.[66] The faculty of judgment itself constitutes a *middle term* or *intermediary* between *understanding* and *reason*.[67] On the one hand, *understanding*, as a cognitive faculty, is concerned with the *theoretical* discharging of the concepts of *nature*.[68] *Reason*, as a cognitive faculty, is concerned, on the other hand, with the *practical* discharging of laws by means of the *freedom of the will*.[69] Several conceptual pairs illuminate this description. These pairs are "understanding and reason," "theoretical and practical," and "nature and freedom of the will." Hence, the terms "understanding," "theoretical," and "nature" are linked on one side, while the terms "reason," "practical," and "freedom of the will" are linked on the other.

Between the sides within these pairs, an important contrast appears. "Understanding" and "reason" represent two different cognitive faculties that our minds engage in as we relate our minds to the *phenomenal* world; namely, to the world that we experience. These cognitive faculties are wholly separate and do not interfere with one another.[70] The categories of *nature* and *freedom* shed further light on the separation between the faculties of *understanding* and *reason*, because nature operates *mechanistically* and is governed by set laws, while freedom operates *voluntarily* and according to moral precepts that free moral agents may or may not obey but *ought* to obey.[71] Kant's contrast between nature and freedom is an important one that reveals his abandonment of Gottfried Leibniz's principle of sufficient reason and his adaptation of David Hume's perspectives on causality. In abandoning

Leibniz's understanding of causality, Kant upholds human free will as a causal agent that is in no way restricted to the mechanistic sorts of cause-and-effect relationships that occur within the operations of nature. I have discussed a similar idea in my treatment of the gap between stimulus and response in chapter 3.

In the phenomenal world (the world of experience), *nature* and *freedom* can limit one another. Still, our ability to exercise *judgment* means that we are free (1) to reflect on the ways that nature and freedom interact in the phenomenal world (i.e., through what Kant calls *reflective judgment*),[72] and (2) to impose our will upon the phenomenal world in order to alter it in certain respects (i.e., through what he labels *determinant judgment*).[73] Nature, therefore, may *impair* or *restrict* our ability to act in ways that we might wish; though this does not mean that nature *necessarily* impairs our ability to engage in reflective judgment. Consequently, even when our wills *participate* in nature, they retain an *autonomous freedom* that remains separate from nature's involuntary and mechanistic laws. Freedom, in this regard, represents a dimension in human nature that *transcends* mechanism.

One of the principle functions of judgment, according to Kant, is its ability to *subsume particulars under universals*. This subsuming ability is accomplished in differing ways by *aesthetic* judgments and by *teleological* judgments.[74] *Teleological* judgments are those that ascribe ends or purposes to *nature* and the *things in nature*.[75] Teleological judgments are thus judgments of a *conceptual* kind. Expressed in another way, teleological judgments are concerned with *discovering the universal laws governing nature.* *Aesthetic* judgments, by contrast, are judgments based upon the *feeling of pleasure* and, for this reason, they are not conceptual. Aesthetic judgments, like teleological judgments, are concerned with subsuming the particular under the universal, but they accomplish this by providing adequate justification for our *feelings of pleasure* and not upon any attempted justification based on *concepts of the understanding*.

In his discussion of aesthetic judgments, Kant distinguishes three levels: judgments of the agreeable, judgments of taste, and judgments of the sublime.[76] Although judgments of the agreeable are judgments based on the feeling of pleasure, they fall well below what Kant thinks comprises the *standard* of the beautiful. That which is merely agreeable falls short of attaining to the standard of the beautiful because it exists as an *interested* rather than *disinterested* pleasure.[77] The statement "I like tattoos" could be translated as "Tattoos are agreeable to me"; but such a statement cannot be extended into the more universal statement, "Tattoos are beautiful." What is truly beautiful is therefore determined by *judgments of taste*. However, to qualify as a judgment of taste, Kant suggests that there must be *four moments* that, taken together, govern what is *tasteful* and, hence, *beautiful*: (1) The feeling of pleasure we experience when we perceive a certain object must qualify as a pure and *disinterested* pleasure that is untainted by the influence of mere charm or emotion.[78] Tainted aesthetic judgments are "empirical" rather than "pure."[79] Something that we find to be merely agreeable does not also qualify as *beautiful*.[80]

(2) What is truly beautiful must have *universal appeal and validity*.[81] Since the universality of judgments of taste have their basis not in *nature* but in *freedom*, not everyone will of necessity recognize a beautiful thing as beautiful.[82] Yet because the element of "will" is present, everyone *ought* to recognize a beautiful thing as beautiful.[83] Hence, judgments of taste are always *subjective* rather than *objective*, and in this respect, they are not based on *concepts*.[84] Furthermore, because they are subjective, judgments of taste *cannot be proved* in the way that judgments based on concepts can be proved.[85]

(3) Judgments of taste are *not teleological*[86] because they do not presuppose an end or a purpose that the beautiful object is intended to satisfy. However, judgments of taste do entail a *nonpurposive purposiveness*. "Beauty is the form of finality in an object," Kant says, "so far as perceived in it apart from the representation of an end."[87] Though judgments of taste entail both the faculties of *imagination* and *understanding*, they are governed by "free play." This means that they lean more in the direction of imagination than understanding.[88] Kant here reverses Plato's understanding of the relationship between imagination and understanding, for where Plato always considered understanding to *govern* imagination, Kant believes, in the case of judgments of taste, that the imagination ought to govern reason. Since in Plato's view, understanding *restricts* imagination, the freedom of imagination must always be brought into conformity with the understanding. Unlike Plato, Kant lands very close to Hume's notion that "reason is and ought to be the slave of the passions." For Kant, the free play of the imagination is what makes possible the *liberation* of the imagination from the strictures that the understanding imposes upon it. This explains why judgments of taste must not be governed by *concepts* because *concepts* belong to the *understanding*. *Judgments of taste* should, rather, be governed by the *feeling of pleasure*.[89]

(4) A judgment of taste must declare that an object of beauty is *universally beautiful*, though this does not mean that *all* persons will necessarily agree with this declaration. Nevertheless, Kant does claim that everyone *ought* to agree with it. Kant in this way tries to interject a concept of *necessity* as it relates to aesthetic judgments, though he emphasizes again that this necessity cannot be based on *determinate concepts* or *rules*. The necessity Kant speaks of is neither of a theoretical nor a practical kind. Rather, it is of a kind that requires the assent of all to a judgment "regarded as an example of a universal rule that one cannot produce."[90] The kind of necessity here is not *objective* but *subjective*. Furthermore, because it is subjective, this type of necessity is *conditioned*. The judgment of taste must presuppose the existence of

common sense (*sensus communis*) as the means of making possible the universal communicability of a feeling.[91] Only in this way can what is subjective in a particular way be extended into a universal rule for everyone.

Kant further prescribes in this fourth moment his own remedy to the problem of diversity,[92] which is a problem that found earlier treatments in the writings of John Locke (1632–1704); Anthony Ashley-Cooper, Earl of Shaftesbury (1671–1713), and Francis Hutcheson (1694–1746). The problem of diversity, which was a special one that arose out of the British empirical tradition, can be explained as follows: Since empiricism focuses on the world of particulars, it has difficulties providing an adequate criterion by which more universal kinds of aesthetic judgments can be justified.[93] Anthony Ashley-Cooper tries to rectify this problem, which Locke was the first to recognize, by borrowing from Stoicism the idea of the innate principles (*koinai ennoiai*) and the *sensus communis*, but these concepts can only at best sustain a theory of *prolepsis*—the innate propensity, tendency, or disposition that is latent in the individual until it is drawn out by the individual's interactions within community.[94] However, empirical evidence of moral diversity and disagreement among cultures seemed to prove that no such thing as a *universal human nature* exists. Shaftesbury argues, however, that the same empirical evidence can be used to prove that some cultures cannot qualify as *fit examples* of human nature. Indeed, they can only serve as examples of what human nature should not be.[95] Kant's position that the universality of taste depends upon an *ought* rather than an *is* reveals here his indebtedness to Shaftesbury.

Akin to aesthetic judgments of *taste* are aesthetic judgments of the *sublime*. In the tradition of Hutcheson, Dennis, and Addison, Kant refers to the sublime as an immensity that overwhelms and, in doing so, elicits wonder and awe in the one experiencing it.[96] He disagrees, however, with their idea that certain objects in nature, like high mountains or turbulent oceans, are *in themselves* sublime.[97] For Kant, the sublime is related to the concept of space and to the category of *quantity* rather than *quality*. In this respect, the sublime must be distinguished from the beautiful, which, being concerned primarily with form and limitation, is related to the category of *quality* rather than *quantity*. The beautiful, furthermore, is directly attended with a feeling of the furtherance of life. In the experience of the beautiful there is an immediate pleasure that contains no trace of repulsion or fear. Such is not the case, however, with the feeling of the sublime. The feeling of the sublime is a pleasure that arises indirectly because that feeling is mixed with elements of repulsion and fear. Because the delight of the sublime evokes admiration or respect, it should be thought of as a negative pleasure.[98] It is, therefore, distinguished from the kind of direct positive pleasure that the aesthetic feeling of beauty evokes. To echo my previous discussion, the sublime entails what Rudolf Otto calls *the mysterium tremendum et fascinans.*

Beauty is therefore concerned with objects (what I refer to as the *tangible*), while the sublime (in my words, the *transcendental*) cannot refer to any object in nature. The sublime cannot be contained in any sensuous form, but depends upon ideas of reason that transcend the senses.[99] Kant therefore disagrees with Hutcheson and Addison that a broad ocean agitated by storms can be referred to *in itself* as sublime.[100] Hutcheson and Addison cannot be correct in this opinion because the sublime *cannot be located* in any sensible object.[101] However, one's experience of some scene like a turbulent ocean can present an opportunity for *one's intuition to be elevated to the level of a sublime feeling*, but first one must have stored a rich stock of ideas in one's mind prior to having such an experience.[102] The elevation of one's intuition to the level of the sublime can only happen when the mind is incited to abandon sensibility and to focus upon ideas involving higher purposiveness.[103]

Kant proceeds to subdivide his analysis of the sublime into the *mathematically* sublime and the *dynamically* sublime.[104] The notion of the mathematically sublime is concerned with that which is *absolutely great and unbounded*,[105] while the *dynamically* sublime is concerned with our aesthetic judgment of the "might of nature."[106] Both concepts of the sublime combine what Otto refers to as the *mysterium tremendum et fascinans.* Hence, whether we look upon nature as mathematically sublime or dynamically sublime, nature must be represented as a source both of fascination and fear.[107]

Having briefly surveyed Kant's comparison of the beautiful and the sublime, it becomes clear that we experience beauty differently from sublimity. We experience the beautiful as immanent within the objects we perceive, but we do not experience the sublime in the same way. The sublime is not experienced as *immanent* in an object, but as *transcendent*. We thus perceive beauty *in* an object, but we experience the sublime as mediated *through* objects. Returning to the Neoplatonic cataphatic-apophatic distinction discussed in the previous chapter, we can then affirm that our experience of the beautiful is more *cataphatic* because such elements as form and similitude are *affirmed*. Our experience of the sublime, by contrast, is more *apophatic* because inconceivable divine transcendence *negates* form and similitude.[108]

Although Kant's theory of beauty generally focuses on the category of *natural beauty*, he also discusses beauty in relation to fine art. Freedom and play are factors that stimulate the creation of fine art. By contrast, labor and drudgery are factors that produce handicraft. Fine art is thus superior to handicraft for several reasons.[109] First, the creation of fine art depends on "genius," which, as a product of nature, is an innate mental aptitude (*ingenium*) that cannot be learned.[110] Second, genius is a talent for producing something for which no definite rule can be given. Genius, for this reason, is not identical to *cleverness*, for the latter natural endowment heavily depends on what is *learned* according to some set rules or standards. Cleverness in this respect is also inferior to *originality*,[111] which only genius can produce. Third, genius cannot be communicated, or learned by another person.[112] Genius, as the source of originality, therefore stands in complete opposition to the spirit of imitation, which lacks originality because it seeks only to copy with exactitude.[113]

As Kant transitions from the topic of the *production* of fine art to the question of how fine art is to be *judged* aesthetically, he invokes again his concept of taste. Judgments of taste are not *analytical* in the way logical judgments are analytical. Rather, they are *synthetical* insofar as they join the feeling of pleasure as a predicate to the object being perceived.[114] The basis for judgments of taste can thus be found only in the synthetic *a priori* that makes possible the synthetical unity of manifold intuitions.[115] The synthetic *a priori* also makes judgments of taste *necessary* in a way that cannot be true of merely empirical judgments that are based upon sensation alone. From this synthetic *a priori,* it follows that our judgments of taste are also *communicable* to others.[116] Consequently, the ultimate standard for determining valid taste must be the *sensus communis* (common sense),[117] which serves as a corrective to prejudiced, narrow, and inconsistent thought.

Taste, like judgment in general, is also the discipliner or corrective of genius. Taste severely clips the wings of genius and makes it orderly while at the same time giving guidance by directing and controlling its flight.[118] Taste introduces clarity and order into the plentitude of thought, gives stability to the ideas, and qualifies them for permanent and universal approval. However, when taste clashes with genius, Kant believes genius should make a sacrifice for the sake of taste by abating the freedom and wealth of the imagination. In this way, taste will keep understanding from being compromised.[119]

In summing up Kant's understanding of the relationship between ethics and aesthetics, we thus find him attempting to achieve unity through a systematic understanding that originates from a "transcendental freedom" that exists in the individual human will. This emphasis distinguishes Kant from Aristotle who oriented his ethics and aesthetics in a principle of *transcendental limit*. Thus, we have two very different attempts to ascertain the connecting link between ethics and aesthetics. Aristotle's principle of transcendental limit, which stands outside the self, functions as one version of this link. Kant's principle of "transcendental freedom," which is located within the self, functions as another. Can there be, then, a rapprochement between these two methods of linking? Or is it necessary for us to choose between them? To answer, we must proceed first to investigate some other ways of linking the ethical and the aesthetic dimension.

THE LINK BETWEEN ETHICS AND AESTHETICS IN THE
THOUGHT OF THE UTILITARIANS

Unlike Kant, British utilitarians Jeremy Bentham, James Mill (1773–1836), and John Stuart Mill (1806–1873) focus on how the *effects* or *consequences* of actions upon society could inform ethical theory. *Like* Kant, however, the utilitarians tried to orient ethics in the dimension of the tangible, while, at the same time, elevating the principle of liberty or freedom over the principle of limit.

The Tangible Dimension as a Source of Conflict for Ethics

Earlier I mentioned how the shift from an emphasis upon the dimension of the transcendental to an emphasis upon the dimension of the tangible runs parallel to the shift from an emphasis on the principle of limit to an emphasis on the freedom principle. Because the dimension of the tangible is itself characterized by disunity and ambiguity, it was perhaps inevitable that this transition would give rise to a set of problems that earlier ethical and aesthetic theorists did not have to face. The problem of *disunity* and *ambiguity* surfaces when we consider how Kant's deontological approach to ethics conflicts with the consequentialist moral theories proposed by the British Utilitarians. On the one hand, Kant's transcendental approach to philosophy elevates the role of the *individual* as a free moral actor, while the utilitarians emphasize the role *society* plays in determining the good. The cleavage between these respective ethical approaches derives from the stark divide between widely differing epistemological perspectives and philosophical methodologies. The attempts of Kant and the utilitarians do, however, share a common concern; namely, to make some principle derived from the dimension of the *tangible* the most suitable foundation for their ethical theories.

Kant's solution is to try to anchor his deontological ethic firmly in the dimension of the tangible by demonstrating the possibility of a *transcendental link* within *one aspect* of the tangible dimension. As I have previously discussed, Kant locates the *possibility* of this link specifically within the *free will* of individuals. Still, free will alone hardly guarantees that the individual will automatically embrace the good. Such can only happen if free will is exercised in terms of *duty*; and duty, in turn, must be informed by the categorical imperative that universal reason supports. *Duty* represents a *voluntary* way of *limiting* freedom. *Limit* in this way is brought into the orbit of *freedom* and not the other way around as Aristotle advocated.

Kant, in his attempt to locate the transcendental good in the will of *individuals*, nonetheless fails to embrace *all aspects* of the dimension of the tangible. Indeed, his locating of the transcendental good in *one* aspect of the tangible *only*, viz., in *human individuality*, leads him to minimize the role that *another* aspect of the tangible, viz., the *social dimension*, could play in revealing what the good might consist of. Kant's deontological ethic, with its transcendental bent, was not only too *formalistic*, but it is also too little concerned about how the *consequences* of actions could play a role in determining whether actions might be deemed ethical. Kant's ethic thus makes his understanding of the transcendental dimension too vague, while it ignores the dimension of the tangible in its *social* aspect to too great an extent.

The Greatest Good for the Greatest Number

The Utilitarians prioritized the tangible dimension differently from Kant; for while Kant virtually *ignores* how the consequences of actions could inform ethical theory, the utilitarians *elevate* the consequences of actions performed within the tangible dimension to a position of critical importance. In doing so, they also lose sight of the transcendental dimension in a manner different from Kant. Utilitarian ethicists adhere to the maxim "the greatest good for the greatest number," though considerable ambiguity stems from the way they define "the greatest good." In his approach, Bentham espouses a *quantitative* definition. This appears in the way that he relies upon the most rudimentary of the value-indicators, *pain* and *pleasure*, to provide the principle determinates that could assist him in calculating *how* he should define the good. The quantitative nature of his approach also comes to light in his "happiness calculus," for he defines the *good* as a garnering of the maximal number of pleasures and as an elimination of the maximal number of pains. Bentham's moral philosophy thus succumbs to the charms of *hedonism*.

While achieving the "greatest good" qualifies as one central goal of ethics, it hardly comprises the only goal. The statement "for the greatest number" entails the other central criterion of Bentham's "happiness calculus." "The greatest number" functions as the *social criterion* for determining the good. Hence, the "greatest good" and the "greatest number" become the means of arbitrating and negotiating between the extent to which individual human liberty can pursue happiness in an unrestrained way and the extent to which society can justifiably impose limits upon individual human liberty. As does Kant, the utilitarians also bring the principle of limit into the orbit of the principle of freedom and not the other way around as Aristotle advocated. The utilitarians nevertheless differ from Kant in the way they arrive at the principle of limit. Kant appeals to *universal reason* as the guiding criterion for determining limit. Furthermore, with Kant, the *principle of limit* is brought to bear upon *freedom* through a *voluntary acceptance* of that principle. Hence, duty regulates freedom. The Utilitarians, by contrast, rely upon various *sanctions* to furnish that criterion, and the principle of limit is imposed upon individual freedom from determinates that arise out of these sanctions.

Bentham reveals four kinds of sanctions that work together to impose limitations upon individual human freedom and to regulate it: (1) The *physical* sanction, which is guided by the principle of pain, is ingrained in the physical fabric of human sensation. Bentham follows here the lead of the ancient Epicureans who were the first to explore the ramifications of pain for developing an ethical theory. (2) The *political* sanction is a social sanction imposed on an individual by another person or persons whom society has chosen to dispense justice. (3) The *moral* sanction is a social sanction imposed by social mores that a society popularly agrees upon and accepts as standards that ought to regulate behavior. (4) The *religious* sanction comes from the immediate hand of a superior Invisible Being either in this life or in the life to come.[120]

When compared to his successor, John Stuart Mill, Bentham's focus on the dimension of the tangible appears more extreme. Mill, by contrast, advances a more *qualitative* approach that leads him to alter Bentham's quantitative method of calculating happiness. Mill recognizes that some kinds of pleasure, such as the pleasure derived from intellectual pursuits, transcend the dimension of the physical. Mill thus understands pleasures to be ordered *hierarchically*. He thus advocates the view that one should postpone or curb the kind of gratification that immediate physical pleasure can supply and instead should pursue pleasures that are higher and more long-ranging in their fecundity.[121]

Mill's definition of the good thus conflicts with Bentham's definition in important respects. This conflict in how "the good" should be defined reveals that the proponents of the utilitarian school fail to promote a *unified* definition of the good. This failure, in turn, introduces considerable ambiguity into efforts to determine exactly what the ethical purpose of individuals living a common life together in a society should consist of. Their failure to achieve clarity in defining the good guarantees that the Utilitarian idea of the good remains ambiguous. Indeed, the attempt to root ethics solely in the dimension of the tangible poses the danger that the good would inevitably be redefined in radically individualistic terms, thus endangering the continued prospects of social cohesiveness.

A further weakness of the Utilitarian approach lies in its *experimental* approach to ethics. Experimentation allows for the principle of freedom to play a maximal role in determining what limitations should be placed upon society. Again, the principle of limit is made to orbit the principle of freedom but not vice versa. Freedom, having now been elevated to a place of central importance, becomes, on the one hand, a vehicle for arbitrarily imposing limit; but on the other hand, it becomes the scalpel that arbitrarily cuts away excessive limits that are perceived to be too restrictive of freedom. Unfortunately, the sanctions that Bentham originally identified would eventually succumb to this scalpel. The first sanction to be cut away would be the religious sanction because it seemingly had the least amount of experimental evidence to support it.

The second and third sanctions to suffer amputation from the utilitarian ethical system would be the moral and political sanctions, respectively. In place of sanctions suggested by past wisdom, new kinds of moral and political sanctions would be imposed that looked very different from those that had been forged and tested in the crucible of tradition. The present moral and cultural situation that exists in Western democracies can largely be traced to these arbitrary processes of cutting away old sanctions and introducing new ones. As a result, behaviors, attitudes, and actions that were once considered highly *immoral* are now arbitrarily deemed *moral*, and behaviors, attitudes, and actions that were once considered *moral* are sanctioned as *immoral*. The only one of Bentham's sanctions that remains is, predictably, the *physical* sanction; but this sanction has proved not to furnish an adequate foundation that can support the other three.

The experimental approach to ethics fostered by utilitarianism also fails to consider the lag time that often exists between causes and their effects in the *moral* realm. I have previously mentioned that this gap between stimulus and response is wider in the personal dimension than it is in the purely physical dimension where cause and effect operates mechanistically. This time lag proves to be another weakness in Utilitarian moral philosophy for one important reason: Its experimental approach can only determine a basis for ethics, first, by sifting through the salutary and deleterious effects of various sorts of human actions and, second, by extrapolating moral principles from these salutary and deleterious effects. However, by the time any adequate assessment of these effects can be fully made, it is possible that the moral experiment will have already proved disastrous. Any ethical insights gleaned from a such a moral experiment would then come too late to benefit individuals who ended up serving as guinea pigs in some failed experiment. Rescue that comes too late is, of course, no kind of rescue at all; and unfortunately, people who willingly allow themselves to be used as guinea pigs in elaborate social experiments often become *victims* when these social experiments go terribly awry. Indeed, the consequences of such failed social experiments can prove even more tragic than what Aristotle had imagined.

I blame the inadequacy of the solutions proposed by Kant and the Utilitarians on their failure to connect adequately the tangible and transcendental dimensions of the value-compass. The Utilitarians, on the one hand, were too preoccupied with the tangible dimension to be able to view the transcendental dimension with any clarity. On the other hand, Kant was too preoccupied with connecting the transcendental dimension with the free will of the *individual* to bring that dimension adequately to bear upon all aspects of the dimension of the tangible. The resulting cleavages between the tangible dimension and the transcendental dimension only resulted in blind spots, particularly in ethicists' understanding of how these two dimensions should intersect.

The weaknesses of these modern theories might lead one, then, to conclude that they did not really offer any truly substantial improvements over Aristotle's ethical theory. Instead, they only provided additional perspectives by shifting the emphasis from limit to freedom and from the transcendental to the tangible. Aristotle, of course, had already proposed that freedom and limit would best coexist when individuals voluntarily live in accordance with virtue. A recovery of certain aspects of Aristotle's approach might, in fact, serve as a corrective to the split between deontological and consequentialist ethical theories. Aristotle's concept of virtue might also aid in identifying the *channels* through which duty ought to flow. Duty, after all, can become a rather vague notion and can be easily misdirected if it is not guided by virtue.[122] Because Aristotle's ethical approach is teleological or goal-oriented, it also takes into consideration circumstances in which the exercise of particular virtues is brought to bear upon specific situations in such a way as to produce the most effective outcome.

Aristotle's method of determining the "golden mean" with respect to the cardinal virtues could also serve as a counterbalance to Kant's overly abstract and formalistic understanding of duty and his attempted rational justification for it. Already for Aristotle, prudence, as the virtue that governs the head, is deeply immersed in and informed by experience, and experience has as its content the actual practical application of all the other virtues. Aristotle's method also can serve as a corrective to the approach of the Utilitarians that too often becomes trapped in the muck and mire of the tangible because it lacks a clear understanding of virtue. Because Utilitarianism and other consequentialist types of ethical theories end up lopping off the dimension of the *transcendental*, they are forever using tangible reality as the petri dish for ill-conceived experiments that ultimately require the petri dish to be discarded in the hazardous waste bin of history. Unfortunately, society is infinitely more valuable than a petri dish, and one can hardly expect to clean up a failed social experiment by disposing of society itself.

John Stuart Mill on the Link between Ethics and Aesthetics

In his 1843 edition of *A System of Logic*, Mill discusses the *Art of Life*.[123] Though he uses the word "art" in the broad sense to denote all human practical enterprises, he promotes the art of life as the highest level of art that persons can and should pursue. According to Mill, art encompasses virtually every kind of human practical endeavor. In this comprehensive sense, art differs from science, which deals with matters of fact and speaks in the *indicative* mood. Art does not belong to the province of *science* but to the province of *practical reason*, which speaks in the *imperative* mood.[124]

Art nonetheless relies on scientific insights to assure practices that can prove ultimately beneficial to all human beings. However, in doing so, science must be conceived as an *inductive* rather than *deductive* enterprise. Mill thus rejects the tendency of the French "geometrical school" to assume a general rule and reason deductively from the general to particular applications.[125] Rather than forcing particulars to conform to an order simply because it is convenient for thought, art must take its cue from inductive science before it arranges the truths it discovers into an order deemed suitable for *practical use*.[126] Thus, whereas science begins with causes and reasons to their various effects, art reasons backward from a singular overall effect to that effect's multiplied and diversified causes and conditions. Art must therefore visualize the *overall effect* that it intends to bring about before it can determine what resources and skills it needs to achieve that effect.

Because art focuses on *effect*, it attempts to define *teleology* or the *doctrine of ends* in a way that differs from scientific objectives. Whereas science investigates the *means* that lead to a given end, art defines *what those ends should be*. Art thus *enunciates* the object aimed at and *affirms* that object as *desirable*.[127] In its more replete form, the art of life exemplifies the highest level of art practicable. Hence, the art of life, as the highest of all arts, is the art to which all other arts must be subordinated. The art of life therefore includes as its aspects *morality*, the making of *policy* (i.e., *prudence*), and *aesthetics*.[128] Expressed in another way, the art of life aims, by means of human conduct and work, to achieve three goals: the *Right*, the *Expedient*, and the *Beautiful* or the *Noble*.[129]

Interestingly, Mill's *teleological* emphasis seems not to rest entirely on an Epicurean foundation, but upon one that more closely approximates the ideas of Aristotle and the Stoics.[130] He echoes Aristotle, for instance, when he asserts that the ultimate principle of teleology is the promotion of the happiness of all sentient beings.[131] What nevertheless becomes apparent is the way that the *qualitative* emphasis in Mill's utilitarianism lends itself to his accepting the role of aesthetics in a manner that seems quite foreign to Bentham's *quantitative* version of Utilitarianism. Unfortunately, Mill did not undertake to develop a more comprehensive aesthetic theory but refers to his art of life as an art "which, in the main, is unfortunately still to be created."[132] Consequently, we can only speculate about what his fully developed art of life might have looked like, though we can assert with some confidence that it would likely adhere to the kind of hierarchical arrangement of pleasures to which Mill alludes elsewhere in his works. Mill suggests as much when he speaks of the various arts fitting into the "scale of desirable things."[133]

What then does Mill believe that the link between the ethical and the aesthetic consists of? Because his aesthetic theory is sketchy at best, its link to ethics seems fraught with an internal inconsistency. This inconsistency derives from the enormous leap that Mill must make as he compares the

lower kinds of pleasures with the higher ones. There seems to be no justification for his appeal to teleology apart from the fact that he finds it useful, but
this raises the question, "Why should this *telos* be found in the higher pleasures instead of the lower ones?" There seems to be no rationale for deferring
the kind of gratification that the pursuit of lower pleasures assures apart from
subjective opinion. Certainly, there is no way of deducing any absolute principle from a comparison of the pleasures themselves, since morality and
aesthetics are dependent upon an inductive enterprise. Through experimentation, one could find a way to balance the pursuit of lower pleasures with the
pursuit of higher ones. The pursuit of the higher would not necessarily have
to preclude the pursuit of the lower. Unfortunately, the inability to find a
clear principle of teleological purpose means that the same ambiguity that
haunts the ethical theories of the Utilitarians haunts their aesthetic insights as
well. Without a clear understanding of how the transcendental dimension
connects to all aspects of the tangible and purposively directs them, one is at
best left with opinions, personal preferences, and sentiments. The way of
escaping this haze of ambiguity is thus as unclear as Kant's concept of duty
is vacuous.

VIEWING ETHICAL AND AESTHETIC CATEGORIES IN DIALECTICAL RELATION

In post-Kantian philosophy, the use of dialectical reasoning assisted philosophers in bridging to some degree the impasses that resulted from attempts to
impose rigid categories on various aspects of the dimension of the tangible.
To cite one example, Kant preferred *one* of these rigid categories to the
exclusion of the *other*. By elevating the *individual* aspect of the tangible
dimension to a place of central importance in his deontological ethical theory, he was left with a rigid category that took the role played by the social
aspect into too little account.

A similar thing happened with the utilitarians who elevated the social
aspect of the tangible dimension to a place of central importance. In doing so,
they, too, produced a rigid category that allowed too little attention to be paid
to the *individual* aspect. Such attempts at rigid categorization predisposed
philosophers on both sides to ignore the obvious connection between these
two aspects. Dialectical thinking, by contrast, allowed both aspects to be
reconnected; and this, in turn, relaxed these categories and restored fluidity to
understandings of how they were interrelated. I shall now look at some
representative versions of dialectical thinking that sought in various ways to
bridge the impasse between these aspects.

Using Dialectical Thinking to Bridge Dimensions of the Tangible: Hegel, Bradley, Marx, Schopenhauer, and Nietzsche

G. W. F. Hegel criticizes Kant for espousing "empty formalism" and "empty subjectivity."[134] Kant's view of duty, Hegel believes is vacuous because Kant fails to ask the question, "Duty in relation to what?" Duties based on an idea of transcendental subjectivity quite frankly lack an emphasis on an "immanent doctrine of duties."[135] Following the cue of Hegel, F. H. Bradley (1846–1924) specifically applies Hegel's dialectical understanding to his moral philosophy when he develops his notion of "my station and its duties."[136] The "station" aspect of Bradley's thought links up well with the thinking of the Utilitarians, while the "duty" aspect reflects Kant's deontological ethic. Bradley mirrors Hegel's understanding of the dialectical link between station and duty. The former's dialectical approach thus signals an advancement over the two opposed ethical perspectives that he links. Bradley's ethical philosophy does, however, harbor one inherent weaknesses that was also attributable to Hegel's view; viz., his preference for collectivism (i.e., holism) over individualism.[137] Bradley is thus conservative in his view that station should determine duty. This view echoes Hegel's belief that the individual exists for the State and not the State for the individual. Furthermore, the variety of collectivism that Hegel and Bradley advanced privileged the *status quo*, and this would inevitably invite Karl Marx's critical analysis. Marx's collectivism equals that of Hegel's but turns it topsy-turvy. Marx entirely reenvisions the concept of duty by redirecting it toward an abolition of the present status quo and an establishment of the "dictatorship of the proletariat."[138]

Just as Bradley and Marx could not agree on how to value the respective roles of station and duties in their dialectical relationship to one another, Arthur Schopenhauer and Friedrich Nietzsche disagree in the ways they value the principle of the will as it exists in nature and the will as it exists in man. This disagreement, in turn, shape their views concerning ethics and aesthetics. Schopenhauer views the will in nature as a negative and destructive force,[139] while Nietzsche views the will in man as a creative, life-engendering, vital potency that, if anything, needs to be vindicated and nurtured. Schopenhauer thus views ethics and aesthetics as an escape, albeit temporary, from nature's *devouring will*.[140] Nietzsche, on the other hand, advocates not for an *escape* from the human "will to power" but a full immersion in it.

Related to Nietzsche's will-to-power concept is his understanding of the *Dionysian principle*, which he discusses at length in *The Birth of Tragedy*.[141] In this work, Nietzsche contrasts Dionysius, the god of wine and the orgy, with Apollo, the god of the sun and of reason. While Nietzsche holds that both the rational Apollonian principle and the irrational Dionysian principle are necessary elements in tragedy, he also observes among the Greeks, begin-

ning with Euripides and culminating in Socrates and Plato, a gradual elevation of the Apollonian principle over the Dionysian.[142] The waxing of the
Apollonian and the waning of Dionysian subsequently eroded and even
threatened to destroy aesthetics. The privileging of the Apollonian principle
also allowed ethics and morality to be elevated at the expense of the aesthetic
dimension. We can perhaps understand, then, why Nietzsche so often derides
morality and its champions at the same time that he seeks to vindicate aesthetics from Apollonian oppression.[143] Clearly, *he* champions the ascendency of the Dionysian principle over the Apollonian and the aesthetic dimension over the ethical.

We thus find, even with these versions of dialectical thinking, that philosophers will invariably privilege one aspect of tangible existence over another. Conflict that arises in the outworking of dialectical processes aims at
some synthesis that is *teleological*, but one cannot find agreement concerning
what that synthesis should look like. The means of achieving certain ends are
brought into conflict as persons in a society pursue a variety of different
ends. The reason for this is that the ends themselves have become proliferat-
ed and confused.[144]

Aesthetic Insights from Schiller to Hegel and
Their Relation to the Ethical

Friedrich Schiller

Kant's aesthetic theory would influence another eighteenth-century thinker,
Friedrich Schiller (1759–1805), who in 1794 produced his *Aesthetic and
Philosophical Essays*.[145] Schiller acknowledges his indebtedness to Kant;[146]
however, Schiller's aesthetic theory is less structured than his predecessors in
that it allows for greater reciprocity in the dialectical interplay between *nature* and *freedom*. Perhaps most important is Schiller's attempt to *reunite*
aesthetics and ethics where Kant has managed to make too sharp a distinction
between them. Kant rejects Hume's contention that sentiments such as sympathy or fellow feeling should serve as the basis for ethical motivation.
Instead, Kant, as previously mentioned, proposes a reason-based, duty-moti-
vated ethical theory. On the other hand, when Kant grounds his aesthetic
theory of taste *solely* in human subjectivity and feeling, he seems to follow
Hume's lead.

Schiller thought this theoretical bifurcation between Kant's ethical and
aesthetic theories was unnecessary. Instead, Schiller proposes that the concept of "grace" could reunite ethics and aesthetics without doing damage to
either.[147] The Greeks, he declares, distinguished grace and the Graces from
the goddess of beauty. Yet, when Schiller asserts that "all grace is beautiful,"[148] he allows grace to include an *aesthetic* dimension. However, this

inclusion does not, however, contradict Kant's idea that *duty* should be based on reason and not on inclination.[149] Schiller's concept of *grace* entails neither a repudiation of duty-based morality nor a reduction of grace to pure sentimentality.[150] On the contrary, grace *includes* the concept of duty while raising duty to a higher level.[151] When the concept of duty is joined to that of grace, duty is performed joyously, not begrudgingly. Therefore, grace, far from *negating* moral duty, *elevates* it.

Johann Georg Hamann

Johann Georg Hamann (1730–1788), who just so happened to introduce Kant to the works of David Hume in the first place, reacted even more extremely to Kant than Schiller did. Hamann was the principle thinker behind the highly influential *Sturm und Drang* (Storm and Stress) movement (1762–1780), which was a proto-Romantic movement that sought to vindicate the use of *emotional extremes* in aesthetics. By contrast with Kant, Hamann's thinking was both unsystematic and reactive to Enlightenment ideas. Indeed, the ideas of rationality and universality that Kant treats with such high importance becomes Hamann's principle targets. Though Hamann agrees with Kant's recognition of the *limits* of reason, he disagrees with Kant's attempt to *vindicate* reason.

In his *Metacritique of the Purism of Reason*, Hamann objects to what he calls Kant's "purifications" of reason.[152] The first attempt at purification, Hamann notes, involves Kant's attempt to make reason independent of all tradition, custom, and belief in them. The second even more transcendent purification is to make reason completely independent from experience and its everyday induction.[153] The third and highest purism in Hamann's view is Kant's failure to concern himself with language, which Hamann claims constitutes the only, first, and last organon and criterion of reason.[154] Hamann thinks that a good many of Kant's analytic judgments imply "a gnostic hatred of matter" or "a mystic love of form," and he chides Kant for harboring a cold prejudice for mathematics when Kant uses it to support his concept of the synthetic *a priori*. He accuses Kant of using language so esoteric that it is on par with the very language of scholasticism that the denizens of the Enlightenment so despised.[155]

Kant's failure to be concerned with language, Hamann believes, is rooted in Kant's "violent, unjustified, willful divorce of that which nature has joined together"—namely, the two stems of human knowledge, the *sensibility* and the *understanding*. These, Hamann asserts, grow from one common root, but when that root is ruptured both stems wither and dry up.[156] Specifically, Kant's rigid segregation of knowledge into *a priori* and *a posteriori* categories is responsible for hacking asunder what nature, through language, had joined together. In his attempt to rescue language from the violent divorce that Kant imposes between nature and spirit, Hamann appeals to a Christo-logical doctrine that was of the greatest importance to Martin Luther; viz., the doctrine of the *communicatio idiomatum* or the "communication of prop-erties" between Christ's divine and human natures.[157] Luther uses this doc-trine to support his view of the Lord's Supper. According to this view, the real presence of Christ was present not only in the elements of the Lord's Supper, but it pervaded the entire universe as well. The idea that the physical body of Christ permeates the universe is, in fact, part and parcel of Luther's doctrine of the "ubiquity of Christ," and he supports this doctrine by arguing as follows: (1) The physical body of Christ has ascended to the right hand of God; (2) the right hand of God is everywhere; (3) therefore, the physical body of Christ is everywhere.[158]

According to Kenneth Haynes, Hamann extends Luther's ubiquity of Christ doctrine well beyond the doctrine of the Real Presence of Christ in the Eucharist to include the entire physical world. Because of this move, human language, which joins the sensibility and the understanding, becomes the means that makes the word (*Logos*) incarnate in the physical world.[159] Ha-mann's idea of incarnation, however, very much reflects Luther's emphasis upon the *earthy* aspects of Jesus' human physical experience, such as his birth from the Virgin's womb, his being nursed at Mary's breast, his sharing of the peasant's lot, and his suffering and death on the cross. Like Luther, Hamann believes there are no human conditions or emotions that cannot ultimately be sanctified by God's participation in them. Even the original act of human procreation (which Kant views with outright disgust), Hamann believes reflects the very image of God; though this reflection admittedly became distorted because of the shame that the fall of man brought.[160]

Against Kant's insistence on reason, Hamann employs Hume's insights concerning how knowledge is obtained. Because Hamann was a German Pietist Christian, he disagreed entirely with Hume's rejection of Christianity. He nonetheless accepted Hume's view that all our knowledge is ultimately based on *belief*.[161] Developing Hume's notion of belief, Hamann uses the German word "*Glaube*" to refer both to "*epistemic belief*" and to "*faith*" in the religious sense.[162] In so doing, he reveals that even thinkers of the En-lightenment had put their *faith* in such notions as "reason" and "universal-ity," thus contradicting their own confidence that reason alone was the basis of their knowledge.[163] For Hamann, relationality and the "union of oppo-sites" is the best way to understand how human knowledge functions as a totality. Ultimately, relationality contextualizes all human experience and suggests ways that opposites can be reconciled.[164]

Up until Hamann, aesthetic theories had allowed only the nobler human emotions to be explored artistically. This had produced an "asceticism" in art of the kind that was apparent in French classicism, where order, balance, and simplicity were the rules that governed what could be classified as good art.

Hamann, by contrast, shows how all aspects of the physical dimension, and not merely the "tasteful" ones, can be reunited with the spiritual. He thus proposes a way in which the despicable and the ugly elements of man's physical and emotional experiences can be integrated in a redemptive way into an aesthetic theory. The *Sturm und Drang* movement, which Hamann's insights initiated, ultimately included such figures as Johann Gottfried Herder (1744–1803), Johann Wolfgang von Goethe (1749–1832), and Schiller.

Sturm und Drang and August Schlegel

The *Sturm und Drang* movement had a significant impact on German Romanticism, which, as a movement, began with a group known as the Romantic circle whose members included brothers Friedrich Schlegel (1772–1829) and August Schlegel (1767–1845), Novalis (Georg Philipp von Hardenberg) (1772–1801), Friedrich Schleiermacher (1768–1834), Friedrich Wilhelm Joseph von Schelling (1775–1854), Ludwig Tieck (1773–1853), and Wilhelm Wackenroder (1773–1798). Of this group, the most important contributor to the field of aesthetics was Friedrich Schlegel. Initially influenced by Schiller's work on "Naïve and Sentimental Poetry," Schlegel eventually moved beyond Schiller and began to prefer the Romantic ideal to the classical. Schlegel, following Herder's insights concerning the widely varying differences between peoples living during different historical eras and different cultures, abandoned the idea that pieces of art should be judged by a *general* ideal. He advocated instead the role of the *individual* ideal in the judgment of every work of art.[165] At the same time, he embraced Immanuel Kant's contention that judgments of beauty are internal and subjective and cannot be made based on objective external rules.

Schlegel's work, like that of the other Romantics, engages in the problem of how to reconcile the holism of Baruch Spinoza's pantheistic philosophy with the subjective emphasis on the freedom of the will found in J. G. Fichte's absolute idealist philosophy. Schlegel, along with his contemporaries, inaugurated new features into their poetics and aesthetics: the novel,[166] Romantic poetry,[167] the literary fragment,[168] the concept of irony,[169] and the use of wit and allegory.[170] The novel as an art form allows for the swinging back and forth between the subjectivity of lyric poetry and the objectivity of the epic, and between chaos and system. The novel, in this latter respect, is an example of "shaped chaos." The literary fragment functions as a means of relating the finite to the infinite, for the fragment itself is finite and in conflict with other fragments while remaining nonetheless open to the Infinite.[171] The unity and universality of the Infinite, however, is not a *rational* and *harmonious* unity and universality like that imagined by Kant,[172] but an *emotional* and *dynamic* unity and universality. In a similar way, the literary modes of irony, wit, and allegory reveal the fluctuation between the fragmentary and

the universal,[173] and between the Fichtean emphasis on the subjective freedom of the will[174] and the Spinozan emphasis upon objective holism.[175]
These literary modes all allow for the dynamic interplay of these two emphases.[176]

F. W. J. Schelling

A further attempt to move beyond Kant by using dialectical thinking comes
from Schelling. In his work, *The Philosophy of Art*, Schelling advances his
theory of "three potencies," which are *truth*, *goodness*, and *beauty*.[177] He
accommodates to the first two potencies Kant's views concerning nature and
freedom.[178] However, Schelling's view of the third potency departs significantly from the way Kant conceives of the relation between nature and freedom. Schelling's idea of *truth* as the *first* potency corresponds to Kant's
understanding of *nature* and the *necessity* of nature. Moreover, Schelling's
idea of *goodness* as the *second* potency corresponds to Kant's conception of
the human will and the freedom of the will. Schelling, however, in the vein of
Hamann and Friedrich Schlegel, cannot accept Kant's absolute divorcing of
nature from freedom. Instead, Schelling advances the idea that *beauty* as the
third potency achieves the "indifference" (identity or synthesis) of nature and
freedom.[179] This synthesis is more than a subjective occurrence as it was for
Kant. It is, rather, an *ekstasis* that entails "the All"; viz., the originally undif-
ferentiated infinite from which both nature and freedom emerge and in which
they eternally subsist.[180]

We see in this concept of the *All* that Schelling has managed to jettison
the subjectivism of Kant in favor of a synthesis that combines the objecti-
vism and determinism of Spinoza's nature pantheism with the subjectivism
and voluntarism of Fichte's "I" or ego. This synthesis of truth (na-
ture=objectivity) and freedom (will=subjectivity) is, itself, "beauty." In advancing this idea, Schelling subsumes beauty under "the Concept," which is
a move that Kant never would have countenanced. Nevertheless, Schelling's
rooting of all three of his potencies in "the All" move him beyond the rationalism of Kant's Transcendental Idealism to mysticism. Hence, where Kant
seems stuck in the rationalism of Plato, Schelling moves beyond Plato to the
mysticism of the Neoplatonists. Furthermore, while "truth" for Schelling is
entailed in the "first potency," this potency is not, as it is for Kant, an
ultimate objective standard. Schelling's mysticism serves as that deeper reality in which even "truth" is rooted. In a similar way, "beauty" cannot be
reduced to rationality, for the mystery of the All continues to be mediated
through the beauty of concrete forms. The mystery of the All extends as well
to Schelling's discussion of the beauty of nature, the development of Greek
and Christian civilization, and the forms of art. Schelling seeks to demonstrate how beauty appears when the Eternal or the Infinite becomes one with

the finite and is mediated through it. No individual thing can be beautiful apart from its participation in this Absolute.

Schelling, like his predecessors, also recognizes that the production of beauty involves *conflict* and *suffering* in addition to *catharsis* and the *resolution of conflict*. The conflicts between freedom and nature, and between the Infinite and the finite, are causes of human suffering. Suffering and catharsis are evident in tragedy where the sublime in nature cleanses the soul by liberating it from mere suffering.[181] "Only within the maximum of suffering," Schelling states, "can that principle be revealed in which there is *no* suffering, just as everywhere things are revealed only in their opposites."[182]

G. W. F. Hegel

Perhaps the most significant contributor to the dialectical understanding of reality during the nineteenth century was Hegel. In the vein of Schiller, Hegel rejects the Kantian project, which divorces sense from reason and subjectivity from objectivity and leaves Kant with no other alternative but to ground his aesthetic theory solely in subjectivity.[183] What Hegel sees lacking in Kant is any notion of the *external* and *objective embodiment* of beauty in works of fine art.[184] Hegel has some difficulty with the use of the word "aesthetics" for a similar reason, for this word, which originally referred to "sense," is too narrow to encompass a theory of beauty that weds subjectivity to objectivity.[185] For this reason, Hegel proposes a twofold approach to the "scientific (Ger=*Wissenschaftlich*) ways of treating beauty and art."[186] One aspect of such an approach is *empirical*. It begins with the examination of external pieces of art, proceeds to arrange them into a history of art, and finally arrives at general considerations that aid in both criticizing and producing works of art.[187] This more empirical approach, which can be found in Aristotle's *Poetics* and Horace's *Ars Poetica*, leads to the formation of what Hegel terms the "Concept" (Ger=*Begriff*) of beauty.[188] The *Concept* entails four syntheses that can be summarized as follows: 1) The synthesis of subjectivity and objectivity (or the synthesis of the inner and the outer),[189] 2) the synthesis of metaphysical universality with the precision of real particularity,[190] 3) the synthesis of nature and freedom,[191] and 4) the synthesis of sense and reason.[192]

Whereas the *empirical* mode of treating art starts from the particular and existent and moves to the general, a second mode starts from a purely *theoretical* reflection that labors to understand the beautiful as "Idea."[193] In this theoretical mode, Hegel uses Platonic terminology at the same time that he departs from the Platonic understanding of the "Idea" as an abstraction.[194] For Hegel, the Idea must be grasped *concretely*; and in order for this to be done, the Idea must be concretely *embodied* in art.[195] Hegel calls this concrete embodiment of the "Idea," the "*Ideal*."[196] The "Concept" of beauty and the "Idea" of beauty thus serve as two vantage points (one, the empirical; the other, the theoretical) for approaching beauty. The *Concept* of beauty, however, is insufficient to provide a full understanding of beauty unless it is combined with the Reality of the Absolute. Thus, whereas the *Concept* of beauty is the widest possible apprehension of beauty available from the vantage point of the world, the *Idea* of beauty goes even further in that it contains within itself the Concept of beauty while at the same time transcending the Concept by joining it with the Absolute.[197] The Idea of beauty thus encompasses the totality of God and the world.

Since for Hegel both the Concept and the Idea of beauty are only conveyed through the synthesis of the finite and the infinite, this means that beauty cannot reside in nature alone.[198] Nature, which is finite, bounded, and determined, must first be transformed by the agency of human free will and harmonized with it. Hegel calls this agency "spirit."[199] The mere imitation of nature in a production does not yet accomplish this transformation that spirit brings about. In producing by mere imitation, human agency becomes a slave to exactness and, hence, is in no way free. By contrast, spirit, as the infinite penetrates the finite and elevates it. In doing so, spirit transcends mere imitation and leaves its mark upon the truly artistic production.

Hegel thinks that the Romantic form of art refers to art's third and final form; for in this form, the principle of inner subjectivity triumphs.[200] At this stage "the spirit knows that its truth does not consist in its immersion in corporeality. . . ."[201] On the contrary, the spirit posits external reality as an existence inadequate to itself and withdraws from eternal reality to its own internal intimacy with itself. In these ways, the spirit becomes sure of its truth.[202] The true content of Romantic art is thus *absolute inwardness*. Beauty in this artistic form becomes the *spiritual beauty of the absolute inner life* as an inherently infinite spiritual subjectivity that grasps its own independence and freedom.[203] For Hegel, this sense of infinite spiritual subjectivity possesses an absolute and universal content that entails the absolute negation of everything particular. It dissipates all the external relations of the processes of nature, such as birth, passing away, and rebirth; it annuls all forms of restrictedness in spiritual existences; and it dissolves all particular gods into pure and infinite self-identity.[204] This infinite spiritual subjectivity, as the one God, the one spirit, and the one absolute independence, dethrones all gods from their pantheon. As the absolute knowing and willing of itself, this God remains in free unity with itself.[205]

Hegel holds that the God of the Jews represents this highest expression of *infinite spiritual subjectivity*;[206] however, this absolute subjectivity would elude art and would be accessible only to thinking if it did not enter back into the dimension of the finite. Here, Hegel invokes the *Christian* idea of the Incarnation of God in Jesus.[207] This idea entails the idea of the self-knowing, sole, and universal God whose birth, life and suffering, death, and resurrection reveals the eternal and infinite spirit in all its truth to finite human consciousness.[208] This universal in Jesus is not restricted to individual, immediate existence in the shape of Christ but through the giving of the spirit of God unfolds until the universal is possessed by the whole of humankind. The freedom of infinite subjectivity entering into the finitude of nature now appears as redemptive *love*.[209] *Love* is the depth of feeling that alone corresponds to the essential nature of the spirit, which in itself is free and satisfied.[210] Finally, love transitions from its *individual expression* (in Jesus) into a reality that is *communal*.[211] This is accomplished when Christ, through death and resurrection, negates the negativity of his immediate individuality, which makes possible the rise of the individual person to freedom and to peace in God.[212]

In all Romantic forms of art, what becomes of paramount importance for Hegel is the idea of the *community* as the *repository of the inner subjectivity of spirit* expressed in terms of *love*.[213] Painting, music, and poetry are art forms that require the highest level of communal participation. The participation of the community represents a synthesis of nature and spirit in which not nature, but the spiritual principles of individuality and inner subjectivity are transmuted into love.[214] Love, on the one hand, retains the element of spiritual freedom inherent in individuality. On the other hand, the person who loves freely chooses to be restricted and compelled by love itself.[215]

Assessing Dialectical Links between Ethics and Aesthetics

Various kinds of dialectical links appear in the thought of the philosophers I have discussed. These suggest ways that one might proceed when attempting to integrate and reconcile ethical and aesthetic insights. Particularly illuminating are the ideas of Hamann and Schlegel. Hamann makes it possible for one to imagine how the universal can become incarnate in the dimension of the tangible despite the way the particulars that populate the tangible dimension are prone to come into conflict. His understanding of language also allows for the kind of flexibility that I argued for in chapter 5—a flexibility that can allow the concept of *logos* to include rather than exclude elements of *différance*. Schlegel, too, points out ways that conflict and chaos, and not only rational and harmonious unity, can become vehicles that can mediate unity and universality. Such mediation can be accomplished through literary forms such as the literary fragment, the concept of irony, the allegory, and the novel, for these are linguistic vehicles through which *chaotic* unity and universality can find expression. Schlegel's thought is particularly helpful in finding ways to link the tangible dimension, with all its conflicts, to the dimension of the transcendental.

Hegel, however, allows the universal scope of his dialectical system ultimately to eclipse particularity. As a result, Hegel comes down too heavily on the side of objectivity while giving too little attention to subjectivity. This move on the part of Hegel, in my estimation, diminishes the value that Hamann and Schlegel accord to particularity. This neglect of the element of particularity would prove extremely problematic to one who became unsettled by Hegel's emphasis; notably, Søren Kierkegaard.

However, two important insights from Schiller and Hegel are worth noting here; namely, Schiller's view of "grace" and Hegel's view of "love." Schiller speaks of the way that *grace* weds the moral and the aesthetic, but I argue that grace does not wed the moral and the aesthetic in a *dialectical* fashion. Grace, in fact, stands apart from the dialectical nature of tangible reality even though it can be mediated through that reality. Grace, furthermore, does not arise out of the dimension of the tangible. Rather, it originates from the dimension of the transcendental. This is similarly true of Hegel's conception of *love*. *Love* begins in Hegel's thought as a transcendental category, for Hegel, in his *Philosophy of Religion*, speaks of the Trinitarian life itself in terms of "playing love."[216] The concept of play links *love* with the principle of *freedom*; and *freedom* belongs to the workings of *spirit, not* of nature. Hegel goes on to speak of a "serious love" that originates in God and embraces "serious otherness."[217] This embrace inaugurates the process of elevation (Ger=*Aufgehoben*) that is so central to Hegel's philosophy.[218] Since "serious otherness" represents the tangible dimension of reality—which is riddled with finitude, sin, and guilt—*serious love* is the only remedy that can accomplish the redemption of the tangible dimension.

Unfortunately, Hegel's focus on love, while rooted in a concept of freedom, does not adequately incorporate a concept of human *libertarian freedom* into his dialectical system. Instead, the freedom of Absolute Spirit *overrides* the free will of man; and this, in turn, makes faith on man's part seem unnecessary for love to succeed. Hegel subsumes all *particular* forms of human freedom under the *universal* freedom of *spirit*. This move results in a determinism that closes Hegel's dialectic off from *truly free* human participation and assures that the dialectic will continue to operate smoothly because it will be kept safe from too much human interference.

ETHICS AND AESTHETICS IN PARADOXICAL RELATION: SØREN KIERKEGAARD

Hegel's dialectical system inevitably falls short because it collapses the transcendental dimension into the dimension of the tangible and conflates the two. In doing so, it also allows transcendental universality to eclipse tangible particularity, thus making the role of particularity in the scheme of things inconsequential. Danish philosopher Søren Kierkegaard vehemently reacts to this propensity in Hegel. Borrowing from the insights of Hamann and Friedrich Schlegel, Kierkegaard develops a philosophical perspective that radically opposes the very essence of Hegel's system. In his works, *Either/Or*, *Repetition*, and *Stages on Life's Way*, Kierkegaard departs significantly from Hegel's universally all-encompassing and totalizing dialectic by relating the dimension of the tangible to what I am calling "paradoxical transcendence."

Kierkegaard rejects Hegel's dialectic principally because it tips the scales in favor of a determinism that operates chiefly by means of a principle of reason. As reason imposes its inexorable march through history, it assures the eventual sublation of everything particular and individual. As an alternative to Hegelianism, Kierkegaard offers a version of the dialectic that preserves particularity by allowing the free choices of individuals to settle outcomes. Kierkegaard's dialectic is consequently one which is open to the Infinite and which can mediate the Infinite through the dimension of the finite. Because Kierkegaard respects individual libertarian freedom, he believes that individuals may choose either to progress or not to progress through a series of stages that he labels "the aesthetic," "the ethical," and "the religious." His respect for individual choices also allows divergent voices to resound clearly and distinctly from a wide range of particular perspectives and in such a way that a singular voice, which purports to speak in the name of the universal, cannot cancel them out. In the vein of Schlegel, he thus scatters here and there throughout his writings aesthetic insights that are unsystematically arranged at the same time that they are artistically textured and presented from a wide array of individual perspectives.

Kierkegaard's earliest treatment of the aesthetic and ethical stages occurs in his first work, *Either/Or*, a pseudonymous work wherein he assumes the name "Victor Eremita."[219] In this work, Kierkegaard touches on the preliminary role that the dimension of the *aesthetic* plays, but which later appears as a component in the "leap of faith" that propels and transitions one into the "religious stage." However, one cannot yet discern in Eremita's discussion Kierkegaard's more comprehensive view of aesthetics, so all discussions at this point must remain preliminary.

The Aesthetic Stage

The topic of aesthetics, however, is broached by Eremita, who claims to be the editor of the works of an unidentified proponent of the aesthetic view of life (whom he calls "A"), on the one hand,[220] and a proponent of the ethical view of life named Judge William (whom he calls "B"), on the other.[221] The discourses of "A" are comprised of personal reflections, fragments, discourses, letters, and a diary that champion the living of a life motivated by desire and aimed solely at the pursuit of pleasure. In "A's" aesthetic reflections, he discusses musical and literary interpretations of legendary figures, such as Don Juan and Faust.

"A" begins by speaking of the poet's sufferings, which the nonpoet or critic of poetry has no capacity to understand.[222] "Life's supreme and most voluptuous moment of pleasure," "A" stresses, is like that of insects that die in the moment of fertilization—a moment that "is attended by death."[223] Everything human is characterized by the opposition between 1) the desire for an object, and 2) the boredom and melancholy that ensue once the object is possessed.[224] As "A" embarks upon "an ecstatic lecture," he introduces the concept of "regret" as it relates to *Either/Or* kinds of choices.[225] If one marries, says "A," one will regret it; and if one does not marry, one will also regret it.[226] "A" recites a litany of other examples in which one will live to regret whatever decision one makes "for" or "against" something. Regret, "A" believes, is inevitable once a decision is made. In the vein of Solomon in the Book of Ecclesiastes, "A" points out that life lived in pursuit of any goal is vain. The aesthete must therefore live in a state of perpetual indecision and refrain from making choices; for once he decides, his decision will invariably be attended by regret.

"A" proposes here one way of avoiding any form of entrapment in the Hegelian dialectic with its thesis and antithesis. If one does not choose, then he will not have posited a *thesis* (or starting principle) that must inevitably encounter its *antithesis*. The aesthete, therefore, *must not live dialectically.* Rather, he must stand always poised on the *precipice* before the "*Either/Or*," a precipice from which he must perpetually refrain from leaping. His life must also be lived in *aeterno modo* (the mode of eternity) this being a mode that is always *before* or *prior to* the *Either/Or* and not *behind* it or *following* it.[227]

"A" in *Either/Or* extensively discusses Don Juan as the *sensual aesthete* who opposes the spirit at all costs.[228] Don Juan, says "A," is an "expression of the demonic specified as the sensual."[229] His *love* does not flow from the soul but from *pure sensuality.* Such love is *faithless* because it seduces all and exists only in the moment. The seductive aims of the sensual aesthete are preoccupied with *sheer quantity.* Don Juan, for instance, can seduce 1,003 women in Spain alone without making a single commitment.[230] "A" considers a number of interpretations of the character of Don Juan, but out of all of them, he argues that Mozart, in his opera *Don Giovanni*, best captured the essence of Don Juan's character. The art of seduction is superlatively reflected through *music*; for music, like the comings and goings of Don Juan, *happens in the moment.*[231] Music seduces the listener and then vanishes until it is played again.[232] "A," for this reason, rejects all interpretations—such as those of Molière and Lord Byron—that try to make Don Juan reflective.[233] If Don Juan lives in the moment, "A" argues, then how could he be reflective?[234] Don Juan's seductiveness, like champagne, effervesces and bubbles.[235] Like wine, he seduces and intoxicates. His figure can never be serious. It must always be comic.[236] Here, Kierkegaard links the idea of *comedy* to the *aesthetic* stage, but the element of the tragic cannot yet be linked to it. For tragedy to be possible, the element of the ethical must first be introduced,[237] and Kierkegaard introduces it with the figure of *Faust*.[238]

In *Either/Or,* Victor Eremita next transitions his discussion from the *sensual* aesthete to the *spiritual* aesthete. Victor Eremita cites Faust as representative of the latter because he has in him the *category of spirit*.[239] Faust's contract with Mephistopheles is evidence of his spiritual interest, for Faust quests to know the secrets of the universe. Faust therefore operates on a spiritual level that is higher than the one on which Don Juan operates. Thus, unlike Don Juan, he does not try to seduce *many* women but aims instead to seduce only *one*—the innocent and pure Margrete (Gretchen).[240]

Since Faust's method of seduction is spiritual, he is plagued by doubt in a way that the sensual seducer is not. He suffers doubt because the art of spiritual seduction is riskier than sensual seduction. It is riskier, first, because of the amount of time needed to weave a web to entrap the victim; and second, because it entails a conquest of one victim alone and of no other.[241] Besides facing doubt, the spiritual seducer also faces the prospect of boredom.[242] A main objective, therefore, is to forestall boredom by fashioning highly creative and interesting schemes of seduction. Here, Faust's seduction is again unlike the kind Don Juan engages in, for the latter's seduction is neither carefully planned nor craftily executed. Instead, it is based upon the genius of sheer sensuality and momentary pleasure. Faust, by contrast, engages in elaborately and imaginatively devised schemes of deception.[243] By means of speech, which is his primary instrument of seduction, he weaves lies that are intended to deceive and to entrap.[244] Insofar as it must be carefully planned and meticulously implemented, Faust's seduction takes time. He does not mind this, however, for he finds his pleasure not so much in the *accomplishment* of seduction as in the *art* of seduction itself. Faust fails nonetheless to achieve happiness through his art of seduction because his reflective nature causes him to experience subjective guilt and despair over his mistreatment of Margrete.

In *Either/Or,* "A" concludes his section with the diary of a seducer named Johannes. Johannes, I suggest, represents a synthesis of Don Juan and Faust, for he combines the *sensual* and *spiritual* aspects of the two others in his art of seduction.[245] Like Faust, Johannes is calculating and reflective. However, unlike Faust, his reflective nature does not catapult him into an experience of subjective guilt, regret, and remorse.[246] Instead, Johannes has managed, like Don Juan, to live in the moment; though, unlike Don Juan, he does so *reflectively* rather than *immediately*. Johannes the Seducer manages to achieve this balance by refusing to allow his spirit to become emotionally entangled in a commitment. He simply does not choose but lives on the *precipice* before the *Either/Or* and the choice it calls upon one to make.

The Ethical Stage

In the next section of *Either/Or*, Kierkegaard's Victor Eremita transitions from the aesthetic papers of "A" to the ethical responses of Judge William ("B").[247] "B," however, does not abandon the topic of the aesthetic but appeals to ethics as a means of contextualizing the aesthetic dimension. Rejecting "A's" philosophy of seduction, "B" argues in favor of marriage as the ethical means that not only preserves the aesthetic experience of erotic love but also elevates that experience.

In part two of *Either/Or*, "B" scolds "A" in a fatherly way for being like an unbroken horse. By not submitting to the reins, "B" contends, "A" raises above his head the scourge of an overpowering fate.[248] "B" rebukes "A" for sarcastically taunting and making a mockery of marriage and claims that "A's" life will consist of nothing but approach runs.[249] "B" maintains that "A" hides in a dreamy, love-intoxicated clairvoyance while weaving all around himself the finest spider's web by which to entrap his victim.[250] "B" cautions that "A's" life is passing and warns him that the time will come when his life must draw to a close. "A" will then find no further ways out in life but will only be left with *recollection*.[251] This recollection that remains, however, will not consist of the intoxicating mixture of poesy and truth. Instead, it will contain the serious and faithful recollection of *conscience*. This recollection, "B" warns, may not unfold into a personal record of genuine crimes. Rather, it will unfurl a remembrance of wasted possibilities and phantom images that are impossible to chase away.[252] "B" continues by warning that "A" will look back over his life, recognize the whole of it as tragic, and forthwith be catapulted into regret and lamentation.[253]

Because "A" tries to live *before* the choice demanded by the *Either/Or*, "B" claims that "A" represents the epitome of possibility; viz., the possibility of his own ruin and of his own salvation.[254] By avoiding commitment, "A" will never experience the aesthetic element in marriage called *love*. *Lust* is not the same as love because lust does not bear the stamp of the eternal.[255] Even in Romantic literature, says Kierkegaard, love is put to work fighting hard-hearted fathers, ogres, and monsters, albeit love in this type of literature is put to work in a purely *external* way.[256]

To bring about the true eternity of love, "B" argues, there must be a determination of the will through an act of freedom.[257] In such cases, the free act expresses itself not in the *external* (as in the case of person's living in the aesthetic stage). Rather, free will is an *internal* determinative power that issues into a free act.[258] At this point, we can detect how Kierkegaard's distinction between the aesthetic and the ethical both correlates with and departs from Hegel's nature-spirit dialectic. For Hegel, nature represents limit, while spirit is the principle of freedom that permeates nature and transforms it. However, once spirit has accomplished its transformation of the external reality of nature, spirit is objectified and, hence, no longer free to make further determinations. The opposite is the case with Kierkegaard, who focuses on the transformation of the *internal* self as it encounters external reality. The aesthetic, for Kierkegaard, does not represent *limitation* (as it does for Hegel) but *possibility*. Moreover, the *ethical* for Kierkegaard does not represent *possibility* (as for Hegel) but *self-limitation*.

Here also, Kierkegaard presents a concept of the "existential self" that is an alternative to earlier philosophical characterizations of the self in terms of "nature," "essence," or "substance." This free determination of the will involves the forward movement of what Kierkegaard calls "repetition," which is a "forward recollection" that is opposite from the backward movement involved in aesthetic "recollection."[259] With aesthetic recollection, one can only remember the first experience of erotic love. Such an experience, however, remains unrepeatable no matter how much the aesthete may try to recapture it through his endless diversions and erotic exploits. For "B," the aesthete therefore has no self because he lacks the unity and continuity of existence that ethical commitment insures.[260] Therefore, marriage has the power to transform and elevate the aesthetic in an ethical way.

On the one hand, marriage ideally presupposes love, for it incorporates the "pagan move" of "being in love," which is the aesthetic element that is taken up into marriage. On the other hand, marriage also involves what "B" calls "the Christian move," which involves the will's act of commitment.[261] This is the ethical component that takes up the aesthetic into itself. Only through commitment can true transformation be accomplished, because the commitment of will involves from the first the promise of the future, and it entails a propulsive infinite that is expressed in terms of constant unfolding and rejuvenation.[262] This "first love," instead of *recollecting* the past in a purely aesthetic way, constantly *reaffirms* itself in the present. This kind of love entails "the unity of freedom and necessity";[263] for at the same time the person feels himself irresistibly drawn to the other, he feels freedom in being irresistibly drawn. Such love is also the unity of the universal and the singular, but not in such a way that the singular, having been taken up into the universal, is annulled by it. Rather, it is the universal *as* the singular, for the universal (love) is immediately experienced by the *individual*.[264]

Married love has its conflict, its victory, and its blessings in time, but it cannot be understood in terms of a simple progression in which what was there originally is automatically preserved.[265] It is, rather, a growing progression in which what was originally present increases. In married love, aesthetic recollection becomes wedded to hope. Married love, therefore, does not merely seek to recapture the past, but through repetition it progresses forward toward the future. Because it seeks only to recapture the past, aesthetic love fades, while the aesthetic value of married love increases because of repetition. "B" realizes, however, that repetition must not be confused with "habit," for this word denotes uniformity, total uneventfulness, and incessant vacuity.[266]

"B" suggests that repetition in one respect should be more on the order of mystical experience than mundane habit, though it should not lose respect for tangible reality as mysticism so often does. "B" thinks that mystical experience is misguided because it does not choose the ethical.[267] Indeed, one can only choose the ethical through acts of repentance. Through repentant acts, the one who chooses becomes concrete, and it is only as a concrete individual that one is also a free individual.[268] The mystic "repents" only metaphysically by *running away* from the world.[269] In doing so, the mystic also only *chooses himself.* The one who repents ethically, on the other hand, *chooses himself back into the world* after he chooses himself out of it.[270] His choice is concrete. Instead of seeing possibilities everywhere as the aesthete does, the person who lives ethically sees tasks everywhere. This gives the person who lives ethically a sense of security that the person living aesthetically altogether lacks. As living aesthetically inevitably leads to despair, despair can either remain as a permanent breech or become the occasion for metamorphosis for the one who chooses ethically. Only when life is regarded ethically does it acquire beauty, truth, meaning, and security.[271]

The Religious Stage

"B's" preoccupation with the "ethical stage" does not, however, satisfy Kierkegaard's full development of the dialectic of the self, for the ethical stage itself may present an obstacle if it fails to transition to what Kierkegaard designates "the religious stage." Indeed, the ethical stage is an intermediate stage between the aesthetic and the religious. The transition from the ethical to the religious is briefly introduced in *Either/Or* in the form of a sermon delivered by a priest in Jutland's barren heaths. The priest, who is a friend of Judge William, argues that "no one is right before God."[272] In *Stages on Life's Way*, the subject is further explored when the question "Guilty/or not guilty?" is raised.[273] The ethical thinker considers the aesthete to be "guilty" and himself to be "not guilty." However, the priest's sermon reveals that even the ethical thinker cannot think of himself as "right" before God, since that thinker's sense of ethical rightness can very easily lure him into the sin of pride. Before the holiness of God, all stand guilty. For this reason, despair flows from the life of the one who has made the ethical stage final and all-encompassing just as it does from the life of one stuck in the aesthetic stage.

The concept of the religious stage is fully developed by Kierkegaard's pseudonymous character Johannes de Silentio in *Fear and Trembling*;[274] and it is further developed in *Stages on Life's Way* by another pseudonymous character, Frater Taciturnus.[275] Silentio and Taciturnus are obviously meant

to be parallel personas for Kierkegaard, because their names are both syno-
nyms for "silence." Silentio introduces Abraham as one who is commanded
by God to sacrifice the son whom he loves with his whole heart.[276] In this
act, Abraham is faced with a horrific choice that violates the ethical injunc-
tion against murder. What renders God's requirement even more horrific is
the degree to which Abraham loves Isaac. Abraham is faced with a personal
dilemma: Obeying God's command will wholly violate the *aesthetic* sense
by bringing him unimaginable pain.[277] But Abraham is also faced with an
ethical dilemma: By obeying God's command to sacrifice Isaac, Abraham
risks becoming a murderer.[278] Furthermore, Abraham is faced with a *religious* dilemma: By not obeying God, he will fail to become a "knight of faith."
To become a knight of faith, Abraham must therefore risk murdering
Isaac.[279]

In *Fear and Trembling*, Abraham must, through "infinite resignation,"
show that he is willing to enter into what Silentio calls "a teleological suspension of the ethical." The idea of "suspension" here actually runs contrary
to the concept of repetition that is such an important mark of the ethical
stage. Indeed, "suspension" is more a characteristic of the *aesthetic* stage
than it is of the ethical stage, for with the aesthetic stage, possibility never
gives way to actuality. The teleological "suspension" of the ethical on Abraham's part, however, *does not* result in inaction by remaining only in the
realm of possibility.[280] Resignation on Abraham's part is not enough, for
God also requires the action of faith when he requires Abraham to sacrifice
his son.

Because entrance into the religious stage requires a *teleological suspension of the ethical* as well as a *leap of faith*, Silentio reveals that the religious
stage transcends the ethical stage. Indeed, the religious stage represents a
different kind of synthesis of the ethical and the aesthetic stages, for the
religious stage recaptures aspects of the aesthetic stage that the ethical stage
had too rigidly suppressed.[281] At the same time, the religious stage requires
"repetition" like the ethical stage, but its repetition is the repetition of *faith*,
and not the repetition of *frail and sinful human effort*. In the religious stage,
Kierkegaard also achieves a synthesis of the *tragic* and the *comic*, which is a
synthesis that is parallel to the synthesis of the *ethical* and the *aesthetic*
stages.[282] Abraham is one representative of this tragicomic synthesis. In his
story, the tragic element is preserved in the horrific fate that haunts Abraham
and Isaac and to the pain Abraham experiences in having to carry out the
horrendous divine command to sacrifice his son. The comic element, on the
other hand, is revealed in the outcome, in which God provides a ram to be
sacrificed in Isaac's stead. The story of Abraham thus represents a way that
the tragic and comic elements of human experience may be united. This
uniting is not, however, *logical*, but in many ways it defies logic. Kierkegaard expresses the union of the tragic and the comic through his use of the

concept of irony, for irony becomes manifest when the *expected* is invaded by the *unexpected*, and *closed* perspectives become *open* to a God who *surprises*.[283]

THE CHRISTIAN VIRTUES AS MEDIATORS OF PARADOXICAL TRANSCENDENCE

Kierkegaard's emphasis upon the infinite qualitative distinction between God and the world in one important respect can rescue the Christian virtues of faith, hope, and love from entrapment in overly dialectical categories and free them to become maximally opened to the dimension of paradoxical transcendence. But having been freed from dialectical constraints, these virtues must not then become entrapped in the purely interior dimension of human subjectivity. Catholic theologian Hans Urs von Balthasar observes that such relegations of aesthetics to inward subjectivity is a hallmark of Reformation thought harking back to Luther himself, who insisted that God's revelation was most intensely expressed in its opposite; namely, in its veiledness.[284] Because of Luther's paradoxical focus, in which he rejected Thomas Aquinas' "theology of glory" in favor of a "theology of the cross," von Balthasar observes that the progression of aesthetic thinking in Protestantism came to an either/or crossroads.[285] On the one hand, aesthetics was eliminated from theology by means of the dialectical system, which, like that of Hegel, conceived of God's exteriorizing of himself in nothingness only to adopt that nothingness back into himself.[286] On the other hand, what von Balthasar calls a "paradoxical 'aestheticization' of theology" would logically bring about a "new and sweeping iconoclastic controversy."[287] Von Balthasar credits Kierkegaard with the *banishing* of aesthetics from nineteenth-century theology, for though Kierkegaard had achieved a meeting of religion and aesthetics in *Either/Or*, he finally accomplished the eradication of the aesthetic element from religion in *Stages on Life's Way* by sharply distinguishing "the apostle" and "the martyr of truth" from the "genius" and by making a severe distinction between *agape* as Christian love and *eros* as sensual human love.[288]

At this point, Kierkegaard's insights on aesthetics must be judged as too one-sided insofar as they focus on the interiority of human subjectivity to the exclusion of how the aesthetic dimension can be validly exteriorized. Likewise, the Christian virtues must not be imprisoned in human subjectivity but must be exteriorized by reflecting them back into the concrete world where they will become embodied through language and action. The Christian virtues in this way can serve as vehicles that dialectically mediate paradoxical transcendence into the fullest possible range of the tangible dimension of human experience. Paradoxical transcendence can then be understood in terms of a divine purpose and a divine meaning that, though unified paradox-ically in the dimension of the Infinite, are experienced in an interior, subjec-tive way by finite sentient beings in terms of the *mysterium tremendum et fascinans*, on the one hand, and are exteriorized in terms of ethical and aesthetic language and action, on the other.

At the beginning of this chapter, I discussed Aristotle's account of the cardinal virtues. Now I will appeal to the insights of Kierkegaard and attempt to counterbalance his insights by considering the critique of von Balthasar in order to consider the views of the one theologian against whose theological perspectives Luther most harshly reacted; namely, *St. Thomas Aquinas*. Lu-ther's belief that the image and likeness of God in man was lost because of the fall precludes him from presenting a fair account of how pre-Christian philosophers such as Aristotle could have developed any concept of virtue in the first place.[289] His bias against Aristotle is clear,[290] and it extends to his opinion concerning Aquinas as well. For the sake of balance and fairness, I must therefore examine Aquinas' insights on the relation of the classical virtues to the theological virtues.

Specifically, how did Aquinas treat the three Christian or theological virtues in relation to Aristotle's view? (See figure 6.6.) To contextualize what Aquinas understands the relationship between the four classical and three Christian virtues to be, I will first consider how Aquinas contrasted and compared the image of God and the likeness of God in man. His contrast and comparison reveal that the divine likeness is superior to, and more compre-hensive in its essence and perfection than, the divine image.[291] Indeed, not only is the likeness compared to the image as the genus is to a species, but the likeness serves both as the preamble to the image and as a consequent to it.[292] Aquinas thus understands the likeness to be the *perfection* of the divine image.[293] The divine likeness is, moreover, the repository of the three Chris-tian virtues of faith, hope, and love, which together constitute the superadded gift (*donum superadditum*) that Adam possessed prior to his fall. Therefore, Adam *in a sense* possessed all the virtues.[294] Aquinas, however, qualifies this *sense* by pointing out that some virtues, such as love and justice, do not admit imperfection since imperfection is inconsistent with the perfection of man's prefallen state.[295] Faith, hope, and love thus exist in the prefallen state with respect to *habit*, though not with respect to *act*; for *acts* of penance and mercy already presuppose the fallenness of human beings who are in need of repentance or who are in need of mercy. Since the perfection of Adam is summed up in the idea of habit, Aquinas sees how it is possible to speak of Adam as both innocent and perfect; though this perfection is one of degree lying somewhere midway between man's present fallen state and the eschat-ological state in which the beatific vision will be enjoyed.[296]

The sin of Adam, however, effectuates the loss of the superadded gift, along with a loss of the habitual possession of the virtues of faith, hope, and

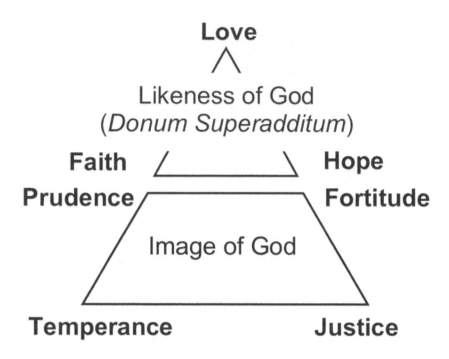

Figure 6.6. Aquinas's Configuration of the Virtues.

love. Consequently, the fall also results in the loss of the divine likeness. Aquinas considers the *image of God*, on the other hand, to be intact after the fall of Adam, with the image serving as the repository of the *four cardinal virtues*—prudence, fortitude, temperance, and justice.[297] Even fallen human beings thus remained capable of exercising the *cardinal* virtues. However, fallen humans were incapable of exercising the theological virtues apart from the restoration of the *donum superadditum* through salvation in Christ. Still, this restoration does not occur completely all at once but requires the process of sanctification.

In further distinguishing himself from Aristotle, Aquinas also makes a distinction between (1) Aristotle's idea of *eudaimonia* as an intrinsic end attainable through natural principles that entail the cultivation of the four cardinal virtues, and (2) the happiness surpassing human nature—supernatural happiness—that one can only receive by the power of God alone and eventually culminates in one's participation in the Godhead.[298] Thus, whereas the four cardinal virtues are cultivated by means of *habit*, the three theological virtues are not cultivated by human natural powers but are *God-infused*. Together, the theological virtues constitute the avenue that leads the Christian to eventual participation in the Divine.[299] Of the three theological virtues, love stands as the perfect virtue. As such, it is the root of faith and hope; though, when viewed from a different angle, faith and hope are also the precursors of love. [300]

Aquinas's view of the virtues fits neatly into his Aristotelian version of Neoplatonism. It also allows for some fluidity between categories, especially in the temporal way that the image of God grows over time into the divine likeness. I think, however, that the *fluid* and *dynamic* relationship between the Christian and cardinal virtues remains to too great a degree restricted by the overly *formalistic* categories he imports from the Aristotelian and Neo-platonic traditions. This restriction makes me think that Aquinas simply stacked the Christian virtues on top of the cardinal virtues. His formalistic approach in this way precludes an adequate exploration of the way that Christian virtues might relate to the more *dynamic* aspects of the human soul, such as *libertarian freedom*. In Aquinas's view, faith appears as something the human being receives *in addition* to his freedom, not as an *expression* or *mode* of freedom itself. Aquinas, I think, succumbs to a category mistake here that is unfortunate, because faith seems to become for him an element completely foreign to present human nature until it is infused into human nature supernaturally.

I thus shall need to ask a couple of questions here: "Is faith a *component wholly separate* from human freedom that is given to humans as a gift *added to* that freedom?" or "Does faith represent God's rehabilitation and redirec-tion of a human freedom already possessed as an innate capacity?" I believe that in one sense, faith should be emphasized as entailing both these alterna-tives. However, understanding faith as a *rehabilitating* of human freedom and a *redirecting* of that freedom toward the Infinite would help us better understand what *kind* of gift faith entails. To illustrate, faith as a gift given *in addition* to freedom could perhaps be likened to the gift of crutches presented to a lame person. The crutches may help the lame person to walk, but they remain an *added* external aid. Faith as the *rehabilitation* and *redirecting* of freedom toward the Infinite, on the other hand, would entail something more on the order of the gift of healing itself, whereby the lame person's ability to walk is fully restored. Here the gift is characterized not as an external ena-bling, but as an internal one. Faith could be thus understood as a rehabilita-tion, restoration, and redirection of libertarian freedom as it reaches out to the true Infinite. I must, however, proceed to explain what such a rehabilitation, restoration, and redirection might entail.

First, the causes that disable libertarian freedom are those that result in the bondage of the will, as Martin Luther observed. [301] Bondage occurs when libertarian freedom directs its trust toward and bonds itself to aspects of the dimension of the finite, and it does so to the extent that its trust in and its bonding to finitude imprisons freedom. On the religious level, this phenome-non is called *idolatry*, while on the practical level it is characterized by bondage to sinful patterns of behavior that become fueled by compulsions and obsessions and are driven by addictions. When, for instance, libertarian freedom directs its energies towards the unbridled pursuit of pleasure or power, the will can become turned in upon itself to the extent that it becomes spiritually paralyzed. Initially, the deception that accompanies idolatry and human behavioral choices provides a kind of tentative justification of one's excessive pursuit of pleasure or power. This deception hides from one's view the consequences normally associated with the kind of lifestyle the seeker after pleasure or power pursues.

Deception gradually gives way to habit, habit to addiction, and addiction to entrapment. These consequences reveal eventually that the original justification of one's lifestyle was in error. Libertarian freedom consequently becomes dysfunctional, and one cannot escape what in effect has become a prison of one's own making. However, the realization that this is a self-made prison often comes too late to offer help of escape. At this late stage, cognitive enlightenment will usually do little if any good; for the person will find himself caught firmly in the grip of an addiction from which he has already suffered disablement.

Nothing short of a rehabilitation of libertarian freedom can make escape from this kind of paralysis possible, and this rehabilitation can only be extended from the Transcendent by the issuing of *grace*. *Grace*, which belongs to the categories of the *beautiful* and the *sublime*, bathes the immoral person with its healing properties. It regenerates, rehabilitates, and restores libertarian freedom by breaking down the walls of the prisons that are built out of the stones and bars of idolatrous deception and addictions to immorality. The beauty of grace restores the moral and opens channels to the Infinite from whom continued grace will flow. Faith, as the medium or conduit through which this grace flows, is thus not alien to libertarian freedom. Rather, it is a special mode of libertarian freedom that, having been transformed, becomes redirected toward and reconnected to the Infinite.

Here, the virtue of faith appears to differ from the cardinal virtues of Aristotle in one important respect; and the kind of virtue that faith exemplifies applies to the virtues of hope and love as well. Whereas the cardinal virtues have *limit* as their regulating principle, the Christian virtues employ *libertarian freedom* as the channel through which divine transcendence is mediated. This transcendence then sustains and feeds the very virtues through which it is mediated.

The Christian virtue of hope, like faith, serves as a channel that mediates divine transcendence. Hope promises a means past obstacles that limit human progress. Therefore, it is fitting that the resurrection of Jesus in Christian theology serves as the foundation for the virtue of hope because his resurrection reveals the overcoming of the most formidable obstacle that any human being can face; namely, the obstacle of *death*. Hope, by assuring that the obstacle of death will be surmounted, assures by extension that all other obstacles that exist between Infinite God and finite man will be surmounted as well, so that a human being's participation in divine transcendence becomes assured.

Like faith, hope channels the divine transcendence through human libertarian freedom, but faith differs from hope in several important regards. First, whereas faith links with divine transcendence in the *present* moment, hope links with divine transcendence as a *future* certainty. Since faith links with God's transcendence in the present moment, it must accept the reality of the distance that now exists between the divine purpose and the tangible dimension of human existence with all its dialectical conflicts. *Faith*, however, by accepting the divine purpose, discerns and imagines how that purpose can direct tangible human existence in beneficial ways. *Hope*, meanwhile, inspires and incentivizes persons to adjust their own purposes in such a way that these will coincide with the divine purpose. So, while *faith* focuses on how the divine purpose *rectifies* and *redirects* human purposes so that they correspond to that purpose, *hope* focuses on how the divine purpose eventually *will prevail* over every obstacle.

Faith also differs from hope in a second respect. *Faith*, in linking human libertarian freedom to the divine purpose, emphasizes the *causal* aspect that human libertarian freedom now shares with the *divine purpose* in *its* causal aspect. Since faith is the vehicle through which humans are enabled to connect with the causal aspect of the divine purpose, this further implies that human *action* will be brought into concert with the divine action. With both the divine purpose and human free will, however, this causal aspect is *personal* rather than *impersonal.* Thus, while faith in the causal sense is an *active* virtue, the linking of human *libertarian freedom* as a causal agent to the transcendent freedom of God as a causal agent makes faith *personal* as well. The *freedom* of God as a causal agent is, furthermore, implied in the *Judeo-Christian understanding* of the divine purpose as *personal* rather than *impersonal.* Faith, therefore, entails a commitment and reliance of the total *personhood* of *human individuals* upon the *personhood of God.*

In contrast to faith, the virtue of hope has its basis more in the *effects* that the divine purpose realizes rather than the divine purpose in its *causal* aspect. Hope is thus based upon ways that the divine purpose is repeatedly vindicated through history despite all oppositions to that purpose. Insofar as they are *effects* of the divine purpose, these episodes of vindication lend credibility to the conviction that the divine purpose will also be vindicated as well. As is the case with the virtue of faith, the *effects* of the divine purpose are personal in the same way its *causal* aspects are personal. The effects, therefore, are not *impersonal* and *mechanistic*, as, for instance, the way that effects appear impersonal and mechanistic in the outworking of karmic law.

The elevation of effect to the dimension of the personal thus becomes apparent not only when the vindication of the divine purpose entails *redemption* but also when the vindication of the divine purpose entails *judgment*. In both respects, hope is the *guarantor* that ultimate vindication will be realized and that final justice will be accomplished. Furthermore, hope as vindication assures that one will, at a future time, participate in a dimension of transcendent life that extends beyond a world where the cycles of life and death seem forever fixed, closed, and impossible to escape. To accept such a closed, cyclical world as final is to embrace fatalism, but hope remedies this worldview by offering an escape from fate's entrapment. Hope offers the opportunity to reverse the closure that fate accepts and offers the assurance that inescapable and closed cycles, which are so characteristic of tangible existence, do not represent the final state of things. Instead, hope provides a means of seeing beyond what seems a final closure toward which tangible existence points and of glimpsing the divine transcendence beyond the veil of tangibility. The resurrection of Jesus reveals in a superlative way how divine purpose blasts open the door of finality that death has slammed shut and fashions it into a gateway to the life everlasting.

Of all the Christian virtues, however, *love* stands as supreme. The Apostle Paul portrays love as the summation of the other Christian virtues.[302] It represents a summation because love "*believes* all things" and "*hopes* all things."[303] Love thus takes faith and hope up into itself. Faith and hope, as partial virtues, are in this way completed by love. Indeed, regarding love as the transcendental virtue that eternally endures, it represents the *perfection* of all virtue.[304] Thus, when love, as that which is perfect, comes then that which is partial shall be done away with. Love represents a *transcendentally* oriented virtue that mediates the purest form of infinite divine meaning.

Love is simultaneously the *most sacrificial* of all the virtues and the *freest*. Like faith and hope, the virtue of love transforms libertarian freedom into the channel through which infinite divine meaning is mediated into the dimension of the tangible. Love, as the highest of all virtues, connects the divine purpose to the divine meaning. In so doing, it weds the ethical and the aesthetic so that they operate dialectically within the tangible dimension of existence in ways that are maximally beneficial for the survival and flourishing of human life, individually as well as collectively. In the realm of paradoxical transcendence, on the other hand, love joins together the dimension of the moral and the dimension of the beautiful, harmonizing them in a way that may be best described as *ecstatic*. What is commonly called "the beatific vision" expresses well the idea of blessedness entailed in this state of ecstasy.

How, then, do the cardinal virtues relate to the Christian virtues? Do they differ to such a degree that they have nothing in common? Do they correlate and intersect at points? On the one hand, the Christian virtues may first appear to contradict the cardinal virtues. For instance, the *leap of faith* may be viewed from the standpoint of the virtue of prudence as an *imprudent* action. The virtue of *courage*, too, normally operates in such a way that it actively opposes evil; however, martyrs for the Christian faith, though seemingly courageous, hardly exhibited courage in the way Aristotle prescribed. Courage in the Aristotelian sense may motivate one to be *willing* to sacrifice oneself. Still, this willingness can hardly be thought to extend to an *active embrace* of sacrifice in the way that Christian love actively embraces it. In addition, justice as Aristotle understood it does not line up well at all with Jesus' words, "Father, forgive them, for they know not what they do."[305] If anything, Jesus' utterance suggests that he might have been complicitous with those engaged in the very act of crucifying him. If anything, the sacrificial love that Jesus demonstrates appears foreign to the Aristotelian understanding of justice, and especially to the notion of *retributive* or *corrective* justice. Furthermore, when persons are moved by the virtue of love to make sacrifices to care for those whom life has treated unfairly, such sacrifices appear to violate Aristotle's emphasis upon the principle of *proportionality* toward which distributive justice as a virtue should aim. Grace, like love, is also *undeserved*: It is not given based on what is *merely deserved*. Joy, as the fruit of Christian hope, is also too emotionally exuberant to match well Aristotle's virtue of temperance, for joy is too excessive. Consequently, the hope that produces joy must be held suspect, too.

In certain respects, the Christian virtues thus reveal the *incompleteness* of the cardinal virtues. The cardinal virtues, being governed by the principle of *limit*, will never find a legitimate reason to go the extra mile. The Christian virtues, on the other hand, will always do so. Paul Ricoeur expresses this when he refers to the "logic of superabundance." The words of Jesus, "Father forgive them for they know not what they do," seem to violate the "logic of equivalence" that one finds in such a statement as "an eye for an eye and a tooth for a tooth." Still, the "logic of superabundance" is not illogical. Rather, it contains a transcendental element that reason simply cannot pin down. If anything, reason resigns itself and reduces itself to silence in the face of the transcendental goodness that the "logic of superabundance" mediates.[306]

I maintain here that the Aristotelian virtues are more *impersonal* than the Christian virtues, and this means that they are perhaps more effective in creating general guidelines for fostering polite behavior within a greater society. The Christian virtues, on the other hand, are *maximally personal* in that they are channeled through individual libertarian freedom. This means that they are incapable of being legislated in the same way that moral laws based upon the principle of limit are legislated. The Christian virtues, being exercised through voluntary freedom, are best inculcated through inspiration and persuasion, not through coercive attempts to modify behavior. This distinction between the way Christian and cardinal virtues are inculcated may help explain why societies as a whole cannot "turn the other cheek" in the way individuals separately can do. Only voluntary aggregates can attempt to do such. Since churches are social units formed through voluntary associations, these come closest to accomplishing a *collective* practicing of the Christian virtues, but this differs greatly from collective efforts to force society to conform to certain ethical standards by legislating edicts and enforcing them. When churches do try to legislate and enforce the higher ideals of Christian morality, they invariably fall short of success; however, when they embody the Christian virtues through their lives and actions, they influence others by means of inspiration. Unfortunately, Christians often experience the cognitive dissonance of trying to straddle two spheres in which they are trying to maximize good and minimize evil. There often is very little choice but to embrace this dissonance and to effect as much of a reconciliation between the two spheres as possible.

There are also ways in which the cardinal and Christian virtues can be integrated. Prudence can inform and temper faith so that faith does not become synonymous with mania. Hope can help foster courage by providing it with a transcendental basis. Temperance can add the element of discipline to love and prepare it to become sacrificial. Justice can help to anchor love and keep it from sliding into pure sentimentality. The discipline that comes through the practice of the cardinal virtues can prepare one to become more effectual in exercising the Christian virtues. The exercise of the Christian virtues, on the other hand, can keep the practice of the cardinal virtues from becoming too routine and mechanical.

JOINING LANGUAGE AND ACTION

We find numerous examples in the foregoing discussion of how the integration and the reconciliation of the virtues make possible the mediation of value through virtue-guided actions. The mode of these actions is both ethical and aesthetic, and the virtues that guide these actions and mediate value through them are the four cardinal virtues and the three Christian virtues. The cardinal virtues I have discussed, of course, represent a minimum, for this realm can be extended to include Aristotle's other virtues, such as magnanimity and generosity. Value itself is mediated through virtues as they guide persons to engage in ethical and aesthetic action. This value itself entails the dimensions of the moral and the beautiful, and these dimensions have their ultimate origin in paradoxical transcendence experienced in terms of the *mysterium tremendum et fascinans*. The art and skill needed for the practice of the virtues, of course, must be developed within and be purposively and meaningfully related to a context that the full range of the value-compass provides. The same, of course, is true of language; for language best mediates value when it is contextualized in the light of the value-compass's full range.

At this point, I believe we ought to make every effort to join language and action. On the one hand, language without action resembles seed cast on barren ground. That is, language divorced from action tends to be sterile and ineffectual. The embodiment of *Logos* in language alone is therefore only a partial embodiment, and as such it lacks both moral force and aesthetic appeal. On the other hand, action apart from language risks drifting into purposelessness and meaninglessness, for action that separates itself from the light of the *Logos* or refuses to follow the Ariadne thread that the *Logos* provides can come to resemble the actions of directionless rats running through a dark maze. Language and action together, however, can mutually support one another, for whereas action gives language authenticity and saves it from becoming a tool of hypocrisy, language has the capacity to infuse action with moral and aesthetic truth.

NOTES

1. Aristot. Nic. Eth. 1.4.2. *Eudaimonia* translates "well-being." It refers not just to *emotional* happiness but to *happiness regarding one's total estate.*
2. Aristot. Nic. Eth. 1.7.1095b1.
3. Aristot. Nic. Eth. 1.1.1094a1–4.
4. Aristot. Nic. Eth. 2.1.1103b3.
5. Aristot. Nic. Eth. 2.6.1106b13–14.
6. Aristot. Nic. Eth. 2.6.1106b14–15.
7. Aristot. Nic. Eth. 2.1.1103b1.
8. Aristot. Nic. Eth. 2.2.1104a6–7. Excess and deficiency impair and destroy virtue, just as too much or too little exercise impairs health.
9. Aristot. Nic. Eth. 2.7.1104a2.
10. Aristot. Nic. Eth. 2.7.1104b3.
11. Aristot. Nic. Eth. 2.3.1104a2–2.3.1104b4.
12. Aristot. Nic. Eth. 3.12.1119a1.
13. Aristot. Nic. Eth. 3.12.1119a2.
14. Aristot. Nic. Eth. 3.10.1118a9–11.
15. Aristot. Nic. Eth. 3.11.1119a5–8.
16. Aristot. Nic. Eth. 5.1.1129b15–19.
17. Aristot. Nic. Eth. 5.1.1129b19.
18. Aristot. Nic. Eth. 5.1.1129b20.
19. Aristot. Nic. Eth. 5.1.1129b15.
20. Aristot. Nic. Eth. 5.2.1130b8.
21. Aristot. Nic. Eth. 5.2.1130b12.
22. Aristot. Nic. Eth. 5.3.1131a4–5.3.1131b7.
23. Aristot. Nic. Eth. 5.4.1132b4–6.
24. "Not every action or emotion however admits of the observance of a due mean. Indeed, the very names of some directly imply evil, for instance malice, shamelessness, envy, and of adultery, theft, murder. All these and similar actions and feelings are blamed as being bad in themselves; it is not the excess or deficiency of them that we blame." Aristot. Nic. Eth. 2.6.18–19, in *The Loeb Classical Library*, Vol. 19, trans. H. Rackham, Cambridge: Harvard University Press (1975), 97. (Bekker numbers 1106b–1107a not included in the Rackham edition.)

25. Aristotle, *Poetics*, trans. Stephen Halliwell, in *Loeb Classical Library* (Cambridge, MA: Harvard University Press, 1995), 1.1447b2–13; 9.1451b 9–10.

26. See Plato, *Republic*, ed. and trans. Christopher Emlyn-Jones and William Preddy, in *Loeb Classical Library* (Cambridge, MA: Harvard University Press, 2013), bk. 10.

27. Aristot. Poet. 9.1451b1–3.

28. Aristot. Poet. 9.1451b1–3.

29. Aristot. Poet. 9.1451b4–8.

30. Aristot. Poet. 4.1448b1–7.

31. Aristot. Poet. 6.1450a19–21.

32. Aristot. Poet. 6.1450a19.

33. Aristot. Poet. 6.1450b28.

34. Aristot. Poet. 6.1449b1–3.

35. Aristot. Poet. 13.1453a5.

36. Aristot. Poet. 6.1449b2–4.

37. Aristot. Poet. 6.1450a12.

38. Aristot. Poet. 13.1453a5–13.

39. Aristot. Poet. 14.1453b1–3.

40. Aristot. Poet. 13.1452a11–12.

41. Aristot. Poet. 13.1452a5–6.

42. *Brahma Sūtra Bhāṣya*, trans. Sri Swami Sivananda (Tehri-Garhwal, Uttarakhand, Himalayas, India: The Divine Life Society, 2008), ch. I, sec. 1, topic 1.

43. See, for example, Shlomo Giora Shoham, *The Measure of All Things: Anthropology* (Newcastle upon Tyne, UK: Cambridge Scholars Publishing, 2013), 123.

44. That is, using a crane or pulley attached to a car to lower a god (Grk=ἀπὸ μηχανῆς θεός; Latin=*Deus ex machina*) or hero who can artificially "cut the knot" of the plot and resolve it. Aristot. Poet. 15.1454a10b–10d.

45. Aristot. Poet. 26.1461b1–26.1462a8.

46. Craig Martin, *Subverting Aristotle: Religion, History, and Philosophy in Early Modern Science* (Baltimore, MD: Johns Hopkins University Press, 2014), 147–48.

47. Matt 7:12.

48. Immanuel Kant, *Groundwork of the Metaphysics of Morals* [hereafter referred to as *GMM*], trans. and ed. Mary Gregor and Jens Timmermann (Cambridge, UK: Cambridge University Press, 2012), 33–34 (4:421). Parenthetical references are to the German–English volume based on the second original edition of 1786.

49. Immanuel Kant, *The Metaphysics of Morals* [hereafter abbreviated as *MM*], trans. Mary Gregor, ed. Lara Denis (Cambridge, UK: Cambridge University Press, 2017), 20 (6:225). Parenthetical references are to *The Metaphysics of Morals*, ed. Paul Natorp in vol. 6 [1907] of the Prussian Academy of Sciences edition of Kant's work.

50. Kant, *GMM*, 14–15 (6:211–213).

51. David Gauthier, *Rousseau: The Sentiment of Existence* (Cambridge: Cambridge University Press, 2008), 9–14.

52. David Hume, *Treatise of Human Nature*, ed. L. A. Selby-Bigge (Oxford: Clarendon, 1888), 2.2.9; 3.1.2; and 3.2.5.

53. *GMM*, 34 (4:421).

54. *GMM*, 17 (6:221–22).

55. *GMM*, 44–45 (4:432–33).

56. Kant, *Critique of Pure Reason*, trans. and ed. Paul Guyer and Allen W. Wood (Cambridge, UK: Cambridge University Press, 1998), 535–37 (A538/B566–A542/B570). ("A" refers to the 1781 German edition of the *Critique* and "B" to the 1787 German edition).

57. That is, the *noumenal* self and not the *empirical* self. See Kant, *Critique of Pure Reason*, 232–34 (A106–11), 236–37 (A115–17), 240–41 (A123–25), and 246–48 (B132–37).

58. *GMM*, 34–35 (4:422); *MM*, 185–88 (6:417–420).

59. *MM*, 187 (6:419).

60. *GMM*, 34–35 (4:422); *MM*, 189–91 (6:421–24).

61. *GMM*, 34–35 (4:422); *MM*, 206 (6:442–43).

62. *GMM*, 35 (4:423–24); *MM*, 163–66 (6:390–93).

63. *GMM*, 36 (4:423); *MM*, 166–67 (6:393–94).

64. *MM*, 167 (6:394).

65. *MM*, 187 (6:419).

66. Kant, *Critique of the Power of Judgment* [hereafter cited as *CJ*], trans. Paul Guyer and Eric Matthews, ed. Paul Guyer (Cambridge: Cambridge University Press, 2000), 55 (5:167). Parenthetical references are from the Academy edition volume and page numbers of Kant's *Gesammelte Schriften*, 29 vols., ed. Königlich Preußischen (Berlin: Walter de Gruyter, 1902).

67. *CJ*, 64 (5:177).

68. *CJ*, 62 (5:174).

69. *CJ*, 62 (5:174–75).

70. *CJ*, 63 (5:175–76).

71. *CJ*, 63 (5:176).

72. *CJ*, 67 (5:179–80).

73. *CJ*, 67 (5:179–80).

74. Kant uses the term aesthetics in the sense set forth by Alexander Gottlieb Baumgarten (1714–1762), who was the first to use the word "aesthetic" regarding the study of good and bad taste. Before this, the word was used to refer to "sensibility" or "sense."

75. *CJ*, 79 (5:193–94).

76. *CJ*, 89–95 (5:203–11), 97–101 (5:212–17), 128–31 (5:244–48).

77. *CJ*, 97 (5:212).

78. *CJ*, 89–90 (5:204–5).

79. *CJ*, 90–91 (5:204–6).

80. *CJ*, 91–95 (5:206–11).

81. *CJ*, 99–100 (5:213–15).

82. *CJ*, 98 (5:212–13).

83. *CJ*, 98 (5:213).

84. *CJ*, 98 (5:213).

85. *CJ*, 167–68 (5:286–87).

86. *CJ*, 105 (5:220).

87. *CJ*, 120 (5:236).

88. *CJ*, 102–3 (5:217–18).

89. *CJ*, 95 (5:209–10).

90. *CJ*, 121 (5:237).

91. *CJ*, 122 (5:238).

92. *CJ*, 123 (5:238–39).

93. Daniel Carey, *Locke, Shaftesbury, and Hutcheson: Contesting Diversity in the Enlightenment and Beyond* (Cambridge: Cambridge University Press, 2006), loc. 48–74 of 4154, Kindle.

94. Carey, *Locke, Shaftesbury, and Hutcheson*, loc. 165–73 of 4154.

95. Carey, *Locke, Shaftesbury, and Hutcheson*, loc. 171–72 of 4154.

96. Dabney Townsend, "From Shaftesbury to Kant: The Development of the Concept of Aesthetic Experience," *Journal of the History of Ideas*, 48, no. 2 (April–June 1987), 287–305.

97. Kant's view, which reduces the sublime to feeling, is countered by C. S. Lewis in *The Abolition of Man* (Oxford: Oxford University Press, 1943), 2–3.

98. *CJ*, 129 (5:245).

99. *CJ*, 129 (5:245).

100. *CJ*, 249 (5:245–46).

101. *CJ*, 249 (5:245–46).

102. *CJ*, 129 (5:246).

103. *CJ*, 129 (5:246).

104. *CJ*, 131 (5:247).

105. *CJ*, 131–32 (5:248–49).

106. *CJ*, 143–44 (5:260–61).

107. *CJ*, 147–48 (5:264).

108. I maintain, however, that the apophatic tradition within Neoplatonism relates more to Kant's understanding of the mathematically sublime than to the dynamically sublime. The

Hebrew tradition, on the other hand, seems to reflect the dynamically sublime to a greater extent.

109. *CJ*, 183 (5:303).

110. *CJ*, 186–87 (5:307–8).

111. *CJ*, 187–88 (5:308–9).

112. *CJ*, 187–89 (5:309–11).

113. *CJ*, 187–89 (5:309–11).

114. *CJ*, 169–70 (5:289).

115. *CJ*, 168–69 (5:287–89).

116. *CJ*, 102 (5:217), 185 (5:306).

117. *CJ*, 173–74 (5:293–94).

118. *CJ*, 197 (5:319).

119. *CJ*, 197 (5:319).

120. Bentham, *Principles of Morals and Legislation* (Oxford: Clarendon, 1907), 3. 2–6.

121. Colin Heydt notes that Mill's transition to a qualitative approach to "the good" was based upon aesthetic concerns that he gleaned from William Wordsworth and John Ruskin. Mill accepts Wordsworth's opposition of poetry to science, in which the *emotive* opposes the *rational*. From Ruskin, Mill inherited the distinction between "agreeableness" and "beauty." Mill was particularly influenced by Ruskin's championing of *moralism* in art. Heydt, *Rethinking Mill's Ethics: Character and Aesthetic Education*, London: Continuum (2006), 15–32.

122. Kant relates the virtues only to the imperfect duties (*MM*, 155–81 [6:397–413]), and, as such, performing them results in merit. However, the transgression of them does not necessarily result in demerit.

123. John Stuart Mill, *A System of Logic Ratiocinative and Inductive: Being a Connected View of the Principles of Evidence and of the Methods of Scientific Investigation*, ed. J. M. Robson, in *The Collected Works of John Stuart Mill*, Vol. 8 (Toronto: University of Toronto Press, [1981] 1974), bk. 6, ch. 12.

124. Mill, *System of Logic*, bk. 6, ch. 12, sec. 1.

125. Mill, *System of Logic*, bk. 6, ch. 12, sec. 4.

126. Mill, *System of Logic*, bk. 6, ch. 12, sec. 4.

127. Mill, *System of Logic*, bk. 6, ch. 12, sec. 6.

128. Mill, *System of Logic*, bk. 6, ch. 12, secs. 1 and 6.

129. Mill, *System of Logic*, bk. 6, ch. 12, secs. 1 and 6.

130. Antis Loizides, "The Socratic Origins of John Stuart Mill's 'Art of Life,'" in *John Stuart Mill: A British Socrates*, ed. Antis Loizides and Kyriakos M. Demetriou (Basingstoke, UK: Palgrave-Macmillan, 2013), 75.

131. Mill, *System of Logic*, bk. 6, ch. 12, sec. 7.

132. Mill, *System of Logic*, bk. 6, ch. 12, sec. 6.

133. Mill, *System of Logic*, bk. 6, ch. 12, sec. 6.

134. Allen W. Wood, *Hegel's Ethical Thought* (Cambridge: Cambridge University Press, 1990), 254.

135. Wood, *Hegel's Ethical Thought*, 254.

136. F. H. Bradley, *Ethical Studies* (Oxford: Oxford University Press, 1970), 160–206.

137. Bradley, *Ethical Studies*, 163–74.

138. Karl Marx and Friedrich Engels, *The German Ideology: Including Theses on Feuerbach and Introduction to the Critique of Political Economy* (Amherst, NY: Prometheus Books, 1998), 52, 69, 97.

139. Arthur Schopenhauer, "On the Vanity and Suffering of Life," in *The Essential Schopenhauer: Key Selections from The World as Will and Representation and Other Works*, ed. Wolfgang Schirmacher (New York: HarperCollins, 2010), 33, Kindle.

140. Schopenhauer, "The Artist and the Sublime," in *The Essential Schopenhauer*, 137. Schopenhauer, "On the Metaphysics of the Beautiful and Aesthetics," ch. 19, sec. 205 in *Parerga and Paralipomena*, 2 vols., trans. Christopher Janaway (Cambridge: Cambridge University Press, 2015), 2:374–75. Translated from Schopenhauer, *Sämtliche Werke*, Vol. 6, ed. Arthur Hübscher (Mannheim: F. A. Brockhaus, 1988), 442–44.

141. Friedrich Nietzsche, *The Birth of Tragedy and Other Writings*, trans. Ronald Speirs, ed. Raymond Geuss and Ronald Speirs (Cambridge: Cambridge University Press, 1999), 4, 6–7, 17–21, 27–28.

142. Nietzsche, *Birth of Tragedy*, 55–59, 60–75.

143. Nietzsche, *Beyond Good and Evil*, trans. Judith Norman, ed. Rolf-Peter Horstmann and Judith Norman (Cambridge: Cambridge University Press, 2002), 1.5–6 (pp. 8–9), 2.25 (pp. 26–27), 5.187 (p. 77), 7.219 (p. 111), 7.221 (pp. 112–13), 7.228 (pp. 118–19).

144. For example, Albert Einstein writes, "Perfection of means and confusion of goals seem, in my opinion, to characterize our age." Einstein, *Out of My Later Years* (New York: Philosophical Library, 1950), 113.

145. For further discussion of the influence of Kant upon Schiller and Hegel, see Stephen Boos, "Rethinking the Aesthetic: Kant, Schiller, and Hegel," in *Between Ethics and Aesthetics: Crossing the Boundaries*, ed. Dorota Glowacka and Stephen Boos (Albany: State University of New York Press, 2002), 15–27.

146. Johann Christoph Friedrich von Schiller, *Letters on the Aesthetic Education of Man*, trans. Elizabeth M. Wilkinson and L. A. Willoughby, in *Essays*, ed. Walter Hinderer and Daniel O. Dahlstrom (New York: Continuum, 2001), 86–88.

147. Schiller, *On Grace and Dignity*, trans. George Gregory (New York: New Benjamin Franklin House, 1982 [Schiller Institute]), 365.

148. Schiller, *On Grace and Dignity*, 337.

149. Schiller, *On Grace and Dignity*, 365–68.

150. Schiller, *On Grace and Dignity*, 341, 349–50.

151. Schiller, *On Grace and Dignity*, 363–65.

152. Johann Georg Hamann, "Metacritique on the Purism of Reason," in *Writings on Philosophy and Language*, trans. Kenneth Haynes (Cambridge, UK: Cambridge University Press, 2007), 205.

153. Hamann, "Metacritique," 207.

154. Hamann, "Metacritique," 208.

155. Hamann, "Metacritique," 209–10.

156. Hamann, "Metacritique," 212.

157. Hamann, "The Last Will and Testament of the Knight of the Rose-Cross," in *Writings on Philosophy and Language*, 99–100.

158. Bernhard Lohse, *Martin Luther's Theology: Its Historical and Systematic Development*, trans. and ed. Roy A. Harrisville (Minneapolis, MN: Fortress, 1999), 172–77.

159. See Haynes, "Introduction" to Hamann, *Writings on Philosophy and Language*, xv.

160. Hamann, *Essay of a Sibyl on Marriage, Nadler's Edition of Hamann's Werke*, Vol. 3, 198–200, cited by Gwen Griffith Dickson, *Johann Georg Hamann's Relational Metacriticism* (Berlin and New York: Walter de Gruyter, 1995), 507–8.

161. Hamann, "Golgotha and Sheblimini!" in *Writings on Philosophy and Language*, loc. 5943 of 9058.

162. Haynes, "Introduction," to Hamann, *Writings*, xvi–xvii. Hamann, "Golgotha," 202–3.

163. Haynes, "Introduction," to Hamann, *Writings*, xv.

164. Haynes, "Introduction," to Hamann, *Writings*, xv.

165. Friedrich Schlegel, *Literary Notebooks* (London: The Athlone Press, 1957).

166. Schlegel, "Critical Fragment," no. 89, in *Philosophical Fragments*, trans. Peter Firchow (Minneapolis: University of Minnesota Press, 1991).

167. Schlegel, "Critical Fragment," nos. 42, 65, "Athenaeum Fragment," no. 116, in *Philosophical Fragments*.

168. Schlegel, "Critical Fragment," nos. 14, 90, 103, in *Philosophical Fragments*.

169. Schlegel, "Critical Fragment," nos. 42, 48, 108.

170. Schlegel, "Critical Fragment," nos. 51, 56, 59, 67, 90, 96, 104, 109.

171. Schlegel, "Athenaeum Fragment," no. 77.

172. Schlegel, in his veiled belittling of Kant, writes, "Maxims, ideals, imperatives, and postulates have now all become the small change of morality." "Critical Fragment," no. 77.

173. See Schlegel, "Athenaeum Fragment," no. 121.

174. Schlegel, "Athenaeum Fragment," nos. 216, 281.

175. Schlegel, "Ideas," in *Philosophical Fragments*, nos. 135 and 137.

176. Allen Speight, s. v. "Friedrich Schlegel," in *The Stanford Encyclopedia of Philosophy* (Winter 2015 edition), ed. Edward N. Zalta, plato.stanford.edu/archives/win2015/entries/schlegel/.

177. F. W. J. Schelling, *The Philosophy of Art: An Oration on the Relation between the Plastic Arts and Nature* [hereafter cited as *PA*], trans. A. Johnson (London: John Chapman, 1845), 10–11.

178. Schelling, *PA*, 1–16.

179. Schelling, *PA*, 10–12.

180. Schelling, *PA*, 13, 17.

181. Schelling, *PA*, 13, 22.

182. Schelling, *Ideas for a Philosophy of Nature*, trans. Errol Harris and Peter Heath (Cambridge: Cambridge University Press, 1995), 176.

183. Georg Wilhelm Friedrich Hegel, *Hegel's Aesthetics: Lectures on Fine Art, Vol. 1* [hereafter cited as *LFA*], trans. T.M. Knox (Oxford: Clarendon Press, 1975), 56–58, 60–63.

184. Hegel, *LFA*, 57–58.

185. Hegel, *LFA*, 60.

186. Hegel, *LFA*, 14.

187. Hegel, *LFA*, 14–15.

188. Hegel, *LFA*, 14–15, 22–25.

189. Hegel, *LFA*, 98.

190. Hegel, *LFA*, 22.

191. Hegel, *LFA*, 62, 70, 100.

192. Hegel, *LFA*, 61, 108.

193. Hegel, *LFA*, 13–14.

194. Hegel, *LFA*, 21–23.

195. Hegel, *LFA*, 21–22.

196. Hegel, *LFA*, 19, 38.

197. Hegel, *LFA*, 111.

198. Hegel, *LFA*, 2.

199. Hegel, *LFA*, 2.

200. Hegel, *LFA*, 518.

201. Hegel, *LFA*, 518.

202. Hegel, *LFA*, 519.

203. Hegel, *LFA*, 519.

204. Hegel, *LFA*, 519–20.

205. Hegel, *LFA*, 519–20.

206. Hegel, *LFA*, 70, 325.

207. Hegel, *LFA*, 532.

208. Hegel, *LFA*, 532–34.

209. Hegel, *LFA*, 533.

210. Hegel, *LFA*, 527.

211. Hegel, *LFA*, 543.

212. Hegel, *LFA*, 522–23.

213. Hegel, *LFA*, 533, 540.

214. Hegel, *LFA*, 505, 522, 543, 596.

215. Hegel, *LFA*, 463–64.

216. Hegel, *Lectures on the Philosophy of Religion*, trans. E. B. Speirs and J. Burdon Sanderson (London: Routledge & Kegan Paul, 1895), 3:35.

217. Hegel, *Philosophy of Religion*, 3:38, 92.

218. Hegel, *Philosophy of Religion*, 3:71, 93–98.

219. Søren Kierkegaard, *Either/Or*, 2 vols. [hereafter abbreviated as *E/O*], ed. and trans. Howard V. Hong and Edna H. Hong (Princeton: Princeton University Press, 1987), 1:1. Victor Eremita means "victorious hermit."

220. Kierkegaard, *E/O*, 1:7 (1.ix). Parenthetical notations are marginal references in the Hong translation to volume numbers and pages in *Søren Kierkegaards Samlede Værker*, I–XIV, ed. A. B. Drachmann, J. L. Heiberg, and H. O. Lange (Copenhagen: Gyldendal, 1901–1906).

221. Kierkegaard, *E/O*, 1:11 (1.xiii).

222. Kierkegaard, *E/O*, 1:20 (1.3).

223. Kierkegaard, *E/O*, 1:20 (1.4).

224. Kierkegaard, *E/O*, 1:20 (1.4).

225. Kierkegaard, *E/O*, 1:38 (1.22–23).

226. Kierkegaard, *E/O*, 1:38 (1.22–23).

227. Kierkegaard, *E/O*, 1:39 (1.23–24).

228. Kierkegaard, *E/O*, 1:87 (1.69).

229. Kierkegaard, *E/O*, 1:90 (1.72–73).

230. Kierkegaard, *E/O*, 1:91 (1.72–75).

231. Kierkegaard, *E/O*, 1:96–97 (1.76–77).

232. Kierkegaard, *E/O*, 1:101 (1.81).

233. Kierkegaard, *E/O*, 1:105–106 (1.85–87).

234. Kierkegaard, *E/O*, 1:106–107 (1.86–87).

235. Kierkegaard, *E/O*, 1:133 (1.111–12).

236. Kierkegaard, *E/O*, 1:92 (1.73–74).

237. Kierkegaard, *E/O*, 1:98 (1.79–80).

238. Kierkegaard, *E/O*, 1:88 (1.69).

239. Kierkegaard, *E/O*, 1:98 (1.80).

240. Kierkegaard, *E/O*, 1:204 (1.180).

241. Kierkegaard, *E/O*, 1:206 (1.181–82).

242. Kierkegaard, *E/O*, 1:286 (1.258).

243. Kierkegaard, *E/O*, 1:289–91 (1.261–63).

244. Kierkegaard, *E/O*, 1:98 (1.79).

245. Kierkegaard, *E/O*, 1:306–307 (1.278–79).

246. Kierkegaard, *E/O*, 1:361 (1.330–31).

247. Kierkegaard, *E/O*, 1:7 (1.ix)

248. Kierkegaard, *E/O*, 2:6 (2.6–7).

249. Kierkegaard, *E/O*, 2:6–7 (2.6–7).

250. Kierkegaard, *E/O*, 2:7 (2.7).

251. Kierkegaard, *E/O*, 2:16 (2.15).

252. Kierkegaard, *E/O*, 2:16 (2.15).

253. Kierkegaard, *E/O*, 2:16 (2.15–16).

254. Kierkegaard, *E/O*, 2.:17 (2.16).

255. Kierkegaard, *E/O*, 2:20 (2.20).

256. Kierkegaard, *E/O*, 2:17 (2.16–17).

257. Kierkegaard, *E/O*, 2:21–22 (2.20).

258. Kierkegaard, *E/O*, 2:121 (2.110).

259. Kierkegaard, *E/O*, 2:142 (2.129).

260. Kierkegaard, *E/O*, 1:219–21 (2.196–98).

261. Kierkegaard, *E/O*, 1:36 (2.33–34).

262. Kierkegaard, *E/O*, 2:39 (2.37).

263. Kierkegaard, *E/O*, 2:44 (2.42).

264. Kierkegaard, *E/O*, 2:44 (2.42).

265. Kierkegaard, *E/O*, 2:141–42 (2.128–29).

266. Kierkegaard, *E/O*, 2:125–26 (2.114).

267. Kierkegaard, *E/O*, 2:242–43 (2.217–18).

268. Kierkegaard, *E/O*, 2:241 (2.217).

269. Kierkegaard, *E/O*, 2:242 (2.217).

270. Kierkegaard, *E/O*, 2:248 (2.223).

271. Kierkegaard, *E/O*, 2:271 (2.243).

272. Kierkegaard, *E/O*, 2:337–38 (2.303–304).

273. Kierkegaard, *Stages on Life's Way*, ed. and trans. Howard V. Hong and Edna H. Hong (Princeton, NJ: Princeton University Press, 1988), 185.

274. Søren Kierkegaard, *Fear and Trembling*, trans. and ed. Howard V. Hong and Edna H. Hong (Princeton, NJ: Princeton University Press, 1983), 1.

275. Kierkegaard, *Stages on Life's Way*, 185.

276. Kierkegaard, *Fear and Trembling*, 20.

277. Kierkegaard, *Fear and Trembling*, 82.

278. Kierkegaard, *Fear and Trembling*, 55–57.

279. Kierkegaard, *Fear and Trembling*, 46–59.

280. Kierkegaard, *Fear and Trembling*, 59.

281. Kierkegaard, *Stages on Life's Way*, 476–78.

282. Kierkegaard, *Fear and Trembling*, 28–30. See also *Stages on Life's Way*, 445.

283. Kierkegaard, *Fear and Trembling*, 118–19.

284. Von Balthasar, *Glory of the Lord*, 44–49.

285. Hans Urs von Balthasar, *The Glory of the Lord: A Theological Aesthetics*, trans. Erasmo Leiva-Merikakis, eds. Joseph Fessio and John Riches (San Francisco, CA: Ignatius Press, 2009), 48.

286. Von Balthasar, *Glory of the Lord*, 48.

287. Von Balthasar, *Glory of the Lord*, 48.

288. Von Balthasar, *Glory of the Lord*, 49.

289. See Martin Luther, *Disputation Concerning Man* (1536), thesis 26.

290. See Luther, *Disputation Against Scholastic Theology* (1517), theses 41–44, 50–53. Luther refers to the entire ethics of Aristotle as the "worst enemy of grace" (thesis 41).

291. Aquinas, *ST* I.93.9.

292. Aquinas, *ST* I.93.9.

293. Aquinas, *ST* I.93.9.

294. Aquinas, *ST* I.95.3.

295. Aquinas, *ST* I.95.3.

296. Aquinas, *ST* I.94.1–2.

297. Aquinas, *ST* I–II.62.1; I–II.95.1; 2.5.1.

298. Aquinas, *ST* I–II.62.2

299. Aquinas, *ST* I–II.64.4.

300. Aquinas, *ST* I–II.65.5; 1.62.4.

301. Luther, *On the Bondage of the Will, to the Venerable Erasmus of Rotterdam*, trans. Edward Thomas Vaughan (London: Applegate, 1823), pt. 3.

302. 1 Cor 13.

303. 1 Cor 13:7.

304. 1 Cor 13:10.

305. Luke 23:34.

306. Paul Ricoeur, "The Logic of Jesus, The Logic of God," in *Figuring the Sacred: Religion, Narrative, and Imagination*, trans. David Pellauer, ed. Mark I. Wallace (Minneapolis, MN: Fortress, 1995), 279–92. Ricoeur shows that the logic to which Paul appeals is the "logic of superabundance" that bursts the old "logic of equivalence," which is none other than the logic of the Law (Ricoeur, "The Logic of Jesus," 282).

Chapter Seven

Story, Narrative, and Drama as Mediators of Ultimate Value

THE FUNCTION OF VALUE-INDICATORS IN POETICS

To be compelling, stories, narratives, and dramas must mediate value both ethically and aesthetically by combining language and action. Furthermore, they should mediate both a sense of proximate value and a sense of ultimate value; namely, ultimate value that is both purposive and meaningful. In chapter 4, I used stories and synopses of novels to help contextualize the way that values are applied and sometimes misapplied. I also investigated in a preliminary way how the problem of good and evil emerges from the way human beings, who possess libertarian freedom, either use or misuse the value-compass in their attempt to find meaning and purpose in existence. I want now to build from this preliminary investigation a case for why stories, narratives, and dramas need to receive dominant consideration when providing cumulative evidence for why belief in the existence of God as an ultimate source of value is warranted.

THE NARROW RANGE OF THEISTIC ARGUMENTS

While stories have the power to intrigue and capture the imaginations of most people and transform their lives, there are subsets of individuals for whom this option seems too simplistic to provide a plausible basis for belief in the existence of God as a source of transcendental value. Philosophers of religion have thus believed it expedient to use theistic arguments to convince people of God's existence. Though I am not unsympathetic to this goal, I happen to think that theistic arguments can be made more effective if they are viewed not so much in isolation or as *ends* in themselves, but as *components* of a more *cumulative argument* based on the sorts of axiological insights I have presented thus far in this book.

Traditional Theistic Arguments Reexamined

What are now commonly called the *traditional arguments* for the existence of God first began to be developed in the eleventh century when St. Anselm of Canterbury offered his famous *ontological argument*.[1] The art of framing theistic arguments reached its heyday in the thirteenth century when St. Thomas Aquinas, borrowing from contributions of the Arab philosopher Avicenna and the Jewish philosopher Moses Maimonides, developed *cosmological* and *teleological* arguments for God's existence within a Christian framework.[2]

Aspects of these traditional arguments have from the very start proved compelling for the philosophically minded. The fact remains nonetheless that theists and nontheists alike have found reasons to refute them. Theistic arguments have thus not always fully succeeded in accomplishing for their recipients all that they were intended to do. Still, as challenges have mounted against these arguments, philosophers who argue in support of theism have continued to revise them in ever more sophisticated ways.[3] Indeed, some of their revisions have reached a level of complexity that ordinary people will find virtually incomprehensible. Consequently, as traditional arguments have become more and more complex and abstract, they have become incomprehensible to many; and few persons will find an argument compelling that they fail to grasp intellectually. At the same time, atheists and other nontheists have, overall, found the arguments unconvincing and so have continued to mount their challenges against them.[4]

The Extremes of Abstraction and Reduction

In chapter 4, I asserted that materialistic frameworks are needlessly restrictive because they are *too reductive*, while idealistic frameworks are needlessly restrictive because they are *too abstractive*. In the conclusion of that chapter, I suggested that a 3D lens needed to be furnished that could effectively bring into sharper focus the fuzzy blurs that had resulted from viewing reality *either* with a materialist lens *or* an idealist lens. I intend now to explore this issue further with regard to arguments for the existence of God and their rejection by nontheists.

One principle that underlies all attempts to frame traditional arguments is "the principle of abstraction."[5] Using this principle is always necessary for traditional arguments to succeed in their aim. Anselm employed the principle when he posited the idea of *the Infinite* as the primary cause behind all *ideas* of the Infinite that *exist in the finite mind.* The incongruity between the *idea* of the Infinite as it exists in the mind and the *finitude* of the mind itself begs for resolution. The answer Anselm hit upon was that the Infinite is responsible for reflecting itself into our finite minds as an *Innate Idea.* Expressed in another way, "God has set eternity in the hearts of men."[6]

Aquinas, in another way, employed the principle of abstraction when he began with the dimension of the finite and moved by means of logical deduction to affirm the existence of God. Here, the finite realities that are observed are *external* to the mind, and not so much *internal* as they were for Anselm. These finite realities include the phenomena of *cause and effect* and *design,* which are observable through the five senses. Once the senses have perceived these finite verities, the mind then takes over and does its job of abstracting. Starting with human observation of the finite phenomenon of cause and effect, Aquinas employs the principle of abstraction until he reaches the idea of God as the First Cause. Likewise, he abstracts the human observation of the existence of design in the finite world to affirm that an ultimate Designer—i.e., God—must necessarily exist.

What nontheists have brought into question concerns whether using the principle of abstraction is at all valid or permissible. Indeed, if doubts can be cast upon the very validity of this principle, then all arguments relying on it can be jettisoned at their source. Furthermore, even if using the principle is discovered to be valid in *some* regards, this does not imply that using it in *other* or *all* regards is an equally valid move. All that is needed then is to "cut" the traditional arguments "off at their knees" so that they fail to obtain. This can be achieved simply by demonstrating that the theist's manner of employing the principle of abstraction is arbitrary and, therefore, baseless and unjustified. A case in point is the apophatic-cataphatic divide that has long distinguished Eastern from Western Christian theological outlooks. Because the principle of abstraction employed in the Eastern Orthodox tradition veers in an *apophatic* direction, its use of this principle arrives at an understanding of God through the mode of *negation.*[7] In the Western tradition, by contrast, the mode of *affirmation* dominates. Here, the principle of abstraction veers in a *cataphatic* direction.[8]

Cataphatic theology founders even further when it seeks to resolve the kind of questions some of the medieval scholastics posed; viz., Is God's *will* subordinate to his *intellect* (the opinion of Thomas Aquinas)? Or is God's *intellect* subordinate to his *will* (the perspective of Duns Scotus)?[9] The cataphatic use of the principle of abstraction here reaches the impasse that Immanuel Kant called "the antinomies of reason."[10] The apophatic use of that same principle, on the other hand, reaches a point in which the "solvent" of negation dissolves all particularity into the *not-being* of Neoplatonic theology. A worst-case scenario is that even morality either will be *dissolved,* or else it will be *relegated to a status of inferior importance.* Such seems the case in *Shankara* Hinduism (the nondualist or *Advaita* school) where *Nirguna Brahman* (Brahman without attributes) transcends those polarities of good and evil that humans experience in the world.[11] As a result, any belief that imagines morality to be grounded in some absolute must be judged as misguided. Such examples thus reveal that theistic attempts to utilize the principle of abstraction are at best arbitrary.

Overall, proponents of traditional arguments have fallen short of at least one of their objectives, which is to convince nontheists either of the validity of the principle of abstraction itself or of the way theists employ that principle. Most atheists simply reject the principle from the outset. Instead, they adopt an opposite tool—viz., the principle of *reduction,* which is grounded in skepticism—to interpret the very same evidence that theists observe. They then use this tool to take the evidence in a *nontheistic* direction. Ironically, the theist rejects the validity of this tool, as well as the way the nontheist uses it, for reasons very similar to the ones nontheists use to reject the tool of abstraction that theists employ. Therefore, it appears to be the case that theists use the principle of *abstraction* in an arbitrary fashion, while nontheists use the principle of *reduction* in a manner just as arbitrary.

How then does the principle of reduction succumb to arbitrary usage by nontheists? On one side of the nontheism spectrum are located the hard materialists who employ the principle of reduction in a draconian fashion. Hard materialists seek to explain such higher functions and beliefs of living organisms as the soul and morality solely in terms of the laws of physics, chemistry, and biology.[12] Here, it seems, the mode of negation is employed by hard materialists to deny what theists will interpret as "spiritual." On the other side of the spectrum one finds a soft materialism, as in the vein of E. O. Wilson, who affirms a kind of irreducible complexity in phenomena he calls "consiliences."[13] Consiliences occur, for instance, when the dimension of the biochemical is taken up into the dimension of organic life, or organic life is taken up into the operations of the brain. Hence, life as a phenomenon may contain a biochemical aspect, but this does not make it *merely* biochemical. The same also happens to be true of the phenomenon of *thought* as a product of the human brain. There is here a qualitative leap from one consilience to another that prohibits one from deducing that phenomena such as organic life or thought can simply be collapsed back into what is merely biochemical. According to Wilson, even morality becomes possible as an aspect that emerges from the physical world, though he stops short of positing an *ultimate transcendental basis* for any consilience. For Wilson, the basis is not to be found in a deity but in the world alone.[14]

To clarify the point of my discussion, the way nontheists use the principle of reduction seems just as arbitrary as the way theists use the principle of abstraction. No adequate justification is given for *why one should* adopt the principle of reduction or *why one should* use that principle in one way rather than another.[15] It may be that the atheist is right to think that he has success-fully cut the platform out from under the theist. One could argue convincing-ly, however, that the opposite is also true—that the theist has cut the platform from underneath the atheist—touché!

MORAL AND AESTHETIC ARGUMENTS

In addition to the traditional arguments for God's existence, philosophers have offered moral and aesthetic types of arguments. For instance, Kant, heeding David Hume's rejection of the traditional arguments, proposes his moral argument for God's existence;[16] and recently, philosophers of religion such as Richard Swinburne and Keith Ward have advanced arguments for the existence of God based on beauty.[17] How then can one justify the claim that moral and aesthetic arguments provide a more viable basis for a successful argument for the existence of the Judeo-Christian God than do the traditional arguments? In answering, I would suggest that moral and aesthetic argu-ments are *more successful* because they include the key ingredient of *human libertarian freedom* that is absent in purely physical cause-and-effect rela-tionships and in merely physical instances of order, symmetry, and apparent design in the universe. Purely physical cause-and-effect phenomena fall short of operating at a moral level, and order and symmetry alone do not necessari-ly evoke an experience of the beautiful. For the moral and the beautiful to be plausible as categories, there must first be a human perceiver who possesses the faculty of libertarian freedom. Libertarian freedom provides space for inward *reflection* on categories such as *purpose* and *meaning* as well as for ethical and aesthetic *action*. More specifically, human libertarian freedom provides space in the human psyche (1) for reflection upon the meaning and purpose of objects external to consciousness and (2) for the execution of judgments and performance of actions involving value. I shall now endeavor to expound in greater detail why I think moral and aesthetic arguments are a successful addition to cosmological and teleological ones.

Moral Arguments

It is one thing to recognize *physical* laws operating in the cosmos and to extrapolate from those laws the existence of *a kind* of First Cause, but it is another thing entirely to try to account for the phenomenon of *human moral consciousness* based solely on *mechanistic laws of cause and effect* observ-able in such fields as physics and chemistry. The phenomenon of human moral consciousness begs for a more replete explanation of why it exists than what mechanistic explanations allow for. Laws of cause and effect that oper-ate at a purely physical and mechanistic level simply cannot account for morality, for they fall short of demonstrating why there should be any real *purpose* in the universe that could be construed as *morally significant*.[18]

Furthermore, merely affirming the existence of a First Cause does not tell us *what kind* of cause it happens to be. Though it is true that Aristotle and Aquinas argue from contingent effects to a necessary Unmoved Mover, a comparison of their differing conclusions reveals that the *nature* of this Unmoved Mover is difficult to ascertain by means of the categories of thinking they employ. As I already indicated in chapter 3, Aristotle arrives at his idea of the Unmoved Mover as exerting an impersonal force of attraction that he calls "Love."[19] However, this force, as Aristotle understands it, lacks the fuller insights that Aquinas imports from his Christian theological presuppositions; namely, the presupposition that the God who created all things is an *efficient* First Cause in addition to his being Aristotle's Final Cause (Unmoved Mover). Aristotle's God is the *telos* toward which every contingent activity is directed. However, Aquinas's view falls short of affirming the *necessary* existence of a *personal* God that fully resembles the God described in the Hebrew and Christian Scriptures. The disparity between the conclusions that Aristotle and Aquinas reach demonstrates how the argument Aquinas employs could not extend so far as to prove the existence of the *God of the Bible*. Indeed, the argument from effects to causes could just as easily support a *mechanistic* conception of the relation between God and creation, such as one finds in *deism*. In this regard, the cause-and-effect chain upon which the cosmological argument is predicated is inadequate to account for the existence of phenomena such as moral *power* and *purpose*.

Nevertheless, arguing from the phenomenon of human moral consciousness (though it may be dim, distorted, or underdeveloped) to the existence of God as the necessary ultimate cause of the moral law elevates the causal nexus from a purely *mechanistic* level to a *moral* one (see figure 7.1). The leap from mechanism to morality begs for an explanation. When the mechanistic explanation is weighed against the theistic explanation, it seems more probable that there exists a transcendent Supreme Moral Legislator and Arbiter of the universe whose nature is *personal* rather than *impersonal*.

Aesthetic Arguments

Just as *moral arguments* for God's existence can serve to elevate *cosmological* types of arguments to a higher level, *aesthetic arguments* can serve, in a similar manner, to elevate *teleological* kinds of theistic arguments (see figure 7.1). As I mentioned previously, the component of reflection that is so characteristic of the ontological argument is the component that makes elevation possible in both cases.

Teleological arguments may consider the phenomenon of design in created things, but they do not yet include the possibility that this phenomenon

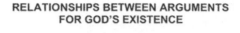

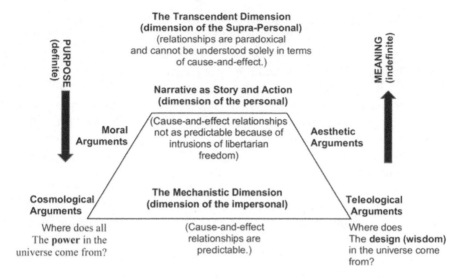

Figure 7.1.   Relationships between Arguments for God's Existence.

may also be assessed and valued as something *beautiful*. Furthermore, just as the transition from the cosmological argument to the moral argument involves a leap from a purely quantitative assessment (that recognizes the phenomenon of sheer mechanism) to a qualitative assessment (that entails the recognition of a universal *purpose*), the transition from the teleological theistic argument to an aesthetic one involves a similar qualitative leap. In the latter case, however, the leap from the quantitative to the qualitative entails the recognition not so much of universal *purpose* as of universal *meaning* (see figure 7.1).

Expressed in another way, leaping from the *cosmological* to the *moral* and from the *teleological* to the *aesthetic* entails a transition from a more purely cognitivist-epistemic approach to an axiological-experiential one. Prior to the Enlightenment, such a leap would have struck the philosophically minded as largely unnecessary, for epistemology as a totally separate field of philosophical inquiry had not yet been caged and tamed by an excessive use of the scientific method. In other words, it had not yet been made to conform to the newly "christened" ideal of "total objectivity." Value-free, neutral knowledge was the desired product of the kind of thinking that severed epistemology from axiology; though in retrospect, the belief that knowledge *should* be neutral and value-free was all along grounded in a presupposition that at its heart was also *axiological*. To put it more simply, the belief that knowledge *should* be neutral and value-free was a belief that was *anything but* neutral and value-free.

TOWARD AN ARGUMENT FOR GOD'S EXISTENCE BASED ON VALUE

I have attempted above to argue for how the intrusion of libertarian freedom makes possible a transition from cosmological and teleological theistic arguments to arguments for the existence of God that find their basis in the human ability to recognize the dimensions moral and the beautiful. This transition entails as well a transition from the more *cognitivist*-based apophatic and cataphatic approaches that utilize the principle of abstraction to *experiential-expressivist* ways (to echo theologian George Lindbeck) of apprehending the Transcendent that will include psychological and volitional human responses to the *mysterium tremendum et fascinans.*[20] With apophatic and cataphatic thinking, a cognitive process of ratiocination functions as the vehicle whereby the finite human mind is propelled toward construals of a transcendent mystery that lies beyond *reason*. On the other hand, the human experience of the *mysterium tremendum et fascinans*, which I have previously discussed in several places at length, introduces psychological responses such as trepidation and fascination into human experience at another level. These elements, in turn, allow the human being to apprehend and express through both emotional and volitional channels moral and aesthetic responses to the transcendent mystery that is perceived as lying beyond one's own will and emotion. This further dimension of human responsiveness to the divine mystery does not necessarily exclude the apophatic/cataphatic apprehension of the Divine, for it is possible to achieve a rapprochement between cognitivist and experiential-expressive models.[21] In what ways, then, can this rapprochement be accomplished?

Lately, philosophers of religion have suggested one way of accomplishing this rapprochement by seeking to view arguments for God's existence *cumulatively* rather than in *isolation* from one another. Philosopher of science Michael Polanyi (1891–1976) anticipated this development when he rejected the assumption that "the whole is *equal* to the sum of its parts" and asseverated that "the whole is always *more* than the sum of its parts."[22] This type of cumulative approach had some success in persuading England's foremost intellectual atheist, Antony Flew, to convert to deism.[23] Roy Abraham Varghese's book *The Wonder of the World* was instrumental in convincing Flew of the insufficiency of his earlier method, which was a method he had inherited from the likes of Hume,[24] Alfred Jules Ayer, and Bertrand Russell.[25]

In his book, Varghese employs a cumulative argument in an effort to show how lower chemical and physical laws and operations are taken up into higher phenomena, but in such a way that the higher phenomena cannot simply be reduced to, or explained in terms of, the lower ones.[26] The laws of organic chemistry, for example, function predictably within the sphere of organic life, but the sphere of organic life cannot be explained solely in terms of organic chemistry. Life forms will indeed utilize organic chemistry in their various biological and even mental functions, but there is no evidence that organic chemicals, when left to operate on their own, can ever join together through their own power to produce more complex phenomena such as organic life and mental activity. A life form utilizes, in addition to organic chemistry, an irreducibly complex information code that transcends the chemical dimension and cannot be derived from that dimension. Though organic chemicals may obey this code, they lack any inherent ability to produce it on their own. Indeed, no amount of combining and recombining organic chemicals can suffice to produce the code necessary to create organic life. Organic chemicals simply lack the necessary qualifications—i.e., the possession of a genetic *language* that is necessary for producing and sustaining life.

Despite his conversion to deism, Flew never goes so far as to embrace the Judeo-Christian worldview, although he does maintain a degree of openness toward further exploration of it. In retrospect, it is obvious that he is still to some degree hamstrung by his earlier method. To use his own words, he is willing to "follow the evidence wherever it led." However, he—much like Zeno of Elea, whose paradoxes on motion cause him to deny the reality of motion—could not, like Achilles, catch up with the tortoise. Flew's method causes him to embark on a series of fitful starts, stops, and reversals that ultimately result in his succumbing to a kind of methodological stalemate. He is mired along the way because he preoccupies himself too intensely with going the first half of the distance before he can even think about completing the second half. If anything, his preoccupation with the first half precludes his ever being able to move on to travel the second half at all. Thus, having used his analytical method to take religion apart, he is never really able to put it back together again. Because of this inability, his theism, predictably, never expanded beyond one of the most minimalistic sort. Aristotle and the deists may have finally started making sense to him, but to embrace the God of Christianity remained for him *a step too far*.[27]

A more cumulative method can, however, provide a springboard for launching one to the next step where a more comprehensive theistic argument can begin to be developed. Thus far, I have tried to take such a first step by suggesting that cosmological and teleological arguments can function as rudimentary components of moral and aesthetic arguments, respectively. Moral and aesthetic arguments, in turn, include elements of the ontological argument because they reflect on transcendental categories belonging to the Infinite such as purpose and meaning in ways that cosmological and teleological arguments do not allow. Moral and aesthetic arguments, however, still may appear disconnected from one another, as though they have little in common. Nevertheless, by appealing to the cumulative strategy, I think that I can now suggest ways that moral and aesthetic arguments can be conjoined to form a more comprehensive *axiological argument* for the existence of a *personal* God. Indeed, stories, narratives, and dramas may provide the best scenario—and the best 3D lens for which we have been searching—for viewing these moral and aesthetic aspects. This 3D lens would then comprise the next step in arriving at a comprehensive *axiological* rationale for the coherence of theistic belief.

THE SUPERLATIVELY GOOD STORY AS A FULCRUM OF VALUE

In the last few decades of the twentieth century, a number of scholars investigated ways of refocusing their ethical and aesthetic perspectives by rescuing them from sterile, lifeless, and reductive systems. They chose instead to emphasize how these dimensions become concretely embodied in extraordinary examples of human character and in compelling narratives. Dallas Willard and Linda Zagzebski are ethicists who, independently of one another, extended Aristotle's view of the *phronimos* to suggest examples of how virtue can become embodied in various kinds of exemplary human character. Willard suggests the possibility of such embodiment in the formed character of what he terms the "good person,"[28] while Zagzebski similarly speaks of the various embodiments of virtuous character in "exemplars."[29] While these are valid insights, we should note that virtuous character neither develops nor exists in a vacuum but already presupposes the virtuous character's situatedness within the whole lived experience of his/her *life story* or *narrative*. Such narratival backdrops serve like settings for jewels in a crown. Like the glittering jewels that are placed in these settings, those possessing virtuous character are displayed. Thus, the approaches of Willard and Zagzebski thus depend upon more comprehensive kinds of approaches, such as those put forward by proponents of "narrative theology."

In my estimation, the arrival of narrative theology signaled an important stage in the transition from ethical and aesthetic systems to the narratival embodiment of ethical and aesthetic truth. Dan Stiver identifies three different strands of narrative theology that appeared during the last several decades of the twentieth century. (1) The Chicago School, composed of such figures as Paul Ricoeur, Langdon Gilkey, and David Tracy, emphasized a broader, cultural, narrative context.[30] This school, which took its cue from continental philosophy, emphasized the *relevance* of narrative to *universal* human values and experience. (2) The Yale School, which included such scholars as Hans Frei, George Lindbeck, and David Kelsey, differed from the Chicago School in that they focused more *particularly* on biblical narratives.[31] This school took its cue from the later Ludwig Wittgenstein's emphasis on language games and from the theology of Karl Barth.[32] (3) The California School, represented by James McClendon, Michael Goldberg, and Terrence Tilley, focused on the biographies of persons who exhibited extraordinary character and on the speech-act theory of J. L. Austin.[33] After summarizing the distinctives of these schools, Stiver, following Tilley, suggests a rapprochement that adopts the best emphases of these three traditions. The *intratextual* approach of the Chicago School, Stiver and Tilley observe, manifested the danger of supporting *relativism*, while the intertextual approach of the Yale School migrated too far in the direction of *fideism*. Stiver suggests that the California approach that Tilley represents, with its focus on the importance of biography and speech-act theory, promises a "nuanced and nonreductionist approach to narrative."[34]

The approach to narrative that Stiver and Tilley favor accords with the one I have adopted here and in the chapters that follow. In this approach, the particularity of stories and their universality are allowed to coexist in paradoxical tension. In embracing a narratival approach, however, I am fully aware of the need to avoid any methodological tendency that allows the doctrine of God to be collapsed into a particular narratival "method." Francesca Murphy observes this tendency among those whom she labels the "story Barthians" (e.g., Frei and Lindbeck) and the "story Thomists" (e.g., Jenson).[35] By considering the reality of God to be virtually synonymous with God's story, these restrictive methodologies allow the fullness and transcendence of that reality to be too greatly obscured. The tendency of these methodologies to reduce the full reality of the divine to the level of narrative takes its cue from the language-game theory of the later Wittgenstein. However, as I noted in chapter 5, Wittgenstein's "game" analogy, though certainly not as reductive as the approaches of logical positivism and linguistic analysis, is still reductive. Expressions of human language and action that entail serious risks should not be viewed as *merely* game-like. If they are viewed in this way, then their seriousness will invariably be diminished.

Any further investigation of the more technical points of the various approaches to narrative theology lies beyond the scope of this book,[36] so my comments here regarding the power of narrative to mediate value will not be overly technical. To broach the subject, I must therefore initially ask, "How can a superlatively 'good story' function as a fulcrum of value by providing a contextual arena in which conflicting values are sorted out and in which the struggle between good and evil can be explored?"

First, a good story will often deal with the conflicts and resolutions of conflicts between the dimensions of the ethical and the aesthetic, if not explicitly, then implicitly. In much nineteenth-century Romantic literature, for instance, the ethical sense of duty that a protagonist's station in life thrusted upon him/her may have thwarted valid aesthetic concerns such as finding true love or achieving lofty aspirations.[37] In such cases, the established *moral* order may have been so overly contrived, arbitrary, or conventional that it kept valid *aesthetic* impulses in check and hampered one's search for meaning. Such restrictive moral contexts force upon the reader of the story a sense of the fundamental unfairness of the protagonist's plight. This sense of unfairness calls for rectification and a restoration of the balance between the dimensions of the ethical and the aesthetic. The reader is compelled by the sense of unfairness to cast his lot with the protagonist's decision to choose, in his or her particular case, the *aesthetic* over the ethical. In this way, a proper equilibrium between the ethical and the aesthetic can be restored.

However, the infringement of the dimension of the aesthetic upon the ethical also remains a danger. As I mentioned in the previous chapter, Søren Kierkegaard understood the transition from the aesthetic stage to the ethical stage in this way. The pursuit of an aesthetic divorced from morality became an emphasis with the transition from nineteenth-century Romanticism to literary realism. Somerset Maugham, for instance, used a section out of Spinoza's ethics as the title for his novel *Of Human Bondage*, which is the story of idealistic artist Philip Carey's tormented and unrequited love for Mildred Rogers, a woman of low reputation. Thomas Hardy's *Tess of the d'Urbervilles* and *Jude the Obscure* also investigate the way that aesthetic pursuits, which are not properly balanced with a focus on the dimension of the ethical, deteriorate into self-perpetuating quagmires of misery. The insights of William Golding in his novels *The Lord of the Flies* and *The Spire* bring to light as well the tragedy that ensues when the ethical is abandoned in favor of a purely sensual aesthetic. Again, these novels are profound in the way that they highlight the human condition and issue "prophetic" warnings about the dangers of abandoning the ethical sense by giving in to the deceptive lure of an immoral aesthetic.[38]

A *second reason* why a "good story" provides a fulcrum of value comes to light in the way that its narrative manages to weave together those disparate threads of value that emerge in the living of life and are reflective of it. Such threads might otherwise appear separate and unrelated, but the good story manages to weave these skillfully into a tapestry. Anyone who has studied literature is, of course, familiar with the common elements of a story: The overall problem of good versus evil; the characters with their internal and external challenges and struggles, needs, desires, dreams, aspirations, inhibitions, duties, risks, failures, successes, phobias, virtues, and vices; the way that a story's plot and subplots unfold as they become entangled and are finally disentangled and resolved; the way that mystery and the devices of veiling and unveiling are employed to carry a plot along; the intensity of conflict between the characters themselves and the dilemmas they face; the manner in which conflict is resolved, whether that manner be constructive or destructive; the story's mode, whether it be comic or tragic or tragicomic; its genre, whether it be adventure, mystery, romance, or some admixture of these.

Truly good stories can further be distinguished from inferior ones by highlighting the way their characters interact individually and collectively with their social, cultural, political, economic, and historical setting. Does a story's setting with all its facets facilitate or thwart the characters' efforts to realize their aspirations and achieve their goals? What kind of challenges and obstacles does the setting present? In what ways do the characters face and overcome obstacles the setting poses, and in what ways do they shrink back from challenges and succumb to failure?

A story's setting provides an arena in which characters, individually and collectively, can either become victims or achieve victory by bravely facing their psychological, moral, social, economic, political, and spiritual struggles.[39] The setting of a story further provides a sphere in which the story's characters, being confronted and challenged by some higher purpose, are compelled to exercise virtue, or else are tempted to succumb to vice. As they are faced with navigating specific dilemmas, they may choose a cowardly means of escape, or they may choose to embrace tragedy courageously.

It is a story's context that provides, as well, the sphere in which the characters can be elevated into an experience of greater meaning. Faced with the opportunity of participating in that greater meaning, the story's characters may either be inspired by it to flourish, or else they may shrink before it in despair and wither. As a place where meaning can be experienced, setting is also the sphere in which the characters may encounter challenges and surmount obstacles that encourage the ennobling of their character, or else they may be distracted by and may succumb to sensual allurements that will thwart the development of noble character.

A good story need not, of course, feature characters that are stereotypically virtuous or vicious. However, what it must do is to strive to portray characters as honestly as possible by highlighting the successes and consequences resulting from their beliefs and actions. If this is done, then a story will ring true and will resonate as such in the minds of its readers. When this occurs, the readers' grasp will be immediate, and the sense of value that is mediated to them will be self-evident.

A *third reason* why the superlatively good story can provide a fulcrum of value is evident in the way good is affirmed and evil is contextualized and overcome. Not every story presents the struggle between good and evil in the same way. However, the superlatively good story will provide a greater context in highlighting what is entailed in this struggle than will an inferior story. Cautionary tales, for instance, may candidly portray scenarios of how certain types of human behavior produce misery by identifying the causal link between the behaviors and their consequences.[40] Tales of heroism, by contrast, will, with the same candor, identify the causal link between the character and actions of the hero, on the one hand, and the outcomes of his or her heroism on the other.

The struggle to realize the good is usually expressed, on one front, as the struggle to maximize human creativity and, on the other front, as the struggle to achieve justice. The struggle to maintain equilibrium in achieving both is parallel to the struggle to maintain equilibrium between the dimensions of the ethical and the aesthetic. Broadly speaking, evil in its various guises usually seeks to elevate one front in the struggle for the good by wholly eliminating the other. On the one side, people obsessed with the struggle to maximize their own creativity may not care how much injustice they perpetrate in the process of their own self-actualization. On the other side, people may become so obsessed with the struggle to achieve justice that they try to abolish all contexts in which the creative impetus can thrive. Evil persistently uses the tools of *deception* and *injustice* to bring about an unbridgeable cleavage between the fostering of creativity and the execution of justice, thereby destabilizing the good and working to bring about its deterioration. Indeed, when the evils of deception and injustice work in concert with one another, they generate scenarios of stagnation and destruction.

THE SUPERLATIVELY GOOD STORY AS EVIDENCE FOR THE EXISTENCE OF GOD

The superlatively good story can concretely anchor a methodology that one can use in framing theistic arguments and refuting atheistic ones. Anchoring methodology in the concrete dimension, I believe, represents a step in the right direction, for doing so helps keep the tools of reduction and abstraction from being overextended and used in ways that seem too arbitrary and too extreme. At the same time, superlatively good stories resonate with concrete human experience by investigating the many different ways that their plots sometimes throw the dimensions of the ethical and the aesthetic into conflict, and at other times achieve equilibrium through the resolution of that conflict. Moreover, while focusing on the twists, turns, conflicts, and dilemmas that plague the dimension of the tangible, superlatively good stories taken as a whole will also be able to mediate transcendent purpose and meaning in a more universal manner.

Philosophers such as Hans-Georg Gadamer and Paul Ricoeur have, in different ways, anticipated the rapprochement between cognitive and experiential approaches to theological and philosophical truth that I am advocating here. Gadamer, on the one hand, decries the overuse in the human disciplines of the scientific method as well as the privileging of this method to serve as the most qualified hermeneutical tool for discovering truth. For Gadamer, forcing an overly rigid method upon the humanities can eclipse truth rather than reveal it.[41] Gadamer appears here to resist the reductive tendencies so often demonstrated by agnostic and atheistic philosophers.

Ricoeur, on the other hand, upholds as primary the role that narrative plays in the disclosure of truth. Not only does narrative invite and precipitate philosophical reflection, but it also serves as the *object* from which the activity of philosophical reflection takes its cue. It must, therefore, always stand as *prior* to all reflection. Ricoeur seems here to offer an alternative to philosophical methods that launch immediately into a rather arbitrary use of the principle of abstraction and, by doing so, quickly lose touch with the concrete dimension.[42]

I shall now offer an illustration that will help explain why a superlatively good story concretely anchors evidence for the existence of God in a way that the traditional theistic arguments cannot. Suppose I learn that you have just seen an interesting play that I have not seen. How would you describe the play if I were to ask you, "What was the play about?" Now suppose that instead of describing the play you launched into a discourse about set design and construction. I would respond, "That's fine and good, but what was the play about?" Suppose that you veer off next in another direction and begin to talk about the resumes of the director and the actors; or suppose that you speak about what a powerful and compelling performance the director and actors produced. I would again respond, "Fine, but you still have told me nothing of what the play was about." Suppose that you then gave me an overly vague emotional response and said, "Well, the play was wonderful— just wonderful." Your forays into these issues are red herrings. They are beside the point. You have told me nothing about the play itself. Instead you have skirted and danced around the original question without providing any satisfactory answer.

Now let's compare aspects of this analogy to the way we philosophers of religion produce arguments for God's existence. Instead of focusing on the plot that reveals the *purpose* and *meaning* of the grand narrative of existence, we spend our time discussing set design and construction, or we speak vaguely of the performance of the actors. In so doing, it seems that we are trying to convince people of the meaningfulness of a play without ever describing what the play is about! Likewise, when we philosophers insist on presenting cosmological and teleological sorts of arguments, we are like the person who discusses set design and the actors' and director's resumes while ignoring what should be given central attention; namely, the plot and story line of the play. In a similar way, if all I have to go on is the claim that the play was "just wonderful," this empty emotional declaration tells me nothing about *why* you thought it was wonderful. Again, it is nowhere obvious that the story is something alive and existentially incarnate that can be experienced through the five senses.

Abstract and ontologically vague ideas simply cannot be substituted for the kind of vital embodiment that the good story provides. In comparison, the realm of pure thought comes closer to resembling more of a sensory deprivation chamber than Plato's cave ever did. Unlike abstract thought, a good story is vibrant with sensations that point to ultimate purpose and ultimate meaning. In a similar way, persons of faith may continue to use hyperbole and superlatives in referring to experiences they have had with God, but these hardly convey to a listener what it was exactly that produced their experiences. Indeed, what difference does it make if we arrive at a vague *idea* or *experience* of the Infinite but continually fail to reveal the *story* of the Infinite? Our failure to connect the Infinite purposefully and meaningfully to the dimension of the concrete leaves us floating in the realm of abstraction.

On the other hand, nontheists would be expected to account for why they hated everything about the play, from the set design, to the director, to the actors, to the play itself. If they can only complain about this or that aspect, then it will become apparent that their disgust with the whole play is unwarranted and exaggerated, and they cannot see the whole for the parts upon which they have become disproportionally fixated. In short, they will appear to be the very kind of insensible, dull, and tasteless people that Aristotle would have banished from his audiences.

These analogies may help reveal the immense disconnection between the cerebral excursions of philosophers, both theistic and nontheistic, and the existential experiences of ordinary people who undertake and conduct their search for some meaning and purpose at a gut level here on *terra firma*.

Sacred Story as the Quintessentially Good Story

I want now to demonstrate how my appeal to the quintessentially good story as a fulcrum of value links up in particular with *sacred* story.[43] Here, I would argue that sacred story functions as the quintessentially *good story* because it provides the most comprehensive arena where the interplay and intersection of the abstract with the concrete dimensions of human existence can be observed and experienced.[44] What is observed and experienced can then provide evidence for the existence not just of some kind of God, but of the *personal triune* God in particular.

Philosophers of religion and theologians have usually made too rigid a distinction between special and general revelation and, in doing so, have created unnecessary philosophical obstacles. Believers and skeptics alike perennially focus on these obstacles much like the five blind men of Hindustan focused on the parts of the elephant without considering the whole elephant. Indeed, they are unable for the most part to move on from the parts to the whole. C. S. Lewis understood well how such barriers stand in our way of grasping the truth that he described in the *Abolition of Man* as the *Tao*.[45] Lewis found in the *Tao* that place of intersection between dimensions of the human psyche that thinkers of his day had compartmentalized and shut off from one another—namely, the passions and reason. The compartmentalization of revelation into the categories of general and special violates the principle of the *Tao* in a similar way by not conveying how one bleeds into the other and completes the other. Just as Lewis used the analogy "men without chests"[46] to describe modern man's inability to find the place of intersection and interplay between reason and passion, I would use the analogy "actors in a play without a stage and without a story" to describe the way many of the philosophers and theologians today engage in their craft. Lewis's analogy of the "chest" can be used analogously of the "stage" because the chest is the "stage" of the human psyche whereupon the actors of desire and reason perform their "story" by playing out their roles in relation to one another.

My contention here is that the *quintessentially good story* similarly conveys the sense of the *Tao* and does so in a way that the overly rigid categories, formalities, and structures of philosophical thought can never do. Not even the dialectic of G. W. F. Hegel could achieve this, for his version of the dialectic was too limited by the principle of reason (and *logos*) as he understood it. *Something* of the Tao appears in the movement of Hegel's dialectic from thesis to antithesis to synthesis, true enough; but his predilection for logical explanation and the synthesis made his understanding of the dialectic too formulaic and inflexible. If Hegel had been a novelist, he almost certainly would have used those formulas that guarantee a novel's status as ranging anywhere from bland mediocrity to sheer drivel. Thus, Kierkegaard was right to pry open the dialectic of Hegel by stressing the importance of the *principle of difference* rather than the *principle of identity*.

Sacred story as the quintessentially good story defies the kind of classification that Hegel attempted. Sacred story has a way of inspiring new vistas, or as Gadamer suggested *new horizons*.[47] Sacred story encompasses all the elements of what makes a story *superlatively good*. All strands of existence ranging from the most mundane and physical, to what is most purposeful and meaningful, are woven together to form a whole that can only lead the spectator to the conclusion that "the whole is indeed more than the sum of its parts." The result of this weaving is not a static fabric, but a living, dynamic, and ever-changing portrayal. Those dimensions of existence, which human beings mistakenly think of as "lower," cease to appear as merely mundane and inconsequential as the higher dimension illuminates and infuses them with significance. In a similar way, the dependence of the higher dimensions on the lower reveals that vulnerability and fragility lie at the very heart of the universe. Vulnerability and fragility, in turn, provide the arena in which ultimate value can be manifested, experienced, and appreciated.

Furthermore, sacred story never just contains *one* plot in the way that it reveals the sacred. If anything, there are *two main* plotlines that at times run separately and at times intersect and even become concurrent (see figure 7.2). One plot reveals the human story with all its successes and failures. The other plot reveals the life of the triune God. Even when the two plots remain distinct and do not intersect, the stark contrast between the human plot and the divine plot reveals truth. The tragic story of humanity cut loose from its source reveals its desperate need to be reunited with that source or else be doomed to an eternity of despair, sorrow, and pain. The human plot, by revealing the absence of ultimate purpose and meaning, conveys a sense of tragedy that begs for some kind of catharsis. The need of the human plot to experience this catharsis anticipates its convergence with the plot of the story of the triune God. At the same time, the love of the triune God orchestrates the way in which the divine plot will intersect with the human plot. In doing so, the redemption of humankind from its void of purposeless and meaninglessness becomes possible. Hope for a comic reversal of man's tragic fate appears possible for the first time, though this comic reversal is hardly something easily accomplished. In order to reverse the human tragedy, the triune God must enter that tragedy and become its victim. Otherwise, comic reversal will never occur. In sacred story, the fullest intersection of the divine plot with the human plot occurs in the incarnation of the Son of God, where "the Word became flesh and dwelt among us."[48] It is here that the divine story takes upon itself the human story. In this way, too, the purpose and meaning of the divine plot are revealed in the midst of the human plot.

The intersection between the two plots, however, is anything but smooth. It is, rather, rife with conflict as certain persons seek, either intentionally or unintentionally, to advance the human plot in a way that opposes the divine purpose and the divine meaning. Still, despite attempts of human beings to advance their own plot by resisting or ignoring the divine plot, God, in a twist of irony, somehow manages to weave this misguided human plot as well into the overall fabric of the divine plot.

Sacred Story and the Trinitarian God

The way that ethics and aesthetics dynamically interrelate in the superlatively good story reveals a Trinitarian pattern (see figure 7.2). I argued earlier in this book that *transcendental purpose* links up more with ethics and the dimension of the moral, and *transcendental meaning* more with aesthetics and the dimension of the beautiful. God the Father, I suggest, is that Person

Sacred Story and the Trinitarian God

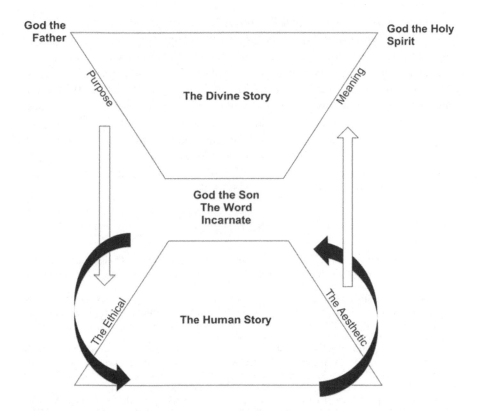

Figure 7.2.   Sacred Story and the Trinitarian God.

of the Holy Trinity who links up with the axiological category I have referred to as the *transcendental purpose*—the divine purpose that channels God's inexhaustible power into the tangible dimension of existence. One should note here, however, that God's *purposive* power is one that guides, directs, and determines human destinies in a manner that is initially *external* to the human soul rather than *internal*. God *internal* working within the human soul is accomplished by the Holy Spirit. The Holy Spirit is the Person of the Holy Trinity who works *within* the human soul to liberate, regenerate, inspire, and transform it. The kind of power that the Holy Spirit engenders is called *dunamis* (δύναμις) in Scripture.[49] The way the Holy Spirit works comports well with my understanding of the way libertarian freedom is unleashed from bondage and reconnected to the Infinite through the Christian virtues of faith, hope, and love. *Dunamis* in the New Testament, however, contains a maximally *positive* significance that is lacking in Aristotle's understanding of *dunamis*. The dynamic enabling that the Holy Spirit accomplishes is a *positive* one that *inspires* the human soul and elevates it into an experience of *transcendental meaning.*

Finally, God the Son is that Person of the Trinity who has to do with the linking and dynamic interplay *between* the divine purpose and the divine meaning. As the Word (the *Logos*), the second Person of the Trinity corresponds to our understanding of what constitutes the quintessentially good story. The incarnation of the Word in Jesus of Nazareth further brings the interplay between the divine purpose and the divine meaning into the context of the concrete so that human beings can grasp it and value it. The story of Jesus Christ—particularly in the way his atonement addresses the problems of deception and injustice, integrates what is fragmented, and reconciles what is alienated—thus ties together the work of the Father and the work of the Spirit in ways that are both paradoxical and dialectical.

NOTES

1. Anselm of Canterbury, "Proslogion," in ed. and trans. Jasper Hopkins and Herbert Richardson, *Anselm of Canterbury Complete Treatises*, Vol. 1 (Toronto: Edwin Mellen, 1974), ch. 2.

2. Thomas Aquinas, *The Five Ways*, in *Summa Theologica*, pt. I, ques. 2, art. 3. See Avicenna, *The Metaphysics of the Healing*, trans. Michael E. Marmura (Provo, Utah: Brigham Young University Press, 2005), ch. 5; Moses Maimonides, *Guide of the Perplexed*, 2nd rev. ed., trans. M. Friedländer (London: Routledge, 1904), ch. 69.

3. See, for example, Richard Swinburne, *The Coherence of Theism* (Oxford: Oxford University Press, 1993); William Lane Craig, *The Kalām Cosmological Argument* (Eugene, OR: Wipf and Stock, 1979), 65–82; Douglas Groothuis, *Christian Apologetics: A Comprehensive Case for Biblical Faith* (Downers Grove, IL: IVP Academic, 2011), chs. 9–13.

4. For example, Richard Dawkins, *The God Delusion* (Boston, MA: Houghton Mifflin, 2006), 24, 73, 100–36, 403; Daniel Dennett, *Breaking the Spell: Religion as a Natural Phenomenon* (New York: Penguin, 2007), 241–42.

5. Also referred to as the "method of remotion." See Aquinas, *Summa Contra Gentiles*, trans. English Dominican Fathers (London: Burns Oates & Washbourne, 1924), bk. I, ch. 14, secs. 1–2, 33.

6. Eccl 3:11.

7. Andrew K. Gabriel, s.v. "Apophatic Theology," in *The Encyclopedia of Christian Civilization* (Oxford: Blackwell, 2012).

8. Alister McGrath, *Christian Theology: An Introduction*, 5th ed. (Oxford: Wiley-Blackwell, 2011), 188–89.

9. Richard Cross, *Duns Scotus* (New York: Oxford University Press, 1999), 48.

10. Immanuel Kant, *Prolegomena to Any Future Metaphysics that Will Be Able to Come Forward as Science*, Akademie edition, trans. Paul Carus, rev. James W. Ellington (Indianapolis, IN and Cambridge, MA: Hackett, 1977), 292, 330, 333, 341–47, 379.

11. I alluded to this problem in chapter 2 in my discussion of the views of Sarvepalli Radhakrishnan.

12. See, for example, Sam Harris, *The End of Faith: Religion, Terror, and the Future of Reason* (New York: W. W. Norton, 2005), 170–73.

13. Edward O. Wilson, *Consilience: The Unity of Knowledge* (New York: Vintage Books, 1999), 8–14.

14. Wilson, *Consilience*, ch. 11.

15. Brian Davies highlights the problem involved in privileging either the principle of credulity or the principle of skepticism in the way he juxtaposes the views of Alvin Plantinga with those of Antony Flew. See Davies, *Philosophy of Religion: A Guide and Anthology* (Oxford: Oxford University Press, 2000), 36–94. He also includes in his anthology an article by Norman Malcolm entitled, "The Groundlessness of Religious Belief," 115–22.

16. Immanuel Kant, *Critique of Pure Reason*, trans. and eds. Paul Guyer and Allen W. Wood (Cambridge: Cambridge University Press, 1998), 680–82 (A810/B838–A815/B843). See also John Frame, *Apologetics: A Justification of Christian Belief*, ed. Joseph E. Torres (Phillipsburg, NJ: P&R Publishing, 2015), 98–110.

17. Swinburne, *The Existence of God* (Oxford: Clarendon, 2004), 145–51; Keith Ward, *God, Chance and Necessity* (Oxford: One World, 1996), 141–45.

18. Examples include the metaphysical speculations of philosophers from Thales to Anaxagoras. All these pre-Socratic philosophers arrived at a view of existence that was fatalistic and impersonal.

19. Aristot. Met. 12.7.1072b4–6.

20. "Cognitivist" and "experiential-expressive" are labels George A. Lindbeck uses to describe two quite different models for approaching theology. Lindbeck, *The Nature of Doctrine: Religion and Theology in a Postliberal Age* (Louisville, KY and London, UK: Westminster John Knox Press, 1984), 16.

21. Lindbeck saw this kind of rapprochement being attempted by ecumenically inclined Roman Catholics such as Bernard Lonergan and Karl Rahner. *The Nature of Doctrine*, 16.

22. Michael Polanyi, *Personal Knowledge: Towards a Post-Critical Philosophy* (Chicago, IL: University of Chicago Press, 1958), 97–98; 377–79.

23. Antony Flew, *There is a God: How the World's Most Notorious Atheist Changed His Mind* (San Francisco, CA: Harper One, 2007), vii–xv, 1–5.

24. A favorite tool of Flew's is "Hume's fork," which allows him to separate "matters of fact" from "relations of ideas." By using this tool, Flew affirms one false dichotomy after another. An example is his insistence that there is no middle ground between "univocal" and "equivocal" sorts of language—in other words, there is no possibility for analogical ways of speaking about God. *God and Philosophy* (Amherst, New York: Prometheus Books, 2005), 44.

25. Flew writes, "A failed proof cannot serve as a pointer to anything, save perhaps to the weaknesses of those of us who have accepted it. Nor, for the same reason, can it be put to work along with other throwouts as part of an accumulation of evidences. If one leaky bucket will not hold water that is no reason to think that ten can" (*God and Philosophy*, 73). However, in *There is a God*, Flew accepts Swinburne's line of reasoning, appealing to the "C-inductive" method of arguing from *cumulative evidence* (143–45).

26. See, for example, Varghese, *The Wonder of the World: A Journey from Modern Science to the Mind of God* (Fountain Hills, AZ: Tyr Publishing, 2003), 145.

27. On May 11, 1996, Flew was awarded the second Phillip E. Johnson Award for Liberty and Truth at Biola University. During his acceptance speech, Flew clarified that he had not accepted the God of Christianity but reaffirmed his deism. In touting deism, he insisted that God is neither interested nor concerned about human beliefs or behaviors.

28. Willard, *The Disappearance of Moral Knowledge*, eds. Steven Porter, Aaron Preston, and Gregg A. Tens Elshof (New York: Routledge, 2018), 102, 358–75.

29. Linda Trinkaus Zagzebski, *Exemplarist Moral Theory* (Oxford: Oxford University Press, 2017), 1–2.

30. Dan Stiver, *The Philosophy of Religious Language: Sign, Symbol and Story* (Oxford: Blackwell, 1996), 134–39.

31. Stiver, *Philosophy of Religious Language*, 149–53.

32. See, for example, Hans Frei, *Theology and Narrative: Selected Essays*, ed. George Hunsinger and William C. Placher (New York: Oxford University Press, 1993), 26–44, 94–116; Lindbeck, *Nature of Doctrine*, 20, 24.

33. Stiver, *Religious Language*, 154–62. Cf. 79–82. See also James McClendon, *Biography as Theology: How Life Stories Can Remake Today's Theology*, new ed. (Philadelphia, PA: Trinity Press International, 1990), 67–88; Michael Goldberg, *Theology and Narrative: A Criti-*

cal Introduction, 2nd ed. (Eugene, OR: Wipf & Stock, 2001), 40–61; Terrence W. Tilley, *Talking of God: An Introduction to Philosophical Analysis of Religious Language* (New York: Paulist Press, 1978), 114–20.

34. Stiver, *Religious Language*, 161–62; Tilley, *Talking of God*, 55–62.

35. Francesca Aran Murphy, *God is Not a Story: Realism Revisited* (Oxford: Oxford University Press, 2007), 5–26.

36. For further discussions of narrative theology, see Gerard Loughlin, *Telling God's Story: Bible, Church and Narrative Theology* (Cambridge: Cambridge University Press, 1996), 17–24; Stanley Hauerwas and L. Gregory Johnson, eds., *Why Narrative? Readings in Narrative Theology* (Eugene, OR: Wipf & Stock, 1997); George W. Stroup, *The Promise of Narrative Theology* (Eugene, OR: Wipf & Stock, 1997), 70–97; Gerhard Sauter and John Barton, eds., *Revelations and Stories: Narrative Theology and the Centrality of Story* (Abingdon, UK: Routledge, 2000); and Francesca Aran Murphy, *God is Not a Story: Realism Revisited* (Oxford: Oxford University Press, 2007).

37. Examples include Jane Austen's *Pride and Prejudice*; Charlotte Brontë's *Jane Eyre*; Emily Brontë's *Wuthering Heights*; Anne Brontë's *The Tenant of Wildfell Hall*; George Eliot's *Middlemarch*; Charles Dickens's *Great Expectations* and *David Copperfield*, also Dickens's *Hard Times* and *Little Dorrit*; and Victor Hugo's *Les Miserables* to name the major ones.

38. One is reminded as well of the heart-wrenching story of the Old Testament prophet Hosea whose wayward and adulterous wife Gomer becomes for him a source of continual agony. This human story deliberately reflects Yahweh's grief over idolatrous Israel. In this way, the human narrative becomes a lens through which the divine narrative can be viewed.

39. Zagzebski, whose understanding of exemplars links closely with the narratival approach I have been advocating, writes, "I think it is a particular advantage of a theory if it can link up with narratives since narratives are one of the primary vehicles for the moral education of the young, and the basic way humans of any age develop and alter their moral sensibilities. Narratives capture the imagination and elicit emotions that motivate action" (Exemplarist Moral Theory, 8).

40. To the realist works of Thomas Hardy, Somerset Maugham, and William Golding, which I have mentioned previously, I should add Joseph Conrad's *Heart of Darkness* and Henrik Ibsen's *A Doll's House* as being representative of cautionary tales.

41. Hans-Georg Gadamer, *Truth and Method*, trans. Joel Weinsheimer and Donald G. Marshall (London and New York: Continuum, 2004).

42. Paul Ricoeur, *Figuring the Sacred: Religion, Narrative, and Imagination*, trans. David Pellauer, ed. Mark I. Wallace (Minneapolis, MN: Fortress, 1995), 35–47.

43. See F. W. Dillistone, *The Novelist and the Passion Story* (New York: Sheed & Ward, 1960). Dillistone, who on one occasion spoke to me of his appreciation for James McClendon's narratival approach to theology, also produced biographies on Anglican clergymen and theologians, including Max Warren, Charles Raven, and C. H. Dodd. My supervisor at Oxford, Paul Fiddes, who, like myself, was a student of Dillistone's, has similarly investigated how an appeal to "creative dialogue" can inform Christian theology. Fiddes, *Freedom and Limit: A Dialogue between Literature and Christian Doctrine* (Macon, GA: Mercer University Press, 1999), 27–46.

44. Recently, for example, Gregory Koukl has focused on the comprehensive nature of the Christian story as true sacred story in *The Story of Reality: How the World Began, How it Ends, and Everything Important that Happens in Between* (Grand Rapids, MI: Zondervan, 2017), 29–39, 173–76.

45. C. S. Lewis, *The Abolition of Man* (Oxford: Oxford University Press, 1943), 27–51.

46. Lewis, *The Abolition of Man*, 1–26.

47. Gadamer, *Truth and Method*, 302–7.

48. John 1:14.

49. Acts 2:8; 2 Tim 1:7.

Chapter Eight

The Struggle of Good against Evil

Value-indicators, at every level of human existence, mediate positive value when they are properly interconnected and contextualized. Instincts, impulses, drives, and aspirations can become interwoven into language and action; and language and action can work together to create a living tapestry of value that has the power to mediate divine purpose and divine meaning into the lives of human beings. No axiological investigation would be complete, however, without considering the ways in which *evil* threatens to unravel the good story in much the same way that a tapestry can be unraveled. Evil threatens to unravel the tapestry of the good and to reduce its component parts to a tangled chaos of immorality and ugliness. Evil can threaten either to destroy or to misdirect even the most basic threads of this tapestry, but its threat certainly does not end there. Evil can threaten to disrupt, halt, and even reverse the process of weaving. It can, as well, devote its energies toward a thwarting of the *purpose that directs*, and a profaning of the *meaning that inspires*, the very process of weaving.

FRAMING THE PROBLEM

To understand why the struggle between good and evil persists, the common source from which the two originate needs investigating. Paul Ricoeur's insights again shed valuable light on the topic. In shifting from his discussion in *Fallible Man* to the one in his work *The Symbolism of Evil*, Ricoeur also transitions from an emphasis on the problem of *finitude* to the problem of guilt.[1] In *Fallible Man*, he investigates how human fragility provides *opportunities* for evil to erupt;[2] whereas in *The Symbolism of Evil*, he examines *narratives* and *symbols* that reflect *actual eruptions* of evil.[3]

203

In these two works, Ricoeur offers valuable reflections concerning what the transition from finitude to guilt entails. For one thing, the symbolism of evil always reveals a particular kind of intrusion of the dimension of the *voluntary* into the dimension of the *involuntary*, especially when the voluntary intrudes into vulnerable and fragile aspects of human existence and does so with damaging consequences. To the degree that nature at its more rudimentary levels does not possess the ability to act *voluntarily*, attempts to ascribe to it either *guilt* or *blame* are pointless. *Natural evil* does not possess a *moral component*. Indeed, no serious person would blame a volcano for erupting and destroying a city in the same way he/she would blame a terrorist for blowing up buildings with people inside them.

There are, however, a couple of places where I believe Ricoeur's approach needs to be further developed. First, while I do not wish to minimize in any way the important ground he broke in his investigations into the symbolism of evil, I do think his treatment of evil focuses too one-sidedly, perhaps, on the dimension of the *ethical* without giving equal attention to the *aesthetic*.[4] Still, since he emphasizes aesthetics elsewhere, this one-sidedness seems easily rectifiable. How, then, does the problem of evil thwart and corrupt the dimensions of the ethical and the aesthetic? With regard to the ethical, on the one hand, evil appears as the *immoral* and the *unjust*. An examination of the *aesthetic* side of evil, on the other hand—such as the one Philip Tallon undertakes in his book *The Poetics of Evil*—might provoke further reflection on the problem of the *deceptive* and the *ugly*.[5]

Second, Ricoeur's investigations into the symbolism of evil could stand to be counterbalanced with a greater emphasis upon the symbolism of the good. I say this because it is clear to me that the fragility that provides occasions for eruptions of evil happens to be the same fragility that provides opportunities for manifestations of the good. This twofold possibility consequently entails that intrusions of the voluntary into places of fragility always hold forth the possibility of producing *good* benefits as well as *evil* consequences. I hope to redress this imbalance in emphasis by keeping the question of the good prior to the question of evil. This is altogether justified insofar as evil, as a negation of the good, *presupposes* the existence of the good.[6] The question of good is thus best not investigated against the backdrop of the problem of evil. Rather, evil as a problem needs to be examined against the backdrop of the question of the good. One cannot, after all, legitimately ask the question, "Why is there a defect?" apart from asking, "What is the defect a defect *of*?"

Efforts in the philosophy of religion to offer solutions to the problem of evil are called "theodicy" (from the Greek words *theos* [θεός] meaning "God" and *dikē* [δίκη] meaning "justice").[7] More specifically, theodicy undertakes to justify how a good and all-powerful God can allow evil to exist in the world. Reputedly, the ancient Epicureans first posed the theodicy dilemma (or *trilemma*) against their Stoic counterparts; and the church father Lactantius, in his *Ira Dei*,[8] discussed its relevance for Christian theology. The problem (with a few of my own insertions) can be framed as follows:

> God is good. God is great. Evil is real. But a trilemma is posed by these three statements that can only be resolved in the following ways:
>
> If evil exists, then God must be good but not great. We may therefore concede that God wishes to eradicate evil but is not fully able to do so.
>
> If evil exists, then God must be great but not good. We may therefore concede that God is fully able to eradicate evil but, for some reason, does not wish to do so.
>
> If evil exists, then God must be neither great nor good, in which case he is feeble. Or else, he does not exist at all.
>
> God may be both great and good, but evil is merely an illusion and is therefore either unreal or not as serious a problem as we human beings, from our limited perspectives, might judge it to be.

Religious perspectives across the world have sought to deal with the problem of evil either by grasping one or more of the horns of the trilemma while sacrificing some or all of the others. Islam, for example, grasps one horn of the trilemma by affirming belief in an all-powerful (omnipotent) God; but it relativizes and compromises God's "goodness" by subsuming it under the "power" category. According to this scenario, power limits and defines goodness, but goodness does not define or restrict how power should be exercised. In the words of the Euthyphro dilemma, "something is deemed right because God wills it." It is not "willed by God because it is right."

Hinduism, by contrast, grasps another horn of the trilemma by affirming an all-wise (good) God, whose power is restricted by the tangible world; viz., the world of illusion (*māyā*). This view curtails God's omnipotence in favor of an emphasis on God's wisdom (goodness). Zoroastrianism, or *Persian dualism*, similarly grasps this horn by affirming the existence of a wise God (Ahura Mazda). In this case, however, God does happen to possess *limited* power; for in Zoroastrianism, the power of Ahura Mazda is challenged by the power of the evil god Ahriman. Hence, while Ahura Mazda can act against evil in the world to a limited degree, he faces an almost equal possibility of defeat because he lacks omnipotence.

Perspectives that seek to grasp the third horn of the trilemma either deny the existence of evil outright (for example, the Christian Science of Mary Baker Eddy [1821–1910])[9] or minimize its radical nature by deeming it necessary for human character development (such as Stoicism and other forms of pantheism). Still, other perspectives see no trilemma because no God exists who needs justifying. Such perspectives accept the evil of this world as a *de facto* characteristic of existence. One such perspective is maintained in Theravada Buddhism. This religious philosophy recognizes that evil in this world is something that must be escaped while leaving aside the question of how evil originated. Likewise, atheism, while arguing that the existence of evil counts against the rationality of belief in the existence of an all-good and all-powerful God, fails to account for why they are so confident that such a thing as evil exists.

With the exception of Theravada Buddhism, the above approaches to the problem of evil share a common element; namely, they employ *reason* as the dominant tool by which to account (1) for why evil does or does not exist, (2) for why only a certain kind of God can exist in the face of evil, or (3) for why God does not exist at all. Whether or not such attempted rational solutions are satisfactory, however, cannot really be decided favorably; for in what sense does a fully rational *explanation* for the problem of evil offer a fully satisfactory *solution* to the problem? At best, rational solutions offer little by way of rectifying the problem of evil in a practical way.[10]

Still, most religions—even those that offer rational solutions—usually do propose certain practical solutions as well. Most of these, however, appear unsatisfactory insofar as they tend to be partial and incomplete. Either they advocate resignation or benign indifference in the face of evil (as with the practical solutions advocated by Buddhism, Hinduism, Stoicism, and pantheism), or they promote endeavors to bring evil to heal through bellicose means (as with radical Islam and early expressions of militant Zoroastrianism).[11] While practical approaches like these enjoy a certain intuitive appeal, as partial solutions they are prone because of their one-sidedness to exaggerations that can make the cure worse than the disease for which the cure was intended. One example is evident in the overzealous jihad philosophy of radical Islam, while another appears in the benign indifference to systemic injustice that characterizes classical Hindu notions of caste. Traditional Hinduism deems people deserving of the social status conferred on them by birth due to sins committed (hypothetically) in a previous existence. These partial solutions to the problem of evil should therefore be set aside in favor of a more comprehensive approach. Can an approach that satisfactorily deals with the theodicy trilemma be found, then, in the perspectives of Christianity?

CHRISTIAN APPROACHES TO THEODICY

Throughout the history of the Christian church, the problem of evil has perhaps not been so much overpondered as it has been overexplained. Among the approaches that have vied to offer satisfactory explanations, *four* have exerted considerable influence: The free will defense, the soul-making theodicy, transformationism, and the eschatological solution.[12] I shall now try to evaluate and examine the relative strengths and weaknesses of these approaches.

Augustine and the Free Will Defense

Of crucial importance to the Augustinian free will defense is the idea of evil as "a privation of the good." Augustine taught that all evil in the world came about as a result of the sin of Adam and Eve.[13] This view affirms that man before the fall was equally "able not to sin and to die" and "able to sin and to die."[14] What, then, is Augustine's particular understanding of the *good* of which evil becomes the privation? The short answer is that *good* equals *perfection*, and he presupposes that this perfection characterizes the state of paradisal bliss that prefallen Adam enjoyed. This perfection further entails, for our purposes here, the harmonious integration of the dimensions of the moral and the beautiful.

The Ambiguity of the Good in Augustine's Theodicy

Nevertheless, while Augustine's view has exerted a pervasive and long-lasting influence on Western theological interpretations of the fall of Adam, I feel compelled here to offer several reasons why I think his understanding of the good, with respect to his interpretation of Genesis 1–3, suffers from several serious misconceptions. First, I must point out that he derives from *Neoplatonism* the lens that he uses to interpret what creation's original goodness as described in Genesis entailed. His use of this lens would not be so problematic if Neoplatonism had actually existed as a philosophical option at the time Genesis was written, but that lens did not and would not exist until the *third century* of the Common Era.[15] Augustine's reliance on Neoplatonism thus commits, first and foremost, the fallacy of *anachronism*.[16]

Second, the Neoplatonic interpretive lens Augustine employs skews his interpretation of the word "good" in Genesis, thus causing him to depart from its lexical denotation and its connotation in the original Hebrew context. The Hebrew word "good" (*tob* [טוֹב]) simply does not convey the idea of perfection as Augustine thought it did, but instead means "good for something" or "for a good purpose."[17] Whereas the Hebrew word implies *potential goodness* with the possibility of further development, the word "perfect" does not imply the same. To say that Adam and Eve in their prefallen state of innocence were also *perfect* thus risks suggesting that they were already *as fully developed as possible*. Unless one equivocates in one's definition of perfection, the choice then becomes clear: either Adam and Eve were *perfect and needed no further development*, or else they were *potentially good and did require further development*. The first option can only preclude the second.

Furthermore, since the first pair apparently could not become *more perfect* than they already actually were in their prefallen state, would this not also imply that they could only change *for the worse*? Why, then, would God allow a change for the worse to be their only option?

The semantic ambiguity concerning the kind of *goodness* man's prefallen nature entails raises even further questions. In the first place, if man were really perfect in his prefallen state, then why would he choose to sin? In the second place, if man were created perfect, then why would God find it necessary to test him? Indeed, if man's goodness could not really be *improved* upon through the test, then what would be the point of the test? Augustine does, of course, appeal to the "*O felix culpa*" theme—*O happy crime that warrants so great a redeemer*. This theme stresses that the *blessedness of those redeemed from the fall will be greater than that of the angels who never sinned*.[18] How, then, does this theme comport with Augustine's suggestion that man is originally created *already* perfect, for now it seems that man *does* have something to gain by sinning, falling, and experiencing redemption?

The original perfection of Adam and the eschatological perfection of the redeemed do not line up either when the two states are compared. The Latin phrase "*posse non peccare*" (able not to sin) characterizes the state of perfection enjoyed by prefallen man. The phrase "*non posse peccare*" (not able to sin) describes the state of perfection enjoyed by the redeemed in their glorified eschatological state. These two statements simply are not semantically equivalent. In the former state of perfection, man possesses free will; while in the latter state, he is sealed by divine grace so that he is *unable* to sin. However, if this sealed perfection is possible eschatologically, then why would God not have endowed Adam with this sort of perfection in his prefallen state as well, especially considering the fact that Adam's free will would only result in his forfeiting of his already-possessed state of perfection?

The problem of Augustine's theodicy is exacerbated again when the question is asked, "Why would an omniscient, all-powerful God create a man whom he knew would fall in the first place?" Surely this could have been avoided if, in the array of all possible worlds that God foresaw *could be actualized*, he had chosen to actualize one in which Adam and Eve would *not* have used their free will to sin. Surely, if God is omniscient, then he would not be surprised when the creatures, whom he does in fact allow to be actualized, commit error. It would also seem that once this actualization has resulted in a fall, an all-powerful God could have chosen to end the failed experiment in a number of ways: (a) He could have isolated Adam and Eve from one another to prevent them from procreating; (b) He could have sterilized them so that they could not have procreated offspring and brought more fallen human beings into the world; or (c) He could have destroyed them for their sin and even sent them to hell as they justly deserved. Finally, why could God not have started the creation of the human race over again using a clean slate?

That an omniscient and all-powerful God could fail in such an experiment is inconceivable enough. However, even more inconceivable is the prospect that God would allow Adam and Eve to reproduce and to bring into being the *"massa damnata"* (mass of the damned) who are doomed to spend eternity in hell.[19] Since God seemingly does nothing to curtail this process, he must at least be charged with negligence; for having the ability and wisdom to intervene and avert such a catastrophe, yet not doing so, raises serious questions about whether he is truly good. Such a God may indeed be all-powerful, but his goodness comes into question. If anything, his goodness is relativized in such a way that "right" becomes entirely relative to "might," so that it must necessarily be defined in terms of it.

Of course, by invoking Plotinus's doctrine of evil as a privation of the good,[20] Augustine seeks to exonerate God of any complicity whatsoever in the appearance of evil in the world. Evil comes into the world—natural and otherwise—solely because of Adam's sin. All nature is cursed as well because of the fault of Adam. However, this explanation again raises the question, "Why did God curse nature instead of intervening on its behalf?" Is it not the case that nature is now doubly victimized? Not only does nature become the victim of Adam's sin, but it becomes the victim of God's curse as well.

In an even more incomprehensible way, this double victimization seems also to apply to Adam's descendants. They are deserving of hell simply by virtue of the fact that they have been born. Though they did not ask to be born, now that they have been thrown into this world through the actions of their parents, they are the victims (1) of Adam's transgression that they themselves did not choose to commit, and (2) of a God who punishes them for a flaw in their nature that they were not responsible for causing. One would have to say here that God seems to become an accomplice to the unfolding of a drama resembling a Greek tragedy.

A further difficulty with Augustine's free will defense concerns how an all-powerful God could choose to elect persons to salvation by illuminating some while passing over the *massa damnata,* whom he, for no apparent reason, chooses not to illuminate. An all-powerful God, after all, has the ability to illuminate everyone, so why does he not do so? Augustine seeks to get around this difficulty by saying that God is justified in sending everyone to hell, but that he has shown himself gracious in saving *some.* Pierre Bayle (1647–1706), who once had been a French Huguenot who espoused fideism, reacted to this idea when he claimed concerning Augustine's portrayal of God: *God seems very much like a surgeon who deliberately allows the bones of his patients be broken just to show them how good he is at setting bones.*[21]

I should point out now, however, that most of the difficulties associated with Augustine's theodicy stem from an understanding of "the good" that is too narrow. I would ask my reader at this point to revisit my discussion in chapter 5, where I considered how Plato and Aristotle, and much of the tradition stemming from their insights, maintained an axiologically *negative* view of the principle of *différance*. From this, it follows that elements such as dynamism, change, and becoming are, for them, *axiologically negative* as well. Unfortunately, any possible *positive* notion of the role of libertarian freedom is precluded by this axiologically negative bias. This bias at the same time allows a *positive* axiological emphasis to be placed upon elements such as form, limit, and actuality, so there is little wonder that the concept of the *good* became equated with the concept of *teleological perfection*. Unfortunately, these axiological presuppositions were carried over into Augustine's thought.

Rescuing Valid Elements of Augustine's Theodicy by an Appeal to Narratival Truth

Despite the difficulties that I have found with some of the ways that Augustine formulated his free will defense, one very important truth remains uncompromised by the metaphysical conundrum that his Neoplatonist-inspired theodicy creates. The *narratival truth* of the story of Adam and Eve endures despite attempts of reflective philosophy to improve upon it. Though Adam and Eve did enjoy the best of circumstances in paradise, they chose to throw everything away for a piece of forbidden fruit. Instead of *flourishing* as God intended them to do, they were catapulted into a downward spiral of *perishing*. The catalyst that occasioned this transition was the evil of *deceptive beauty* that inveigled them into committing an immoral act. The serpent's ruse promised an easy path to flourishing rather than the difficult path that would have required from them obedience and sacrifice. Adam and Eve chose what seemed to them a shortcut, but this "easy pathway to godhood" instead turned out to be a long, steep, and tortuous path that led through the barren valley of the curse before it could lead out of it. Hence, Adam and Eve, by choosing to commit their immoral act, opted to be inveigled by a deceptive beauty that would lead not to beauty's increase, but to its depletion. They consequently found themselves exiled from the beauty of paradise into the curse's territory with its stark ugliness.

The narrative of Genesis 3 preserves an emphasis as well upon divine grace that Augustine, the theologian of grace, seems to miss. Genesis portrays the divine judgment upon the first pair not so much in terms of God's wrath and retribution, for the curse does not entail a final exile into another dimension of existence that turns out to be a dead end. Instead, the pain resulting from the curse turns out to be the soil in which the seeds of divine redemptive grace can germinate; or, as C. S. Lewis commented concerning the problem of pain: "It is God's megaphone through which he rouses a deaf world."[22] A closer examination of Genesis reveals that the curse itself has the potential to become an instrument of redemption. In this respect, the curse's effects can be transitioned from the status of divine retribution to one of divine chastisement. How, then, are divine retribution and divine chastisement interconnected, and what makes the transition from the former to the latter possible? I believe the answer will depend on how persons with libertarian freedom respond to the divine displeasure. Whether it is experienced in terms of retributive judgment or chastisement depends very much on whether human attitudes and responses are favorable or unfavorable. Repentance from evil ways certainly qualifies as a favorable response. There is no guarantee, however, that free moral agents will respond in a favorable way.

The Soul-Making or Irenaean Theodicy

A very different interpretation of the fall of Adam and Eve—one made popular through the writings of John Hick (1922–2012)[23]—was offered by St. Irenaeus of Lyons, a second-century Christian bishop and apologist who countered the heresy of gnosticism. Since Irenaeus rejected gnosticism, we should naturally expect that his view of the fall of Adam and Eve would avoid some of the gnostic categories that had exaggerated Plato's two-world theory into outright dualism. Irenaeus's view of the fall of Adam is often described in terms of an "*upward* fall." As such, it contrasts significantly with Augustine's "*downward* fall" perspective.[24]

Dynamic Goodness as Opposed to Formal Perfection

According to Irenaeus, Adam and Eve are not created as *perfect* but as *innocent* and *childlike*.[25] As Eric Osborn (1922–2007) observes, "Perfection for Irenaeus lies at the end, not at the beginning, of man's education by God, a process which takes account of the fall from the beginning."[26] Adam and Eve are endowed with free will and warned not to eat of the forbidden fruit. However, because they are childlike and inexperienced, they disobey God and are punished accordingly. The catalyst that precipitates this disobedience is *deception*, just as it was for Augustine; but with Irenaeus the deception is aimed not at a perfect creature but an innocent one. Indeed, in the Irenaean account, the deception that the serpent employs gains entrance principally through the *innocence* and *idealism* of youth. Hence, the sin for which Adam and Eve are punished must not be viewed so much a heinous crime (in the way Augustine saw it) as it is a horrible mistake. The sin of the first pair is committed out of a lack of experience instead of in the full light of knowledge and wisdom. The condition this sin brings about, however, is one from which they can recover and through which they can learn, grow, and progress.[27] Irenaeus consequently views the punishment that the first pair received not as a final verdict of condemnation but as a severe reprimand intended to teach them wisdom and help them to develop their character in a proper way. With these facts in mind, Adam's fall becomes an occasion for *moral growth and progress* as well as for the *cultivation of true beauty*.[28]

According to Irenaeus's interpretation, Christ makes possible the growth of human beings from their possession merely of the image of God to the point that they come over time to possess the divine likeness—this being none other than "Christlikeness."[29] Irenaeus accordingly distinguishes between the "image" of God and the "likeness" of God[30] despite the fact that there is no real exegetical basis for deriving this distinction from the Genesis text where the *image* and *likeness* are used synonymously.[31] In Irenaeus's view, then, Adam's state in paradise is not one of formal perfection, which has been lost and which must now be regained by the circular process of *anamnesis* (as Augustine, following the Platonists, taught). Rather, it is an initially incomplete state that is transcended as the faithful, through their moral and aesthetic participation in God,[32] eventually grow into Christlikeness.[33] The idea that certain evils exist as *tests* which aid in the progress of human growth and development is often called "soul-making."[34]

Soul-making further appears as a dominant theme in Hebrew Kabbalah,[35] which I discussed in chapter 5 in connection with the concept of *différance*. According to Kabbalistic theology, the physical world and the human body serve more as the *incubator* of the soul than as the *prison house* of the soul as Plato had supposed.[36] The world contains obstacles that we must overcome and surmount if we are to grow in our understanding and appreciation of God and his meaning. However, these obstacles are all for the purpose of testing human beings and encouraging them to engage in the process that leads to the development of the good.

With regard to powerful narratives and compelling stories, the emphasis upon soul-making shares affinities with a literary genre known as the *bildungsroman*. Indeed, in a *bildungsroman*, the plot revolves centrally around a protagonist's character development in the face of life's numerous challenges. Pip, in Charles Dickens's *Great Expectations*, and David Copperfield, in another of the author's novels by that name, are examples of *masculine* character development; while Charlotte Brontë's *Jane Eyre* exemplifies a perspective on feminine character development belonging to this genre. In the twentieth century, the fantasy novels of J. R. R. Tolkien use a *bildungsroman* theme in the stories of Bilbo and Frodo Baggins.

The Optimistic Assessment of Free Will in Soul-Making Models

The soul-making theodicy does serve as a useful counterbalance to the Augustinian free will defense. Whereas the Augustinian defense maintains a more negative assessment of the role free will plays in bringing *evil* into the world, the soul-making view makes the point that our freedom is the means by which *good* also is established. This latter view is closer, as well, to Jewish interpretations of the transgression of Adam and Eve. Some Christian interpreters fall short of recognizing this view in the Book of Genesis. Evidence from the Genesis text nonetheless reveals a subtle comparison between Adam and Eve, on the one hand, and Abram and Sarai, on the other. The faithless rebellion of Adam and Eve are countered by the faithful obedience of Abram and Sarai.[37] The first couple through disobedience lose their access to land (i.e., paradise).[38] The second pair, Abram and Sarai, through their faithful obedience to God, inherit for themselves and their offspring the land of promise.[39] The curse upon Adam and Eve, which entails pain in childbirth and the thorns and thistles that inhibit cultivation of the land, is countered by the blessings bestowed upon Abram and Sarai. These blessings include the birth of Isaac and their habitation of the land of Canaan.[40] One further sees the idea of soul-making unfold especially in the journey of faith and in the process involved in the Christian process of sanctification.

Inherent Deficiencies of the Soul-Making Idea

Despite certain attractive elements in the soul-making theodicy, this approach to theodicy nonetheless harbors several deficiencies. One major deficiency is this model's failure to provide an adequate explanation for why evil is so unevenly distributed in the world or why some people seem to have to suffer to a greater extent than others. Because this theodicy focuses so heavily on the soul-making of *individuals*, it fails to pay enough attention to the role the human social dimension plays in providing ideal contexts that can facilitate human flourishing. Systemic social evil can erect serious obstacles that can limit—and even eliminate—opportunities of individual human souls to engage in soul-making. The world is hardly an enormous Montessori school where everyone is furnished the best of circumstances and ample opportunity to undertake growth. Indeed, certain versions of the soul-making view may justify the most horrific types of social inequity and atrocious of evils as being necessary for character development. The notion of soul-making in Hinduism certainly deserves such an indictment, not to mention the philosophy of Stoicism. Nietzsche, too, in his *Twilight of the Idols* says, "that which does not destroy me, makes me stronger;"[41] but counterevidence suggests that some people can indeed become utterly demoralized and debilitated by the tragedies they are forced to endure. Psychologist Viktor Frankl, for instance, observed cases among Nazi death-camp survivors whom he treated.[42] Frankl observed that human constitutions differ from person to person, for some possess a stronger psychological disposition, while others are more fragile.[43] Thus, evil appears to be unevenly distributed not only because of sociological inequities, but also because of inequities in individuals' capacity to succeed in facing challenges to their psychological development.

A second deficiency of the soul-making model is that the advancement of *individual souls* does not necessarily guarantee *social advancement* as well. In short, soul-making fails to address the need for *distributive justice*. Though it is true enough that the soul-making of individuals can have a positive transformative effect upon society, the opposite can also happen. The disintegration of society is an equal possibility when individuals become too negligent, withdraw from their social and political obligations, and decline to take an unyielding stance against perpetrators of social injustice.

Again, if taken as a *rational explanation* for the problem of evil, the soul-making theodicy can no more epitomize an *all-encompassing solution* for why evil exists than can Augustine's free will defense model. The problem of radical evil defies rational explanation and neat categorization. The existence of radical evil thus demands approaches that venture beyond the scope of both these paradigms.

Balancing the Strengths and Weaknesses of the Soul-Making Theodicy with Those of the Free Will Defense

Still, to abandon every element of the soul-making and free will defense paradigms due to their incapacity to be extended into universal solutions would prove foolish. These two theodicies do, in fact, relate to the wider contexts of human experience in the same way that the choices of individual characters within a story relate to the whole. Aspects of the two models are therefore combinative because they share a common hinge; namely, that hinge where human freedom of choice is capable of producing manifestations either of good or of evil. Elements of both models can be recovered by appealing to a concept of libertarian freedom in an effort to connect them. Thus, instead of claiming that the good is a prepossessed perfection that is forfeited by an act of free will, the soul-making view can demonstrate that free will is itself a "good"—a good potential—that can function as an instrument for developing a greater good than what man's original state entailed. If free will is to be capable of producing good, then it must at least have the equal capability of producing evil. The concept of "the good" can in this way be broadened to include the dimensions of both *potentiality* and *actuality*, and not of *actuality* only. Libertarian freedom, which entails *good potential*; and *perfection*, which entails *actualization* of that potential; can then both be viewed as *species* of a good that transcends formal and dynamic categories while at the same time embracing them, directing them, and inspiring them.[44]

Appealing to the concept of libertarian freedom as a hinge that combines the best elements of the *free will defense* with the *soul-making theodicy* can also prevent one from falling into the trap (as G. W. F. Hegel did) of making *actual* evil necessary for the realization of the good. It would nonetheless be correct to affirm that the *possibility* of evil is necessary for the realization of the good, because one cannot have the possibility of good without an equal possibility of evil. Evil as a possibility is therefore implied in the nature of real human freedom just as the possibility of good is implied in the same. The possibility of producing *great* good, furthermore, must also entail the possibility of committing *great* evil. Indeed, all cultural advancements that prove beneficial can bring the concomitant risk of producing evil consequences. The discovery of nuclear power is just one example of this truth. Persons living in the Middle Ages did not need to fear the destructive consequences of nuclear power because that technology did not yet exist. They were therefore limited in the degree of evil they could cause because the degree of good (as least as it pertains to technological advancement) was limited. However, as technologies develop, so do the opportunities to use them for good or for evil increase in tandem. Unfortunately, putting the "genie back in the bottle" once it escapes is impossible; for once a development unfolds, it is more than likely here to stay.

Transformational Approaches to the Problem of Evil

"Transformational approaches"[45] to theodicy are not new but appear throughout Christian history. Indeed, the *whole story* of Christianity can be viewed at one level as a *grand* story that includes numerous smaller stories of persons who have engaged *individually* in the development of their own character as well as *collectively* in the process of world transformation. The individual stories of human beings, in fact, form narratival clusters as these stories become linked through transformative social networks. Transformational approaches thus entail practical ways of initiating and fostering the good, and of preventing and curtailing evil, with regard to individuals and their social relationships.

Returning to my earlier discussion of the value-compass, I must point out here that the two aspects of the compass's tangible direction, *life* and *survival*, come to mind when characterizing various kinds of transformational approaches. These two aspects can be either hampered or facilitated by the particular ways in which the compass's liberating and limiting directions (i.e., freedom, limit, power, and order) either produce destructive conflict that results in manifestations of evil or interconnect in constructive ways to foster the good.

Intentionally Perpetuating Contexts that Enable Flourishing

One transformational approach addresses the problem of evil preemptively by focusing on the *ordinary and regular tasks of life*. Persons who engage in this kind of transformationism typically endeavor to establish and foster the development of the good by caring, nurturing, teaching, guiding, and aiding in processes of individual and cultural transformation. Advocates of this approach thus seek to initiate and develop the good by instituting social covenants, agencies, and structures that, ideally at least, intentionally promote contexts in which soul-making and human flourishing are made maximally possible both for individuals and for the societies in which they live and to which they contribute. Advocates of this type of transformationism seek furthermore to embody its ideals and to establish their permanence in institutions such as homes, churches, and schools. As agents of transformation, these institutions, in turn, aim through their day-to-day operations at improving individuals and the societies in which they live, and to do so in extraordinarily meaningful ways.

In his now classic work, *Christ and Culture*, H. Richard Niebuhr observes this kind of transformational model operative in the thought of St. Augustine, to whom he attributed the "Christ-transforming-culture" vision of how Christ and culture should interact.[46] As a central theme of the Christian story, the Christ-transforming-culture vision entails something more than just a bandaging up of the wounds of the afflicted. Though the church is indeed called to this task of ministry, she is not restricted to accomplishing *only* this task: She is called as well to be an agent of "cultural formation" (Ger=*Bildung*).[47] Andy Crouch has recently set forth this vision in a fresh way in his book *Culture Making*.[48] The transformational vision is more comprehensive than the vision that merely promotes individual soul-making. While this larger vision must include the soul-making model of theodicy as one of its components in order to be fully effective, its scope and aim also extend well beyond the limitations of *individual* soul-making to include the prospect of *world* transformation through culture-building. Thus, as St. Augustine recognized, the scope and aim of this vision must encompass the story of the *City of God* and all that the building of that city entails.

The story that the City of God encompasses extends well beyond a return to the paradise of the beginning. As such, it extends beyond the highly restrictive Platonic narratives of salvation that merely envision a return of individual souls to the same state of being from which they fell.[49] The story of the City of God is driven by a vision of forward progress that embraces the best accomplishments of the earthly dimension of reality as the church progresses towards its final destination. This destination accomplishes the integration of the ideals of the *garden* and the *city*.[50] The Apostle John envisions this destination as a garden-city symbiosis in the Book of Revelation.[51] The individual's enjoyment of heaven (or the beatific vision) may therefore stand as one principal goal of soul-making, though it is not the only goal. The goal of soul-making is surpassed by the promise of the redemption of *civilization* as well, so that it includes the salvation not just of *isolated individuality* but of the *meaningful relationality* that individuals form with one another as they journey through the present world in the company of others.

N. T. Wright, in his book *Surprised by Hope*, develops this fuller under-standing of redemption as one that includes within its horizon the expectation of *cosmic redemption*.[52] This cosmic-redemption expectation, he observes, appears in the eighth chapter of Paul's Epistle to the Romans.[53] The Apostle John's description of the Celestial City in Revelation further reveals that this city comes down out of Heaven from God as a bride adorned for her hus-band.[54] Its location is on a "great and high mountain."[55] John's description suggests that the City of God is a place or state of being where heaven and earth at long last meet.[56] However, while this "place" is not described as some disembodied spiritual plane of being, it is not characterized as a mere earthly utopia either. Indeed, this city already presupposes that "the new heavens and the new earth" have arrived before it comes down on "the great and high mountain." Such imagery suggests that the present physical or material dimension will somehow be refined and transmuted into something *transphysical.* The present physical world is thus not entirely left behind, as so much of the Platonic tradition taught. Just as the resurrected body of Jesus had qualities that qualified as physical—he could eat fish and could be touched[57]—this body had at the same time qualities that were transphysi-cal—for example, he could appear inside a locked room without entering through a door, and he could appear and disappear at will.[58] There is thus a continuity between the story of the present life and the story of the life to come; not an absolute break where one story (i.e., the spiritual) wholly re-places the other (i.e., the physical). At the same time, the use of the Greek word for "new" (*kainos* [καινός]), which John uses in Revelation 21:1, sug-gests a *qualitative* difference: The new heavens and the new earth are not merely new in *time*, they are even more so new in *kind*.

The transformational approach I am describing also ventures beyond the idea of soul-making because it holds forth the possibility that not just ordi-nary, but *extraordinary* goodness may be actualized in the present world. In Roman Catholic and other liturgical church traditions, there has always been room for this idea of extraordinary goodness in its understanding of what *sainthood* entails.[59] For instance, persons like Saint Teresa of Calcutta exem-plified in recent history an extraordinary degree of dedication to bringing about good in situations of extreme deprivation. In Catholicism, such saints serve as embodiments of an inspiring ideal of what we can become if we choose to surrender ourselves to God. In Protestantism, the idea of sainthood has often been diluted to the category of the common (every saved person is considered to be a saint), but even Protestantism has recognized extraordi-nary heroes of faith such as Martin Luther, John Calvin, John Wesley, and Billy Graham. The extraordinary lives of persons such as these serve to inspire us to be extraordinary in the ways we engage in our individual soul-making and seek actively to foster and encourage the soul-making of others. In these ways, the stories of the saints feed and enrich our own stories.

Extraordinary goodness, in fact, serves as the counterbalance to the problem of radical and senseless evil. In the face of the absurd evil perpetrated by the likes of Adolf Hitler, for instance, there appeared the extraordinary goodness of Dietrich Bonhoeffer who stood up against the evil of the Third Reich and was martyred for his faith because he dared to do so. In the face of the absurd evil of social inequality in the Southern United States during the days of racial segregation, Martin Luther King exhibited an extraordinary courage that transformed a society even though the effort ended up costing him his life. The stories of persons like Bonhoeffer and King demonstrate what Ricoeur calls "the logic of superabundance"—the same kind of "logic" Jesus exercised when he cried from the cross, "Father, forgive them, for they know not what they do."[60] To the world, giving one's life in the way martyrs do may indeed seem irrational—even absurd—but it is one powerful response to the problem of irrational and absurd evil. Extraordinary goodness furthermore has the power to overcome and outlast absurd evil, and this should encourage us to devote ourselves to committing "random acts of goodness" as we progress through this world and as our own stories unfold.

To give one's life over entirely to one's own individual "soul-making" is, therefore, insufficient because it is too narrowly focused upon the story of the self to the exclusion of a greater story; viz., one that includes the lives of *others*. We should therefore also devote ourselves to helping others in their progress through this world. The call to this kind of devotion is, in fact, entailed in the Great Commission in the New Testament where Jesus enjoins his followers to go into all nations and "teach" whatsoever Christ has commanded.[61] This task turns out to be immensely large in its scope. Though important, the practice of Christian evangelism is insufficient in its scope to fulfill what the Great Commission requires, and people are mistaken if they think that the Great Commission can be reduced to evangelism alone. Fulfilling it must, rather, entail nothing short of one's dedication to the task of the building of the Kingdom of God in all its facets.

Just as the stories of extraordinary *individuals* may intrude into our world during certain times in history, there have also been extraordinary *epochs* in history when stories of goodness have broken through in significant ways to transform entire societies. Theologian Paul Tillich referred to these as *kairoi* moments (from *kairos* [καιρός]), which is a Greek word for a kind of time infused with significance.[62] Among these *kairoi* moments were the acceptance of Christianity as the religion of the Roman Empire, the theological and philosophical strides made during the High Middle Ages, the Reformation, and the Great Awakenings of the eighteenth and nineteenth centuries that spiritually revitalized England and the United States. Many more of these *kairoi* moments have occurred throughout history, emerging unexpectedly when vast numbers of people have become energized to participate in social movements that achieve human betterment. Finally, if the transformational vision that I have been discussing is to be maximally effectual, then it must entail consistent and long-term commitment, work, and self-sacrifice. In this respect, investment in the *process* of transformation becomes just as important as reaching its goal. There can be no standing still.

Transforming Radical Evil

Transformational approaches are concerned not only on one front with the *ordinary* and *regular* tasks of life that establish and foster the development of the good in both individuals and societies, but they are also faced on another front with the transformation of situations where individuals and societies have had to face times of *extraordinary* crisis, testing almost beyond the limits of human endurance, and circumstances that can lead to eclipses of faith. In such cases, the good story must somehow be manifested meaningfully in the midst of *absurd evil*. With regard to the tangible direction of the value-compass, the transformational emphasis here happens to be placed more upon *survival* than upon the *flourishing of life*. The shadow-side of the possibility that extraordinary good may be actualized in our world is the possibility that absurd and senseless evil may be actualized as well. Indeed, it is on the problem of radical evil that most people focus; for we are prone always to ask "Why?" when faced with senseless evil, but we are less likely to ask "Why?" when we encounter extraordinary goodness. More often than not, we seem to dwell upon the negative while ignoring the positive.

Again, I must stress that the actualization of radical evil is *not necessary* for the realization of good. A transformational approach nonetheless offers hope that the most radical experiences of evil can be contained and even transformed in such a way that they can be turned *toward* good. In chapter 2, I pointed out that the *tenacity* of the human species entails the possibility that high degrees of meaning can be actualized. However, meaning only appears *as* meaningful when set against the backdrop of human fragility. The ability to experience meaning increases as tenacity and fragility increase in tandem. Because we are fragile, this means we are vulnerable; and our vulnerability, in turn, can serve as the backdrop against which absurd evil may be experienced to higher degrees among humans than may be possible among other species.

When faced with absurd evil, we are usually affected on two fronts. One is the *psychological* front and the other is the *sociological*. Events of *natural* evils such as hurricanes, tornadoes, earthquakes, and tsunamis can leave people *psychologically* wounded. Events such as these may cause, as well, enormous *social* setbacks for which the resources and recovery time needed to return to a state of normality may be lengthy. Even worse than natural evils, however, are acts of *moral* evil that free moral agents perpetrate against individuals and groups. Weather cannot be blamed for being destructive in the same way terrorists can be blamed, for terrorism is a moral evil that indicates malice aforethought. If a psychologically insane person commits an atrocious act of evil, then this factor may make that evil act easier to process than a planned and premeditated act of moral evil. On the other hand, genocide registers as one of the greatest of all acts of moral evil because genocide, being socially orchestrated, cannot be blamed on the psychological illness of only one person. It was, in fact, the evil of genocide that Frankl encountered in his own account of being interned in a Nazi concentration camp. Frankl's story, recounted in his work *Man's Search for Meaning*, provides help for anyone who has suffered the more extreme kinds of victimization that the Jews experienced in the Nazi death camps.

Frankl noticed that those who lost hope in trying to survive in the Nazi death camps were inevitably the first to die. On the other hand, those who did survive were those who never lost the will to do so.[63] Frankl derived from this experience an approach to psychological healing that he called "logotherapy."[64] He encouraged each patient to accept the fact that the evils each had suffered were patently absurd, but he also presented each with a choice. Either one could dwell upon the evils suffered to the extent that the memory of this suffering would develop into a full-blown psychological cancer that would eventually eat away whatever else remained of the good in one's life, or else one could choose to contain this suffering and even to transform it into a force that could be turned toward good. Frankl urged persons not to waste their suffering, but to use it as a tool to help give wisdom and courage to others.

The psychological-transformational approach, however, is at best one-sided because it does not go far enough in changing the status quo of a society so that it becomes conducive to fostering the good rather than perpetuating evil. To stop short of changing the status quo is to accept patterns of moral and spiritual depravity and apathy as normative. The facile acceptance of status quo structures in which patterns of social evil have become entrenched invariably guarantees that future eruptions of irrational evil will continue to occur. Karl Marx's insights are valuable in this regard. In his eleventh thesis on Feuerbach, he made the now-famous statement, "Philosophers have only interpreted the world in various ways; the point is to change it."[65] Marx's advocation for change can be directed against what is most unacceptable in the models offered by Platonic philosophy, whether Christian or otherwise; and this is the Platonically inspired idea that we simply must endure psychologically the present world and its evils because they are to be expected as a matter of course. Thus, this Platonic perspective survived in the opinion of Augustine, who believed that the institution of slavery resulted from the sin that Ham committed against his father Noah.[66] Augustine unfortunately viewed slavery as a result to be expected in a fallen world. For this reason, it was a condition of present existence that people simply had little choice but to endure. He consequently found no place in his Christian Neoplatonism for an incentive to abolish slavery. This same perspective was upheld by Martin Luther, who, after the Peasant's Revolt of 1525, reemphasized his understanding of Christian freedom to entail only a freedom of the soul. Christian freedom did not extend to include *political* freedom.[67] Hence, in Luther's estimation, the freedom of the Christian could not entail a license for peasants to rebel against their unjust overlords. Instead, it was the peasants' lot to endure the cross and to suffer just as Jesus had suffered. Systemic social injustice is thus tolerated and endured because of viewpoints that happen to be too rigidly Platonic.

Fortunately, Martin Luther's namesake, the Reverend Dr. King, would not accept these views but would make a push through nonviolent means to bring about a new status quo in the post-slavery context of the Southern United States. Interestingly, Martin Luther King's own story was heavily influenced by Mohandas Gandhi's (1869–1948) Satyagraha movement, which did much to transform India from a society based on caste into a democracy.[68] Gandhi, in turn, was influenced by the Christian socialism of Leo Tolstoy (1828–1910) and John Ruskin (1819–1900).[69] The effort to overcome *systemic injustice* thus stands as a counter-balance to models of *psychological transformation*, but one should remember that solutions that divorce the psychological dimension from the social dimension, and that migrate either to one pole or the other, always end up being half-solutions.

Approaches that try to achieve total equitability in society often destroy, as well, the incentive necessary for human creativity to flourish. Marx therefore may have been accurate about the need to change the world, but he was mistaken about the *best way* to go about it and *to what end*. The cure he advocated ended up being worse than the disease the cure was intended to remedy. His cure was inadequate because it was merely a socio-economic remedy, but the sociological consequences of his cure provide evidence for why it was inadequate. The lack of attention given to the importance of individual incentive and initiative in fostering economic success provides a major explanation for why the Soviet Union went bankrupt.[70] The attempt of the Soviets at the redistribution of wealth destroyed the very individual incentive and initiative that, by fostering competition, could have effectively led to the creation of wealth. Consequently, when all the wealth had been depleted and no more of it was left to redistribute, the Soviet Union faced bankruptcy. The Marxian experiment thus ended abruptly before its imagined end, utopia, could ever hope to be realized. The outcome of this experiment reveals, however, that the transformation of the *inner lives* of persons must be deemed just as important as the transformation of *social structures* where extreme inequities exist. The best approach is, therefore, two-pronged rather than singular in the way it addresses social problems. The back-and-forth movement between cooperation and competition should thus be kept in a state of equilibrium as much as possible, for social stagnation usually occurs when this equilibrium is jeopardized.

While the transformational approaches I have presented above do offer a way of further contextualizing the free will defense and soul-making theodicy, and of overcoming some of the inherent weaknesses of these efforts to deal with the problem of evil, these models do tend to fail if they offer no basis on which to hope for a better future other than human strength and ingenuity. As the Reformed theologian Jürgen Moltmann once said of the Marxist utopian ideals of atheist sociologist Ernst Bloch, "Bloch knows a hell on earth in which there is no Easter and a dying where the principle of hope accomplishes nothing."[71] Moltmann means by this indictment that the hope that some human utopia will be reached at the end of history gives little comfort to those who have had to sacrifice their lives along the way to see this utopia become a reality. Those who are now dead will never enjoy the utopia when it is finally reached; if, indeed, it ever *is* reached.

Secular utopias, as I have already indicated in chapter 4, are thus limited in their capacity to inspire because only those fortunate enough to live to see them come to pass will become their beneficiaries. The rest, who work feverishly to bring them to fruition, may also become so driven to see them bear fruit in their own day that they "shipwreck" themselves on the rocky shores of reality. In such cases, dashed ideologies offer little comfort to those holding them. Instead, they only serve to highlight how one's life has been misspent in a futile cause directed toward an unattainable, if not unfulfilling, end. The inadequate forms of social transformationism thus beg for a solution that extends beyond tangible existence to a dimension where the ultimate purpose of the Transcendent prevails and where the ultimate meaning of the Transcendent abounds.

Eschatological Approaches to the Problem of Evil

Because so many of the stories of secular utopias tend to end unsatisfactorily, tragically, or not at all, they fail to qualify as "good stories." Every "good story" must have a satisfactory denouement and ending, and eschatology points to these aspects of my narratival approach to understanding the struggle of good against evil. Denouements and satisfactory endings usually reveal what in literature is called "poetic justice," and Christian eschatology reveals ways that poetic justice renders its verdict. Eschatology, in Christian theology, concerns teachings about "last things," and these teachings must inevitably entail a discussion about heaven and hell, what the future state consists of, and logical reasons for believing that God's purpose for humanity will be vindicated and that God's meaning will become further opened to human experience in a future state. The vindication of God's purpose will necessitate the triumph of ultimate justice and fairness over injustice and inequality, while the further opening up of God's meaning must entail the ascendency of truth and clarity over deception and ambiguity. With regard to our present existence, the eschatological approach to theodicy entails the promise that all of the evils of the here and now will pale in comparison with the glory that shall be manifested in the world to come, as St. Paul writes in Romans 8:18, "For I reckon that the sufferings of this present time are not worthy to be compared with the glory which shall be revealed in us."

The Role of the Christian Virtues in the Mediation of Transcendence

Because the eschatological approach to theodicy is linked to divine meaning and divine purpose, it provides an ultimate standard for measuring justice in the world as well as offering grounding for living a good life in the present state. One must, however, consciously and deliberately choose to allow one's libertarian freedom to become open and linked to divine meaning and purpose. This linkage entails a transformation and redirection of one's libertarian freedom by means of the virtues of faith, hope, and love. These virtues, in turn, become the vehicles and channels through which that divine meaning and purpose begin to be mediated further into one's tangible existence. Apart from this transformation, libertarian freedom will remain disconnected from the dimension of the Transcendent.

Blaise Pascal expresses the idea I am presenting here in terms of the role faith plays when he offers his celebrated wager. He argues that if God exists and I believe, then I have everything to gain and nothing to lose; but if God exists and I choose not to believe, then I have nothing to gain and everything to lose. [72] Pascal argues as well that if I believe and God does not exist, then I still would have lived a better, more fulfilling life in this world than I would have done had I chosen otherwise. His wager, however, involves more than mere mental assent. It also involves the element of risk-taking.

I surmise that John Hick was the first modern philosopher of religion to offer a version of this wager in his "eschatological verification theory." [73] Hick, in a manner that seems Bunyanesque, couches his theory in the story of two pilgrims on the road to the Celestial City. One believes there is a Celestial City; the other does not. Neither of them, however, will actually know whether there is such a city until one of them finally arrives; but it is almost guaranteed that the one who chooses to disbelieve will never arrive because he will have too soon given up the journey, thinking it all a waste of time, effort, and investment.

Hick's story helps illustrate how belief in the afterlife provides a transcendental basis for both ethics and aesthetics in the present world. [74] (1) With regard to *ethics*, the eschatological *hope* of heaven provides a positive incentive for one's living out the story of *faith*. The story of faith, in turn, entails the living of a morally upright life marked by obedience to God's commandments and submission to his purpose. The fear of punishment by an infinitely good and just God can serve as a deterrent to living out a story in opposition to faith and hope. Lived apart from the virtue of faith, one's life story becomes marked by faithlessness, rebellion, immorality, and the unjust treatment of others. Lived apart from hope, the soul becomes tarnished by hopelessness, apathy, and despair. (2) With regard to *aesthetics*, the *beauty* of heaven provides positive inspiration for living out a *sacrificial* story that mediates transcendental beauty into the lives of others. Optimally, one who lives out such a story does so in accordance with the Christian virtue of *love*, which is the virtue most capable of mediating divine meaning into the lives of ourselves and others. The ultimate grounding for both ethics and aesthetics thus lies in eschatology, and this fact is repeatedly pointed out in the New Testament. [75]

The Weakened Emphasis on the Mysterium Tremendum et Fascinans in Modern Conceptions of the Afterlife

Traditionally, Christian theological concepts of the afterlife pointed to more intensified experiences of the transcendent God as the *mysterium tremendum et fascinans* than are possible for persons living out their stories in the tangible existence. These concepts, however, seem to have become less attractive to modern people. All too often we are prone to cry out against the evils of this world while taking its goodness for granted. At the same time, we willingly forfeit the belief that there can be such a thing as an ultimate basis for either justice or goodness. However, if this ultimate basis is scrapped, then all attempts to bring justice to bear upon evil will wholly depend upon accomplishing them inside the tangible dimension and within its timeframe. The results of such efforts, however, will always disappoint. [76]

The modern "enlightened" mind is prone, as well, to reject the idea of an eternal hell and to treat it as a deplorable remnant of medieval theology that needs to be jettisoned. However, at the same time modern people are prone to reject the possibility of hell as a story ending, many will presume that heaven is the destination to which every person's story leads. Such presumption explains why the belief in universalism (that ultimately everyone will go to heaven) remains a perennial attraction for many. It seems unthinkable to them that God would punish a person infinitely for sins committed in a finite existence.

In such modern permutations of ideas about the afterlife, one observes that the *mysterium tremendum et fascinans* is extracted from concepts of *both* hell *and* heaven. That which remains in these pared-down versions of the afterlife resembles whatever the individual deems are the best aspects of the present existence, with the bad being entirely filtered out and left behind. The story of the present world with all its evils is thus sometimes envisaged as "hell"; but this "hell" comes to an end once one's temporal story concludes. Heaven, on the other hand, becomes an infinite extension of whatever pleasures made a person happiest while living out his or her earthly story. If a person's life story revolved around fishing, for instance, then heaven will be for him/her an eternal fishing trip. Or, if one loved to play baseball, heaven will be a "field of dreams" where every hit is a homerun. [77] In such anemic views of the afterlife, the concept of the Holy has been filtered out completely. On the one hand, heaven, by losing something of its beauty and its sublimity, also loses its ability to inspire fascination and awe. It is either re-envisioned as a hedonistic paradise, or it is imagined as a rather bland and boring state of being. Few seem aware of the possibility, however, that the *hedonistic* and the *bland* may turn out to be two sides of the same coin. [78]

On the other hand, the vision of hell loses its power to incite fear and trepidation when it ceases to represent a real future threat to anyone's existence. At worst, hell, according to this diminished view, is identified with all the bad experiences of one's present life story that are left behind at death. Since hell, then, no longer represents a real future threat, caricatures of it can be invented for entertainment purposes. Such caricatures, when they belong to the horror genre, may try to shock and terrify audiences, but audiences are conditioned as well to believe these caricatures are as fantastical as dragons, goblins, and trolls. Other caricatures may make light of hell by presenting the devil and his demons as comical or mischievous pranksters. So it is in such views that the veil of the tangible too greatly obscures the reality of the Holy. The only remedy is to rip away the veil of the temporal, the transitory, and the illusory to reveal the unchanging and eternal permanence of the Holy. Only by increasing eschatological awareness can the full purpose and meaning of the Transcendent again be mediated to the soul.

The sort of anemic renditions of the afterlife I have described are species of *universalism*; namely, the view that guarantees heaven as the destination everyone will eventually reach postmortem. I maintain, however, that universalism is a flawed construct because it portrays the Infinite too much in terms of the finite. The finite is, in effect, projected onto the Infinite in such a way that the Infinite becomes merely an idealized version of the finite. Because it is obsessed with finitude as its starting point, the universalist perspective on the afterlife entails a *dialectical* and *quantitative* understanding of the relation between sin and divine holiness. This dialectical-quantitative understanding assumes that God can tolerate a little sin—just not a lot. The universalist, for instance, will find it incomprehensible that someone like Mohandas Gandhi would ever fall into hell. [79] Such a possibility strikes the universalist as absurd. But to give a counterexample, it seems equally incomprehensible and absurd that someone like Adolf Hitler might turn up in heaven. Such a possibility would absolutely defy the outworking of poetic justice, much less *divine* justice. The absurdity thus cuts both ways, and this reveals one Achilles' heel of the universalist position.[80] Universalism seems fine to affirm if we think of friends and people like ourselves. However, the full ramifications of the logic of universalism seem not quite so appealing when we consider the possibility that God will wink at the most heinous and contemptible exhibitions of evil, or that he will let such horrific evil go unpunished. However, since this model presents the relation between human sin and the divine infinity (i.e., holiness) dialectically, one must ask of it the following questions: Exactly how bad or how good would a person have to be to tip the scales in the direction of either hell or heaven? What would be one's destiny if one just happened to find oneself exactly on the borderline?

Recovering the Elements of the Qualitative and the Paradoxical in Conceptions of Divine Holiness, Human Sin, and Salvation

How the above-stated questions are answered may depend upon what kind of analogy is used to characterize acts of sin and righteousness. Are sinful and righteous acts weighed in a balance or tallied *quantitatively*, as if on some kind of balance sheet? Or, is sin much more *qualitative* in its effects—like arsenic, for instance, in which *a tiny bit poisons the whole*? Or can sin be thought of as an incurable, terminal disease that once contracted will progress until its full and final consequences are realized? If it is anything like these latter examples suggest, then sin represents a *qualitative* break that initiates a downward spiraling process that cannot be eradicated by a solution that is merely *quantitative*. A *qualitative* approach, by contrast, must consider the relation between human sin and divine holiness not *dialectically* but *paradoxically*. As Søren Kierkegaard maintains, there exists an *infinite qualitative distinction* between God and humanity.[81] This qualitative emphasis explains why the concept of the Holy in the biblical texts calls for the *complete* eradication of any form of contamination before one can expect to enter the precincts of the Holy. Furthermore, if sin is approached *qualitatively*, then the *solution* must be qualitative as well. The mainstream of Christian orthodoxy has always maintained that it is the *quality* of the sacrifice of Jesus Christ, not the *quantity* of sacrifices, that accomplishes salvation for human beings.[82] One act of sin is thus enough to break one's relationship with the holy God and to initiate a downward spiraling tendency that results in one's life story becoming a story of habitual sin and the hardening of the human heart. Likewise, one act of grace is sufficient to restore that relationship, to rescue one from a downward spiraling into ever greater compulsion and addiction to sin, to bring about a reversal through a regeneration of the heart, and to set one on a journey that becomes one's unique story of sanctification.

A proper understanding of the relationship between the qualitative and the quantitative reveals that we must again think of the Infinite as *transcending* the finite at the same time that the Infinite *includes* the finite. This means that the paradoxical *includes* the dialectical at the same time that the paradoxical *transcends* the dialectical. With regard to the doctrine of salvation, the idea of justification by grace through faith points to the *paradoxical* dimension of salvation, whereas sanctification reveals the *dialectical* outworking of salvation that is grounded in the *paradoxical*. In this respect, justification by grace through faith forms the basis of sanctification, and not vice versa.

Hell, Libertarian Freedom, and the Dimension of the Personal

Soul-making, as a theodicy, closely parallels the Christian theological doctrine of sanctification in that it entails a dialectical process. However, like the doctrine of sanctification, soul-making must be rooted in a *paradoxical* and *qualitative* understanding of salvation. Otherwise, soul-making cannot commence and be sustained as a process. Unless it is linked to the reality of the Transcendent that is its life source, it will instead starve for lack of nourishment. Additionally, without the element of transcendence directing and inspiring the soul, the soul will at best become engaged in living out an uncompelling and bland story characterized by purposeless ethical repetition and meaningless aesthetic pursuits. By contrast, whenever libertarian freedom is allowed to become a receptacle for the Transcendent, the divine purpose directs the soul and the divine meaning inspires it. The story of the soul then becomes a loom upon which the threads of the moral and the beautiful are interwoven into a tapestry that both reflects and mediates the ultimate value of the Transcendent into the tangible dimension of human experience.

When human libertarian freedom rejects the Transcendent and becomes emptied of it, on the other hand, the phenomenon of the process of soul-making is precluded. Being cut off from the divine purpose and meaning has as its consequence a phenomenon that moves in an opposite direction from the process of soul-*making*. I shall call this phenomenon "soul-*disintegration*." Soul-disintegration logically follows from the premise that human libertarian freedom entails at least the equal possibility of manifestations of evil as it does manifestations of good. The phenomenon of soul-disintegration cannot be understood simply in terms of isolated and disconnected manifestations of evil. These manifestations are connected by the very fact that they are rooted in and flow from a libertarian freedom that not only has become disconnected from the Transcendent but also persists in this state of disconnectedness. As manifestations of evil continue to flow from this cut-loose libertarian freedom, certain human dispositions take on more of an obsessive, compulsive, and addictive quality. Over time, these dispositions become "concretized." Habituation finally produces ignoble and vicious character; and when this kind of character becomes set, the odds of its changing become less and less probable. The story of the life that follows this trajectory turns out to be a *cautionary tale* at best.

The danger posed by soul-disintegration justifies why Christian theology encourages persons to pursue lives of continual repentance from sinful impulses and behaviors, as these, unless constantly remediated, invariably become habitual. What is habitual typically becomes further hardened into fixed character. Fixed character over time then becomes less and less likely to undergo any transformation that heads a person in the opposite direction. As human libertarian freedom persists cutting itself off from divine purpose and meaning, the soul experiences within itself the dwindling of both. The consequence of soul-disintegration then appears not as a tapestry that reflects and mediates value but as a tangled and confused web that reveals only what is morally vicious and aesthetically ugly.

How, then, do the doctrines of heaven and hell correlate with the ideas of soul-making and soul-disintegration? In one respect, heaven can be viewed as the story ending of persons, who by virtue of the fact that they allowed their libertarian freedom to become receptacles linked to the Transcendent, engaged in soul-making. Hell, on the other hand, exists as the story ending of those, who, having allowed their libertarian freedom to become unlinked from the Transcendent, suffer the consequences of soul-disintegration. Hell, in this respect, represents the final tragic ending of a process that begins with the hardening of a disposition that opposes God and ends with a disposition that has become fixed in its state of eternal opposition. Soul-disintegration can thus be described in terms of a deterioration of the soul that involves a dissolution of the unity of any remaining purpose or meaning. Reflecting on Augustine's idea of disordered love, hell would then represent the irreversible *terminus* that this disordering process eventually reaches. This comports with C. S. Lewis's view that hell contains the remains of what used to be human.[83]

At the same time, soul-disintegration brings with it the realization that one has lived a life in opposition to the meaning and purpose of all things, so even though the soul is continually confronted with meaning and purpose, it experiences ceaseless pain and regret because it simultaneously persists in its rejection of them. Hell, in this respect, should not be interpreted as an eternal torture chamber but as the final outworking of justice. As such, it is the revelation of what the paradoxical disjunction between a holy God, who is infinitely good and beautiful, and sinful humans entails. In this respect, it may be that Lewis's contention that "the door to hell is locked from the inside"[84] is at least partially true—that somehow the soul has become so fixated in its sinful opposition to God that it cannot find within itself the power to repent. The fixation of the soul in impotence derives from its having voluntarily and irretrievably forfeited the very willpower necessary for repentance. The effect of the divine light would be not so much to melt this kind of opposition to its brilliance, truth, and clarity, as to harden it in the way fire hardens clay. A persistent state of sinning and opposition to God thus characterizes how the life story ends of those who choose hell rather than heaven as their eternal destination.

Hell and the Dimension of the Social

I have used two analogies describing sin as a poison or as a disease. These comport well with my emphasis upon the way sin influences *individuals*. Certainly stories, whether their endings are tragic or happy, include individual characters; but good stories always bring in the social dimension as well. Analogies that are overly psychological are thus insufficient to account for how sin disrupts and damages *society*, or how it creates ripple effects that spread down the corridors of history into eternity. To speak of ourselves as victims of our *own* sin is one thing. To consider sin as a force that brings devastation to *others* and damages human society is another thing entirely. Lewis's idea that the door to hell is locked from the inside may thus turn out not to be as comprehensive as it could be. Though Lewis's suggestion fits well with the idea that hell is the destiny of those caught in the downward spiral of soul-disintegration, his view seems not to place a great enough emphasis upon the consequences of sin from a *sociological* perspective. If Lewis's view were plausible (as well as believable), then we might ask why it is the case that prison doors in the present world are not also "locked from the inside." Lewis's view, I think, depends too heavily on the idea that the denizens of hell in some respect freely choose their fate. This assumption, however, is not always sustained by what we know of human behavior. Lewis might have us believe that we should expect no attempted "prison breaks" by the denizens of hell, but this is contraindicated in our present experience by the fact that prisoners who are locked up are restricted by the greater society as to curtail further damage that they might inflict upon society. Inmates do not choose to lock themselves up in prison. If anything, they seek to find ways to escape incarceration.

Jesus' story of the rich man and Lazarus serves to clarify the point I have been making about the imbalance in Lewis's view. The rich man wants to alleviate his pain by invoking the familiar social status quo that he had depended upon while he was alive; namely, he wants Lazarus to resume his former servile function and to fetch water to cool his tongue as to relieve his torment in the flame.[85] This story reveals that a barrier between heaven and hell has been fixed, and this to the rich man's disadvantage. The door to hell in this regard seems not only locked from the inside, but from the outside as well.

Hell and the Conflict between the Divine Love and the Divine Justice

No discussion of the topic of hell would be complete, however, without examining questions of how this doctrine reconciles with the divine justice and the divine love: For instance, "Would God be *justified* in punishing someone eternally for a sin committed in a finite existence?" and "Would a *loving* God ever condone eternal punishment?" One is tempted to give negative answers to both these questions. However, arguments that conclude that the doctrine of hell is inconsistent with divine love and divine justice tend to proceed with assumptions that again are dialectical. They are, as a consequence, limited in scope by the very nature of the dialectical method of reasoning. Such arguments are restrictive because they assume that *finite* conceptions of love and justice can be projected onto the dimension of the Ultimate. Such finite conceptions must then, by their very nature, envisage a *boundary* between love and justice that mutually *limits* them both. In limiting both, they fail as well to grasp that the divine love and the divine justice belong to the dimension of the Infinite and are thus not subject to the kinds of limitations that dialectical thinking imposes. By contrast, a paradoxical understanding of the relationship between divine love and divine justice must locate their source in the dimension of the Holy and, hence, in the unity of the Holy as *mysterium tremendum et fascinans*.

A doctrine of the infinity of God consequently removes the boundaries that dialectical thinking tries to impose. At the same time, however, the idea that the Infinite also *includes* the finite disallows the assertion that God's being is wholly *beyond* the world or that God's knowledge is *oblivious* to the world. Such assertions would entail a reversion to a doctrine of the impersonality of God of the sort found in Aristotle or in *Shankara* Hinduism. Again, I wish to maintain that God's love and justice are *personal* though not personal in a purely *individualistic* sense. God exists as *tri*personal, not *uni*personal. Furthermore, God must also be conceived of as *supra*personal, meaning that the quality of his personality is maximally inclusive of, and not only transcendent to, what we as finite humans imagine are the superlative qualities of personhood.

An adequate understanding of what it means that God is *supra*personal helps us rethink how the divine love and the divine justice line up with the doctrine of hell. A truncated understanding of the divine personhood might, for instance, rest upon a purely individualistic notion of personhood. Such a notion might visualize God as the supreme egotist of the universe. Every offense against God would then be evaluated against the backdrop of God's egocentricity. All sin in this respect would be construed as *an affront to God's ego*. Such views of the egocentricity of God, however, only lead to a narrowing and limiting of the way one imagines God to be affected by human sin.

At this point, I suggest that considering a concept of the vulnerability and the suffering of God might provide a more adequate basis for conceiving how human sin opposes the nature of a God who is *tripersonal* as well as *suprapersonal*.[86] Egocentric views of personhood tend to cut persons off from one another. Consequently, to project such a view of personhood onto the Holy Trinity would be to promote tritheism. What is missing here, however, is an adequate doctrine of the *divine unity*. Is the divine unity a self-enclosed egocentric unity? Or, is it a communal kind of unity, such as that which John of Damascus envisaged in his doctrine of the perichoretic unity of the Trinity?[87]

One way of imagining the divine unity would be to view it as entirely *transcendent* to and *exclusive* of the dimension of particularity. Christian theology, however, opposes this view and teaches that the divine unity, while transcendent, is *inclusive* of the dimension of particularity. This means that the divine unity is also *inclusive* of the dimension of particularity where value is mediated through those aspects of human vulnerability and fragility, and where negations of value pose a threat to those aspects. How, then, is the divine unity inclusive? I suggest here that a doctrine of the vulnerability and suffering of God can be based upon an understanding of divine omniscience that includes divine participation in the suffering of the creation.[88] Human ways of knowing tend to be characterized by unconsciousness and forgetfulness; however, the same would not be true of divine ways of knowing. God's knowing of creation involves both memory and consciousness that extends infinitely beyond the three human capacities of logos, ethos, and pathos. An adequate understanding of the divine nature would thus affirm God's *maximal investment* in the creation. God maximally invests in his creation by risking, but God cannot undertake risks without also voluntarily taking upon himself creation's fragility, vulnerability, and suffering on its behalf.

An investigation into certain biblical texts and theological concepts reveals the superlative degree to which God invests in creation. Matthew 25:3 –6 points to the correlation between divine judgment and the ways that individuals love or mistreat others. Two verses stand out: "Inasmuch as ye have done it unto one of the least of these my brethren, ye have done it unto me"[89] and "Inasmuch as ye did it not to one of the least of these, ye did it not to me."[90] These references point to God's nature as being a nature that is *maximally invested* in the creation, not an *isolated* apathetic nature belonging to some oblivious, detached cosmic ego. In a similar vein, the Apostle John states in his First Epistle:

> He that saith he is in the light, and hateth his brother, is in darkness even until now. He that loveth his brother abideth in the light, and there is none occasion of stumbling in him. But he that hateth his brother is in darkness, and walketh

in darkness, and knoweth not whither he goeth, because that darkness hath blinded his eyes.[91]

This passage also points to the correlations and contradictions between human attitudes and behaviors, on the one hand, and the divine nature, on the other.

The doctrine of the Incarnation underscores this identification of the divine nature with the totality of the human context and all its ranges of value as well. Because the divine nature resides in Jesus of Nazareth, this means that Jesus assumes the human psychological perspective as well as social, cultural, and historical situated-ness. T. F. Torrance (1913–2007), following Karl Barth, thus spoke of the incarnation of God in Christ in terms of *inhistorization*.[92] God in Jesus shows that he is invested in the entire fabric of human connectedness, including time and history, and not merely individual psychological isolated-ness.

At this point, I want to offer several illustrations that may help shed light on how the divine love and the divine justice are consistent with the idea of hell. Often, when human beings engage and invest in the work of marriage and parenting, they will find themselves transitioning over time from perspectives that are initially ego-centered to perspectives that become other-centered. In such cases, the protective instincts of individuals may come to focus less on self-protection and more upon the protection of family members. As the well-being of the family consequently takes precedence over individual well-being, altruism trumps egoism. Affronts to the well-being of the collective in which the individual has become maximally invested then begins to be viewed as more serious than affronts to oneself. If it is the case that the divine nature is maximally invested in creation, then affronts to creation also become serious affronts to the divine nature.

Human sin thus represents an affront to a divine nature that is maximally invested in the creation; not to an apathetic divine nature that remains entirely separated and disconnected from the creation. To use another illustration, sin becomes the proverbial "bull in the china closet" of God's creation. The china closet functions here as an analogue for the value of the creation. The bull, which functions as an analogue for sin, represents a dangerous affront to the contents of the china closet. Sin thus represents an affront to the *value* of creation; and for this reason, it cannot be tolerated. Sin jeopardizes and actively destroys the interconnectedness of all that is valuable, vulnerable, fragile, and personal. It does this in one way by unleashing forces that damage and destroy that interconnectedness. It does so in another way by failing to engage and invest in ways that could both preserve and facilitate that interconnectedness. Sins of commission and sins of omission must then be viewed in the light of the fabric of goodness that God expects his creation to weave. From the standpoint of God's glory, human sin presents an intolerable violation and a thwarting of the good that God intends not so much for himself, but for the other in whom he is maximally invested. Thus, hell represents the ultimate contradiction; namely, the negation of all *possible* and *actual good.*

The Inadequacy of Analogies of the Afterlife

If anything, analogies that attempt to explain what lies beyond present experience cannot help but be deficient, though analogies are all we have on this side of the divide between time and eternity. One would do best, however, to reject caricatures that represent hell as an eternal chamber of horrors. Similarly, analogies that present heaven as a static, dull, and boring place should be rejected. In place of static portrayals, heaven could be envisioned as an endless journey into ever profounder depths of God's infinite goodness and beauty. The analogy of the marriage nuptials of the Lamb seem to support this superior portrayal; for the marriage ceremony symbolizes not a final goal, but an initiation into a life that promises a further progression into the depths of the divine and a continued deepening of the bonds of love. Because the doctrines of the resurrection and the life everlasting entail the transmutation of the physical dimension into a transphysical one, particularity and individuality are not objects needing to be annihilated by some "universal solvent" that is the Ultimate Being. If anything, particularity and individuality are elevated into something even higher, richer, and profounder than what could ever be experienced in the present world. In this respect, the "good story" of God and his people does not end but continues into eternity.

At the same time, one would expect that *relationships* will be profounder and more meaningful in the world to come. Heaven is not portrayed biblically as a retreat for the weary, wounded soul,[93] but as an eternal city. The "city" analogy adds richness and diversity to the concept of heaven. Such notions appear absent in views where particularity, individual personality, and meaningful social relationships are swallowed up in some sea of being or extinguished by "something" resembling nirvana. Drawing upon the culture-making analogy, heaven must be thought of as a supremely "civilized" place; a place where not only individuals forever journey into the ever-expanding story of the divine meaning and purpose, but a place where meaningful and purposive social relationships continue to be deepened by an eternal adventure into the ever-expanding novelty of the Divine Life.

Strengths and Weaknesses of Eschatological Approaches

Finally, I must offer a few critical remarks regarding eschatological approaches. Though such approaches to theodicy complete the overall Christian approach to the problem of evil, they still do not in themselves answer the questions, "Why does evil *continue* in the world when an all-powerful and good God presumably possesses both the power and the desire to stop it?" and "Why does God delay in bringing about a total eradication of evil?"

By coupling the eschatological view with soul-making and transformationism, we are provided with several important rationales for why God has not yet brought about a full eradication of evil. Though God intends to bring his story of creation and redemption to its full conclusion, *time* is an indispensable vehicle for accomplishing this goal. Both soul-making and transformationism require time if they are to bring to fruition concrete embodiments of the good. Furthermore, God's delay in bringing his story to a conclusion need not imply that he has failed to superintend history, for many historical episodes have occurred that demonstrate God's repeated reining in of evil over time. Of all these episodes, the resurrection of Jesus stands as the most important guarantee that God will eventually and finally defeat all evil, including death. This guarantee provides sufficient reason to hope, to persevere, to endure, and to overcome evil as much as possible on this side of the divide between time and eternity. Both individuals and civilizations sometimes face great challenges, but the passage of time usually sees these resolved.

Something also could be said for the way that a good storyteller uses mystery and suspense to engage his/her readers. If God is the author of the cosmic story, then it is conceivable that he might allow elements such as mystery and suspense to serve the greater purpose of making that story more enticing and compelling. In such a case, God would not prematurely interfere with the present world story that unfolds in this "vale of soul-making." Nor would he choose to short-circuit his mission of ongoing creation and world transformation by bringing about a hasty and premature end to the human story. Something of this idea may be found in the response of 2 Peter 3:9 as to why the world seems to continue on its way as it apparently has always done: "The Lord is not slack concerning his promise, as some men count slackness; but is longsuffering to us-ward, not willing that any should perish, but that all should come to repentance." At the same time, persons are warned that God has brought judgments in the past, such as the judgment of Noah's flood. These judgments remind us that God will not endure evil forever but will at some point execute a final justice that will contextualize evil and reveal it for what it is.

GOOD, EVIL, AND THE DIVINE-HUMAN STORY

In the previous chapter, I wrote of the convergence of the *divine* and *human* stories. I must stress here again that this convergence must entail God's maximal involvement and participation in the human story, but how should this divine involvement and participation be comprehended? The Christian church has long affirmed that God's involvement and participation in the human story should be fathomed in the light of Christ's incarnation and atonement. Admittedly, however, theologians have at times lapsed into views that fall short of affirming God's full embracement of tangible existence. One example was degree Christology, which, from the time of Friedrich Schleiermacher and Albrecht Ritschl, abandoned the metaphysical underpinnings of Christology in favor of reductive explanations that viewed the "divine" nature in Jesus in terms of his superior intuitive or moral faculty. In more recent times, the Christological formulations of Rudolf Bultmann, Paul Tillich, and a majority of the process theologians have tried to resolve the Christological *paradox* that Christ is fully God and fully man by resorting to types of *dialectical* thinking that produced pared-down existentialist interpretations. Invariably, these interpretations sever the Christ of faith from the Jesus of history. Because these views rely on outcomes that are reached through dialectical thinking, they can at best only affirm a *partial* divine involvement and participation in the world. Not only do they fall short of what the mainstream of Christian orthodoxy has always taught, but they also have more in common with some of the partial solutions to the question of theodicy discussed early on in this chapter than they do with traditional Christian orthodoxy.

Hence, to affirm Christ's status as a good teacher or a superior inspirational figure is to settle for an understanding of the Incarnation that is too anemic a remedy for the problem of evil. So, what would a doctrine of the *full* involvement and participation of God in tangible human existence require from the standpoint of the doctrines of Christ's incarnation and atonement? A full immersion would necessitate God's *voluntary assumption and suffering of the universal consequences of human evil and his victory over it*. This voluntary act of God, which acknowledges Christ both as *victim* and *victor*, must be affirmed in such a way that the paradoxical relatedness of these two aspects is fully upheld. The affirmation of Christ as victim cannot, therefore, be surrendered in favor of the affirmation of his role as victor, or vice versa.

In affirming that Christ is both victim and victor in the sense of paradoxical relatedness, one understands more fully what it means that Christ is simultaneously both Savior and Lord. These titles, which themselves stand in paradoxical relation to one another, fully entail Christ's status as victim and victor. These titles must further be conceived of in their fullest *cosmic* sense, and not merely in a restrictive intuitive, moral, or existential sense. Conceiving of the titles of Savior and Lord in this way is critically important because the two main evils that prevent the fostering of *creativity* and the establishment of *justice* in the cosmos that humans inhabit happen to be *deception* and *injustice*.

Often in the world, the human desire to maximize creativity and the struggle to bring about justice are thrown into destructive conflict. This conflict runs parallel to the conflict between the quest for height and the search for centeredness, which I discussed earlier in this book. I suggest here that the two evils of *deception* and *injustice* are largely responsible for this conflict. Deception, on one front, leads to a thwarting or short-circuiting of human creative impulses and processes. Obstacles to creativity appear when a given "ideal of inspiration" promises persons a way to achieve success without the need for any sacrificial expenditure or investment on their part. The *ideal of inspiration* in such cases ceases to be *divine* and instead becomes a *demonic* lure: That is, it promises an easy shortcut to achievement, success, and prosperity, but it always fails to deliver what it promises. The deception that inhibits and curtails human creative processes, in turn, produces *injustice* as its fruit. Injustice, in turn, can trigger in those who have suffered its consequences attempts to establish a *semblance* of justice through acts of violence and vendetta that are inspired by resentment and hatred. In such cases, "justice," which is purported to be a right *principle of direction and determination,* appears in fact as something *demonic* and far from divine. Furthermore, where deception represents the attack of evil on one front, injustice represents its attack on the other.

Deception and injustice are evils that must therefore be overcome and contained by means of the truth conveyed by Christ's incarnation and atonement. Otherwise, the divine purpose and the divine meaning cannot begin to transform humanity both individually and collectively. How, then, do Christ's incarnation and atonement provide the means of accomplishing this task? How shall a true understanding of the divine purpose and the divine meaning be restored in a tangible dimension of existence that is fraught with conflict and beset with deception and injustice? These important themes will need to be explored at length in the chapter that follows.

NOTES

1. Walter J. Lowe, "Introduction," in Paul Ricoeur, *Fallible Man*, trans. Charles A. Kelbley (New York: Fordham University Press, 1986), xxiv–xxvi.

2. Ricoeur, *Fallible Man*, 81–132.

3. Ricoeur, *The Symbolism of Evil*, trans. Emerson Buchanan (Boston, MA: Beacon Press, 1967), 3.

4. The words "moral" and "ethical" copiously occur throughout Ricoeur's *The Symbolism of Evil.* On the other hand, "aesthetic" appears only one time (p. 174), and beauty only four times (pp. 156, 210, 321).

5. Philip Tallon, *The Poetics of Evil: Toward an Aesthetic Theodicy* (Oxford: Oxford University Press, 2012). See, for example, 199–203.

6. As Ricoeur states, "...evil is not symmetrical with the good, wickedness is not something that replaces the goodness of a man; it is the staining, the darkening, the disfiguring of an innocence, a light and beauty that remain. However *radical* evil may be, it cannot be as *primordial* as goodness" (*The Symbolism of Evil*, 156).

7. The word was coined by Gottfried Leibniz in the eighteenth century. See Leibniz, *Theodicy: Essays on the Goodness of God, the Freedom of Man and the Origin of Evil*, trans. E. M. Huggard (LaSalle, IL: Open Court Publishing, 1985).

8. Lactantius, *On the Anger of God*, ch. 13.

9. Mary Baker Eddy, *Science and Health with Key to the Scriptures* (Boston, MA: Christian Science Publishing Co., 1875).

10. Hence, Karl Marx's comment on his eleventh thesis on Feuerbach, "Philosophers have only interpreted the world, in various ways; the point is to change it" ("Theses on Feuerbach," in *Marx/Engels Collected Works*, Vol. 1 [Moscow, USSR: Progress Press, 1969], thesis 11).

11. Yuri Stoyanov, *The Other God: Dualist Religions from Antiquity to the Cathar Heresy* (New Haven, CT: Yale University Press, 2000), 101.

12. I have long been indebted to my former professor Yandall Woodfin for his delineation of this fourfold schema. See Woodfin, *With All Your Mind: A Christian Philosophy* (Nashville, TN: Abingdon, 1980), 210–11. In my present chapter, I have further developed his approaches to theodicy, especially the *transformationist* view.

13. Augustine, *City of God* 13.

14. Augustine, *City of God*, 12.30.

15. Indeed, the option of Platonism available at the time Paul lived was Middle Platonism; and one of its permutations, gnosticism, was stringently opposed by the early church. It is highly unlikely that Paul would have used Platonism in an affirmative way to undergird his theological perspectives.

16. Recently, some scholars have attempted to downplay Augustine's reliance on Neoplatonism and to focus more on the biblical aspect of his thought. However, while one would not want to downplay Augustine's indebtedness to the Bible, it would be very wrong to ignore the influence of Neoplatonism upon him.

17. Jeff A. Benner mentions that the Hebrew word *tob* is best translated "something that functions properly," while the Hebrew word for evil, *ra*, could be translated "something dysfunctional, wrong, evil, or wicked." Benner, *The Ancient Hebrew Lexicon of the Bible: Hebrew Letters, Words and Roots Defined Within Their Ancient Cultural Context* (College Station, TX: Virtualbookworm.com, 2005), entry 1186, p. 134; and entry 1460, p. 269.

18. Augustine of Hippo, *On Christian Doctrine* (Radford, VA: SMK Books, 2013), 7.

19. Augustine, *City of God*, 21.12.

20. Augustine of Hippo, *Confessions*, trans. Carolyn J.-B. Hammond, in *Loeb Classical Library* 26 (Cambridge, MA: Harvard University Press, 2014), 3.7.

21. Pierre Bayle, *Historical and Critical Dictionary: Selections*, trans. Richard H. Popkin (Indianapolis, IN: Hackett Publishing, 1992), 76.

22. C. S. Lewis, *The Problem of Pain* (New York: HarperCollins, 1996), 91.

23. John Hick, *Evil and the God of Love* (New York: Palgrave McMillan, 2010).

24. See, for example, Norman Powell Williams, *Ideas of the Fall and Original Sin: A Historical and Critical Study* (London: Longmans, Green & Co., 1927), 317–23.

25. Irenaeus, "Against Heresies," in eds. Alexander Roberts, James Donaldson, and Cleveland Cox, *The Writings of the Ante-Nicene Fathers* Vol. 1 (Grand Rapids, MI: William B. Eerdman's, 1973–74), 3.23.5; 4.38.1–2.

26. Eric Francis Osborne, *Irenaeus of Lyons* (Cambridge: Cambridge University Press, 2001), 219.

27. See John Hick, *Evil and the God of Love*, 213.

28. Hick, *Evil and the God of Love*, 212.

29. Hick, *Evil and the God of Love*, 211. Irenaeus, "Against Heresies" 5.16.2. The movement from image to likeness is suggested to Irenaeus by the distinction between the first and second Adam. The first Adam is created in the image and is in need of development. Christ, as the second Adam, is created in the image but reestablishes the likeness that the first Adam lost.

30. Irenaeus, "Against Heresies" 4.38.3

31. See, for example, Gen. 5:1.

32. According to Osborne, Irenaeus's doctrine of participation includes a strong aesthetic emphasis. For the full discussion, see Osborne, *Irenaeus of Lyons*, 193–210.

33. Hick, *Evil and the God of Love*, 212. Cf. Augustine, *City of God* 13.13–14.

34. The terminology referring to the world as a "vale of soul-making" is not terminology Irenaeus uses but is derived from the poetry and thought of nineteenth-century literary figure John Keats. John Keats, "Letter to George and Georgiana Keats," April 21, 1819, in *Letters of John Keats to His Family and Friends*, ed. Sidney Colvin (Project Gutenberg e-book), www.gutenberg.org/files/35698/35698-h/35698-h.htm.

35. Moses de Leon, *The Zohar ha Sefirot, Bereshith*, trans. Daniel C. Matt (Stanford, CA: Stanford University Press, 2004), 1:29a.

36. Plat. Phaedo 80–85; Plat. Phaedrus 250c.

37. Cf. Gen 3:6–7 and Gen 12:4–5.

38. Gen 3:23–24.

39. Gen 12:7.

40. Cf. Gen 3:16–19 and Gen 21:1–7.

41. Friedrich Nietzsche, *Twilight of the Idols*, "Maxims and Arrows," 8 loc. 69 of 1644, Kindle, n.d.

42. Viktor E. Frankl, *Man's Search for Meaning: An Introduction to Logotheraphy*, trans. Ilse Lasch (Boston: Beacon Press, 1992), 49–50.

43. Frankl, *Man's Search for Meaning*, 70–72, 74–76.

44. Semantically, the English language speaks of "better" and "best" in terms of the comparative and the superlative uses of the adjective, respectively. These uses can have the effect of lessening the meaning of the word "good" to stand for something inferior to "better" and "best." What I am advocating here is an understanding of "best" that is predicated as a subcategory of "the good" rather than the other way around. This will prevent the concept of the "good" from becoming mired in the dimension of the *dialectical*. It can instead be elevated into the dimension of the *paradoxical*.

45. See Clyde Rolston Majors on Viktor Frankl's logotherapy and its application to what Majors called "Transformationism," in "Contemporary Emphasis on Transformation: Its Relation to a Christian Approach to the Problem of Suffering," Fort Worth, TX: ThD diss., Southwestern Baptist Theological Seminary, 1973, unpublished.

46. H. Richard Niebuhr, *Christ and Culture* (New York: Harper Colophon, 1975), 206–18.

47. See Hans-Georg Gadamer, *Truth and Method*, trans. Joel Weinsheimer and Donald G. Marshall (London: Continuum, 2004), 9–19.

48. Andy Crouch, *Culture Making: Recovering Our Creative Calling* (Downers Grove, IL: IVP, 2008), 65–77.

49. For example, the Platonic idea of *anamnesis*.

50. Crouch, *Culture Making*, 101–17.

51. Rev 21 and 22.

52. N.T. Wright, *Surprised by Hope: Rethinking Heaven, the Resurrection, and the Mission of the Church* (New York: HarperOne, 2008), 99–108.

53. Rom 8:18–25; Wright, *Surprised by Hope*, 103.

54. Rev 21:2.

55. Rev 21:10.

56. Wright, *Surprised by Hope*, 104–6.

57. Luke 24:42; John 20:26–27.

58. Luke 24:31; John 20:19.

59. See, for example, Edith Wyschogrod, *Saints and Postmodernism: Revisioning Moral Philosophy* (Chicago: University of Chicago Press, 1990), xii–xxiv. See also comment in Linda Trinkaus Zagzebski, *Exemplarist Moral Theory* (Oxford: Oxford University Press, 2017), 24: "The saint casts aside goods that make our own lives worthwhile—family, hobbies, special interests—in order to carry out his 'astounding mission.'"

60. Paul Ricoeur, "The Logic of Jesus, the Logic of God," in *Figuring the Sacred*, 279–92.

61. Matt 28:19–20.

62. Paul Tillich, *The Interpretation of History*, trans. N. A. Rasetzki and Elsa L. Talmey (New York: Charles Scribner's Sons, 1936), 129–36.

63. Frankl, *Man's Search for Meaning*, 66–67 (loc. 885–95 of 2073).

64. Frankl, *Man's Search for Meaning*, 98–99 (loc. 1221–47 of 2073).

65. Karl Marx, "Theses on Feuerbach," in *The German Ideology*, 647.

66. Augustine, *City of God* 19.15; Margaret Mary, "Slavery in the Writings of St. Augustine," *The Classical Journal* 49, no. 8 (May 1954): 363–69.

67. Martin Luther, *Against the Robbing and Murdering Hordes of Peasants* [1524], in Luther's Works, Vol. 46, 47–55.

68. Mary King, *Mahatma Gandhi and Martin Luther King Jr: The Power of Nonviolent Action* (Paris: United Nations Education, Scientific and Cultural Organization, 1999), 93–100, 129–34.

69. King, *Mahatma Gandhi and Martin Luther King Jr*, 18–19. Unfortunately, Richard Dawkins, in pointing out Martin Luther King's reliance on Gandhi, ignores these Christian influences on Gandhi. See Richard Dawkins, *The God Delusion* (Boston, MA: Houghton Mifflin, 2006), 307.

70. Jacek Rostowski, "The Inter-enterprise Debt Explosion in the Former Soviet Union: Causes, Consequences, Cures," *Communist Economics and Economic Transformation*, 5, no. 2 (1993): 131–59.

71. Jürgen Moltmann, *Religion, Revolution, and the Future*, trans. Douglas M. Meeks (New York: Charles Scribner's Sons, 1969), 165.

72. Blaise Pascal, *Pensées* (New York: E. P. Dutton, 1958), 68–69 (*Pensée* 233) (loc. 1345–1351 of 5955).

73. John Hick, *Philosophy of Religion*, 4th ed. (London: Prentice Hall, 1990), 82–89.

74. Jerry L. Walls makes this case in *Heaven, Hell, and Purgatory: Rethinking the Things That Matter Most* (Grand Rapids, MI: Brazos Press, 2015), 163–86.

75. For example, in 1 Thess 5:1–11; 2 Thess 1:5–10; 2 Pet 3:10–12; Rom 13:12; Heb 12:22, Rev 21:1–4, 10–27; 22:1–5. In these passages, the elements of the ethical and the aesthetic are sometimes combined.

76. See, for example, my previous discussion on utopias and dystopias.

77. See Walls, *Heaven, Hell, and Purgatory*, 12–17. "Field of dreams" is an allusion to the motion picture by that name.

78. Interestingly, Rod Serling, who happened to be a unitarian universalist, captured this idea well in one of his *Twilight Zone* episodes, "A Nice Place to Visit," written by Charles Beaumont and aired April 15, 1960.

79. For example, Rob Bell, *Love Wins: A Book about Heaven, Hell, and the Fate of Every Person Who Ever Lived* (New York: HarperCollins, 2011), 1.

80. Douglas Groothuis makes mention of an "argument from damnation." He writes, "Some acts are so desperately wicked that they demand a punishment greater than what earth has to offer" (Douglas Groothuis, *Christian Apologetics: A Comprehensive Case for Biblical Faith* [Downers Grove, IL: InterVarsity, 2010], 341–42).

81. Kristen K. Deed, "The Infinite Qualitative Difference: Sin, the Self, and Revelation in the Thought of Søren Kierkegaard," *International Journal for Philosophy of Religion* 53, no. 1 (February 2003): 25–43, www.jstor.org/stable/40035916.

82. This is the recurring message of the Book of Hebrews. See Heb 7:11–28; 9:11–28; 10:1–14.

83. C. S. Lewis, *The Problem of Pain*, 127–28.

84. Lewis, *The Problem of Pain*, 129.

85. Luke 16:19–31.

86. See, for example, the discussion in Kazoh Kitamori, *Theology of the Pain of God*, 5th rev. ed. (Eugene, OR: Wipf & Stock, 2005), 46–49.

87. The doctrine of the *perichoresis* refers to the mutual interpenetration and circulation of the life of each of the Trinitarian Persons in the Others. John of Damascus, *The Orthodox Faith* I.14.11. See also Gunton, *The One, The Three and the Many*, 222–23.

88. I am unsympathetic here with David Bentley Hart's attempt to defend a doctrine of the divine *apatheia* against the attempt of theologians such as Joseph Hallman and Paul Fiddes to speak of the suffering of God (David Bentley Hart, *The Beauty of the Infinite: The Aesthetics of Christian Truth* [Grand Rapids, MI: William B. Eerdmans, 2003], 155–74). I do, however, agree with his critique against those (I assume like Jürgen Moltmann) who have managed to make God "the metaphysical ground of Auschwitz" (160). Fiddes actually argues against this tendency in Moltmann when he says that Moltmann has not so much made God the supreme

victim or sufferer as "the supreme self-executioner" (*The Creative Suffering of God* [Oxford: Clarendon, 1988], 137). Hart's apophatic theological approach leads to an understanding of God that is less personal than his creatures rather than suprapersonal.

89. Matt 25:40.

90. Matt 25:45.

91. 1 John 2:9–11.

92. T. F. Torrance, *Incarnation: The Person and Life of Christ* (Downers Grove, IL: Inter-Varsity Press, 2008), 7–10. See also Torrance, *Space, Time and Incarnation* (Edinburgh: T & T Clark, 1997), 67–68; Karl Barth, *The Humanity of God* (Louisville, KY: John Knox Press, 1960), 72–75.

93. In this regard, the popular novel by William Paul Young, *The Shack* (Newbury Park, CA: Windblown Media, 2007), presents a view of heaven that is deficient and one-sided.

Chapter Nine

The Divine-Human Metanarrative in a Trinitarian Context

Jean-François Lyotard, in his work *The Postmodern Condition*, speaks of metanarratives (Fre=*métarécit*), master narratives, or grand narratives that attempt to explain all aspects of reality in a totalizing way.[1] The Judeo-Christian metanarrative counts as one such example of a "narrative of emancipation," to use another Lyotardian classification. Qualifying, too, as "narratives of emancipation" are the Hegelian and Marxist systems, which advocate a belief in scientific progress. These systems, Lyotard maintains, are but philosophical or secularized versions of the Judeo-Christian metanarrative. Lyotard further observes a modern skepticism toward metanarratives generally that is leading toward their abandonment in favor of what he calls "little narratives" (Fre=*petits récits*).[2] While metanarratives pretend to be all encompassing and totalizing, *little narratives* are localized and modest. Though his investigation is intended to be descriptive, Lyotard seems to prefer little narratives to grand ones. A common trend in the academy today is to reject all metanarratives as being too ambitious in their explanatory capacity.

Even so, any suggestion that we would be better off dispensing entirely with metanarratives has done little to encourage and to facilitate the building of bridges across the many impasses that exist across a plethora of conflicting human perspectives. Merely accepting the world's diverse narratives, whether small or grand, does nothing to quell the irresolvable destructive conflict that rages among the proponents of these narratives and only leaves the problem of evil unresolved. A retreat into passivity as a way of dealing with evil and the conflict that precipitates it is no stratagem for a way ahead; for it only fosters non-committal and inaction, assuring that all conflict will remain unabated. Others employ stratagems entailing greater activism in an effort to keep conflict at bay. In the previous chapter, I mentioned radical

Islam and militant Zoroastrianism as religious expressions of activism, but nonreligious expressions prove equally problematic. Nonreligious expressions may even favor the promoting of *religious* pluralism; though atheism and secular pluralism represent activist alternatives that promise to reduce conflict and minimize evil as well.

For advocates of activist stratagems favorable to religious pluralism, the rejection of metanarratives in favor of *petits récits* may require that all *exclusivist* tendencies in religion be roundly condemned.[3] Jean-Jacques Rousseau suggested as much when he advocated civil religion as a "religion of tolerance" that favored an attitude of toleration toward all tolerant religions but prescribed a stance of intolerance against any religion that exhibited intolerance. Rousseau thus justified "intolerance against intolerance" as a means of minimizing the religious conflict that perennially arises out of irreconcilable exclusivist perspectives.[4] Still, his attempt to suppress religious intolerance by condoning attitudes and acts of intolerance against intolerance did not prove entirely successful in reducing conflict. This type of approach, if anything, only adds to the mix an *additional intolerant actor*—usually, the *secular state*—which by the superior power granted it as arbitrator merely pits its own intolerance against the intolerance of other actors whose political power has been curtailed. Such an approach does not seem to differ markedly from the way the Roman Empire tolerated the multitude of polytheisms that existed in the days prior to the arrival of Christianity. Rome, which was religiously pluralistic, exercised tolerance but did so with well-known exceptions; for Rome implemented policies of intolerance against "exclusivist" religions like Judaism and Christianity and subjected these religions to intermittent persecution. Ironically, the polytheistic beliefs of Rome eventually faded into irrelevance and were abandoned in favor of the very Judeo-Christian monotheism it once opposed. Polytheism, which was religiously pluralistic, was thus tested in the crucible of history and found wanting; and Christianity, an unlikely candidate for providing a way forward, eventually became the official religion of the Roman Empire.

Advocates of atheism, too, imagine that their approach can provide a better alternative to remedying religious conflict. They advocate as their remedy the abandonment of all religious narratives, whether these are of the polytheistic or monotheistic variety. Atheism, as a stratagem, simply tries to remove religion without supplying any satisfactory substitute. In places where atheism became a state doctrine, such as in the former Soviet Union, the remedy severely curtailed religious freedom. Nevertheless, like a house emptied of comfortable furniture and refurbished with hard benches, atheism as a state doctrine proved too spartan to be satisfying to most human souls over the long term. The following quote attributed to G. K. Chesterton is illuminating in this regard: "The first effect of not believing in God is to believe in anything."[5] Strangely, Chesterton's words characterize the state of today's culture where conflicting religious perspectives continue to emerge and thrive despite, and perhaps even *because of*, the iconoclastic crusading of proponents of the new atheism. Atheism as a stratagem thus also fails to provide a viable means of bridging the impasses, ending conflict, and ameliorating manifestations of evil. Instead, it only does its best to delegitimate and erase all religious perspectives while insisting that its own perspective is superior.

Secular pluralism represents a third stratagem for reducing conflict between the world's diverse narratives. Many consider this stratagem to be the most attractive of all alternatives that have been recommended as replacements for the Judeo-Christian metanarratival option. Secular pluralism, with its pretense to neutrality, may include agnostic and atheistic perspectives, or it may foster benign attitudes that do not consider religious claims with any degree of seriousness. This stratagem has gained increasing political and cultural hegemony in Western culture. Secular pluralism as a stratagem has nonetheless done little to improve the global situation. The so-called "Arab Spring" counters the belief of some convinced secularists that societies, if given enough time, will "naturally" evolve into democracies. Secular pluralists who believe this version of the myth of progress fail to realize that some intellectual infrastructure first had to be in place before democracy as it exists today in the West could even begin to exist, much less flourish. In the case of Europe and America, that infrastructure was originally supported by the Judeo-Christian metanarrative; and this remained the case long after secularist alternatives, inspired by the myth of scientific progress, had begun their experimental march through history.

Furthermore, one cannot deny the historical fact that the Judeo-Christian metanarrative formed the cultural rootstock from which the Western democracies originally sprouted.[6] Consequently, it has turned out that the "secular" branches that eventually sprouted from this rootstock cannot be easily cut away from their original rootstock and successfully grafted onto alien cultural rootstocks. True, some of the world's metanarratives have demonstrated at least some ability to provide cultural rootstocks that can support the various branches that Western secularism claims as its own; for Western-style political and economic systems have been adapted with moderate success by the cultures of India, China, Indochina, and Japan. Still, these grafted-in branches have not always matured in ways resembling their Western counterparts.

Other situations exist, however, in which cultural rootstocks have proved toxic to attempted grafts; and in such cases, the branches quickly wither and die. Such attempts at grafting have proved catastrophic in areas of the world dominated by Islam, where secular alternatives have often assumed overtly totalitarian forms. In such cases, the secular branch, if it survives at all, must adapt to the totalitarian nature of the original cultural rootstock of Islam into which it is grafted. Religious backlashes against the intrusion of secularism in the Muslim world have also proved virulent. Such backlashes, which typically come in expressions of radical Islam, only demonstrate that Islam as a religiopolitical philosophy and secularism are inimical. Unfortunately, the religious cure that radical Islam offers in place of secularism proves even more horrific than the disease needing to be cured. Sadly, the idealism that inspires and drives attempts to return to Islam's central religious metanarrative has produced not another Islamic Golden Age but unspeakable human suffering and horror wherever its "pure" form has been steadfastly practiced.

Secular pluralism as a stratagem for fostering good and minimizing evil thus not only fails to provide viable answers to the many dilemmas that afflict our globe, but it has also proved inept at maintaining the health of Western culture itself. The loss of the West's Judeo-Christian metanarrative explains why the West is now in a state of rapid cultural decline. Pervasive root rot can be cited as the main cause. The rot has indeed become endemic as secularist, pluralist, and atheistic philosophies, along with their alternative moralities, continue to poison the original root system from which Western culture has sprung and flourished. Ironically, some are promoting the poison as fertilizer for the tree of culture. Consequently, as we face terrorism from without, a turmoil of our own making confronts us from within. Sexual, racial, and gender politics have become the most recent of many "hot-button" issues that drive wedges of animosity and outright hatred into whatever semblance of social solidarity and civility remains.

Unless the West attends to the deep roots of its culture by identifying the rot, cutting it out, and restoring health to the root system, the future seems quite bleak. I am confident, on the other hand, that a restoration of the Judeo-Christian metanarrative can provide the best stratagem for reversing the present demise, though I do not think that the shallow, myopic, and contemporary forms of Judeo-Christian culture that exist today are at all adequate to the task. These forms are much too anemic and powerless to generate vital and lasting cultural transformation. Nothing short of a rediscovery of, and a maximal investiture in, the full form and content of the Judeo-Christian metanarrative will help shape an adequate stratagem for a path forward.

THE PARADOXICAL CONVERGENCE OF SMALL AND GRAND NARRATIVE IN THE JUDEO-CHRISTIAN METANARRATIVE

Throughout this book, I have discussed the importance of story, narrative, and drama. Now I want to suggest ways that the human story and the divine story can be connected by means of an understanding of the Judeo-Christian grand metanarrative that, while moving *toward* a kind of totality in paradoxical transcendence,[7] at the same does not allow the grand metanarrative to dominate, eclipse, abolish, subsume, or dissolve the various *petits récits* that it encounters as it moves towards its destination. This sort of grand metanarrative I speak of is thus not identical to the kinds of metanarrative that Lyotard rejects. I maintain that the kinds he does reject are of a *dialectical* variety that are too greatly restricted by the determinations of logic.[8] Such dialectical metanarratives do tend to dominate, eclipse, abolish, subsume, or dissolve all the *petits récits* they encounter.[9] This kind of dialectical metanarrative in fact resembles a juggernaut that rolls over the *petits récits* standing in its way and crushes them mercilessly beneath its weight. In what way, then, can the Judeo-Christian grand metanarrative qualify as a metanarrative of another kind—namely, a metanarrative that "moves *toward* a kind of totality in paradoxical transcendence" but does so in such a way that it fully preserves the particularity of all *petits récits* that it encounters and takes up into itself along the way?

Translated into Lyotardian parlance, the story of Jesus Christ would qualify *paradoxically* as a *petit récit* at the same time that it meets the criteria of a *métarécit*. On the one hand, the *petit récit* of the humble and obscure Galilean found in the four Gospels attests to the humanity of Jesus. On the other hand, the *métarécit* of the divine story contained in the total fabric of the Bible attests to Jesus' divine nature. These two inseparable narratival aspects are just as much paradoxically related as Christ's human and divine natures are related according to the Christological affirmations of Chalcedon. Interestingly, the story of Jesus as a *petit récit* corresponds well to the so-called "scandal of particularity," which has always presented itself as a palpable feature of Christianity.[10] Taking these insights into consideration, I must therefore advocate for a view of the grand metanarrative that is *paradoxically* rather than *dialectically* grounded. How, then, might such a metanarrative function within a comprehensive Trinitarian context?

THE TRINITY AND THE INCARNATION AS VIABLE MONOTHEISTIC CONCEPTS

A major issue facing Christian theology concerns how to defend the doctrine of the Trinity against the charge that other monotheistic religions have leveled; namely, that *Three* simply cannot equal *One*. On its face, the assertion "Three equals One" seems absurd, especially to the Muslim who insists upon maintaining the doctrine of the unity of Allah against all attempts to ascribe partners or a Son to him,[11] or to suggest that God could ever take on human form. The Muslim finds it hard to see how the Christian can escape the charge of polytheism; but despite this fact, reverence for the Qur'an as the Holy Book, and for the Ka'ba Stone of Mecca as the Holy Site, demonstrates that Muslims do retain something of a sacramental understanding of the way that Allah's will is mediated into the world through these vehicles. In this respect, Allah's mediation of his will through his prophet Muhammad demonstrates that he must have a *means* of communicating that will.

Islam also has its own metanarrative, apart from which the acceptance of Allah as the Sovereign of the universe becomes impossible; hence, the words of the *Shahada*, "There is no God but Allah, and *Muhammad is his Prophet*."[12] The question thus raised concerns not *whether* there are means Allah employs to mediate his will to the world, but *what* those means consist of and *how* those means are to be employed properly. There can be no doubt that *language* and *action* play a central role in the mediation of Allah's will to humankind; but again, the question remains, "*What kind* of language and *what kind* of action?" Certainly, the emphasis regarding both language and action is placed on the principle of *limit*, for the only holy language is Arabic. The Qur'an, which was communicated in this holy language, cannot, therefore, be accurately translated into any other tongue. The principle of *limit* also governs the kind of actions prescribed, for the Five Pillars of Islam must be performed in accordance with strict standards.

In contrast to Islam, Judaism shows a great deal more flexibility in its understanding of the One God. Already in Judaism, prior to the appearance of the Christian Scriptures, certain "bridge terms" were employed to express God's ways of communicating with his people: Among these were Wisdom, Word, Torah, *Memra*, and *Shekinah*.[13] Angels also functioned as intermediaries between God and humans, most notably the Angel of the Lord. The bridge terms Judaism uses, however, are unidirectional, extending from God to the world, but not vice versa. The personification of Wisdom in Proverbs 8:22–31 and elsewhere cannot, therefore, be in any way construed as *a* Person in addition to Yahweh. Only Christianity ventures to cross this barrier when it proclaims that Jesus is both *Lord* and *Christ*. This represents a step too far for Judaism.

Judaism does, however, combine language and action as means of mediating God's purpose and meaning into the world. The Torah guides Jewish religious life through the liturgical year, and the Hebrew festivals provide a dramatic backdrop wherein ethical and aesthetic themes are combined. The Torah and the festivals further serve as vehicles that mediate the divine transcendence. Judaism has, however, remained resistant to the Christian idea of the incarnation of God in Jesus despite the fact that Jewish theology during the days of Kabbalistic speculation in the fourteenth and fifteenth centuries began to develop a doctrine of the suffering of God.[14] There can be no doubt that this resistance stems from the Torah's prohibitions against idolatry.[15] Despite these prohibitions, however, Jewish reverence for the Torah and the Temple demonstrates the sacramental nature of these symbols that are believed to mediate the divine transcendence. This reverence runs parallel to the reverence Muslims show toward the Qur'an and the Ka'ba stone.

In Defense of the Incarnation

Perhaps one way of connecting to Jewish and Muslim theological understandings of *sacred word* and *sacred place* is to emphasize parallel claims in Christianity; viz., that Jesus is understood by the writers of the New Testament to be the *incarnate sacred Word* and *the Temple* (sacred place). These interrelated symbols connect to a concept of metanarrative that finds its totality in the idea of divine paradoxical transcendence, for sacred word and sacred place can never be detached from their transcendental orientation if they are to remain *sacred*. The Christian theological concept of the *Logos* is thus meant to function as a comprehensive symbol that gathers up and weaves together the many disparate threads of the divine-human story into a single tapestry. The same is true of Jesus' claim to be the Temple of God,[16] for the Temple functions as a conduit through which the divine purpose and meaning are mediated to the world.

Christianity, by contrast with Judaism and Islam, affirms that the conduit through which transcendence is mediated is maximally *personal* in that it is a *human* conduit. Though one might attempt to advance the reductive claim that the Torah and the Qur'an consist *merely* of parchment and ink, this claim by itself would not suffice to render the Torah or the Qur'an *ineffectual* conduits of divine transcendence. The same could be said of the Hebrew Temple and the Ka'ba stone. The fact that these sacred places are composed of stone does not preclude them from being mediators of divine transcendence. Yet, following this line of argumentation further, one might ask, "What basis is there for claiming that parchment, ink, and stone, as mediators of divine transcendence, are *superior to* a human mediator?" To say that a human mediator *cannot* function as such a conduit is to demote the value of the human being to a status inferior to books and buildings.

On the other hand, Judaism and Islam, like Christianity, have always had their human instruments through which transcendence is believed to be mediated. In Islam, these instruments of mediation have included prophets, caliphs, imams, and mullahs; while in Judaism, they have consisted of prophets, priests, kings, and rabbis. Thus, in these two religions, as in Christianity, there have always been human actors who played significant roles in the divine-human drama.

Missing from the Islamic and Judaic perspectives concerning these human actors, however, is the notion that God *qua* God could have taken on the role of a human actor in such a way that a full reciprocity between the divine and human became possible.[17] Books and buildings, for instance, may serve as one-way vehicles through which the Transcendent is mediated, but they have no power in themselves to *reflect upon* or *respond to* the Transcendent. In the same way that a computer can mediate ideas, books and buildings can also mediate ideas; however, computers can neither reflect upon nor respond to the ideas they mediate, and the same can be said of books and buildings.

God's full embracement of the human drama cannot, therefore, be fully achieved by a divine manifestation that has all the substance of a holographic image. A failure to affirm God's full embracement of the human drama was the mistake of gnosticism, the heresy that affirmed that Jesus only *appeared* to be human when, in their view, he was only divine.[18] To the same effect, but in a manner different from gnosticism, the ancient Ebionites severed the divine-human connection by claiming that Jesus was *merely* human but not divine.[19] The Ebionite viewpoint would thus have God remain merely a *spectator* of the human drama, but not a full *participant* in it. Full participation therefore demands something on the order of the incarnation of God in Jesus, though theologians who have attempted to explain this doctrine have often fallen short of clarifying *how* God participates in human reality.

The Need to Rehabilitate Religious Language

Especially important for Christology are the symbols of prophet, priest, and king.[20] These three primary symbols constitute focal points upon which networks of other related symbols converge and in which they find their unity. As such, these symbols entail the narratives to which they point. The symbols of prophet, priest, and king, in turn, find an even higher unity in another more comprehensive symbol—viz., the symbol of the *messiah* or the *anointed one*. This more comprehensively inclusive symbol points to and participates in a diverse and interwoven narratival tapestry as well.

Unfortunately, symbols such as prophet, priest, king, and messiah have sometimes been ripped from the more replete narratival tapestry that originally gave them fuller context. This fuller context, which illuminated their value, also filled them with purposive and meaningful content. As these symbols became cut away from their original context, however, they became drained of content and were reduced to overly formalized categories that no longer adequately conveyed the meaning and purpose that they once had conveyed. As a result, a gap ensued between the original meaning of the theological symbols and our modern culture's capacity to understand them. Meanwhile, as modern culture has increasingly come to depend on communication through sound bites, the communication gap has only further widened.

The demise and death of symbols in the contemporary world can thus largely be attributed to the loss of the fuller narratival contexts to which these symbols originally pointed and in which they once participated. Indeed, the demise and death of symbols has occurred as many in Western society have transitioned to what Edward T. Hall terms a "low-context culture";[21] namely, a culture in which higher contexts must be elaborately explained to people who have become victims of decontextualization. Unless sufficient explanation is provided, people coming from low-context scenarios otherwise will typically remain clueless.

Consequently, when theologians throw out bits and pieces of disconnected and decontextualized symbols like so many table scraps from the banquet of replete narratival significance, these scraps will invariably fail to provide intellectual and spiritual nourishment to those receiving them. If anything, most people lacking context will simply view them as so much nonsense. The only way to restore the power of religious symbols is thus to restore to them the fuller narratives for which these symbols are merely the shorthand. I shall thus attempt this feat in the sections that follow by providing *context* for these symbols and restoring *content* to them.

CONNECTING THE DOCTRINES OF TRINITY, INCARNATION, AND ATONEMENT THROUGH NARRATIVE

The Purpose of Power in Relation to Kingly and Prophetic Roles

Clearly, the Hebrew Scriptures never look favorably upon attempts to combine the prophetic and kingly roles but advocate their separation. This separation had its rationale in an understanding of the nature of power itself and the way that the exercise of power typically produced destructive conflict and evil consequences in universal human experience.[22] The entire Deuteronomic history of Israel appears rife with examples of tension, struggle, and conflict that arise when kingly power and prophetic caution collide. After King Saul abused his power by acquiring spoils of war from his battle with the Amalekites, the prophet Samuel confronted him with the pronouncement that God had rejected him as Israel's King.[23] Similarly, the prophet Nathan confronted King David over his abuse of power; namely, his committal of the sins of adultery and murder.[24]

The kingly role, as a role dedicated to the exercise of power, often demonstrates a proneness to disregard restraints and overstep boundaries. The prophetic role, on the other hand, warns kings who would transgress proper boundaries that God will have the final say and that divine judgment upon sin will inevitably and certainly be meted out. The prophetic voice thus urges caution, restraint, and limit as it enjoins the powerful to rein in their power and curb their abuses of it. Furthermore, prophetic verdicts condemning the misuse of power by kings contained God's final word regarding the proper use of power as well as its abuse. Such verdicts, which were pronounced upon one after another of the kings of Israel and Judah, are encapsulated in the oft-repeated refrain, "He did evil in the sight of the Lord."[25] The presumptions of human kingship invariably seem to result in the corruption of power; and the Hebrew Scriptures, with brutal honesty, reveal and condemn the immoral and unjust behavior of the kings of Israel and Judah.

Kingly Power as Evidence of Divine Status

The broader scenario in which Hebrew prophetic proclamations were issued appears even more telling than that which existed inside Israel and Judah. Claims of human kings to possess divine status pervaded Ancient Near-Eastern cultures. The Egyptians imagined their Pharaoh to be the incarnation of all the gods of Egypt;[26] while the Babylonians believed their king to be the son of Marduk, the high god of Babylon.[27] Myths and rituals accompanying ancient kingship institutions served as propaganda tools that bolstered, empowered, and promulgated divine-kingship ideologies. These ideologies became culturally and politically entrenched in all the nations surrounding the people of Israel.

Divine-kingship ideologies reveal that both warfare and the subjugation of enemies were religiously, and not just politically, motivated. Examples from Ancient Near Eastern and Mediterranean cultures demonstrate how the category of *power* became inextricably linked to the category of the *divine*.[28] To *possess power* is *to be divine*, and the degree of power possessed determines the degree of divine status attained. Of course, power by itself means very little unless it is employed in specific ways towards specific people in specific situations. The use and abuse of power must therefore always be assessed in relation to the *contexts* in which that power is exercised. The issue of context, in turn, raises the question, "What purpose should power serve?"

Just and Unjust Uses of Power

Two obvious extremes come to light when assessing the kinds of relations that the exercise of power entails. One extreme entails the *just* use of power; the other, its *unjust* use. Consequently, when power is abused so that justice is not served but injustice is promulgated, the *purpose* of power appears wholly *negative* and *ignoble* in its aim. Power exercised unjustly usually aims at achieving the self-aggrandizement of the individual who exercises it. The ideology of self-aggrandizement is promoted through the worship of power gods. Deities such as Ashur, Marduk, Baal-Hadad, Zeus, and Jupiter epitomize the essence of raw, destructive, and traumatizing power. Usually, the element in power of *unpredictability* is magnified.

In their attempts to hold on to power, kings would often co-opt and weave into royal ideologies the notion that *all* manifestations of unpredictable power are manifestations not only of the god's power but of the king's power as well, since the king claims to be the god's authorized representative or visible manifestation on earth. Kingship ideology also co-opts, as its components, traumatizing phenomena found in tangible existence. Tempestuous and destructive spectacles in nature such as wind, lightning, thunder, and earthquakes; and aggressive or predatory animals, such as bulls, lions, and eagles—all these function as tangible vehicles through which the power of the god is thought to be channeled. When combined, these tangible vehicles of power become focused in the fulcrum of the royal personage in whom the power of the deity is believed to be maximally concentrated.

Divine-kingship ideologies were thus devised to delude intended victims into believing that their god and his representative on earth possess unlimited power. All manifestations of unpredictable power are made to align with the power of the king and his god in such a way that those whom they rule and conquer become overwhelmed with an experience of *terrible holiness*. This kind of experience entails none other than a sense of the *mysterium tremendum*, for it is this sense of the holy that the exercise of raw power most notably evokes in those who encounter and endure its awfulness. Indeed, the more that the manifestation of power appears arbitrary, capricious, and unfettered, the greater is the sense of terrible holiness that it projects. Those whom this holy power constrains and terrifies are reduced in its presence to a state of blind, absolute, unquestioning, and groveling submission. This terrible holiness is, however, a *demonic* holiness in that it usurps the proper prerogative of the *divine* holiness. It is thus evil at its very core.

Power and Purpose in Nature as the Exclusive Possession of the God of Israel

The kind of raw, arbitrary, uninhibited power attributed to pagan kings of nations surrounding Israel also happens to be attributed to the God of Israel. The God whom Israel recognizes is, after all, the true creator of the phenomenal world—that sphere in which raw and unpredictable power is commonly manifested—and this implies that all others claiming to control such power, be they gods or kings, are usurpers who must be deposed. Yahweh's exclusive claim to be the *only* God of his people, and a *jealous* God at that, is one that demands from his people absolute loyalty and submission. This kind of relationship between a deity and his devotees is already a normative feature of Ancient Near-Eastern religions generally.

Nevertheless, the arbitrariness and capriciousness of the God of Israel is at the same time moderated by the fact that he is a *good* lawgiver concerned above all with *justice*. This ethical component qualifies the purpose of the God of Israel as being *positive* rather than *negative* in its aim. The inclusion of the element of the ethical reveals that the divine power, despite all its severity, becomes directed toward constructive purposes that are just and good. What exactly, then, does this inclusion of the ethical entail? First, it is important to acknowledge that the ethical element does not, as such, *regulate* the divine purpose in any way that may appear predictable or mechanical. The negative dimension of the divine holiness (*mysterium tremendum*) as inexhaustible power still overshadows and dominates whatever positive ethical regulations may appear to originate from the holy God. Second, it is critical to understand that the divine power and purpose link up primarily with the concept of *freedom* and only secondarily with the concept of *limit*. Because this linkage with freedom is primary, the power and purpose of God must also be conceived of as maximally *personal*. God is wholly free and unrestrained in the way he rules and commands his people.

Considering the divine omnipotence in terms of *inexhaustible power* is, I believe, of crucial importance for understanding what it means that God is the ultimate progenitor and continuing cause of existence, and that God has the power to conquer all limit, including death. Because God as the Transcendent Original is a reservoir of inexhaustible power, all manifestations of power in the universe must be derived from their ultimate origin in him who is the source of all power. We can thus speak in one way of the divine transcendence as a *transcendence of God in origin as the God of inexhaustible power*. Such inexhaustible power, when manifested, appears to be *directed* in certain ethical ways. In this respect, the inexhaustible power of the Transcendent Original becomes *purposive* power as well.

Contextualizing the Divine Power

The *purposive* power of God finds its basis in a doctrine of the *ordinating power* of God (*potentia ordinata*), and this polarity within the divine power relates more closely to our concept of *limit* than to *freedom*. More specifically, God's ordinating power points to the divine purpose as *just*; and this, in turn, supports the belief that the God of the Bible is also *trustworthy*. Affirming the trustworthiness of God requires, notwithstanding, a careful examining and a full understanding of the *contexts* in which biblical passages describing God's exercise of arbitrary power appear; though admittedly an element of the inscrutable will remain. The historical-political milieu, the beliefs, the ideologies, and the practices of the Ancient Near East in general constitute what may be called the *external* context; while the whole of biblical narrative, which forms the *internal* context, provides the most reasonable standard for contextualizing narratives where God appears to act arbitrarily.

The external context in which the God of purposive power acted was tumultuous, chaotic, and rife with brutality. Consequently, the God whom the Hebrew Scriptures describes is *moral* but not *benign*. If he had been benign, he more than likely would have gotten little if any traction in the aforementioned context. Such a "politically correct" God would have instead appeared impotent, ineffectual, and unable to garner even a modicum of respect from Israel's enemies. Most likely, he would have elicited little if any respect from his own people of Israel either. The God of the Bible sometimes acted capriciously: that much is true. However, if we can find an adequate rationale for his acting thus, then in what sense would we still have to consider his actions *capricious*?

Apparent capricious actions are not the same as *authentic* capricious actions. Neither are "capricious" actions necessarily indicative of moral weakness or evil on God's part. Indeed, displays of passionate anger, displeasure, and disgust might be wholly warranted in circumstances where terrible injustices have been perpetrated, and the Ancient Near-Eastern context was certainly one rife with some of the most horrible episodes of injustice that have ever transpired throughout human history. Mild-mannered responses, in which the element of arbitrary power has been tamped down, are impotent to redress circumstances where injustices are rife. Such responses would instead appear tepid, cowardly, disloyal, half-hearted, lacking in passion, and bereft of commitment. Indeed, attempting to remain cool and aloof in the face of scenarios demanding combative action would, if anything, appear *less* moral, not *more* so—and *less* moral because coolness and aloofness will be perceived as evidence of *apathy*. Apathy, in turn, can itself be interpreted as an indicator either of *passive cruelty* or *cowardly complicity with evil*. Atrocious injustice, if anything, calls for a vigorous response in which one's entire heart, soul, and will are dedicated to the struggle to defeat injustice and establish justice.

An examination of the context *inside* of Israel also helps us gain a more complete understanding of the purposive power of God. Since this internal perspective is provided by the Bible itself, we need to consider the Bible in its entirety as the context for understanding how the divine power is directed and channeled through the divine purpose. Two concepts are especially important; viz., the concepts of *creation* and *covenant*. First, the doctrine of creation suggests that God is a God who creates an *"other"*—a *counterpart* that is external to God's being. God then freely invests this counterpart with power and libertarian freedom of its own.

This counterpart God created has a beginning; a point at which it starts to possess its own power and freedom (see figure 9.1). However, creation's beginning also points to another type of beginning in God as well. This is not an *ontological* beginning, since God's being is eternal. Rather, it is a *relational* beginning, in which we can observe God's initiation on his part of a gradual voluntary limiting, focusing, directing, and channeling of his actual power in ways that are ultimately constructive. The Greek word *ktisis* (κτίσις) expresses the way in which God's inexhaustible power becomes purposively directed (see figure 9.1). *Ktisis* here thus points to a voluntary self-restraint of God the Father as he channels his inexhaustible potential toward the realization of a special divine purpose. This element of limitation, when juxtaposed to the element of divine freedom, renders necessary the usual distinction that is made between God's *potentia absoluta* and his *potentia ordinata*. Expressed in another way, God's absolute *potential* is infinitely great, free, and without limit; while his *actual* power is characterized by various degrees, kinds, and episodes of limitation, restraint, and purposive direction. The personal God channels his power in certain ways and at certain times to achieve certain good purposes.

Second, in addition to God's special directing of his power in his decision to create the world, his purposive channeling of his inexhaustible power involves the establishment of *covenants* (see figure 9.1). The covenant concept reveals a deepening of the *relational* quality between God and the individuals or groups with whom he forges covenants. To the degree that a covenant is more particular in its focus than creation, this relational quality exceeds the quality of the relationship God established with his creation when God brought creation into existence. Again, the idea of a voluntary self-restraint on the part of God the Father is implied in the very idea of *covenantal* relationship.

There are, however, two interrelated levels on which the concept of covenant operates. On one level, this relationship appears to focus on the covenantal recipients' external tangible concerns such as material blessings and

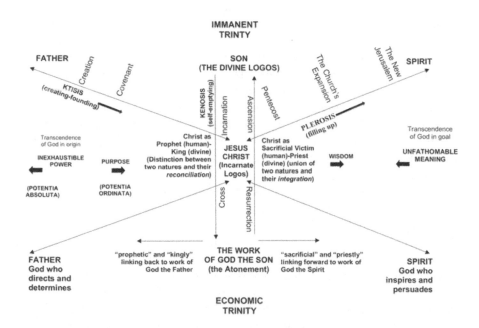

Figure 9.1.   Trinitarian Doctrine Related to Christ's Person and Work.

the possession of land in exchange for their obedience and loyalty to the provider of these privileges. The focus on external tangible concerns links up more closely with the doctrines of creation and common grace than it does with the doctrine of salvation. The kind of covenantal relationship concerned with external tangible concerns usually falls into the category often referred to as a *conditional covenant*.

A conditional covenant, however, does not yet reach the depths of intimacy that touches the dimension of the human soul. This deeper aspect of relationality between God and individuals depends upon an *unconditional covenant*. This second kind of covenant links with the doctrine of salvation in a way that the conditional covenant does not. The unconditional covenant is of the kind that God makes with Abraham in Genesis 15. The cutting of an unconditional covenant thus points to a deepening of the divine self-restraint that is more personal than in either the conditional covenant or creation. Specifically, the qualitative nature of the divine self-restraint that one finds executed in the unconditional covenant looks forward to the incarnation and the cross of Jesus Christ. Hence, one already finds in the unconditional-covenant concept support for a doctrine of the vulnerability and suffering of God. The divine self-restraint, which entails a channeling of the power of God through the limits imposed by the divine purpose, thus entails a gradual deepening that points to the sacrificial love of God that reaches its full expression in the person and work of Jesus Christ (see figure 9.1). Retrospectively, one can thus consider the cross and the incarnation of Christ to be lenses through which one can view and contextualize the earlier moments of the divine self-restraint that transpired when God created the world and forged covenantal relationships with his people.

Furthermore, since the divine purpose is eternal, it does not appear arbitrary in the way the divine power appears arbitrary. God's purpose is, rather, constant, unchanging, and unwavering in its aim. On this basis, the Apostle John can affirm that Christ is "the Lamb slain from the foundation of the world."[29] By using the fullest possible context as a framework, we can thus discern what the aim of the divine purpose entailed from the very beginning. The divine purpose thus becomes one important ingredient of a divine-human drama that reaches its denouement in the cross and resurrection of Jesus.

Because the idea of the covenant is especially significant for discerning how the divine power is channeled in specific ways through the divine purpose, examining more specifically what the prophetic role entailed with regard to God's purposive power is also paramount. The prophets constantly reminded Israel and its kings of their obligations to the God with whom they enjoyed a covenantal relationship.[30] In this regard, the prophetic office functioned as an important counterbalance to the kingly office. The prophet also pointed out ways that Israel and its kings had violated the terms of God's covenant by breaking the laws God had prescribed. The Torah emphasized the idea of limit as well and thus served to curb power and keep it from being raw and unbridled in its exercise. In keeping with this emphasis upon *limit*, the prophetic voice also bore witness to the same divine purpose that informed and issued forth into God's voluntary restraining, focusing, and directing of his actual power in constructive ways.

Furthermore, the prophetic understanding of the divine purpose most notably included concepts of morality, with the greatest focus being placed on *justice*.[31] The theme of divine justice is therefore a key element entailed in the divine purpose. This fact becomes evident throughout the prophetic writings where warnings of divine judgment were issued against those who used power in manipulative, deceptive, and exploitive ways. Exploitation of the poor, the disenfranchised, widows, and orphans was roundly condemned.[32] Related in an insidious way to this kind of exploitation were vices of intemperance, self-indulgence, greed, and pride.[33] These vices, in fact, precipitated unjust behavior. Sins of hypocrisy were also condemned, as were acts of worship that had become superficial, routine, lacking substance, and devoid of the quality of mercy.[34]

Injustices and evils perpetrated through the exercise of unjust political power included among their consequences the persecution, suffering, and martyrdom of prophets.[35] Their fate reveals their all-too-human vulnerability. Kings exercising unbridled political power, on the other hand, often felt threatened by prophetic warnings. Consequently, where the prophet's recourse sometimes entailed martyrdom, kings sometimes chose as their recourse the leveling of the full force of their power against the prophets and their message.

Combining or Reconciling the Prophetic and Kingly Roles

Since the prophetic and kingly roles are largely kept *separate* throughout the Hebrew Bible, a question arises: Can these two roles ever be adequately combined or reconciled in such a way that one individual becomes the bearer of both? This issue must be investigated, because a central claim of Christianity is that Jesus' qualifications as Messiah must include both the prophetic and kingly roles.

Only a couple of personages in the Hebrew Bible, Moses and Samuel, fit a paradigm where political power combined with the prophetic office. In these cases, the corruption of power looms either as actual (as with Moses' sin at Meribah)[36] or as possible (as with the corrupt sons of Samuel).[37] In both cases, the divine response is judgment. Indeed, the Hebrew Bible consistently maintains a thoroughgoing polemic against the presumption of all human kings or power brokers—be they pagan or Israelite—to exercise power *carte blanche*. One could, in fact, discern the Bible's verdict concerning human kingship: It is for the most part a failure; and there is, in fact, *no king but God*.

Here I must note that Islamic understanding of the prophetic and kingly roles represents a fundamental departure from the Hebraic perspective. In Islam, the role of prophet is made *identical* to the office of political ruler. Muhammad is proclaimed to be the greatest of all the prophets of Islam at the same time that he is upheld as its quintessential military leader. His role as caliph and prophet thus qualifies him as one kind of representative of the prophet-king combination that the Bible never condones. Because these roles have become combined, checks upon the one who holds absolute power become virtually nonexistence. Persons living in the Western democracies find it difficult to understand that Islamic culture, ideally at least, rejects the notion of a separation of the religious and political domains. In keeping with the total identification of religion with the state, all power tends to be concentrated in the supreme leader. Without adequate checks and balances, however, power tends much more easily to be corrupted than it does in places where checks and balances of the exercise of power are in effect.

The Reconciliation of the Prophetic and Kingly Roles of Christ in New Testament Theology

Both the prophetic and kingly offices are entailed in the affirmation, "Jesus is the Christ," but the way that these offices are combined and applied to Jesus in the New Testament differs substantially from the Islamic understanding of how these offices converge in the person of Muhammad. The New Testament, like the Hebrew Scriptures, affirms that the two offices are separated. Unlike the Hebrew Scriptures, however, the New Testament narratives achieve a *reconciliation* of the two offices that surpasses the way they are combined in the Hebrew Bible in figures such as Moses and Samuel. The way that the separation and reconciliation of the two offices are upheld cannot be fully appreciated apart from a consideration of the narratives and theological insights of the New Testament concerning what it means that Christ is both divine king and quintessential human prophet. A reading of the New Testament leaves one with no doubt that Jesus' understanding of his own kingship remained out of step with the majority opinion concerning what the messiah's role should entail. The Maccabean revolt against the Seleucids inspired the model that the Jews endorsed after Rome's invasion of Palestine. This model imagined the coming of a military messiah who would throw off the yoke of Roman domination.

Of the four Gospels, Matthew seems more intent than any to portray Jesus as a king. However, equally important for Matthew is the theme of Jesus' servant role. In fact, Matthew integrates the themes of kingship and servant-hood so thoroughly in his theology that they become inseparable, and he rarely refers to one without at least hinting at the other. Clearly, Matthew intends in his gospel to bring the servant theme to the forefront by emphasizing Jesus' willingness to undergo the rite of baptism and to endure the wilderness temptations. In Matthew's account of the third temptation of Jesus, Satan takes Jesus into a high mountain and promises him all the kingdoms of the world if Jesus will only bow down and worship him.[38] Jesus' rebuke, "Get thee behind me, Satan!" reveals already at this early stage of Jesus' career that he has completely rejected the popular Jewish idea of a militaristic messiah.

Jesus' rejection of popular messianism becomes further explicated when, at Caesarea Philippi, Peter utters his Great Confession, "Thou art the Christ, the Son of the living God!"[39] During Jesus' conversation with him, it becomes ironically apparent that Peter, despite his commendable confession, has retained the current Jewish view of "Christ" or "Messiah" as a military figure. After Jesus talks about going to Jerusalem to suffer, Peter rebukes him, "Far be it from you Lord that this should ever happen to you."[40] Jesus then repeats words that he had spoken earlier after his third wilderness temptation, "Get thee behind me, Satan!"[41] By repeating this statement, Jesus demonstrates that the messianic understanding that Peter has allowed to become lodged in his mind is, in fact, *satanically inspired!*

Throughout the Synoptic Gospels as well, instances occur where Jesus enjoined his disciples and others not to spread the word that he was the Messiah or the Son of God, and not to broadcast his displays of miraculous power. The German scholar Wilhelm Wrede (1859–1906) constructed a rather elaborate theory to explain this phenomenon, labeling it the "Messianic Secret Motif" (Ger=*Messiasgeheimnis Verein*).[42] Wrede claimed that the writer of Mark's Gospel puts the phrase "Tell no man that I am the Messiah"[43] into the mouth of Jesus to explain why Jesus never claimed to be the Messiah. Wrede's view, however, which has had considerable influence upon the secular study of the New Testament, offers an unnecessarily complicated explanation for a phenomenon that can be explained more easily if one considers the context in which Jesus discouraged the use of the term "messiah" in reference to himself. Since the term from the Jewish perspective possessed a militaristic connotation, it would have to be redefined before Jesus could validly apply it to himself. This redefinition could not have been possible, however, apart from the context provided by Jesus' suffering and death on the cross, and by his resurrection.[44]

A further redefinition of the messiah idea, and one that could be interpreted as a refutation of the current Jewish view, appears in the passion narratives of the Gospels. The suffering servant poem from Isaiah 52:13–53:12, which is thoroughly interwoven into these narratives, serves as the basis for such a refutation. If the Gospel writers were seeking to unseat the Jewish militaristic interpretation of "messiah," then no better counterbal-

ance to the Jewish view could have been provided than that of the aforementioned Isaiah passage. Isaiah speaks in detail of a suffering servant who
would be "pierced for our transgressions" and "bruised for our iniquities." As
one might expect, the Jewish doctrine of the messiah would have contained
no such element of suffering. As a consequence, by focusing attention on the
suffering element, the Gospel writers kept insisting that their fellow Jews
needed to return to their own Scripture to see plainly for themselves what
they had neglected to emphasize in their own messianic viewpoint.

The sacrificial imagery throughout Isaiah 52:13–53:12 is clear, and the
fact that the suffering servant being described is referred to in Isaiah 53:2 as
the "shoot" (Heb=*yōwnêq* [יוֹנֵק]) or the "root" (Heb=*šōreš* [שֹׁרֶשׁ]) clearly
identifies the suffering servant figure with the ideal of kingship as well.
Elsewhere the term "branch" (Heb=*nêṣer* [נֵצֶר]) is used;[45] but more frequently, the Hebrew word used for branch is *ṣemaḥ* (צֶמַח).[46] In all these cases, the
concept is linked to servant as well as kingship themes. One interpretation of
Matthew's reference, "and he shall be called a Nazarene,"[47] is that Matthew
had the word *nêṣer* in mind. This interpretation would be supported by the
fact that no prophecy exists in the Hebrew Scriptures containing this exact
phraseology. Further complicating the notable absence of such an exact
phrase is Matthew's attribution of it to *prophets* and not just to a *single*
prophet. The issue can be resolved, however, if Matthew happens to be
correlating Nazareth, the place where Jesus grew up, with the *nêṣer* that the
prophets indicated would "grow out of dry ground." Nazareth was, after all, a
place of obscurity,[48] so the spirit of the verse certainly supports Nazareth as a
candidate that aptly alludes to the "dry ground" out of which the branch
would grow.

The point repeatedly made throughout the New Testament is that Jesus'
role as prophet and suffering servant must always be kept prior to the event
that ratifies his kingship. This event is the resurrection of Jesus, as St. Paul
expresses in Romans 1:4, "he was *declared* [emphasis mine] to be the Son of
God with power, according to the spirit of holiness, by the resurrection from
the dead." Here, the sequencing of events is critically important. Jesus' martyrdom as a prophet—namely, his crucifixion—*precedes* his resurrection in
such a way that the resurrection *contains* within itself the event of the cross.
This sequence cannot be reversed. More importantly, the resurrection removes one important linchpin of the dialectic that governs tangible reality;
namely, the principle of *limit*. As I stated previously, *death* represents for
human beings in their tangible existence the most universal and final manifestation of the limit principle. Therefore, only paradoxical transcendence
could contain and contextualize the dialectic of the life-death cycle by replac-
ing this principle of limit with a principle that has its basis in interminable
life, limitless freedom, and inexhaustible power.[49] The resurrection of the
Son of God thus represents a breaking in of divine power into tangible

existence where, for the most part, the dialectic that hinges on the principle of limit still holds sway. The effect of Jesus' resurrection, however, is to transform the *horror* and *ugliness* of death into a thing of *fascination* and *beauty*. In the resurrection, the balance shifts *away* from the *mysterium tremendum* and *toward* the *mysterium fascinans*. Thus, while the death of Jesus removes the moral impediments that separate a holy God from sinful human beings, his resurrection demonstrates the victory of sublime beauty over the supreme ugliness of death.

The relationship between the two natures in Christ thus focuses on the prophetic and kingly roles, with the human nature being more closely correlated with the prophetic, and the divine nature being more closely aligned with the kingly. In both Islam and Judaism, by contrast, these roles are only *dialectically* related because, as in the cases of such figures as Muhammad, Moses, and Samuel, all must succumb to the *ultimate limit of death*. No transcendental principle beyond the limit of death appears in these cases that is capable of recontextualizing death by reversing it. Only in the resurrection of Jesus is this reversal and recontextualization accomplished. Normally in tangible existence, life, from the time of birth, already contains within itself the certainty of eventual death. No example exists, however, of death containing the certainty of eventual life. Only the inexhaustible power of God can bring about such a state. Ordinarily, the purpose of God, as we have seen, is manifested in God's restriction of his power in certain ways; however, the resurrection signals a reversal of the principle of restriction. In one sense, it could be said that God's purpose, which guides the self-restraint of his inexhaustible power, reaches its terminus in Jesus' cross, only to make through his resurrection a radical turn in the opposite direction toward a new beginning. Clearly, God's voluntary restraint of his actual power is not one by which God irrevocably binds himself to the effect that his power must remain forever restrained. Jesus makes this clear even of himself when he says, "I have the power to lay down my life, and I have the power to take it up again."[50] What is true of Jesus here is true of God as Trinity; for in God, freedom does not abolish limit, nor does limit necessarily restrain freedom. Rather, the two mutually coexist in the paradoxical unity of the divine totality. The opposite, however, would be true in tangible existence where freedom and limit do come into dialectical conflict.

At this point, however, it is also essential to note that such paradoxical divine unity does not eclipse dialectical conflict, nor does it act as a universal solvent that dissolves particularity entirely. The doctrine of God's incarnation in Jesus cannot be allowed to tip in the direction of mysticism or gnosticism. The dialectical conflict that Christ suffered must therefore be fully retained at the very heart of paradoxical transcendence. One image in the Book of Revelation preserves this idea; namely, the vision of the Lamb slain in the midst of the Divine Throne.[51] The Divine Throne, identified in the

Hebrew Scriptures with the Ark of the Covenant, was the place where the blood of the Day of Atonement sacrifice was sprinkled. Now sitting upon it is the Lamb who was slain. Thus, situated at the center of the Apostle John's vision of heaven, in all its transcendent mystery and glory, is the cross of Jesus Christ. The tangible realities of the suffering and death of Jesus are thus in no way obliterated by paradoxical transcendence; rather, they are retained and contextualized by it. If anything, these tangibles are elevated so that they become symbols through which the beauty of paradoxical transcendence is mediated.

The distinction between the two natures in Christ is thus retained in the way the prophetic and kingly roles are related. How, then, should we conceptualize the union of the two natures and the two roles that correspond to them? Certainly, the union is best understood in terms of a *reconciliation* of roles that, in many of the Old Testament descriptions of them, were in a state of *tension* or even *alienation*. Reconciliation, however, usually marks a kind of dialectical synthesis that is achieved when alienated parties reach some agreement. An agreement, in this case, would be a *synthesis* that would have to adhere to the strictures imposed by the principle of limit. Such a synthesis would result in a *tertium quid*, which, in the case of the prophetic and kingly roles, would have to exist somewhere midway between the two offices. Speaking of the union of the divine and human natures in Christ as a *tertium quid*, however, does nothing to preserve the Christological paradox—that Christ was fully human *and* fully divine. Since the divine transcendence is what accomplishes this reconciliation, the reconciliation that this transcendence brings about cannot be understood as some kind of admixture of the human and the divine natures, or as a compromise between the prophetic and kingly roles. Rather, the human and the divine natures, as well as the prophetic and kingly roles, must be fully retained in their distinctiveness while being united in a *coincidence of opposites*. This coincidence of the distinct natures and the distinct roles can only be accomplished by the unity of the divine transcendence.

The Meaning of Wisdom and its Relation to Priestly and Sacrificial Roles

A correlation exists not only between *power* and *purpose*, but also between *wisdom* and *meaning*. As we transition from the power-and-purpose discussion to one that concerns the relationship between wisdom and meaning, we also move from an emphasis on the *external* dimension of human tangible existence to an emphasis on the *internal* dimension. On the one hand, in saying that power and purpose are largely concerned with the external dimension, I should point out that *survival* is the chief tangible goal that the purposive exercise of power intends to achieve. I do not speak here so much in terms of the survival of *individuals* as in the survival of the *collective*. For *power* to become *purposive*, it must be directed in a beneficial way for all concerned. For this reason, purposive power must uphold the ideal of *justice* as its supreme directing principle, and it must seek to bring that ideal to bear in a beneficial way upon tangible existence.

The *external* focus becomes evident in the *social* character of the power-order dialectic. This dialectic is reflected in the roles of king and prophet, respectively, for the king ideally should exercise *power* on behalf of the collective that he represents, while the prophet calls for the kind of justice that will provide the best possible *order* for society. While the *collective* receives the dominant emphasis in this model, the *individual* within the collective expects to be governed by standards that are largely behavioral and that are intended to promote social order. Certain freedoms that manifest themselves in antisocial or socially corruptive kinds of behavior must therefore be restricted for those who act in such ways. Restrictions upon individuals who work against the ideal of social order are often accomplished by the imposing of penalties; and in cases where threats to survival are at their highest, such penalties can be quite severe.

On the other hand, the focus upon the categories of wisdom and meaning is concerned more directly with the *internal psychological* dimension of tangible human experience. Here the preoccupation shifts from the *survival* emphasis of the tangible direction of the value-compass to an emphasis on *life* and the *flourishing of life*. Hence, while purposive power makes *survival* possible, meaningful wisdom makes *flourishing* possible. Furthermore, where purposive power is concerned primarily with bringing *justice* to bear upon situations plagued by injustice, meaningful wisdom is concerned above all with the fostering of *creativity* against the forces of destruction.

The search for meaningful wisdom tends to become the central focus of societies or enclaves that enjoy relative stability over time. Thus, in places like Egypt, Greece, and India, wisdom traditions developed. Though episodes of calamity threatened these cultures at various times, long interludes of stability provided contexts in which the pursuit of wisdom could thrive. One element that virtually all wisdom traditions shared was *diversity*, for numerous philosophical schools emerged in places like Greece and India. Among the Hebrew people, the wisdom tradition received its greatest emphasis during the postexilic period, though the tradition itself harked back to the time of Solomon—the greatest period of peace, prosperity, and stability the united Hebrew Kingdom had ever known. Solomon's reign of peace certainly qualifies as the kind of setting that would spawn wisdom, for it marked a time when Israel had transitioned from living in a survival mode to one that fostered creativity and facilitated flourishing. The building of the first Hebrew Temple in Jerusalem reflects this transition in one respect; while in another respect, priestly Judaism, which reached its heyday following the

Temple's construction and dedication, became the conservatory of the wisdom tradition.

The wisdom literature attributed to King Solomon seems somewhat foreign when compared to the royal and prophetic traditions of the Hebrew Bible. Notably absent is a clear emphasis upon the *covenant*, which had held such a privilege of place in prophetic preaching.[52] Despite this absence, the Book of Proverbs may have retained at least one important covenantal symbol in its elevation of the role of Lady Wisdom.[53] Her words reflect the wisdom of the Torah over against the *deceptive* allurements of the adulterous woman Folly. If the commandment, "Honor your father and your mother," were employed as a lens through which Lady Wisdom's role is viewed, then that lens would reveal that she is like a worthy mother whom her son should honor and whose wisdom he should heed. Her maternal wisdom nonetheless lacks the degree of harshness that one might expect from a father figure. Instead, she represents the *inspiring ideal* of the *feminine*. By means of her own power of attraction, she persuades her listener to avoid Folly's deceptive words. Wisdom's advice appears simultaneously nonthreatening and enticing. Her powers of persuasion appeal to the "better angels" of the young man whom she advises. She brings to light the dangers of succumbing to Folly's *deception.* She warns him that Folly will only bring him a life of misery and hasten his own demise and death, and she advises him that living by her precepts will protect him from ruin.

Proverbs not only personifies Wisdom as feminine, but it also calls her the architect of creation.[54] Wisdom is in the beginning with God, and through her, God framed the world.[55] These designations anticipate the later doctrines of the *Logos* and the Holy Spirit. Connections between Wisdom and the Holy Spirit are not, however, made explicit until the Wisdom of Solomon,[56] where the "Spirit of Wisdom" is described.[57] Wisdom, like the Spirit, "is the breath of the power of God, and a pure influence flowing from the glory of the Almighty: therefore can no defiled thing fall into her."[58] Like the Holy Spirit, she is active and pervades all things, "more moving than any motion," and passing and going "through all things by reason of her pureness."[59] Other characteristics are attributed to her as well: She is viewed as the "throne partner of God" and she knows all the works of God.[60] As the spotless mirror that reflects God's power, she is the image of God's goodness, reflecting God's eternal light.[61] Wisdom orders and orchestrates all things;[62] and by her, the workings of nature are revealed.[63] Also through her, God ordained that man would have dominion over the creatures he had made;[64] hence, she enables kings to rule.

Wisdom's association with a doctrine of the Holy Spirit does not, however, appear in other wisdom books such as Ecclesiastes or Job, though these books do seem open to interpretation in the light of this doctrine.[65] Ecclesiastes and Job seek to provide wisdom from the standpoint of persons experiencing failure or suffering. Ecclesiastes represents a condition of inner psychological experience where wisdom has become detached from meaning. The phrase, "there is nothing new under the sun," expresses a condition of human existence that, despite all the external marks of flourishing, is internally bereft of meaning. The "all" or "whole" of the matter that the Preacher sought to obtain could not be found "under the sun;" for in this mundane realm of existence, everything seemed to operate predictably, repetitively, and meaninglessly.

The Jewish rabbinic tradition would go on to emphasize that a life lived by the Torah, which came from the transcendent divine reality that resides "above the sun," could restore meaning to life.[66] However, the conclusion of Ecclesiastes gives advice that raises further questions about what it means to live one's life guided by the Torah. The pieces of advice Ecclesiastes gives are to "remember your Creator in the days of your youth" and to "fear God and keep his commandments, for this is the whole duty of man."[67] These answers seem drenched with the pessimism that is typical of the book overall. The word here for "Creator" (בּוֹרְאֶךָ) can also mean "cistern" or "grave," as Rabbi Akiba notes.[68] Also, the motivation to obey God's commandments out of *fear* falls short of what Wisdom offers in, for example, the Wisdom of Solomon where she inspires obedience out of *love* rather than fear.[69] Those who earnestly seek Wisdom find her, love her, and keep her laws.[70] The Great Commandment, "Thou shalt love the Lord thy God with all thy heart, soul, mind, and strength,"[71] certainly provides an incentive superior to fear as well. Love has the capacity to elevate duty from the level of the mundane and the repetitious into the sphere of the meaningful.

Whereas Ecclesiastes deals with the difficulty of self-inflicted misery, Job deals with that of misery inflicted by external circumstances and, hence, with the problem of innocent suffering. The issue here, as in Ecclesiastes, concerns how one is to find meaning in a situation seemingly sapped of meaning. Meaningless suffering that happens not to be self-incurred denotes Job's situation. His story subverts the mistaken explanation that one's own sin is always the cause of all one's suffering. Hence, as a sole explanation of human suffering, this explanation falters and fails, for Job is a *righteous man*.[72] Another explanation falls short of the mark as well; namely, the one that the young Elihu gives. In a series of four speeches, he contends that God is trying to teach Job a lesson in humility.[73] Though more theologically sound than those of Job's other detractors, Elihu's analysis cannot entail any significant degree of empathy on his part. He is after all inexperienced, with many life lessons himself yet to learn.

It is not the advice of Job's detractors, but God's answer from the whirlwind, that prevails as the Book of Job's central focus. God's answer marshals forth traumatic images, evoking in Job a sense of the *mysterium tremendum* that reduces him to a state of abject submission and repentance.[74] The array of traumatic and awe-inspiring images that God parades before him are, nonetheless, also contextualized. The holy God, whom Job has chosen to trust, has, after all, *created* all the awesome phenomena that strike terror into his heart. The assurance, too, that God could easily vanquish such monstrous creatures as Behemoth and Leviathan provides a context that helps Job endure his sufferings as he waits for God to vindicate him.[75] Thus, Job's sufferings, though extraordinarily great by human standards, dwarf in comparison to the power and enormity of the God whom he chooses to trust. The portrayal of the sublime beauty of God found in God's answer to Job thus reunites the *mysterium tremendum* with the *mysterium fascinans* and makes possible for Job an experience of the *sublime*. We can imagine that Job experiences some degree of comfort as he stands aloof from these images and compares them with the actual suffering he has endured. God's sublime grandeur, which overshadows Job's sufferings, thus appears as a source of consolation.

Books such as Ecclesiastes and Job highlight the psychological and existential crises that persons undergo when aspects of the dimension of the tangible become divorced from the dimension of the Transcendent. *Meaning* becomes the only thread that can help one navigate through the multiple and divergent threads of tangible existence that seem endlessly to proliferate. As the number of threads multiply, we tend to lose sight of the Ariadne thread of meaning and turn our attention instead to finding answers to the plurality of problems we encounter *from* the labyrinth of tangible existence itself. At the same time, we lose track of that Ariadne thread of meaning that can lead out of the labyrinth of meaninglessness and instead become so focused upon the dimension of particularity that the multiple and diverse threads of existence loop in upon themselves and become hopelessly tangled. We are consequently left with the feeling of being trapped with no means of escape.

The Book of Ecclesiastes depicts the sense of meaninglessness the author experiences when he, having been cut off from the divine transcendence, becomes mired in the rut of tangible life. Job, too, finds no escape from his plight as long as he remains fixated on the particulars of his suffering. Indeed, not until he glimpses God's transcendental meaning does he gain some relief from his misery. The human need to allow transcendental meaning to cut through life's Gordian knot calls for an understanding of wisdom that leads *away* from the ugly and *toward* the beautiful and the sublime. Such a view of wisdom establishes a pathway between the diverse ways of the tangible world and the transcendental unity of Meaning-Itself. Wisdom is already immanent in the world, and creation itself bears her imprint for all to see. However, when wisdom becomes unlinked from the Transcendent, it deteriorates into a treadmill of meaninglessness.

Wisdom bereft of transcendence thus lacks the quality of the Holy; viz., the *mysterium tremendum et fascinans*. Ideally, the twofold mystery of the Holy is here grasped in terms of the *beauty of the sublime*, or what David

Bentley Hart calls "the beauty of the Infinite."[76] However, one additional element often appears missing from ideas concerning how wisdom links with the Transcendent; namely, the element of the *personal*. I have mentioned previously how Shankara Hinduism links wisdom to transcendence in an *impersonal* way. Christian theology rejects this view. Instead, the Christian doctrine of the Holy Spirit links the immanence of Wisdom to the transcendence of the sublime in a manner that is intensely *personal*. Since Christian theology views the Holy Spirit as a *Person* within the Holy Trinity, it teaches that the Holy Spirit provides for individual souls a superior ideal of inspiration that can lift *persons* out of their ruts of meaninglessness and despair and can reconnect them with the dimension of the Transcendent. The personal quality that the Christian doctrine of the Holy Spirit embraces is supported by the Spirit's concrete relatedness to the work of Jesus Christ as priest and sacrificial victim. It is, after all, *Jesus* who *sends* the Spirit, even though orthodox theology first affirms that the Spirit proceeds from the Father. The priestly and sacrificial roles that Jesus' atoning work link together thus provide the concrete support on which the Christian doctrine of the Holy Spirit is based and by which the Holy Spirit's own salvific work is shaped. As Jesus' priestly and sacrificial work—far from being ritualistic, routine, and mechanical—is maximally *personal*, the Holy Spirit's work is maximally personal as well. The Holy Spirit's personhood transforms ritual formality and traditional uniformity into freedom and novelty in a way that impersonal conceptions of God are simply incapable of achieving.

Finding Meaning and Wisdom in Priesthood and Sacrifice

Earlier I discussed how the prophetic and kingly roles in the ancient world related to the categories of power and purpose, and how justice stands at the heart of the Judeo-Christian view of the outworking of these roles. As we move now to a discussion of the priestly and the sacrificial roles, we find that these roles interrelate in a manner that differs significantly from the way the prophetic and kingly roles interrelate (see figure 9.1). In ancient sacrificial religious systems, the priest's role aimed at bringing unity out of diversity. He was tasked with gathering up and uniting the many diverse strands of human experience and elevating them into a state of unity with the divine meaning. His task could be accomplished through rites which, on the one hand, eliminated all forms of pollution and kept the forces of destruction at bay and, on the other hand, fostered purification and creativity. Just as pollution was believed to be the cause of decay and disintegration in tangible life, purification was thought to be the best means of overcoming pollution's effects. Once pollution was removed, health and the potential for creativity could be restored.

In one sense, sacrifice itself represents a process that results in dismemberment and *diversification*. In Hinduism, for instance, the sacrifice of Purusha, or primordial or cosmic man, brings creation into existence with all its marks of diversity. The head, arms, thighs, and feet of Purusha form the four principle castes of Hindu society. Thus, the human body becomes an important model for describing the universe in all its diverse aspects. The body not only possesses within itself a multiplicity of parts and functions, but it has a mind or soul that animates the whole and gives unity to the body's diversity. The question then becomes one of how to rescue the world from the destruction that evil precipitates. One of the earliest answers appears to have been *human sacrifice*.

A full knowledge of the extent to which rituals of human sacrifice occurred in the world's ancient cultures is difficult to ascertain. Still, the substitution of animals in place of human beings, such as one finds in the Hindu Ashvamedha or horse sacrifice, and in the sacrifice of sheep, goats, rams, and cattle in place of human beings, seems to attest to earlier times when human sacrifice was widely practiced. In the Old Testament, the event of Abraham's near sacrifice of Isaac provides an important rationale for the Jewish sacrificial system where animal sacrifice replaces human sacrifice. At the heart of this event is a struggle between the powers of destruction and creation. In the case of Abraham and Sarah, their capacity to produce offspring seemed cursed even before the event of Isaac's near sacrifice transpired. In one way, their attempt to help the creative processes triumph over the forces of death and destruction is mirrored in their struggle to conceive a child while in a state of barrenness and infertility. In another way, the struggle between the powers of creativity and the forces of destruction comes to a head when God commands Abraham to travel to Mount Moriah and sacrifice Isaac.[77] From a merely human standpoint, the triumph of the forces of destruction over the powers of creativity would have succeeded if Abraham had actually sacrificed Isaac. The issue here, however, is whether Abraham fully trusts God as the true and final source of creative power. The Bible confirms Abraham's trust in the way he obeys God to the very end. Through this willingness to sacrifice Isaac, Abraham verifies that his trust in Yahweh is unwavering. In response to Abraham's faith, Yahweh provides the ram in the thicket in place of Isaac.[78] Human sacrifice is averted, but the powers of destruction are quelled notwithstanding.

The event of the angel staying Abraham's hand in Genesis 22:11–12 is repeated in the angel's ending of a plague mentioned in 2 Samuel 24:16. God sent the plague upon Israel because David inappropriately took a census without requiring the one-half shekel atonement fee prescribed in Exodus 30:12. The geographical site where the destroying angel appears in the 2 Samuel account is the same as the one mentioned in Genesis 22. The threshing floor of Araunah the Jebusite is none other than Mount Moriah where

Abraham went up to sacrifice Isaac. Consequently, when David commanded the Temple to be built on this site, his command ensured that the burnt offering altar of the Temple would become the place where the people of Israel would offer in perpetuity sacrifices that commemorated God's provision of the ram in place of Isaac.

However, other interconnections provide further insight into these narratives. For instance, the birth of Isaac and his near sacrifice appear in the aftermath of the destruction of Sodom and Gomorrah. Destroying angels are present both at Mount Moriah and at these two cities. The angels do not, however, spare Sodom and Gomorrah from annihilation.[79] Yet, what happens in the aftermath of the obliteration of these cities is significant for several reasons: First, the two daughters of Lot commit incest with their father, become pregnant, and give birth to sons who become the forebears of the Moabites and the Ammonites.[80] Second, these two people groups adopted the custom of burning their children on sacrificial altars to the gods Chemosh and Molech.[81] Third, during the reign of Solomon, these repugnant forms of worship were allowed to invade Israel; and their practice ensued in the valley variously known as Hinnom, Topheth, or Gehenna.[82] Fourth, two of Judah's kings, Ahaz and Manasseh, engaged in this depraved practice by "causing their sons to pass through the fire."[83] Finally, the eventual exile of Northern Kingdom of Israel into Assyria resulted from their engagement in human-sacrifice rituals.[84]

What, then, do the correlations between child sacrifice among the ancient Canaanites, the importation of child sacrifice into Ancient Israel, and ideas about Gehenna reveal? The answer may be delineated as follows: The sacrifice of children marked an abandonment of the rite of animal sacrifice that God had instituted and had commanded to be performed in the worship of the Temple. One interpretation holds that the Temple rock, as a possible location of the sacrificial altar, functioned as the "cornerstone" of the Temple. Isaiah refers to the "precious cornerstone" that God would lay in Zion as a "sure foundation,"[85] and Psalm 118:22 refers to the stone "which the builders rejected" as becoming the chief cornerstone. These curious references may reflect how King Ahaz, under pressure from the Assyrians, erected an altar to the Assyrian sun god Shamash in the very precincts of the Temple. He retained the burnt offering altar only "to inquire by,"[86] suggesting that he resorted to using the altar that Yahweh had authorized for the correct form of sacrifice purely for purposes of divination. Such a perversion of true worship certainly would have signaled a rejection of the proper use God originally intended for the sacrificial altar.

Other sources attest to human sacrifice being performed throughout the Ancient Near East in conjunction with the laying of foundations of houses, temples, and cities, and with attempts to avert catastrophe. Philo of Byblos cited such practices among the Phoenicians who worshiped the god Kronos

(Saturn), a deity reputed throughout the Mediterranean region to devour his own children.[87] Kronos, known by the Phoenicians as *El*, is described as being prior to his deification a Phoenician king who sacrificed his only son, Ieud, to avert destruction during a time of catastrophe.[88] The Carthaginians, who descended from the Phoenicians, also practiced human sacrifice in connection with the laying of foundation stones for temples and cities. The founding of a city by the offering of a human sacrifice seems to have survived, too, in Roman traditions, for Romulus was said to have sacrificed his brother Remus when he founded the city of Rome.[89] Indeed, St. Augustine cited the Romulus-Remus incident in support of his opinion that Cain's murder of Abel was a human sacrifice carried out in conjunction with the founding of the "earthly city."[90] Interestingly, Genesis does attribute the building of the first civilization to Cain.[91]

In trying to reconstruct early beliefs about sacrifice, one fact becomes clear: A major goal of sacrificial practice was to avert the powers of destruction and chaos while at the same time fostering purification so that the powers of creativity could be unleashed. There is further evidence from the ancient world that connects purificatory and creative activities. The Greeks, of course, concerned themselves primarily with a problem of contamination that they called *miasma*, which was a problem that could manifest itself on several fronts. When it manifested itself as disease, miasma polluted and endangered human health.[92] As it pertained to the human intellect, manifestations of *miasma* were responsible for deception, forgetfulness, and ignorance. Psychologically and ethically, *miasma* manifested its corrupting power through moral disordering, perversion, and turpitude.[93]

Not only among the Greeks, but in the Hebrew priestly code as well, examples of contamination are alluded to that infect every dimension of life from human sexual practices, to kosher eating, to the maintenance of health and management of disease, to social relationships. The so-called "Holiness Code"[94] has at its heart a concern to remove all forms of contamination; since contamination, in all its various guises, presents the greatest obstacle to *holiness*. The complete removal of contamination thus comprises the necessary precondition for sacrifice. This precondition is, in turn, twofold: Not only must the one performing a sacrifice undergo ritual purifications that will render him as clean and flawless as possible, but the sacrifice being offered must be deemed clean and flawless as well. If this twofold precondition is met, sacrifice then has the power to maximize those creative impulses that benefit life. Particularly interesting here are the ways that the elements of water and fire both appear as agents of purification;[95] for while these elements certainly could function as agents of destruction, they also had the ability to purify. Fire and water thus not only appear as principal symbols attending the rite of sacrifice in many ancient sacrificial cults; but priestly Judaism, too, made extensive use of these symbolic agents. The purifying effects of fire and water perhaps explain why fire and water also appear in New Testament portrayals of the Holy Spirit.

Clearly, phenomena such as fragmentation, disunity, disintegration, and decay have contamination or uncleanness as their basic cause. The Holy, by contrast, is viewed as the only means of overcoming these phenomena and restoring wholeness. However, any belief that a shortcut to attaining this wholeness is available apart from requiring sacrifice is a belief born of *deception*. In such a case, *demonic*, not *divine*, holiness spins the deception that such a shortcut is available. In fact, deception instigated by demonic holiness usually becomes the very channel through which contamination and uncleanness infect the human soul in the first place. Conversely, sacrifice works as a disinfectant, so it must be applied before wholeness can ever be restored.

Phenomena such as disintegration and decay reach their ultimate nadir in death. Thus, the transference of one's own pollution to a clean and unblemished animal marks a first step in restoring the unity of the Holy. A second step involves the sacrifice of a representative. Such a sacrifice entails a substitutionary death and an offering of that substitutionary death as a payment for sin. As a person is restored to proper relationship with the Holy, the effects of pollution, contamination, fragmentation, disintegration, decay, and death are forestalled. The forces of destruction are kept at bay, allowing the powers of creativity once more to be unleashed.

How Cleavages between Meaning and Wisdom Are Related to the Separation of the Priestly Role from the Sacrificial Role

The Bible, I have maintained, casts suspicion on all attempts to conflate the prophetic and kingly roles or to confuse the categories of *power* and *purpose*. To avoid the corruption of power, these roles and categories must be kept separate. The *opposite*, however, is true regarding our categories of *meaning* and *wisdom* and our understanding of how these correlate with the *priestly* and *sacrificial* roles. Between these latter pairings, there is a perennial tendency toward *cleavage* rather than *identification*, for *meaning* often becomes divorced from *wisdom* in the same way that the *priestly* role becomes divorced from the *sacrificial* role.

As I have already indicated, the divorce of meaning from wisdom already appears as a concern in the Hebrew wisdom literature. Both Ecclesiastes and Job, to cite examples, are concerned with the problem of meaninglessness. The writer of Ecclesiastes especially finds the pursuit of wisdom a meaningless enterprise. Why, then, does pursuit of wisdom tend to become devoid of meaning? One way to understand why this happens is to think of the pursuit of wisdom as a kind of *sacrificial act*. The pursuit of wisdom is hard work, and over time it can easily settle into a seemingly endless and exhausting routine. Qoheleth certainly echoes this sentiment when he says, "of the making of books, there is no end; and much study is a weariness of the flesh."[96]

The pursuit of wisdom is linked to sacrifice in another way as well: One goal of the pursuit of wisdom is to identify and test various *ways* (wise) *of existing* in order to find the best ones. However, the ways of existing turn out to be as multiple as the diversity of the world itself. In a similar way, sacrifice has the capability of disintegrating into meaningless. Sacrifice, after all, aims at death and dismemberment; and there is no going back to what was prior once these acts of death and dismemberment have been executed. In a similar way, the pursuit of wisdom can involve efforts to investigate a seemingly endless array of diverse perspectives that leads farther and farther away from any possibility of unity. Once these diverse perspectives have been evaluated, there often is no going back to the naïve innocence that preceded the evaluation. Instead, the pursuit of wisdom often loses touch with any possibility of unity and turns instead into a foray through numerous blind alleys that lead nowhere but to dead ends. The problem of finding the *Transcendent Unity*, and hence, the *Meaning of Wisdom*, in this respect becomes a perennial problem accompanying the *pursuit* of wisdom. Instead of meaning, futility and meaninglessness haunt each blind alley and every dead end. The pursuit of wisdom thus comes to resemble the proverbial "wild goose chase."

On the other hand, the priestly role has the proclivity to become absolutely separated from the sacrificial role. When this happens, rituals become emptied of their tangible content. Priestcraft in this regard can come to resemble superstition. In fact, it succumbs to the kind of *deception* that is instigated by *demonic holiness*. Here the forays are not into the blind alleys and dead ends of tangible particularity. They are, rather, forays into the vague mystical where all particularity is conveniently left behind or dissolved. One is only left then with the sense of a nebulous "meaning" devoid of wisdom. Ritual begins to be performed for its own sake, and the significance of sacrifice is reduced to meaningless repetition.

How, then, does the tendency to divorce meaning from wisdom and the priestly role from the sacrificial role manifest itself culturally and socially? In its extreme form, the divorce tends to produce hierarchical societies in which the persons at the lower echelons of the social order are viewed as unclean and of lesser worth than persons in the higher echelons. Those at the top must also maintain their distance from those at the bottom so as not to be contaminated by them. Traditional Hindu theology thus taught that even the *shadow* of an untouchable could render a member of the Brahmin caste unclean.

The distance is wide as well between those whose energies are engaged in the pursuit of *meaning* and those whose energies are directed towards accomplishing the ordinary and *mundane* tasks of life. Essentially, those of the lower castes become the "*sacrifices*" that serve as the foundation for the higher castes, while the higher castes—the "*sacrificers*"—endeavor to maintain through their priestly role the unity of the whole body politic. In some ways, the separation of castes along the lines of the meaningful and the mundane already entails the concept of sacrifice by *proxy*. In one sense, this is what sacrifice has always entailed, for the priest does not sacrifice *himself*, but sacrifices something or someone that is *representative* of himself and those on whose behalf he sacrifices.

In its worst form, sacrifice by proxy involved the actual sacrifice of human beings. Of course, in cases where persons sacrificed their own children, we may surmise that the cost of the sacrifice was greater in its *personal* quality than what might otherwise appear to be the case—as for instance, in a scenario where the one *being* sacrificed is deemed of little worth. In this kind of scenario, the identification of the *sacrifice* with the *sacrificer* becomes more routine and less personal as the social distance between the two proportionally increases. The sacrificer in this sort of scenario tends to objectify the sacrifice. When objectification occurs, the sacrificer then becomes incapable of imagining what it is like to live inside the skin of the sacrifice he offers. Empathy and commiseration vanish.

Animal sacrifice in its earlier contexts presupposed, as well, a close bond between the animal and the one offering it. Such a bond often entailed elements of *empathy* and *commiseration*. At least these elements were present in cases where the sacrificer *owned* and *valued* the animal being sacrificed. However, as the practice of sacrifice became institutionalized, money could be used to purchase the sacrificial animal. This practice too easily allowed sacrifices to be reduced to the level of commodities. The development of a socially remote and aloof priestly caste, together with institutionalization of the priestly and sacrificial roles, thus diminished the sense of value and empathy the sacrificer attached to the sacrifice. This seems true in Hinduism even though the *tat tvam asi* (that art thou) doctrine emphasizes the intimate connectedness of all life. Unfortunately, the sacrifice ceases to be truly meaningful where little or no value is any longer attached to it.

The rigid stratification into caste, such as the kind found in traditional Hindu society, thus reveals a *disconnection* between meaning and wisdom of the sort I have been highlighting. As wisdom loses its unifying center in transcendental meaning, it proliferates into a vast number of ways of existing or living that have very little to do with one another apart from the way they facilitate the operation of the treadmill of existence. The ways of salvation proliferate and become disconnected from one another. These phenomena of proliferation and disconnectedness are evidenced by the way that the various yogas—such as *jñanā*, *bhakti*, *karma*, and *raja*—became specialized paths in Hinduism. Though these yogas are supposed to be unified theoretically, in practice they become separate and have little to do with one another. Meaninglessness falls like a pall on such societies, so it is no wonder that they have the tendency to plummet into cynicism, pessimism, and despair. At the same time, those who are at the head of such societies find themselves engaged in rituals that give the appearance of meaning, but these rituals themselves also seem to become vacuous.

The Unification of the Priestly and Sacrificial Roles in Hebrew Theology

Among the ancient Hebrews, one requirement that helped integrate the priesthood into the daily life of the community was the setting up of Levitical cities throughout Israel's tribal lands.[97] The intimate involvement of priests in the total life of the community is observable in figures such as Samuel, who, as the priest of Shiloh, actively participated in virtually every facet of ancient Israel's life. The Israelite priesthood was organized in such a way that its members permeated every stratum of society. Priests, in this respect, were not members of a special caste but were organized in accordance with their various functions as these functions related to the life of the community as a whole.

In actual practice, the Hebrew Scriptures acknowledge the danger that ritual may become too routine. From the beginning of the Bible, a premium emphasis is placed on the *value* of the sacrifice being offered, as the story of Cain and Abel testifies.[98] Later, in the institution of the Hebrew sacrificial system, the quality of the sacrifice is always stressed,[99] though God allows for individuals from different strata of Israelite society to offer sacrifices they can afford.[100] The confession of sin and reparation for damages done against others were always to accompany sacrifices as well.[101] Nevertheless, despite the many ritual and moral requirements that were intended to make sacrifice costly for everyone, sacrifice at times in the history of Israel and Judah degenerated into a meaningless routine. Thus, the prophet Hosea voices the displeasure of the God who says, "I desire mercy, not sacrifice,"[102] and the Lord commands through the prophet Isaiah,

> Stop bringing meaningless offerings! Your incense is detestable to me. New Moons, Sabbaths and convocations—I cannot bear your worthless assemblies.[103]

Later in Israel's rabbinic tradition, sacrifice became connected with the idea of the sacrifice of the *evil impulse*.[104] This idea also stresses the *spirit* of sacrifice rather than its *ritual formality*.

Twice during the year in the rituals of priestly Judaism—at Passover (*Pesach*) and on the Day of Atonement (*Yom Kippur*)—sacrifices were offered that linked up with some of the most important narratives of the Hebrew religion. Passover commemorated the deliverance of the firstborn of Israel from destruction by the death angel and the subsequent deliverance of the Israelite nation from Egyptian bondage.[105] The second important sacrifice entailed the offering of a bull and a goat on the Day of Atonement.[106] The narrative recital of the events that transpired at the first Passover, however, kept the sacrifice of the pascal lamb from becoming a routine ritual. An emphasis on the *mysterium tremendum* of the divine holiness during the "days of awe" leading up to the Day of Atonement rituals kept these from becoming routine as well.[107] Fasting was prescribed for all the people, and the High Priest was expected to keep vigil during the long night prior to his offering of the atonement sacrifices. In addition to these preparations, the High Priest dared not venture into the Holy of Holies in a flippant or unrepentant manner,[108] for God retained the prerogative to strike him dead for his own sins or for the sins of the people.

A high view of the divine holiness thus helped preserve the meaningfulness of rituals that the Jewish priesthood performed. The seriousness of this view also helped prevent these rituals from deteriorating into meaningless routines. By the time of Jesus, however, the role of priests and their offering of sacrifices had indeed begun to deteriorate; hence, Jesus' words at his clearing of the Temple echoed the warnings of the prophet Jeremiah: "My Father's house will be called a house of prayer, but you have made it a den of robbers!"[109] Evidence outside the New Testament reveals, too, that the priesthood by the time of Jesus had developed into an elite caste. The Jewish historian Josephus recalls that many of the priestly elite belonged to the sect of the Sadducees. He speaks of them disparagingly, deploring their lives of luxury.[110] Indeed, some Sadducees were thoroughgoing Hellenists. Thus, for the most part, they remained aloof and had nothing to do with the common people. Josephus reports that their belief system was pessimistic, for the Sadducees highlighted the meaninglessness of life, the certainty of death, and the nonexistence of the afterlife.[111]

The Unification of the Priestly and Sacrificial Roles in Jesus Christ

I referred above to the two most important sacrificial rituals of the Jewish calendar year, these being Passover and the Day of Atonement. Writers of the New Testament allude to both these rituals in relation to Jesus. In doing so, they show a keenness to maintain a close identification between Jesus as Great High Priest and Jesus' sacrifice on the cross. Before discussing this identification in greater detail, however, it is important to recognize how the priestly and sacrificial roles that Jesus embraces correspond, respectively, to his divine and human natures. Priests, like kings, are mediators of divine transcendence, though priests mediate this transcendence differently than kings do. Whereas kings mediate divine transcendence understood more in terms of *power*, priests mediate divine transcendence understood more in terms of *meaning*. Prophetic and sacrificial roles, by contrast, tend to focus on the dimension of the tangible, though in different ways. The prophets, in representing one side of the tangible dimension, were concerned to provide direction amid the terrible crises that punctuated the history of Israel. In this respect, they pointed more to the *survival* aspect of the tangible direction of the value-compass. On the other side of the dimension of the tangible, sacrifice correlates with the role that *wisdom* plays amid the normal aspects and ordinary rhythms of *life*. The life lived in accordance with wisdom should ideally be a sacrificial life, for it is concerned with embracing fragmentation, disunity, and disintegration, and working to reverse them.

At the heart of the concept of sacrifice stands the virtue of love, for love inspires and motivates individuals to sacrifice themselves in service to others and for the greater good. Sacrificial love at its best thus embraces the problematic aspects of ordinary life, discovers strategies for directing individuals away from paths that lead to misery and meaninglessness, and identifies superior ways that individuals can flourish by creatively investing their energies. At one level, love links to the Transcendent. At a second equally important level, the exercise of love is guided by a certain economy; namely, an economy informed by Wisdom. Another way of expressing the *economy* of love is to speak of the *stewardship* of love. Indeed, sacrificial love at its best entails the practice of stewardship.

There are thus *two* ways of viewing Jesus' divine and human natures, and *two* ways in which they ideally are related. The first way, as we have seen, is to view Christ in the roles of king (divine) and prophet (human). The relation here is one in which the *distinction* of the two natures is stressed, although the two become *reconciled,* principally through the events of the cross and the resurrection of Jesus. In a second way, the priestly and sacrificial roles that Christ embodied also correspond to the divine and human natures, respectively. However, the divine and human natures, understood from the standpoint of Christ as priest and sacrifice, are closely identified and integrated at every point, and this differs from the way that they are to be kept separate when they are viewed in the light of the kingly and prophetic roles.

The Unity between the Divine and Human Natures in Johannine Narrative

Both in his Gospel and in the Book of Revelation, the Apostle John portrays Jesus Christ in the light of Passover symbolism. The most obvious way that Jesus himself used the elements of the Passover meal to highlight the meaning of his death appears when he institutes the celebration of the Eucharist. In the context of Passover, Jesus reinterpreted the meaning of the eating of the matzah and drinking of wine as the eating of his body and the drinking of his blood. In John's Gospel, the Eucharistic symbolism is not mentioned in detail at the Last Supper,[112] though it is alluded to in the sixth chapter.[113] Passover symbolism is evident in other ways in his Gospel as well. It appears at the beginning of his Gospel when John the Baptist proclaims, "Behold the Lamb of God, who takes away the sins of the world."[114] Passover references appear especially in the nineteenth chapter of the Fourth Gospel where they are related to the crucifixion of Jesus. John recounts that Jesus was crucified at the same time the Passover lambs were being slaughtered in preparation for the Passover celebration.[115] John refers to the hyssop used in Passover, though he may be using his well-known device of irony to allude in a special way to the spear (*hyssos*) being held up to Jesus mouth.[116] John notes that Jesus' legs needed not to be broken because he was already dead. John interprets this as a fulfillment of the requirement governing how the Passover lamb was to be treated—that "not a bone of it shall be broken."[117] References to Christ as the Passover lamb recur as well throughout the Book of Revelation.[118]

Perhaps the most interesting of John's use of Passover symbolism, however, appears in his references to Christ as the *bridegroom*. The bridegroom symbolism is derived from the Song of Solomon, a scroll of the Megilloth that, in Jewish tradition, was read during Passover. The correlation of Song of Solomon with this Jewish festival might at first seem arbitrary; nevertheless, the correlation appears perfectly reasonable considering how the Song of Solomon was used as a lens through which the romance between God and his bride Israel could be viewed. On a tangible level, the Song of Solomon functions as a story of human love, while on a higher level the story of human love mirrors God's passionate devotion to his people Israel.

Would it be correct, then, to say that an *all-powerful God* could risk anything in delivering his people from bondage? If one understands sacrificial love as a love that takes vulnerability upon itself, then one would have to say that the *God who loves* is also the *God who risks*. As I have indicated previously, the vulnerability of God can best be understood against the backdrop of a divine nature that is maximally invested in preserving and increasing the value of his creation. Hence, the mistreatment of God's creatures is tantamount to a mistreatment of God himself. It is perhaps this perspective that John saw revealed through the cross of Jesus, for this was the place where the victorious deliverer of Israel was revealed to be the ultimate victim as well.

By combining Passover lamb and bridegroom symbolism, John thus established a further connection that Judaism had not yet made explicit.[119] However, the Fourth Gospel and the Book of Revelation do make this connection quite explicit, for the Bridegroom *is* none other than the Passover Lamb. Therefore, just as the older Passover symbolism portrayed Israel as the bride of Yahweh, so now does John portray the church as "the bride of the Lamb." John, of course, is hardly unique in making this comparison. The Apostle Paul, too, speaks of the marital union as representing the *mystery between Christ and his church*.[120] Significant here is the way that the human and divine dimensions converge in the symbol of the Lamb as Bridegroom. The pascal lamb symbol points to the tangible dimension and, hence, to the human nature of Christ. The bridegroom symbol, on the other hand, points to Christ's divine nature.

The Union of the Priestly and Sacrificial Roles in the Epistle to the Hebrews

The Book of Hebrews stresses the close identification of Christ's priestly and sacrificial roles, particularly in relation to the sacrificial rites that the High Priest carried out on the Day of Atonement. Several points contrast the all-sufficiency of Christ and Old Testament dispensations involving priestly qualifications and the efficacy of its sacrifices. First, by pointing out the repetitious nature of Old Testament sacrificial rituals, the writer of Hebrews highlights their inadequate, inferior, and tentative status. These rituals, and the priests who perform them, are therefore but a shadow of the final, permanent, all-sufficient, and superior reality manifested by Christ in his priestly and sacrificial work.[121]

A second point of contrast concerns the greater degree of identification between the priestly and sacrificial roles that Christ achieves. The High Priest in the Old Testament offered not his own blood, but the blood of bulls and goats. Christ, by contrast, offers his own blood. In this way, he perfectly unites the priestly and sacrificial roles.[122] Jesus' blood also represents a better sacrifice than the sacrifice of animals because his perfection is superior to theirs. His is not an already-possessed perfection, but an earned one. The writer of Hebrews insists that "He learned obedience through the things that he suffered"[123] and that he "was made perfect" through his sufferings.[124] "Because he himself suffered when he was tempted, he is able to help those who are tempted."[125] "For we do not have a high priest who is unable to empathize with our weaknesses, but we have one who has been tempted in every way, just as we are—yet he did not sin."[126] As Great High Priest, Jesus therefore experiences the *value* of the sacrifice he offers to a greater degree than could any priest who offers a mere proxy sacrifice.

The Unification of the Sacrificial and Priestly Roles in the Incarnation and Ascension of Christ

Throughout the New Testament, Christ's sacrificial role is related to the theme of God's condescension to become human in Jesus of Nazareth. One of the clearest examples appears in Philippians 2:5–6, which reads, "Have this attitude in yourselves which also was in Christ Jesus, who, although He existed in the form of God, did not think equality with God a thing to be grasped, but emptied Himself, taking the form of a bond-servant, and being made in the likeness of men."[127]

Theologians at least from the time of Martin Luther have recognized that Christ, though fully human, was more than a mere human being.[128] They have insisted that he was God in flesh and that his act of humiliation resulted in his becoming a real man who would experience real trials and real temptations. One line of thought, called kenotic Christology, developed in the nineteenth century among theologians who focused upon the meaning of the word "emptied" in Philippians 2:7. The Greek word used in that text, ἐκένωσεν, is based on the Greek word *kenon* (κενόν) meaning "void"[129]—a principle from which the ancient Pythagoreans believed all evil originated.[130] Kenotic theologians appealed to the word *kenosis* to describe how Jesus "emptied himself" when he relinquished his independent exercise of the relative attributes of divinity; namely, omniscience, omnipotence, and omnipresence.

Other theologians argued, however, that Christ could not have remained *fully* God if he had relinquished even a single divine attribute. They maintain instead that Christ would only have existed as God in a *diluted* or *attenuated* form. Against this postulation, the neoorthodox theologian Karl Barth insisted that classical definitions of God were to blame for the conflict over kenotic Christology, as theologians in both camps depended more upon Greek philosophy as the source of their doctrine of God than upon biblical revelation.[131] Barth insisted that any adequate formulation of the doctrine of God needed first to observe what God had revealed of himself through the Bible. Consequently, God's revelation of himself in the humanity of Jesus merely revealed a mode of God's being that he previously had not made known to humankind.

Barth's thinking here must be understood paradoxically rather than dialectically, for only paradoxical thinking allows one to construe the divine attributes apophatically and cataphatically at the same time. On the one hand, speaking apophatically of the divine omnipotence, one might inquire, "In what respect would a God who could not limit himself still be an all-powerful God?" On the other hand, speaking cataphatically, one might ask, "Can we consider God's ability to limit himself voluntarily as one proof among others of his omnipotence?"

Regardless of how one interprets this kenotic passage, one centrally important truth must be upheld; viz., that God *fully* assumes human nature. Any manner of "self-emptying" that falls short of understanding this as a "self-emptying of God" undercuts the very basis for claiming that the sacrifice that Christ offers as a man is none other than the sacrifice of God himself. In this respect, the concept of Christ's *kenosis* follows from the doctrine of *ktisis* as it relates to God the Father, for Christ's self-emptying of certain of his divine prerogatives follows in the same trajectory that God's purpose follows in relation to his creation of the world and his establishing of covenants. The trajectory begun by the Father's *ktisis* thus continues with God's incarnation and *kenosis* in Jesus and culminates in God's suffering and death upon the cross. In the suffering and death of Christ, *kenosis* thus reaches its deepest point (see figure 9.1).

God's *kenosis* in Jesus, by reaching its profoundest depth in Jesus' death on the cross, in one important respect represents a superior fulfillment of the proper function of *tragedy*; for Jesus' tragic death produces *catharsis*. Catharsis—which entails an overcoming of miasma, contamination, or impurity in those who witness Jesus' crucifixion—makes possible, in turn, their experience of the Holy as both *tremendum* and *fascinans*. The rite of sacrifice, to which Jesus willingly submits, thus properly belongs to the dimension of the tragic as well; for the tragic figure, despite suffering a fate more terrible than what the average person undergoes, is also *nobler*, and infinitely so, since he is also God. The tragic figure reveals the contradiction between a life lived in accordance with Wisdom—i.e., Jesus' life—and the meaninglessness and senselessness of lives destined to succumb to fate—the lives of sinners who stand in need of cleansing. As "sorrow and love flow mingled down," fear and pity also combine to purge and purify the souls of those who behold the tragedy of the crucified God.

The resurrection, however, contextualizes the cross of Jesus in such a way that the Apostle Paul can speak of *wisdom* in the message of the cross, though he describes it as foolishness to those who are perishing.[132] Yet, the wisdom of which Paul speaks is based not just upon any sacrifice but upon the sacrifice of God himself. True divine wisdom thus always entails sacrifice; and sacrifice, in turn, is embraced, transmuted, and elevated by divine transcendence. Furthermore, in the wisdom of Jesus' cross, the divine process of *kenosis* transitions to another divine process—the process of *plerosis* (Grk=πλήρωσις) or "filling" (see figure 9.1). This word occurs in Ephesians 4:10 where the Apostle Paul writes, "He [i.e., Christ], the very one who descended, is also the one who ascended above all the heavens, in order to *fill* [πληρώσῃ] all things."[133] Paul further states, "But practicing the truth in love, we will in all things grow up into Christ, who is the head."[134]

The process of filling begins with the *ascension* of Christ, which, of course, relates to his work as Great High Priest. The goal of this "filling up" process is different from the kenotic process that is entailed in the outworking of the divine purpose; for whereas the aim of the divine purpose is to restrict, limit, and direct the inexhaustible power of God, the aim of the divine wisdom is to liberate, expand, and increase the richness and beauty of the divine meaning (see figure 9.1). Wisdom does this by inspiring the sacrifices necessary for the engendering of creativity and flourishing. The result of this process is the ever-increasing manifestation of the divine *glory*, which theologians from Barth to von Balthasar have interpreted as *divine beauty*. Furthermore, just as the divine purpose guides the divine power, divine wisdom manifests and increases divine meaning within the dimension of the tangible.

The Holy Spirit's Unification of Wisdom and Meaning

I have already discussed how the cleavage between meaning and wisdom correlates with the cleavage between the priestly and sacrificial roles. On the one hand, the cleavage between these roles promotes a segregated and hierarchical kind of society that divides along the lines of the meaningful and the mundane. In the Hindu doctrine of God, this cleavage is reinforced by the belief that Brahman, as a transcendental ideal of inspiration, stands aloof from the illusory tangible world. Though *māyā*, or the veil of illusion, casts its negative pall over the dimension of the mundane, Brahman inspires individual souls to escape the world of illusion and achieve reunification with him by leaving the mundane dimension behind. Despite these cleavages, however, one cannot deny that Brahman's chief influence over souls caught in the web of illusion is to *inspire* their liberation *from it*. Such liberation entails one's leaving the dimension of the tangible behind to become absorbed into a dimension of transcendental meaning. This view of God is, of course, very different from the Islamic view where Allah *directs* and *determines* all that happens in tangible existence. It is thus no wonder that Hinduism does not have a doctrine of divine revelation through history; in Hinduism, history and time are themselves cyclical and illusory.

The doctrine of the Holy Spirit in the New Testament provides an alternative to the Hindu version of the *God of inspiration*. Like Brahman in Hinduism, the Holy Spirit chiefly works within the human soul by means of *inspiration*. Both in Hinduism and Christianity, divine inspiration incentivizes one's struggle to rid one's own soul of the kind of pollution and contamination that inhibits progress into ever higher prehensions of the divine meaning. In Hinduism, this entails one's attempt to rid oneself of bad karma; while in Christianity, it entails conviction of sin and repentance from it. However, in contrast to Hinduism, where Brahman inspires the soul's *escape* from the dimension of tangible particularity, in Christianity the Holy Spirit *embraces* the dimension of tangible particularity and transforms it. The Holy Spirit's embrace of tangible particularity is shaped by the doctrine of the Incarnation. At the heart of this doctrine stands the unification of divine meaning and divine wisdom achieved through the priestly and sacrificial work of Christ. In respect to this work, the Holy Spirit's chief concern is to extend it into the world through the mission of the church.

One can find no better narrative for understanding the work of the Holy Spirit than the Book of Acts in the New Testament. From beginning to end, the Holy Spirit dissolves and breaks down old barriers and divisions that had existed along lines of class, gender, race, and culture. Because the work of the Holy Spirit extends Jesus' incarnation in the widest possible way, the Spirit's work achieves nothing short of the incarnation of divine meaning in the wider dimension of the mundane. Expressed in terms of the value-compass discussed earlier, *divine meaning* embraces and transforms all aspects of *tangible life*. Because the work of the Holy Spirit is at its heart incarnational, all caste distinctions become irrelevant. Chiefly, the Holy Spirit produces the virtue of *love* from which all the other fruits of the Spirit extend.[135] By inspiring love, the Holy Spirit unites wisdom and meaning in human hearts.

Symbols that Unite the Two Natures in Christ with His Fourfold Work

Theologians in the vein of John Calvin have often spoke of the threefold work of Christ,[136] but I have chosen here to extend this to speak of Christ's *fourfold* work; specifically, his work as Prophet, King, Priest, and Sacrificial Victim. I have tried to show as well how the biblical narratives themselves help us visualize the relationship between Christ's human and divine natures as they interact and intersect with this fourfold work. Clearly, there are symbols that accomplish a bridging of roles, such as a bridging of the roles of priest and king, and of prophetic martyr with that of sacrificial victim. The bridging of the prophetic martyr and sacrificial victim roles demonstrates Christ's relevance to the whole dimension of the tangible—to survival on the one hand, and to life and its flourishing on the other. The intertwining of the New Testament narratives shows that these two dimensions are not airtight categories, but interrelated aspects of the *whole* Christ. In a similar way, certain symbols point to ways the two aspects of Christ's divine nature—the priestly and the kingly—are united. These include Christ as King-Priest in the order of Melchizedek, Christ as the Son of God, Christ as the Son of Man, and Christ as the *Logos*.

Christ as Priest-King—Melchizedek and Son of God

The Book of Hebrews designates Jesus Christ as "a priest forever in the order of Melchizedek." Melchizedek, an enigmatic figure in the Book of Genesis, appears in the aftermath of Abraham's victory at the Battle of the Vale of Siddim.[137] Melchizedek, to whom Abram pays tithes, is described in this context as *King of Salem* and as *Priest of the Most-High God* (*El Elyon*).[138]

The only other Old Testament reference to Melchizedek appears in Psalm 110:4: "The Lord has sworn and will not change his mind, 'You are a priest forever in the order of Melchizedek.'" Psalm 110 is cited in association with some of the most important Christological affirmations that Jesus and his followers used when affirming the superiority of his kingship and priesthood. Psalm 110:1 proclaims, "The LORD [יהוה=*Yahweh*] says to my lord [אֲדֹנִי=*Adonai*]: 'Sit at my right hand until I make your enemies a footstool for your feet.'"[139] Jesus cites this verse when he asks the Pharisees, "What do you think about the Christ? Whose son is he?"[140] When they reply, "the Son of David," Jesus asks them how it is possible for David by the Spirit to call him "Lord." No one can answer his query.[141] The Apostle Peter subsequently uses this same text in his sermon on the Day of Pentecost.[142]

Only the Epistle to the Hebrews in the New Testament relates Christ explicitly to the figure of Melchizedek.[143] This epistle compares Melchizedek to the Son of God by combining Psalm 110:4 with Psalm 2:7. The first passage states concerning the one whom David calls "Lord": "Thou art a priest forever in the order of Melchizedek." The second passage reads, "Thou art my Son, this day have I begotten thee."[144] By combining these two passages, Christ's priestly and kingly roles are intentionally linked.

Other scriptures in the New Testament interpret the *ascension* of Christ both in terms of his kingly and priestly roles as well.[145] The relation of Christ's ascension to his kingly office appears in the way he subjugates his enemies. Again, from the Melchizedek passage in Psalm 110, the Apostle Peter quotes the words of Yahweh to David's Lord, "Sit at my right hand until I make all enemies a footstool for Thy feet."[146] This reference reflects an ancient rite in which a conquering king, having ascended to his throne, would place his foot upon the necks of vanquished enemies as they were paraded before him, thus demonstrating his victory over them.[147] The Apostle Peter similarly reflects on the ascension theme when he indicates that Jesus "went into heaven and is at the right hand of God with angels and authorities and powers subject to him."[148]

In Ephesians 4:8–10, the Apostle Paul cites Psalm 68:16, which speaks of God's exaltation as king and his receiving of tribute from his enemies. The symbolism in Ephesians 4 suggests that Christ, by means of his descent into "the lower parts of the earth," vanquishes and plunders his enemies; and, by his ascension to victory, he distributes the plunder. From this plunder comes his gifts to the church: apostles, prophets, evangelists, and pastor teachers. Again, Paul in 1 Corinthians 15:17 refers to Christ's putting all things in subjection to himself. Paul concludes that Christ will reign until all enemies are put under his feet and that the last enemy that will be destroyed is death.[149]

The theme of ascent and descent also appears prominently in the Johannine literature, where Christ's kingly and priestly roles are typically combined. John 1:51 speaks of the angels ascending and descending on the Son of Man. In this reference, John conflates the Son of Man idea with the theme of Jacob's ladder to demonstrate Christ's authority over the angelic powers.

In the Johannine literature, however, Christ's ascent into heaven as the Son of Man does not begin with his ascension or exaltation. He is the one who descends from where he was before—that is, in heaven—and it is to there that he shall return.[150] The *priestly* aspect of this descent and ascent is evident throughout the Fourth Gospel. Certainly, it is implied in Jesus' washing of his disciples' feet, for this was a ritual of a sacrificial nature that priests performed to remove earthly contamination from their feet before they entered the holy precincts of the Temple.[151] Conversely, the *kingly* dimension of Christ's ascension appears as a more prominent feature of the Book of Revelation where the theme of conquest dominates. To cite an example, Revelation 17:4 reads, "They will make war with the Lamb, but the Lamb will conquer them, because he is Lord of lords and King of kings, and those accompanying the Lamb are the called, chosen, and faithful."[152]

The Son of Man as Priest-King

The theme of ascent and descent may be further reflected in the Son-of-Man symbolism that both Jesus and New Testament writers derived from Daniel 7:13–14. The title "Son of Man" is clearly applied to Jesus throughout the New Testament in the sense meant by Daniel 7:13. Jesus uses it in conjunction with his "authority to forgive sins"[153] and with his lordship over the Sabbath.[154] Most often, the title is used to signify the coming of the Son of Man on the clouds of heaven.[155] Though the title "Son of Man" is not always used, allusions to the one who comes from heaven or comes on the clouds of heaven appear as well in Paul's words in 1 Thessalonians 4:13–17, in Luke's report of the promise of the two angels after the ascension of Christ in Acts 1:9–11, and in John's description in Revelation 1:7. Similarly, Jesus refers to himself as Son of Man, which is a title derived from Daniel 7:13–14 of one who would come on the clouds to receive an everlasting kingdom from the Ancient of Days.[156]

Diverse references to Jesus as Son of Man in the New Testament have recently led New Testament scholars to advocate an unnecessary splintering of the concept.[157] It is beyond my scope to deal with these questions at length here. What I do believe the Son of Man concept builds on is the idea of Adam as a "king-priest." First of all, Adam's *kingly* role is implied especially in his *dominion* over creatures of the Garden of Eden and in his ability to name them. As King Solomon was involved in the activity of naming,[158] so did Adam *name* the animals. In the Ancient Near-Eastern world, the ability *to name* implied the ability to *dominate* and *control*. The loss of dominion over the Garden thus marks the failure of Adam's kingship. The curse carries with it the exile from Eden and, hence, the loss of territory.

The idea of Adam as a king is projected into the future by pointing to the Son of Man as a messianic figure who will restore the dominion that Adam lost. As the descendent of Adam, he receives an everlasting kingdom from the Ancient of Days. Significant here is the loss and restoration of dominion over the *beasts* in particular, but the contrast here is not just one between *loss* and *restoration*. The contrast also points to the lesser *degree* of what Adam loses and the greater *degree* of what the Son of Man restores. Genesis refers to Adam's loss of dominion over the *beasts of paradise*. Adam, in this respect, appears as a kind of glorified zookeeper. In Daniel's visions, however, the beasts are no longer mere animals. They instead have become representative of *world empires*. The restoration of dominion that the Son of Man accomplishes thus surpasses in its scope the dominion that Adam forfeited. Lost dominion over a mere *garden* transitions not only to a restored dominion, but to an extended dominion that includes authority over civilization itself.[159]

The reference in Daniel to beasts arising out of the *sea* may also be significant, for the sea, in places throughout the Hebrew Scriptures, symbolizes the realm of the *chaotic*, the *unpredictable*, and the *destructive*. John Day, in his Cambridge monograph, examines the idea of God's conflict with the dragon and the sea both in Canaanite myth and in the Old Testament.[160] In his conflict with the dragon and the sea, God appears as a warrior king. Such common battle themes appear across the Ancient Near-Eastern world from Marduk's battle with Tiamat in the Babylonian myth of creation to Baal's battles with the seven-headed dragon Leviathan and with Prince Yam (Sea). Yahweh's battle with Leviathan is alluded to in Job, Psalms, and Isaiah.[161] Another name for the chaos dragon in the Old Testament is *Rahab*, who is mentioned a couple of times in Job.[162] Ezekiel also, in two places, identifies Pharaoh and the nation of Egypt with the dragon (Heb=*tannim* [תַּנִּים]) that "lies in the midst of the sea."[163] There thus seems to be a precedent for symbolically linking "beasts" and "dragons" to the "sea."

The figures of Adam and the Son of Man may, furthermore, share a connection with the figure of the Hebrew high priest that is different from the connection between Adam and the Hebrew king. Adam and Eve, in their attempt to make themselves into gods,[164] fail to secure the most important attribute that gods possess; namely, immortality. Their transgression results in a contamination that separates them from the precincts of the Holy. Their way to the Tree of Life becomes barred by cherubim whose flaming swords point in every direction.[165] Death, instead of life, becomes their legacy. The cherubim here serve as guardians of God's holiness, as they are stationed before the Tree of Life to block Adam's access. Later, their figures appear embroidered on the veil that separates the Holy Place in the Hebrew Temple from the Holy of Holies,[166] and their shapes rest upon the Mercy Seat covering the Ark of the Covenant.[167] The rabbinic tradition recognized how the presence of cherubim symbolically linked the Torah with the Tree of Life.[168] Later, a prophecy of Ezekiel repeats the symbolism of the *Merkabah*, or chariot throne of God;[169] and with certain alterations, this symbolism finds its way into the Apostle John's description of the Divine Throne Room in Revelation 4:6–9.

The association of Tree of Life symbolism with the Holy of Holies of the Hebrew Temple suggests a parallel between Adam's expulsion from Eden and the high priest's role of regaining access to the estate that Adam forfeited. Only the high priest could venture beyond the veil of the Temple into the Holy of Holies itself. Even then, he could only do so once a year on the Day of Atonement (*Yom Kippur*).[170] On this occasion, the sprinkling of blood on the Mercy Seat was thought to reestablish the connection between God and his people for the ensuing year. Consequently, while the theme of Genesis 3 centers on Adam's *loss* of access to the Tree of Life, the rituals of the Day of Atonement signaled a *restoration* of access, albeit temporary, to the holy presence of God from which Adam was exiled. The Son of Man symbolism, however, refers not to an incomplete and *temporary* restoration of access, but of a complete and *eternal* restoration. The priesthood of the Son of Man is therefore superior to that of the Hebrew high priest.

Implications for Combining Conflicting Theological Traditions

Two perspectives in the ancient church sought to answer how the human and divine natures in Christ were interrelated. These perspectives emerged as the bishops of Christendom faced off in an ongoing conflict over Christology that spanned four church councils. The fathers of the Antiochene perspective, on the one hand, stressed the *distinction* between the two natures; the fathers of the Alexandrian perspective, on the other, emphasized their *union.* Interestingly, the Antiochene emphasis comports with the biblical view I have delineated of *Christ as Prophet-King,* whereas the Alexandrian emphasis coincides with the biblical view I have presented of *Christ as Priest-Sacrifice.*

In the universal conclave of bishops at Chalcedon in 451 CE, an agreement was finally reached that left some in each of the opposing parties dissatisfied. Yet this agreement seemed the only possible outcome. With four negative adverbs, the Chalcedonian confession framed the question of the relationship between the human and divine natures in Christ, and that relationship was best expressed in terms of *paradox.* Chalcedon affirmed that the "hypostatic union" was such that the two natures related to one another "without change (Grk=*asynchutōs* [ἀσυνχύτως]), without confusion (Grk=*atreptōs* [ἀτρέπτως]), without division (Grk=*adichairetōs* [ἀδιχαιρέτως]), and without separation (Grk=*achōristōs* [ἀχωρίστως])." Although these four negative adverbs expressed what the relationship between the natures was *not* like, little help was given to express what the relationship between the natures was *like.* Thus, by issuing this affirmation, the church veered in an *apophatic* direction. By making this move, the church nonetheless attempted to safeguard the *mystery* of the hypostatic union.

On the other hand, theologians who embraced a more *cataphatic* theological approach to the question of the relationship of the two natures attempted to spell out the doctrine in a more dialectical fashion, and this occurred especially with the conflicts that ensued between Zwingli and Luther over the implications of Christology for the Lord's Supper. Zwingli, in the vein of the Antiochene fathers, emphasized the *distinction* between the two natures; while Luther, following the Alexandrians, emphasized their *union*.[171] The ensuing conflict between Lutheran and Reformed theologians unfortunately centered upon what now amounted to a *dialectical* conflict between two opposing Christological viewpoints.

Throughout this book, I have maintained that the distinction between the Infinite and the finite implies that an incongruity exists between paradoxical and dialectical ways of thinking. The incongruity between paradox and dialectic is already entailed in the proposition that an infinite qualitative distinction exists *ontologically* between the creature and the Creator. This ontological distinction does not have to imply, however, that an *epistemological* impasse also necessarily exists between the two. If this were the case, then we should have to abandon entirely the doctrine of revelation in favor of a dead end; namely, skepticism and the agnosticism to which skepticism inevitably leads. If we accept, on the other hand, the presupposition that divine communication *is* possible, then the epistemological impasse can be bridged. I have argued throughout this book that the human capacity to experience and know value across all the dimensions of existence is an incontrovertible fact that points to God as the ultimate origin and goal of all value. To summarize, humans are, first of all, fully capable of apprehending and appreciating the value of the moral and the beautiful. Second, they have the capacity to reflect upon this value and express it through language and action. Third, they are able to understand, appreciate, and respond to the ways that ethically purposive and aesthetically meaningful language and action combine to form the "good story," especially the quintessentially good story that also happens to be sacred story. Fourth, by means of language and action, humans are able to confront, challenge, and stem the tide of evils that threaten to disrupt the unity of value whenever that unity is jeopardized. Indeed, the quintessentially good story, by means of language and action, suggests how extremism can be avoided or overcome and how an equilibrium between the dimensions of the moral and the beautiful can be achieved or restored. Fifth, the quintessentially good story is one that has fecundity in that it can be reproduced and extended into the greater society through individuals who willingly and gladly receive it and live it.

The dialectical interplay between the ethical and the aesthetic, which operates within the tangible dimension of human existence, does not, therefore, have to become shut off from the dimension of paradoxical transcendence. Neither does that transcendence have to remain a passive objective reality that can only be accessed through human initiative. Rather, if the Trinitarian God is conceived of as truly personal, then it follows that the Divine Trinity would take the initiative in mediating transcendence dialectically through the world's many conduits of value. It is then possible for divine initiative and human receptivity to cooperate in order to achieve the reconciliation and integration of the dimensions of the moral and the beautiful, especially when these dimensions of value fall prey to evil. This mediation indeed becomes possible even in the face of evils such as deception and injustice that threaten to disrupt and to unravel the unity of the good that ranges across the many dimensions of human experience. Revelatory truth brings clarity amid the ambiguities of life and provides contexts that restore to the human vision a sense of the wholeness that the unity of the Divine might entail.

What, then, is the content of this revelatory truth? Here we need to consider how the doctrines of Christology and the atonement respectively provide the *form (Gestalt)* and *content* of the revelatory truth that the Holy Trinity communicates to human beings.[172] The two-natures Christology, on the one hand, expresses the *form (Gestalt)*, which is none other than the Christological paradox; while the atonement provides the *content* by mediating that paradox in ways that overturn and reconfigure the normal dialectical outworkings of ethical and aesthetic values on the plane of human experience.

In examining how the kingly (divine) and prophetic (human) roles of Christ relate more closely to the idea of divine *purposive power*, I have tried to show as well how these roles are best contextualized when they link backward to the revelation and activity of God as Father. This is the God of inexhaustible power who is the ultimate originator of all things and whose purpose has been revealed by what he has spoken and what he has accomplished throughout history. This is the God who *establishes* and *directs* the world by means of his sovereign power (*ktisis* [κτίσις]). The priestly (divine) and sacrificial (human) roles of Christ, on the other hand, relate more closely to the idea of divine *meaningful wisdom* (see again figure 9.1). These roles thus link *forward* to the work and inspiration of God the Holy Spirit, who works first and foremost in the inner lives of individuals, but who, by extending the good, redemptive, creative, and just works of individuals, transforms society into flourishing communities.

THE LOGOS AS A COMPREHENSIVE UNIFYING CONCEPT

How, then, should we conceive of the person and work of God the Father in relation to the person and work of God the Holy Spirit? A short answer might be that we can accomplish this by employing a "Trinitarian model" of God, though I think the term "model" will finally prove to be unsatisfactory. Various analogies of the Trinity, such as Augustine's psychological analogy—or the social analogies of the Cappadocian Fathers—may function as *lenses* through which various aspects of Trinitarian truth are refracted into our understanding.[173] The greatest strength of these analogies lies in the fact that they include dimensions of the *personal* while avoiding the reduction of Trinitarian understanding to analogies that are impersonal—such as St. Patrick's alleged use of the shamrock as an illustration. Psychological and social analogies of the Trinity are nonetheless problematic insofar as they employ lenses with which to view the Trinity that are derived from the finite aspects of human personhood.[174] Apparent once more is the way that the infinite qualitative distinction between God and the world renders suspect all attempts to *reduce* Trinitarian understanding to a singular analogy or model. With psychological and social Trinitarian analogies, a gap still remains between *individual* human personhood and persons existing in *social* relationships. The imprint of the Trinity on the human soul or on human social reality consequently does not suggest ways that the impasse can be bridged between the *psychological*-personal dimension of human existence and the *social*-personal dimension. However, if we maintain that *paradoxical transcendence* is the starting and ending place of Trinitarian conceptualization, then we should exercise care when using lenses based on some aspect belonging to the dimension of finitude. Otherwise, we shall set ourselves up for becoming mired in a *dialectical* kind of thinking from which escape can be difficult.

What I therefore suggest is that the *Logos* concept can be used, on the one hand, to reveal the *dialectical* unity of the Trinity because the biblical narratives I have discussed that reveal Christ's fourfold work in relation to the Father and the Spirit do possess such dialectical aspects. This dialectical unity would thus refer more to the work of the *economic* Trinity than to the *immanent* Trinity, though this kind of unity can be thought of as pointing beyond itself to the *paradoxical unity* of the immanent Trinity as well.[175] A parallel should be pointed out here: In the previous section, I spoke of the form (*Gestalt*) of Christ's person as it relates to paradox Christology and of the doctrine of the fourfold work of Christ as it relates to dialectical categories that effectively mediate the divine paradoxical transcendence into the world. Similarly, the paradoxical unity of the immanent Trinity is mediated through the dialectical operations of the economic Trinity. In the light of this parallel, I believe that the relationship between the *form (Gestalt)* of the

Divine and the *content* that the Divine mediates dialectically can best be affirmed when the *Logos* doctrine is explicated in the way that I attempted to do in chapter 5. My view is that the Johannine concept of the *Logos* accomplishes this not only by virtue of its *comprehensiveness*, but also by virtue of it having its origin (*alpha*) and goal (*omega*) in divine *paradoxical transcendence*. Thus, the *Logos* doctrine must first be explicated in such a way that it functions as a lens through which paradoxical transcendence can be refracted purposively and meaningfully into the dialectical operations of the world. It must not, on the other hand, be viewed in the sense of a *model* in which the Holy Trinity becomes confined and encapsulated.

Apophatic thinking must therefore always play some role in human construals of what the divine essence (*ousia*) entails. The Trinitarian theological concept we propose must therefore not become enclosed in any model that happens to be derived from some aspect of the dimension of the tangible. Rather, an adequate Trinitarian understanding should be one that always remains open to the transcendence of God in origin in terms of inexhaustible power, and the transcendence of God in goal in terms of infinite meaning. The transcendence of the *Logos*, moreover, suggests that somehow inexhaustible power and infinite meaning are paradoxically one in the Divine Life. We, however, can only imagine what this paradoxical transcendent oneness might entail. While reason can serve as one channel through which that transcendent oneness is mediated, reason cannot fully grasp hold of it and pin it down. The ultimate oneness of the Holy, conceived of in a Trinitarian way, therefore remains on one side an *unfathomable* and *paradoxical* mystery, but it is a mystery whose value is mediated through and across the many layers of those interconnected value-mediating vehicles I have explored throughout this book.

Far from being a closed-off mystery then, this mystery intrigues us and draws us into active participation in the sacred story of the triune God through the person and work of the Holy Spirit. The Holy Spirit makes the mystery of the transcendent God—the Holy—immanently present through the Spirit. The Holy Spirit compels us and inspires us—both individually, and collectively as the church—to live purposively and meaningfully within God's story and to extend the good news of God's story into the world. As the one who makes the *mysterium tremendum et fascinans* present to human experience, the Holy Spirit confronts us with a grand vision that unites the dimensions of the moral and the beautiful and ignites in us a passion to live out that vision in relation to ourselves and to others. The Holy Spirit not only calls, convicts, cleanses, comforts, and inspires us to cultivate virtue within ourselves, but the Holy Spirit also transforms us into exemplars in whom ethical and aesthetic truth becomes embodied and shines forth to inspire the transformation of other persons.

Our all-too-human quest for height and search for centeredness also become radically redirected and transformed as the Holy Spirit's power and wisdom brings us into realignment with the transcendent divine meaning and purpose. Our quest for height, as a result of this realignment, will no longer aim to attain as its final objective our own self-aggrandizement. Instead, we are redirected to "press forward toward the mark for the prize of the high calling of God in Christ Jesus,"[176] who relinquished the status of equality he enjoyed with God in the heights of pristine glory to become human and take upon himself the form of a servant.[177] The Holy Spirit, by achieving this realignment, reproduces the sacrificial creativity of Jesus in his people and extends to others the blessings, both spiritual and material, that this creativity generates.

Our search for centeredness, on the other hand, will no longer aim to find its ultimate resting place inside the narrow confines of our closed cliques or our "mutual admiration societies." Though these temporal resting places may deceptively lure us into thinking that our comfort zones will protect us against unwanted alien intrusions that threaten to perturb our tranquility, such insulated zones are destined eventually to become like uncomfortable mattresses upon which the rest-broken soul, far from finding the peace and rest it desires, will continue only to toss and turn. This all-too-human search for centeredness is thus destined to end in the miserable restlessness of the self-centered soul; as St. Augustine said, "Our hearts are restless until they find rest in Thee."[178] The Holy Spirit redirects and transforms our human search for centeredness by compelling us always to turn outward from ourselves toward others and, most importantly, toward God. The Holy Spirit inspires us to seek the "rest that remains for the people of God,"[179] and this means that we will devote ourselves to becoming ongoing mediators of a justice that achieves reconciliation, fosters forgiveness, and aims to bring peace on earth. Our search for centeredness, transformed and redirected by the work of the Holy Spirit, will then seek to find its final and ultimate resting place in the God of peace whose ultimate justice is satisfied by infinite mercy. In this way, the Holy Spirit, working through the church, extends the offer of justification by grace through faith made possible by Jesus' atonement to the greater world.

Even in small ways, then, we are inspired, directed, guided, and compelled by God's Holy Spirit to live out our own little stories in concert with grand story of the Trinitarian God, who is the ultimate source and destination of all value. Our own individual stories, then, become like boats carried along by the currents of the grand metanarrative. More precisely, our particular stories are carried along by the grand universal story that is the story of God. On these boats, our own life stories are being played out, and we constantly make decisions about how best to navigate the story of the greater world. Sometimes the currents of the grand narrative become swift, like river rapids, and we are called upon to show great courage, facility, and adeptness at navigating them. At other times, the waters become more placid, allowing us ample time to explore the depths more fully for hidden treasures waiting to be discovered. The metanarrative itself, however, is something that we avoid at our own peril, for it points to the rhyme and reason of existence itself. At its heart, then, this grand narrative is intensely participatory; for as the currents of eternity flow through human history and create the almost innumerable dialectical eddies of tangible existence, we, too, are carried along to our eternal destination.

NOTES

1. Jean-François Lyotard, *The Postmodern Condition: A Report on Knowledge*, trans. Geoff Bennington and Brian Massumi (Minneapolis: University of Minnesota Press, 1984), xxiv, 31–41.

2. Lyotard, *Postmodern Condition*, 60–61.

3. See, for example, the analysis in David Tracy, *Blessed Rage for Order: The New Pluralism in Theology* (New York: Seabury Press, 1975), 3–14.

4. Jean-Jacques Rousseau, *The Social Contract, and Emile*, trans. G. D. H. Cole and Barbara Foxley, loc. 2511–2654 of 12592.

5. Émile Cammaerts, *The Laughing Prophet: The Seven Virtues and G. K. Chesterton* (Walton-on-Thames, UK: Methuen & Co., 1937), 211.

6. In this regard, Elton Trueblood, a generation ago, referred to Western civilization as a "cut-flower civilization." The suggestion is that Western civilization, having been cut away like a flower from its roots, is doomed to wither and die (Trueblood, *The Predicament of Modern Man* (New York: Harper & Brothers, 1944), 59.

7. Or what Collin Gunton calls "the open transcendental." *The One, the Three and the Many: God, Creation and the Culture of Modernity* (Cambridge: Cambridge University Press, 1993), 141–49. I am using the word "totality" here in a nuanced way to refer to the idea of God as the "all in all" in a transcendental sense.

8. Lyotard refers to the Kantian emphasis on the sublime as an earlier modulation of Nietzschean perspectivism (*Postmodern Condition*, 77–78). The sublime "allows us to have an Idea of the world (the totality of what is), but we do not have the capacity to show an example of it. We have an Idea of the simple (that which cannot be broken down, decomposed), but we cannot illustrate with a sensible object that would be the 'case' of it. We can conceive of the infinitely great, the infinitely powerful, but every presentation of an object destined to 'make visible' this absolute greatness or power appears to us painfully inadequate" (*Postmodern Condition*, 78).

9. See discussion in Lyotard, *The Postmodern Condition*, 62–64, on the severity, arrogance, and terrorist behavior of systems. These, I believe, refer to systems of a dialectical nature.

10. See 1 Cor 1:18–25.

11. Qur'an 5:72 states "Surely, they have disbelieved who say: 'Allah is the Messiah (Jesus), son of Mary.' But the Messiah (Jesus) said: 'O Children of Israel! Worship Allah, my Lord and your Lord.' Verily, whosoever sets up partners in worship with Allah, then Allah has forbidden Paradise for him, and the Fire will be his abode...'"

12. Qur'an 3:18.

13. See G.W.H. Lampe, *God as Spirit* (Oxford: Clarendon, 1977), 121.

14. Lawrence Fine, *Physician of the Soul, Healer of the Cosmos: Isaac Luria and His Kabbalistic Fellowship* (Stanford CA: Stanford University Press, 2003), 59–60.

15. Exod 20:4, Deut 5:8.

16. John 2:19.

17. This full reciprocity is the very thing that necessitated the move of Christianity in the direction of Trinitarian theology. See discussion in Arthur W. Wainwright, *The Trinity in the New Testament* (Eugene, OR: Wipf & Stock, 2001), 37–39, 171–72

18. Irenaeus, "Against Heresies," in eds. Alexander Roberts, James Donaldson, and Cleveland Cox, *The Writings of the Ante-Nicene Fathers* Vol. 1 (Grand Rapids, MI: William B. Eerdman's, 1973–74), 3.19.1; 3.22.1.

19. Epiphanius of Salamis, *The Panarion* 3.1.

20. See John Calvin, *Institutes of the Christian Religion*, trans. and ed. John T. McNeill (Westminster: John Knox, 1960), 3.15.1, for his doctrine of the *munus triplex* or the "threefold work of Christ."

21. Edward Twitchell Hall, *Beyond Culture* (New York: Anchor Books, 1976).

22. See, for example, 1 Sam 15:1–28 and 2 Sam 12.

23. 1 Sam 15:1–23.

24. 2 Sam 12:1–13.

25. 1 Kings 11:16; 15:26, 34; 16:7, 19, 25, 30; 21:20, 25; 22:52; 2 Kings 3:2; 8:18, 27; 13:2, 11; 14:24, 15:9, 18, 24, 28; 17:2, 13, 17; 21:2, 6, 9, 11, 15, 16, 20; 23:32, 37; 24:9, 19.

26. Henri Frankfort, *Kingship and the Gods: A Study of Ancient Near Eastern Religion as the Integration of Society and Nature* (Chicago, IL: University of Chicago Press, 1978), 5, 57.

27. Frankfort, *Kingship and the Gods*, 318–19.

28. My use of "divine" here refers to the gods of polytheism, not to the God of the Bible.

29. Rev 13:8; cf. 1 Pet 1:20.

30. Isa 24:5–6; Jer 11:1–10; 22:9; 33:21; 34:13–15, 18; Ezek 16:1–52, 59, 61; 17:18–19; 44:7; Hos 6:7; 8:1; Mal 2:10, 17.

31. Isa 1:17–21, 27; 5:7, 16, 23; 10:12; 11:4; 16:5; 28:6, 17; 29:21; 30:18; 32:1, 16; 33:5; 42:1–4; 51:4–5; 56:1, 4; 59:4, 8–15; 61:8; Jer 5:28; 9:24; 21:1; 21:12; Ezek 22:29; 34:16; Hos 2:19; 12:6; Amos 2:7; 5:7, 10, 12, 15, 24; Amos 6:12; Mic 3:1, 8–9; Hab 1:4; Zeph 3:5; Zech 7:1, 9; Mal 2:17; 3:5.

32. Exod. 22:22–24; Deut 24:17–20; 27:19; Isa 1:17, 23; 9:17; 10:2; Jer 5:28; 7:6; 22:3; Ezek 22:7; Zech 7:10; Mal 3:5.

33. Isa 2:11, 17; 3:16; 9:9; 10:2, 12; 13:11, 19; 16:6; 23:9; 28:15; 25:11; 28:1, 3; 37:23; 57:17; Jer 5:2; 6:13; 8:10; 13:9, 17; 14:14; 48:29; 49:16; Ezek 7:20, 24; 12:24; 13:6–9, 23; 16:50, 56; 21:9; 22:8; 24:1; 28:2; 29:21; 32:12; 33:31; 59:3; Dan 4:27; 5:20; Amos 6:8; 8:7; Hos 10:4; 11:6; Mic 6:11; Obad 1:3; Zeph 2:10; 3:11; Zech 5:3–4; 8:17; 9:6; 10:11; Hab 2:5.

34. Mic 6:8.

35. Mark 6:4; Matt 13:57.

36. Num 20:2–13.

37. 1 Sam 2:3–5.

38. Matt 4:8–10.

39. Matt 16:16.

40. Matt 16:22.

41. Matt 16:23, repeating Jesus words in Matt 4:10.

42. William Wrede, *Das Messiasgeheimnis in den Evangelien* (Göttingen, 1901). Published in English as *The Messianic Secret*, trans. J. C. G. Greig (London: Clarke, 1971).

43. Mark 8:30. See also Mark 1:23–25, 34, 43–45; 3:11; 5:6, 43; 7:36; 8:26.

44. Mark 9:9–10.

45. Isa 11:1.

46. Isa 4:2; Jer 23:5; 33:15; Zech 3:8; 6:12.

47. Matt 2:23.

48. As implied by Nathaniel in John 1:46.

49. The resurrection of Jesus provides a gateway into what Jean-Luc Marion refers to as the *impossible possibility*. The transition from the impossible to the possible corresponds to the transition from human impossibility to divine possibility. Marion, "The Impossible for Man—God," in *Transcendence and Beyond: A Postmodern Inquiry*, ed. John Caputo and Michael J. Scanlon (Bloomington and Indianapolis: University of Indiana Press, 2007), 27.

50. John 10:18.

51. Rev 5:6.

52. This was the view of James L. Crenshaw (*Old Testament Wisdom: An Introduction* [Louisville, KY: John Knox Press, 1998], 21), who emphasized the divergence of the Hebrew wisdom tradition from the prophetic tradition. Recently, scholars have challenged this view by identifying significant points of contact between wisdom and prophetic traditions. See, for example, Mark R. Sneed, "Introduction," in *Was There a Wisdom Tradition? New Prospects in Israelite Wisdom Studies*, ed. Mark R. Sneed (Atlanta, GA: SBL Press, 2015), 1–8.

53. Prov, chs. 1–8.

54. Prov 8:30.

55. Prov 8:22–39.

56. Wis 1:5–7; 9:17; 12:1.

57. Wis 7:7. Cf. 7:22, 24

58. Wis 7:25.

59. Wis 7:27.

60. Wis 9:4. Cf. 9:10.

61. Wis 7:26.

62. Wis 8:1; 7:22.

63. Wis 7:17–22.

64. Wis 8:2.

65. Eccl 12:1.

66. *b. Šabb.* 30b.

67. Eccl 12:13.

68. Rabbi Akiba gave the word בּוֹרְאֶיךָ a threefold meaning: בְּאֵר, "fountain" (referring to one's origin by means of the human procreative faculties); בּוֹר (referring to one's grave); and בּוֹרַאֲיךָ (referring to one's Creator). See *Midr. Qoh* 12:1.

69. Wis 3:9; 6:12, 17–18; 7:10, 28; 8:2. The Wisdom of Ben Sirach places a dominant emphasis upon *fear* as a motivation. See, for example, Sir 1:8–28; 2:7–10, 15–17; 3:7; 6:16–17; 7:29, 31; 9:13; 10:19–24; 15:1, 13, 19; 16:2; 17:4; 18:27; 19:18, 20, 24; 21:6, 11; 23:27; 24:18; 25:6, 10, 12; 26:3, 23, 25; 27:3; 28:22; 32:14, 16; 33:1; 34:13–14; 36:1; 40:2, 5, 26–27; 45:23. More infrequently, the *love* of God or of Wisdom is emphasized. See Sir 1:10, 18; 2:15–16; 4:12, 14; 7:30; 13:14; 17:18; 24:18; 25:11–12; 34:16; 40:20; 47:8, 22; 48:11.

70. Wis 6:18.

71. Mark 12:31.

72. Job 1:1.

73. Job 32:6–37:24.

74. Job 42:1–6.

75. Job 40:15–41:34.

76. David Bentley Hart, *The Beauty of the Infinite* (Grand Rapids, MI: William B. Eerdmans, 2003), 15–28.

77. Gen 22:1.

78. Gen 22:13.

79. Gen 19:13.

80. Gen 19:30–38.

81. 2 Kings 3:27 attests to the Moabite worship of Chemosh. To avert catastrophe, Mesha, the Moabite King, presented his son on the city wall as a burnt offering to Chemosh.

82. 2 Kings 23:10.

83. 2 Kings 16:3; 2 Kings 21:6.

84. 2 Kings 17:17.

85. Isa 28:16.

86. 2 Kings 16:10–15.

87. Philo of Byblos, *Phoenician History*. See Eusebius, *Praeparatio Evangelica* 1.9 and 4.16. The discoveries of the Ugaritic texts at Ras Shamra seem to corroborate the validity of Philo's writings, which depended upon the earlier work of the Phoenician Sanchuniathon of Berytus. "It was a custom of the ancients in great crises of danger for the rulers of a city or nation, in order to avert the common ruin, to give up the most beloved of their children for sacrifice as a ransom to the avenging daemons; and those who were thus given up were

sacrificed with mystic rites." Eusebius, *Praeparatio Evangelica*, trans. E. H. Gifford (Oxford, 1903), 1.10.

88. See Albert I. Baumgarten, *The Phoenician History of Philo of Byblos: A Commentary* (Leiden, NL: E. J. Brill, 1981), 244–45, 251–52.

89. Gary Forsythe, *A Critical History of Early Rome: From Prehistory to the First Punic War* (Berkeley: University of California Press, 2005), 332.

90. Augustine, *City of God*, book 15, chaps. 1 and 5.

91. Gen 4:17.

92. Purification, in Parker's view, involves a division or separation (*Miasma: Pollution and Purification in Early Greek Religion* [Oxford: Clarendon, 1983], 18–31). See also Paul Ricoeur's discussion of the symbolism of defilement in *The Symbolism of Evil*, trans. Emerson Buchanan (Boston, MA: Beacon, 1967), 25–46.

93. A conceptual correlation exists as well between the Greek understanding of *miasma* and the way some of the Eastern religions view *karma*. Jainism, Hinduism, Buddhism, and Sikhism all view bad karma in terms of pollution or contamination.

94. Lev 17–26.

95. See, for example, 1 Kings 18:35.

96. Eccl 12:12.

97. Num 35:1–8.

98. Gen 4:3–4.

99. Exod 12:5; 29:1; Lev 1:3, 10; 3:1, 6; 4:3, 23, 28, 32; 5:15, 18; 6:6; 9:2–3; 14:10; 29:19; 22:21; 23:13, 18; Num 6:14; 19:2; 28:3, 9, 11, 19, 31; 29:2, 8, 13, 17, 20, 23, 26, 29, 32; 29:36; Ezek 43:22, 23, 25; 45:18; 46:4, 6, 13.

100. Lev 5:5–7; 12:8; 14:21, 32.

101. Exod 22:1–14; Lev 5:16; 6:5; 22:14; 24:18; Num 5:5–10.

102. Hos 6:6.

103. Isa 1:13 (*New International Version*).

104. *Midr. Lev* 9:1; *Midr. Num* 13:15, 16; *b. Sanh.* 43b.

105. Exod 11–12.

106. Lev 16:3–34.

107. Lev 16:31.

108. Lev 16:2.

109. Jer 7:11; Matt 21:13; Mark 11:17; Luke 19:46.

110. Josephus, *Antiquities of the Jews* 18.2.4; *Jewish Wars* 2.8.14.

111. See Jonathan Klawans, "Sadducees, Zadokites, and the Wisdom of Ben Sira," in *Israel's God and Rebecca's Children: Christology and Community in Early Judaism and Christianity*, ed. David Capes, April DeConick, Helen Bond, and Troy Miller (Waco, TX: Baylor University Press, 2008), 261–76.

112. See John 13.

113. John 6:53–58.

114. John 1:29.

115. John 19:14.

116. John 19:29.

117. John 19:32–36, a fulfillment of Exod 12:46; Num 9:12.

118. Rev 5:1, 6, 8, 12, 13; 6:1, 3, 5, 7, 16; 6:16; 7:9; 7:10, 14, 17; 12:11; 13:8, 11; 14:4, 10; 15:3; 17:14; 19:7, 9; 21:9, 14, 22, 23, 27; 22:1, 3.

119. Rev 19:7; 21:9. Cf. Jesus' miracle at the wedding feast of Cana in John 2:1–9 and the discourse of John the Baptist in John 3:27–30.

120. Eph 5:32.

121. The superiority of Christ is stressed throughout the Epistle to the Hebrews.

122. Heb 9.

123. Heb 5:8.

124. Heb 5:8–9.

125. Heb 2:18.

126. Heb 4:15 (*NIV*).

127. Phil 2:5–6 (*New American Standard*).

128. Luther believed Christ's "human" experience of suffering and death were fully experienced by God as well. *Luther's Works*, 30 vols., ed. Jaroslav Pelikan and Helmut Lehmann (St. Louis, MO: Concordia Publishing House, 1958–65), 23:81.

129. For example, Charles Gore and Thomasius of Erlangen.

130. Aristot. Phys. 213b–217b.

131. Gordon Fee states that Christ does not relinquish his deity through this process of *kenosis* as some kenotic theologians have assumed. Fee echoes Karl Barth's solution, which questions the classical assumption that God, as he is in himself, can be known *a priori*. Barth insists that we can only know God by what he has revealed of himself (see Fee, *Paul's Letter to the Philippians* [Grand Rapids, MI: William B. Eerdman's, 1995], 209). In becoming man, God thus does not empty himself *of something*; rather, in becoming a slave, God in Christ reveals *more*, not *less*, of who he is.

132. 1 Cor 1:18.

133. *New English Translation*.

134. Eph 4:15 (*NET*).

135. Gal 5:22–23.

136. As in John Calvin's doctrine of the *munus triplex*—Christ is Prophet, Priest, and King (*Institutes* 2.15).

137. Gen 14:1–22.

138. Heb 7:1.

139. *NIV*.

140. *NIV*.

141. Matt 22:41–46; Mark 12:35–37; Luke 20:41–44.

142. Acts 2:34–35.

143. Heb 5:6, 10; 6:20; 7:1, 6, 10–11, 15, 17.

144. Heb 5:5–6.

145. Acts 2:33; 5:31; 7:55–56; Rom 8:34; 3:1; 1 Pet 3:22.

146. Psalm 110:1 (*NIV*). Jesus cites this text in a discussion with the Pharisees. See Matt 22:44, Mark 12:46, and Luke 20:42.

147. See Josh 10:24; Judg 5:21.

148. 1 Pet 3:22.

149. 1 Cor 15:25–26.

150. John 3:13; 6:62; 20:17.

151. John 13:1–15.

152. *NIV*.

153. Matt 9:6; 12:32; Mark 2:10; Luke 5:24; John 5:27.

154. Matt 12:8; Mark 2:28; Luke 6:5

155. Matt 10:23; 13:4; 16:27–28; 19:28; 24:27–44; 25:31; 26:64; Mark 13:26; 14:62; Luke 9:26; 12:8, 40; 17:24, 26, 30; 18:8; 21:27, 36; 22:69; John 1:51; 3:13; 6:62; 12:23; 13:31; Acts 7:56; Rev 1:13; 14:14.

156. Matt 9:6; 10:23; 12:8; 12:32; 13:41; 16:27–28; 17:9; 19:28; 20;28; 24:27, 30, 37; 24:39, 44; 25:31; 26:64; Mark 2:10, 28; 8:31, 38; 9:9; 10:45; 13:26; 14:62; Luke 5:24; 6:5; 9:26, 44; 12:8, 10, 40; 17:24, 26, 30; 18:8; 21:27, 36; 22:69; John 1:51; 3:13; 5:27; 6:62; Acts 7:53.

157. Géza Vermes and E. P. Sanders suggested that Jesus' use of the title "Son of Man" did not always comport with the imagery found in Daniel ("The Use of *Bar Nasha/Bar Nash* in Jewish Aramaic," in *An Aramaic Approach to the Gospels and Acts*, 3rd ed., ed. Matthew Black [Oxford: Oxford University Press, 1967], 310–30. See also Ragnar Leivestad, "Exit the Apocalyptic Son of Man," in *New Testament Studies* 18 [1971]: 243–67). They thus argued that the Aramaic term "Son of Man" (*bar enoš* [שׁ אֱנָ בַר]) simply meant "human being" in contexts where the Daniel 7:13 themes were absent. I maintain, however, that Jesus could have intentionally redefined the "Son of Man" idea in the light of his humility and suffering just as he had redefined the messiah concept in the same way. See also Delbert Burkett, *The Son of Man Debate: A History and Evaluation* (Cambridge, UK: Cambridge University Press, 1999).

158. 1 Kings 4:33: Solomon "spake of trees, from the cedar tree that is in Lebanon even unto the hyssop that springeth out of the wall: he spake also of beasts, and of fowl, and of creeping things, and of fishes" (*King James Version*).

159. The Apostle Paul's concept of Christ as the second Adam contains, as well, this idea of the surpassing greatness of the second Adam to the first Adam. This is suggested by the words *much more* (Grk=πολλῷ μᾶλλον [*pollō mallon*]) found in Romans 5 where Paul explores the Adam-Christ parallel (5:15, 17). The theme is continued in 1 Cor 15:21–23, 45–49. The first Adam was a living soul through whom came death. The second Adam became a life-giving spirit through whom comes life imperishable.

160. John Day, *God's Conflict with the Dragon and the Sea: Echoes of a Canaanite Myth in the Old Testament* (Cambridge, UK: Cambridge University Press, 1985).

161. Job 41:1; Psalm 74:14; Isa 27:1.

162. Job 9:13; 26:12; Psalm 87:4.

163. Ezek 29:3–7; 32:3.

164. That is, if the word *Elohim* is here taken to be plural rather than singular.

165. Gen 3:24.

166. Exod 26:1, 31; 36:8, 35.

167. Exod 25:18–22; 37:7–9; 1 Kgs 6:23–35.

168. See *Midr. Lev* 35. 6. These connections persuade John H. Sailhamer, *Genesis,* 2 vols. (Grand Rapids, MI: Zondervan, 1990), to say, "The description of the Garden of Eden appears to be deliberately cast to foreshadow the description of the tabernacle found later in the Pentateuch. The garden, like the tabernacle, was the place where man could enjoy the fellowship and presence of God" (Sailhamer, *Genesis,* 2:41). Sailhamer observes that cherubim are not the only connecting symbol. There are also the references to gold and precious stones both in relation to the Garden of Eden and the Tabernacle (Sailhamer, *Genesis,* 2:43).

169. Ezek 1:4–28; 10:1–20.

170. The ceremonies of the Day of Atonement are described in the Talmud in *b. Yoma.*

171. Lohse, *Martin Luther's Theology,* 178–80.

172. I prefer Hans Urs von Balthasar's term *Gestalt* here in place of a Platonic understanding of Form that is abstract and based on the principle of limit. *Gestalt,* which implies a wholeness that always transcends the sum of its parts, is not reductive; hence, von Balthasar speaks of *Gestalt* as "the mystery of form." *The Glory of the Lord: A Theological Aesthetics* Vol. 1, trans. Erasmo Leiva-Merikakis, eds. Joseph Fessio and John Riches (San Francisco, CA: Ignatius Press, 2009), 19.

173. Gunton, for example, considers the strength of the social analogy of the Trinity (*The One, the Three and the Many,* 210–31) and refers to David Hardy's idea of "the social transcendental" (222–23). He does not, however, think that "the social transcendental" idea adequately expresses what he refers to as the "two transcendentals, perichoresis and substantiality" (223).

174. St. Augustine recognized his psychological analogy to be problematic and thus transitioned from his psychological analogy of God as memory, understanding, and love to speak of the soul "remembering God, understanding God, and loving God."

175. Karl Rahner's well-known dictum reads: "The economic Trinity is the immanent Trinity, and vice versa." Michael J. Scanlon observes that Rahner did not fully develop the vice versa of this dictum but left room for others to speak of God's Wisdom/Word and Spirit that has proven highly suggestive for further development (Scanlon, "Trinity and Transcendence," in *Transcendence and Beyond,* 71). Surely the affirmation, "the immanent Trinity is the economic Trinity," must resist any attempt to collapse the transcendence of the immanent Trinity into a merely dialectical process.

176. Phil 3:14.

177. Phil 2:6-8.

178. Augustine, *Confessions* 1.1.

179. Heb 4:9-11.

Bibliography

Adams, Robert Merrihew. *Finite and Infinite Goods: A Framework for Ethics*. Oxford: Oxford University Press, 1999.

Ancient Near Eastern Texts Relating to the Old Testament. Edited by James B. Pritchard. Princeton, NJ: Princeton University Press, 1969.

Anselm of Canterbury. "Proslogion." In *Anselm of Canterbury Complete Treatises*. Vol. 1. Edited and Translated by Jasper Hopkins and Herbert Richardson. Toronto: Edwin Mellen, 1974.

Aquinas, Thomas. *Summa Contra Gentiles*. Translated by the English Dominican Fathers. London: Burns Oates & Washbourne, 1924.

———. *Summa Theologica*. 5 vols. Translated by Fathers of the English Dominican Province. Notre Dame, IN: Christian Classics, 1948.

Aristotle. *Metaphysics*. Vols. 1 and 2. Translated by Hugh Tredennick. *Loeb Classical Library* 286, 287. Cambridge, MA: Harvard University Press, 1933–1935.

———. *Nicomachean Ethics*. Translated by Harris Rackham. *Loeb Classical Library* 73. Cambridge, MA: Harvard University Press, 1936.

———. *Poetics*. Translated by Stephen Halliwell. *Loeb Classical Library* 199. Cambridge, MA: Harvard University Press, 1995.

Armytage, W[alter] H[arry] G[reen]. *German Influence on English Education*. London: Routledge, Taylor & Francis Group, 2012.

Augustine of Hippo. *Confessions*. Vols. 1 and 2. Translated by Carolyn J.-B. Hammond. *Loeb Classical Library* 26. Cambridge, MA: Harvard University Press, 2014.

———. *On Christian Doctrine*. Translator unknown. Radford, VA: SMK Books, 2013.

Aune, James. *Selling the Free Market: The Rhetoric of Economic Correctness*. New York: Guilford, 2001.

Austin, J[ohn] L[angshaw]. *How to Do Things with Words*. Edited by J. O. Urmson. Eastford, CT: Martino Fine Books, 2018.

Avicenna. *The Metaphysics of the Healing*. Translated by Michael E. Marmura. Provo, Utah: Brigham Young University Press, 2005.

Ayer, Alfred J[ules]. *Language, Truth, and Logic*. London: Victor Gollancz, 1936.

Ayers, Michael. *Locke: Epistemology and Ontology*. London: Routledge, Taylor & Francis Group, 1991.

Babylonian Talmud. 64 vols. Translated by Israel W[olf] Slotki. Edited by Isidore Epstein et al. New York: R. Bennett, 1959.

Bacon, Francis. *The Advancement of Learning, The New Organon, The New Atlantis*. Vol. 30 of *Great Books of the Western World*. Edited by Robert Maynard Hutchins and Mortimer Adler. Chicago: William Benton/Encyclopædia Britannica, 1952.

————. *The Essays*. New York: Cosimo Classics, 2007.

————. *The New Organon*. Edited by Lisa Jardine and Michael Silverthorne. Cambridge: Cambridge University Press, 2000.

Baker, David Weil. *Divulging Utopia: Radical Humanism in Sixteenth-Century England*. Amherst, MA: University of Massachusetts Press, 1999.

Balthasar, Hans Urs von. *The Glory of the Lord: A Theological Aesthetics*. Vol. 1. Translated by Erasmo Leiva-Merikakis. Edited by Joseph Fessio and John Riches. San Francisco, CA: Ignatius Press, 2009.

Barker, Jessica L., Pat Barclay, and H. Kern Reeve. "Within-Group Competition Reduces Cooperation and Payoff in Human Groups." *Behavioral Ecology* 23, no. 4 (July–August 2012): 735–41.

Barth, Karl. *The Humanity of God*. Louisville, KY: John Knox, 1960.

Barzun, Jacques. *From Dawn to Decadence: 500 Years of Western Cultural Life, 1500 to the Present*. New York: HarperCollins. Perennial edition, 2001.

Bauerschmidt, Frederick Christian. "Aesthetics: The Theological Sublime." In *Radical Orthodoxy*. Edited by John Milbank, Catherine Pickstock, and Graham Ward. (London: Routledge, 1999).

Baumgarten, Albert I. *The Phoenician History of Philo of Byblos: A Commentary*. Leiden, NL: E.J. Brill, 1981.

Bayes, Thomas. "An Essay Towards Solving a Problem in the Doctrine of Chances." Communicated by Mr. Price, in a letter to John Canton, M. A. and F. R. S. www.stat.ucla.edu/history/essay.pdf.

Bayle, Pierre. *Historical and Critical Dictionary: Selections*. Translated Richard H. Popkin. Indianapolis, IN: Hackett Publishing, 1992.

Beach, Edward Allen. *The Potencies of God(s): Schelling's Philosophy of Mythology*. Albany: State University of New York Press, 1994.

Beaumont, George. "The Beggars Complaint (1812)." In *Factory Production in Nineteenth-Century Britain*. Edited by Elaine Freedgood. New York: Oxford University Press, 2003.

Begbie, Jeremy. *Redeeming Transcendence in the Arts: Bearing Witness to the Triune God*. Grand Rapids, MI: William B. Eerdmans, 2018.

Bell, Rob. *Love Wins: A Book about Heaven, Hell, and the Fate of Every Person Who Ever Lived*. New York: HarperCollins, 2011.

Benjamin, Walter. *Über den Begriff der Geschichte*, in *Gesammelten Schriften* I:2. Frankfurt am Main: Suhrkamp Verlag, 1974.

Benner, Jeff A. *The Ancient Hebrew Lexicon of the Bible: Hebrew Letters, Words and Roots Defined Within Their Ancient Cultural Context*. College Station, TX: Virtualbookworm.com, 2005.

Bentham, Jeremy. *Principles of Morals and Legislation*. Oxford: Clarendon, 1907.

Berdyaev, Nikolai. *Freedom and the Spirit*. Translated Oliver F. Clark. San Rafael, CA: Semantron, 2009.

Berkeley, George. "A Treatise Concerning the Principles of Human Knowledge (1710)." In *The English Philosophers from Bacon to Mill*. Edited by Edwin Burtt. New York: Random House, 1939.

Berman, Marshall. *The Politics of Authenticity: Radical Individualism and the Emergence of Modern Society*. London: Verso, 1970. Revised edition, 2009.

Bernstein, David E. *You Can't Say That! The Growing Threat to Civil Liberties from Antidiscrimination Laws*. Washington, DC: Cato Institute, 2003.

Bingham, Jane. *The Cotswolds: A Cultural History*. Oxford: Oxford University Press, 2010.

Black, Matthew, editor. *An Aramaic Approach to the Gospels and Acts*. Oxford: Oxford University Press, 1967. Third edition.

Blake, William. *The Complete Writings of William Blake*. Edited by Geoffrey Keynes. London: Nonesuch, 1957.

Bloch, Ernst. *The Frankfort School on Religion: Key Writings by the Major Thinkers*. Edited by Eduardo Mendieta. New York: Routledge, 2004.

————. *Gesamtausgabe*. 16 vols. Frankfort am Main: Suhrkamp Verlag, 1969–77.

————. *The Principle of Hope.* 3 vols. Translated by Neville Plaice, Stephen Plaice, and Paul Knight. Oxford: Basil Blackwell, 1986.

Bloom, Allan. *The Closing of the American Mind: How Higher Education Has Failed Democracy and Impoverished the Souls of Today's Students.* New York: Simon & Schuster, 1987.

Boos, Stephen. "Rethinking the Aesthetic: Kant, Schiller, and Hegel." In *Between Ethics and Aesthetics: Crossing the Boundaries.* Edited by Dorota Glowacka and Stephen Boos. Albany: State University of New York Press, 2002.

Bowman, John. *Socialism in America.* New York, Lincoln, and Shanghai: iUniverse, 2005. Second edition.

Bradley, F[rancis] H[erbert]. *Ethical Studies.* London, Oxford, and New York: Oxford University Press, 1970. Second revised edition.

Brahma Sūtra Bhāṣya. Translated by Sri Swami Sivananda. Tehri-Garhwal, Uttarakhand, Himalayas, India: The Divine Life Society, 2008.

Bruce, Susan, ed. *Three Early Modern Utopias: Utopia, New Atlantis, and The Isle of the Pines.* Oxford: Oxford University Press, 1999.

Bulgakov, Sergei. *Sophia, The Wisdom of God: An Outline of Sophiology.* Translated by Patrick Thompson, O. Fielding Clark, and Xenia Braikevikt. Hudson, NY: Lindisfarne, 1993.

Burkett, Delbert. *The Son of Man Debate: A History and Evaluation.* Cambridge: Cambridge University Press, 1999.

Bush, Randall. *Recent Ideas of Divine Conflict: The Influences of Psychological and Sociological Theories of Conflict upon the Trinitarian Theology of Paul Tillich and Jürgen Moltmann.* San Francisco, CA: Mellen Research University Press, 1991.

Calvin, John. *Institutes of the Christian Religion.* 2 vols. Translated and edited by John T. McNeill. Westminster: John Knox, 1960.

Cammaerts, Émile. *The Laughing Prophet: The Seven Virtues and G. K. Chesterton.* Walton-on-Thames: Methuen & Co., 1937.

Camus, Albert. *The Myth of Sisyphus and Other Essays.* Translated by Justin O'Brien. New York: Alfred A. Knopf, 1967.

Caputo, John D. and Michael J. Scanlon, editors. *Transcendence and Beyond: A Postmodern Inquiry.* Bloomington: Indiana University Press, 2007.

Cardwell, Kenneth W. "Francis Bacon, Inquisitor." In *Francis Bacon's Legacy of Texts.* Edited by William A. Sessions. New York: AMS Press, 1990.

Carlson, Elof Axel. *The 7 Sexes: Biology of Sex Determination.* Bloomington: Indiana University Press, 2013.

Carrier, Richard. *Sense and Goodness Without God: A Defense of Metaphysical Naturalism.* Bloomington, IN: AuthorHouse, 2005.

Carey, Daniel. *Locke, Shaftesbury, and Hutcheson: Contesting Diversity in the Enlightenment and Beyond.* Cambridge: Cambridge University Press, 2006. Kindle edition.

Charles, R[obert] H[enry], ed. *The Apocrypha and Pseudepigrapha of the Old Testament in English.* 2 vols. Oxford: Clarendon, 1913.

Cloud, Daniel. *The Domestication of Language: Cultural Evolution and the Uniqueness of the Human Animal.* New York: Columbia University Press, 2014.

Comte, Auguste. *Système de politique positive, ou traité de sociologie, instituant la religion de l'humanité,* vol. 1. Paris: Librairie Scientifique Industrielle de L. Matthias, 1854.

Copan, Paul. *Is God a Moral Monster? Making Sense of the Old Testament God.* Grand Rapids, MI: Baker Books, 2011.

Coward, Harold, Toby Foshay, and Jacques Derrida. *Derrida and Negative Theology.* Albany: State University of New York Press, 1992.

Craig, William Lane. *The Kalām Cosmological Argument.* Eugene, OR: Wipf and Stock, 1979.

Crenshaw, James L. *Old Testament Wisdom: An Introduction.* Louisville, KY: John Knox, 1998. Revised edition.

Cross, Frank Moore. *Canaanite Myth and Hebrew Epic.* Cambridge, MA: Harvard University Press, 1997.

Cross, Richard. *Duns Scotus.* New York: Oxford University Press, 1999.

Crouch, Andy. *Culture Making: Recovering Our Creative Calling*. Downers Grove, IL: IVP Books, 2008.

Cudworth, Ralph. *The True Intellectual System of the Universe: Wherein All the Reason and Philosophy of Atheism is Confuted and Its Impossibility Demonstrated.* Edited by Thomas Birch. New York: Gould & Newman, 1837.

Daley, Brian E. "Antioch and Alexandria: Christology as Reflection of God's Presence in History." In *The Oxford Handbook of Christology.* Edited by Francesca Aran Murphy. Oxford: Oxford University Press, 2015.

Davies, Brian. *Philosophy of Religion: A Guide and Anthology.* Oxford: Oxford University Press, 2000.

Davies, W[illiam] D[avid]. *Paul and Rabbinic Judaism: Some Rabbinic Elements in Pauline Theology.* London: S. P. C. K, 1958.

Dawkins, Richard. *The God Delusion.* Boston, MA: Houghton Mifflin, 2006.

Day, John. *God's Conflict with the Dragon and the Sea: Echoes of a Canaanite Myth in the Old Testament.* Cambridge: Cambridge University Press, 1985.

Deed, Kristen K. "The Infinite Qualitative Difference: Sin, the Self, and Revelation in the Thought of Søren Kierkegaard." *International Journal for Philosophy of Religion.* Vol. 53, No. 1 (February 2003): 25–43. https://www.jstor.org/stable/40035916.

Dennett, Daniel. *Breaking the Spell: Religion as a Natural Phenomenon.* New York: Penguin, 2007.

Derrida, Jacques. *Dissemination.* Translated by Barbara Johnson. Chicago, IL: University of Chicago Press, 1981.

———. *Writing and Difference.* Translated by Alan Bass. Chicago, IL: University of Chicago Press, 1973.

Descartes, René. *Meditations on First Philosophy.* Translated by Ronald Rubin. In *A Guided Tour of René Descartes' Meditations on First Philosophy.* Mountain View, CA: Mayfield Publishing, 1989.

Dickens, Charles. *Hard Times.* Champaign, IL: Project Gutenberg eBook, 1997.

Dickson, Gwen Griffith. *Johann Georg Hamann's Relational Metacriticism.* Berlin and New York: Walter de Gruyter, 1995.

Dillistone, F[rederick] W[illiam]. *The Christian Faith.* Philadelphia and New York: J. B. Lippincott, 1964.

———. *The Novelist and the Passion Story.* New York: Sheed & Ward, 1960.

Dillon, John. *The Middle Platonists: 80 B.C. to A.D 220.* Ithaca, NY: Cornell University Press, 1977. Revised edition.

Donovan, Josephine. *Feminist Theory: The Intellectual Traditions.* New York: Continuum, 2012. Fourth edition.

Dubay, Thomas. *The Evidential Power of Beauty: Science and Theology Meet.* San Francisco, CA: Ignatius Press, 1999.

Dugger, William M., and Howard J. Sherman, eds. *Evolutionary Theory in the Social Sciences, Vol. 2.* London: Routledge, 2003.

Eddy, Mary Baker. *Science and Health with Key to the Scriptures.* Boston, MA: Christian Science Publishing Co., 1875.

Edwards, Jonathan. *A Treatise Concerning Religious Affections, in Three Parts.* Philadelphia, PA: James Crissy, 1821.

Einstein, Albert. *Out of My Later Years.* New York: Philosophical Library, 1950.

Eliade, Mircea. *Cosmos and History.* New York: Harper Torchbooks, 1959.

Empedocles. *The Extant Fragments.* Translated by M. R. Wright. New Haven, CT: Yale University Press, 1981.

Epicurus. *Letter to Menoeceus.* Translated by Robert Drew Hicks. http://classics.mit.edu/Epicurus/menoec.html.

Epiphanius of Salamis. *The Panarion, Vol. 63.* Bk. 1. Translated by Frank Williams. In *Nag Hammadi and Manichaean Studies.* Edited by Einar Thomassen and Johannes van Oort. Leiden, NL: Koninklijke Brill, 2009. Revised and expanded Second edition.

Erasmus, Desiderius. *In Praise of Folly.* London: Reeves & Turner, 1876.

Eusebius of Caesarea. *Eusebii Pamphili Evangelicae Praeparationis Libri XV*. Translated by E. H. Gifford. Oxford, 1903.

Farrington, Benjamin. *Francis Bacon: Philosopher of Industrial Science*. New York: Henry Schuman, 1949.

Fee, Gordon. *Paul's Letter to the Philippians*. Grand Rapids, MI: Eerdman's, 1995.

Ferré, Frederick. *Being and Value: Toward a Constructive Postmodern Metaphysics*. Albany: State University of New York Press, 1996.

———. *Knowing and Value: Toward a Constructive Postmodern Epistemology* (Albany: State University of New York Press, 1998.

———. *Living and Value: Toward a Constructive Postmodern Ethics*. Albany: State University of New York Press, 2001.

Fichte, Johann Gottlieb. *Fichte: Early Philosophical Writings*. Translated and edited by Daniel Breazeale. Ithaca, NY: Cornell University Press, 1988.

———. *Foundations of Transcendental Philosophy (Wissenschaftslehre) Nova Methodo (1796/99)*. Translated and edited by Daniel Breazeale. Ithaca, NY: Cornell University Press, 1992.

Fiddes, Paul. *The Creative Suffering of God*. Oxford: Clarendon, 1988.

———. *Freedom and Limit: A Dialogue between Literature and Christian Doctrine*. Macon, GA: Mercer University Press, 1999.

———. *Seeing the World and Knowing God: Hebrew Wisdom and Christian Doctrine in a Late Modern Context*. Oxford: Oxford University Press, 2013.

———. "The Sublime and the Beautiful: Intersections between Theology and Literature." In *Literature and Theology: New Interdisciplinary Spaces*. Edited by Heather Walton. Farnham: Ashgate, 2011.

Fine, Lawrence. *Physician of the Soul, Healer of the Cosmos: Isaac Luria and His Kabbalistic Fellowship*. Stanford, CA: Stanford University Press, 2003.

Flew, Antony. *God and Philosophy*. Amherst, New York: Prometheus Books, 2005.

———. *There is a God: How the World's Most Notorious Atheist Changed His Mind*. San Francisco, CA: Harper One, 2007.

Forsythe, Gary. *A Critical History of Early Rome: From Prehistory to the First Punic War*. Berkeley, CA: University of California Press, 2005.

Frankfort, Henri. *Kingship and the Gods: A Study of Ancient Near Eastern Religion as the Integration of Society and Nature*. Chicago, IL: University of Chicago Press, 1978.

Frankl, Viktor E. *Man's Search for Meaning*. Translated by Ilse Lasch. Boston, MA: Beacon, 1992.

Frame, John. *Apologetics: A Justification of Christian Belief*. Edited by Joseph E. Torres. Phillipsburg, NJ: P&R Publishing, 2015.

Freedman, H., Maurice Simon, S. M. Lehrman, J. Israelstam, Judah J. Slotki, J. Rabinowitz, A. Cohen, and Louis I. Rabbinowitz, eds. *Midrash Rabbah*. London: Soncino Press, 1961.

Frei, Hans. *Theology and Narrative: Selected Essays*, ed. George Hunsinger and William C. Placher. New York and Oxford: Oxford University Press, 1993.

Freud, Sigmund. "A Difficulty in the Path of Psycho-Analysis (1917)." *The Standard Edition of the Complete Psychological Works of Sigmund Freud, Vol. 17*. 24 vols. Edited by James Strachey. New York: W. W. Norton, 1976.

Fry, Northrup. "Notes for a Commentary on Milton." In *The Divine Vision: Studies in the Poetry and Art of William Blake, Born November 28th, 1757*. Edited by Vivian de Sola Pinto, Kathleen Raine, and William Blake Bicentenary Committee. London: Victor Gollancz, 1957.

Gabriel, Andrew K. S.v. "Apophatic Theology," in *The Encyclopedia of Christian Civilization*. Oxford: Blackwell, 2012.

Gadamer, Hans-Georg. *Truth and Method*. Translated by Joel Weinsheimer and Donald G. Marshall. London: Continuum, 2004.

García-Rivera, Alejandro. *The Community of the Beautiful: A Theological Aesthetics*. Collegeville, MN: Liturgical Press, 1999.

Gauthier, David. *Rousseau: The Sentiment of Existence*. Cambridge: Cambridge University Press, 2008.

Gill, Jerry. *Mediated Transcendence: A Postmodern Reflection*. Macon, GA: Mercer University Press, 1989.

Goldberg, Michael. *Theology and Narrative: A Critical Introduction*. Eugene, OR: Wipf & Stock, 2001. Second edition.

Golomb, Jacob. *Nietzsche and Zion*. Ithaca and London: Cornell University Press, 2004.

Gregory of Nyssa. *The Letters*. Translated by Anna M. Silvas. Leiden, NL: Brill, 2006.

Groothuis, Douglas. *Christian Apologetics: A Comprehensive Case for Biblical Faith*. Downers Grove, IL: InterVarsity, 2010.

Graham, Daniel W. *Explaining the Cosmos: The Ionian Tradition of Scientific Philosophy*. Princeton, NJ: Princeton University Press, 2006.

Gunton, Colin E. *The One, the Three and the Many: God, Creation and the Culture of Modernity*. Cambridge: Cambridge University Press, 1993.

Hall, Edward Twitchell. *Beyond Culture*. New York: Anchor Books, 1976.

Hamann, Johann Georg. *Writings on Philosophy and Language*. Translated by Kenneth Haynes. *Cambridge Texts in the History of Philosophy*. Cambridge: 2007. Kindle edition.

Hare, John E. *God and Morality: A Philosophical History*. Oxford: Blackwell, 2007.

Hare, R[ichard] M[ervyn]. *Essays on Religion and Education*. Oxford: Clarendon, 1998.

Harris, Sam. *The End of Faith: Religion, Terror, and the Future of Reason*. New York: W. W. Norton, 2005.

———. *The Moral Landscape: How Science Can Determine Human Values*. New York, London, Toronto, and Sydney: Free Press, 2010.

Hart, David Bentley. *Atheist Delusions: The Christian Revolution and Its Fashionable Enemies*. New Haven, CT and London: Yale University Press, 2009.

———. *The Beauty of the Infinite: The Aesthetics of Christian Truth*. Grand Rapids, MI: William B. Eerdmans, 2003.

Hauerwas, Stanley, and L. Gregory Johnson, eds. *Why Narrative? Readings in Narrative Theology*. Eugene, OR: Wipf & Stock, 1997.

Hawking, Stephen. *A Brief History of Time*. New York: Bantam Books, 1996.

Hegel, G[eorg] W[ilhelm] F[riedrich]. *Hegel's Aesthetics: Lectures on Fine Art*. Vol. 1. Translated by T. M. Knox. Oxford: Clarendon, 1975. Kindle edition.

———. *Lectures on the Philosophy of Religion*. 3 vols. Translated by E. B. Speirs and J. Burdon Sanderson. London: Routledge & Kegan Paul, 1895. Reprint edition, 1962, 1968.

———. *Lectures on the Philosophy of World History*. Translated by Hugh Barr Nisbet. Cambridge: Cambridge University Press, 1975.

———. *Phenomenology of Spirit*. Translated by A. V. Miller. Oxford: Oxford University Press, 1977.

———. *The Difference between Fichte's and Schelling's System of Philosophy*. Translated by H. S. Harris and Walter Cerf. Albany: State University of New York Press, 1977.

Heraclitus. *The Cosmic Fragments*. Translated by G. S. Kirk. Cambridge: Cambridge University Press, 1954.

Herrick, James A. *The Radical Rhetoric of the English Deists: The Discourse of Skepticism, 1680–1750*. Columbia: University of South Carolina Press, 1997.

Hesiod. *Theogony. Works and Days*. Translated by Glenn W. Most. *Loeb Classical Library* 57. Cambridge, MA: Harvard University Press, 2006.

Heydt, Collin. *Rethinking Mill's Ethics: Character and Aesthetic Education*. London: Continuum, 2006.

Hick, John. *Evil and the God of Love*. New York: Palgrave McMillan, 2010.

———. *Philosophy of Religion*. London: Prentice Hall, 1990. Fourth edition.

Himmelfarb, Gertrude. *Poverty and Compassion: The Moral Imagination of the Late Victorians*. New York: Vintage Books, 1991.

Hobbes, Thomas. *Leviathan* (1651). Produced by Edward White and David Widger. Project Gutenberg e-book, 2009.

Hofstede, Geert. *Culture's Consequences: Comparing Values, Behaviors, Institutions, and Organizations Across Nations*. Thousand Oaks, CA: Sage Publications, 2001. Second edition.

Holmes, Arthur. *Fact, Value, and God*. Grand Rapids, MI: William B. Eerdmans, 1997.

Hume, David. "An Enquiry Concerning Human Understanding." In *Collected Writings*. Oxford: Benediction Classics, 2013.

―――. *Treatise of Human Nature*. Edited by L. A. Selby-Bigge. Oxford: Clarendon, 1888.

Huxley, Aldous. *Brave New World*. Cutchogue, NY: Buccaneer Books, 1932.

Inwagen, Peter van. *An Essay on Free Will*. Oxford: Clarendon, 1983.

Irenaeus. "Against Heresies." In *The Writings of the Ante-Nicene Fathers*. Vol. 1. Edited by Alexander Roberts, James Donaldson, and Cleveland Cox. Grand Rapids, MI: William B. Eerdman's, 1973–74.

Jacquette, Dale. *The Philosophy of Schopenhauer*. London: Routledge, Taylor & Francis Group, 2014.

James, William. *The Will to Believe, and Essays in Popular Philosophy*. New York: Longmans, Green, 1912.

Jenson, Matt. *The Gravity of Sin: Augustine, Luther, and Barth on* "Homo Incurvatus in Se." Edinburgh: T & T Clark, 2006.

Jessop, Bob, and Russell Wheatley. *Karl Marx's Social and Political Thought: Critical Assessments—Second Series*. In *Marx's Life and Theoretical Development*, Vol. 5. London: Routledge, Taylor and Francis Group, 1999.

Johansen, Karsten Friis. *A History of Ancient Philosophy: From the Beginning to Augustine*. Translated by Henrik Rosenmeier. London: Routledge, 1998.

John of Damascus. *An Exact Exposition of the Orthodox Faith*. Translated by E. W. Watson and L. Pullan. In *The Nicene and Post-Nicene Fathers, Second Series, Vol. 9*. Edited by Philip Schaff and Henry Wace. Buffalo, NY: Christian Literature Publishing, 1899.

Josephus, Flavius. *The Works of Josephus*. 4 vols. Translated by William Whiston. Grand Rapids, MI: Baker, 1974.

Jung, C[arl] G[ustav]. *The Collected Works*. 20 vols. Edited by H. Read, M. Fordham, and G. Adler. Translated by R. F. C. Hull. Princeton, NJ: Princeton University Press, 1953–79.

―――. *Modern Man in Search of a Soul*. Translated by W. S. Dell and Cary F. Baynes. North American e-book, 2011.

Kant, Immanuel. *Critique of the Power of Judgement*. Translated by Paul Guyer and Eric Matthews. Edited by Paul Guyer. Cambridge: Cambridge University Press, 2000.

―――. *Critique of Pure Reason*. Translated and edited by Paul Guyer and Allen W. Wood. Cambridge: Cambridge University Press, 1998.

―――. *Groundwork of the Metaphysics of Morals*. Translated and edited by Mary Gregor and Jens Timmermann. Cambridge: Cambridge University Press, 2012.

―――. *The Metaphysics of Morals*. Translated by Mary Gregor. Edited by Lara Denis. Cambridge: Cambridge University Press, 2017.

―――. *Prolegomena to Any Future Metaphysics that Will Be Able to Come Forward as Science*. Translated by Paul Carus. Revised by James W. Ellington. Indianapolis, IN/Cambridge, MA: Hackett, 1977. Akademie edition.

Keats, John. *Letters of John Keats to His Family and Friends*. Edited by Sidney Colvin. Project Gutenberg e-book. http://www.gutenberg.org/files/35698/35698-h/35698-h.htm.

Kelber, Werner. "In the Beginning Were the Words: The Apotheosis and Narrative Displacement of the Logos." *Journal of the American Academy of Religion*. Vol. 58, no. 1 (Spring 1990): 69–98.

Kierkegaard, Søren. *The Concept of Anxiety: A Simple Psychologically Oriented Deliberation in View of the Dogmatic Problem of Hereditary Sin*. Edited and translated by Alastair Hannay. New York and London: Liveright Publishing, 2015.

―――. *Concluding Unscientific Postscript to the Philosophical Crumbs*. Edited and translated by Alastair Hannay. Cambridge: Cambridge University Press, 2009.

―――. *Either/Or*. 2 vols. Edited and translated by Howard V. Hong and Edna H. Hong. Princeton, NJ: Princeton University Press, 1987.

―――. *Fear and Trembling* and *Repetition*. Translated and edited by Howard V. Hong and Edna H. Hong. Princeton, NJ: Princeton University Press, 1983.

―――. *Stages on Life's Way*. Edited and translated by Howard V. Hong and Edna H. Hong. Princeton, NJ: Princeton University Press, 1988.

King, Jonathan. *The Beauty of the Lord: Theology as Aesthetics*. Bellingham, WA: Lexam Press, 2018. Kindle edition.

King, Mary. *Mahatma Gandhi and Martin Luther King Jr: The Power of Nonviolent Action*. Paris: United Nations Education, Scientific and Cultural Organization, 1999.

Kirk, G. S., and J. E. Raven, eds. *The Pre-Socratic Philosophers: A Critical History with a Selection of Texts*. Cambridge: Cambridge University Press, 1962.

Kitamori, Kazoh. *Theology of the Pain of God*. Eugene, OR: Wipf & Stock, 2005. Fifth revised edition.

Klawans, Jonathan. "Sadducees, Zadokites, and the Wisdom of Ben Sira." In *Israel's God and Rebecca's Children: Christology and Community in Early Judaism and Christianity*. Edited by David Capes, April DeConick, Helen Bond, and Troy Miller. Waco, TX: Baylor University Press, 2008.

Koukl, Gregory. *The Story of Reality: How the World Began, How it Ends, and Everything Important that Happens in Between*. Grand Rapids, MI: Zondervan, 2017.

Lactantius. *On the Anger of God*. New Advent. http://www.newadvent.org/fathers/0703.htm.

Lamm, Julia A. *The Living God: Schleiermacher's Theological Appropriation of Spinoza*. University Park: Pennsylvania State University Press, 2010.

Lampe, G[eoffrey] W[illiam] H[ugo]. *God as Spirit*. Oxford: Clarendon, 1977.

Leibniz, Gottfried. *The Monadology and Other Philosophical Writings*. Translated by Robert Latta. Oxford: Clarendon, 1898.

———. *Theodicy: Essays on the Goodness of God, the Freedom of Man and the Origin of Evil*. Translated by E. M. Huggard. LaSalle, Illinois: Open Court Publishing, 1985.

Leivestad, Ragnar. "Exit the Apocalyptic Son of Man." *New Testament Studies* 18 (1971): 243–67.

Lenin, Vladimir. *The State and Revolution*. New York: International Publishers, 1932.

Levinas, Emmanuel. *Totality and Infinity: An Essay on Exteriority*. Translated by Alphonso Lingis. Pittsburgh, PA: Duquesne University Press, 1969.

Levinson, Jerrold. *Aesthetics and Ethics: Essays at the Intersection*. Edited by Jerrold Levinson. Cambridge: Cambridge University Press, 1998.

Lewis, Clarence Irving. *The Mind and the World-Order: Outline of a Theory of Knowledge*. New York, Chicago, IL and Boston, MA: Charles Scribner's Sons, 1929.

Lewis, C[live] S[taples]. *The Abolition of Man*. Oxford: Oxford University Press, 1943.

———. "That Hideous Strength." In *The Space Trilogy*, bk. 3. London: The Bodley Head, 1945.

———. *The Problem of Pain*. New York: HarperCollins, 1996.

Lindbeck, George A. *The Nature of Doctrine: Religion and Theology in a Postliberal Age*. Louisville, KY: Westminster John Knox Press, 1984.

Locke, John. "An Essay Concerning Human Understanding (1689)." In *The English Philosophers from Bacon to Mill*. Edited by Edwin Burtt. New York: Random House, 1939.

———. *The Second Treatise of Government*. Project Gutenberg e-book, 2010. https://www.gutenberg.org/files/7370/7370-h/7370-h.htm.

Lohse, Bernhard. *Martin Luther's Theology: Its Historical and Systemic Development*. Translated by Roy A. Harrisville. Minneapolis: Fortress, 1999.

Loizides, Antis. "The Socratic Origins of John Stuart Mill's 'Art of Life.'" In *John Stuart Mill: A British Socrates*. Edited by Antis Loizides and Kyriakos M. Demetriou. Basingstoke: Palgrave-Macmillan, 2013.

Loughlin, Gerard. *Telling God's Story: Bible, Church, and Narrative Theology*. Cambridge: Cambridge University Press, 1996.

Lovejoy, Arthur O. *The Great Chain of Being*. Cambridge, MA: Harvard University Press, 1964.

Lupton, Robert. *Toxic Charity: How Churches and Charities Hurt Those They Help, and How to Reverse It*. New York: HarperOne, 2012.

Luther, Martin. *On the Bondage of the Will, to the Venerable Erasmus of Rotterdam*. Translated by Edward Thomas Vaughan. London: Applegate, 1823.

Luther's Works. 55 vols. Edited by Jaroslav Pelikan and Helmut Lehmann. St. Louis and Philadelphia: Concordia Publishing House and Fortress Publishing House, 1955–1972.

Lyotard, Jean-François. *The Postmodern Condition: A Report on Knowledge.* Translated by Geoff Bennington and Brian Massumi. Minneapolis: University of Minnesota Press, 1984.

Machiavelli, Niccolò. *The Prince.* Translated by N. H. Thompson. New York: Cosimo Classics, 2008.

MacIntyre, Alasdair. *After Virtue: A Study in Moral Theory.* Notre Dame, IN: University of Notre Dame Press, 1984.

Mahabharata of Krishna-Dwaipayana Vyasa. 12 vols. Translated by Pratap Chandra Roy. Calcutta: Oriental Publishing, 1962.

Maimonides, Moses. *Guide of the Perplexed.* Translated by M. Friedländer. London: Routledge & Kegan Paul, 1904. Second revised edition.

Majors, Clyde R[olston]. "Contemporary Emphasis on Transformation: Its Relation to a Christian Approach to the Problem of Suffering." ThD diss. Southwestern Baptist Theological Seminary, 1973. Unpublished.

Malebranche, Nicolas. *Dialogues on Metaphysics and Religions.* Translated by David Scott. Edited by Nicholas Jolley. Cambridge: Cambridge University Press, 1997.

Martensen, Hans. *Jacob Boehme: His Life and Teachings; Or Studies in Theosophy.* London: Hodder & Stoughton, 1885.

Martin, Craig. *Subverting Aristotle: Religion, History, and Philosophy in Early Modern Science.* Baltimore, MD: Johns Hopkins University Press, 2014.

Marx, Karl. "A Contribution to the Critique of Hegel's Philosophy of Right (1843)." In *Deutsch-Französische Jahrbücher.* Translator unknown. Edited by Andy Blunden and Matthew Carmody. Paris: February 7 and 10, 1844.

———. "Theses on Feuerbach." In *Marx/Engels Collected Works.* Vol. 1. Moscow, USSR: Progress Press, 1969.

Marx, Karl, and Friedrich Engels. *The Communist Manifesto.* Project Gutenberg e-text, 1993.

———. *The German Ideology: Including Theses on Feuerbach* and *Introduction to the Critique of Political Economy.* Amherst, NY: Prometheus Books, 1998.

Mary, Margaret. "Slavery in the Writings of St. Augustine." *The Classical Journal.* Vol. 49, No. 8 (May 1954): 363–69.

Maslow, Abraham. *Motivation and Personality.* New York: Harper, 1954.

McClendon, James. *Biography as Theology: How Life Stories Can Remake Today's Theology.* Philadelphia: Trinity Press International, 1990. New edition.

McGrath, Alister. *Christian Theology: An Introduction.* Oxford: Wiley-Blackwell, 2011. Fifth edition.

Mill, John Stuart. *A System of Logic, Ratiocinative and Inductive: Being a Connected View of the Principles of Evidence and of the Methods of Scientific Investigation.* Edited by J. M. Robson. *The Collected Works of John Stuart Mill, Vol. 8.* Toronto: University of Toronto Press/Routledge & Kegan Paul, 1974. Reprint edition, 1981.

Mokyr, Joel. *The British Industrial Revolution: An Economic Perspective.* Boulder, CO: Westview Press, 1999. Second edition.

Moltmann, Jürgen. *Religion, Revolution, and the Future.* Translated by Douglas M. Meeks. New York: Charles Scribner's Sons, 1969.

Moore, G[eorge] E[dward]. *Principia Ethica.* Mineola, NY: Dover Publications, [1903] 2004.

More, Thomas. *Utopia.* London: Cassell, 1901.

Moses de Leon. *The Zohar, Vol. 1.* Translated by Daniel C. Matt. Stanford, CA: Stanford University Press, 2004.

Mueller, Gustav E[mil]. "The Hegel Legend of 'Thesis, Antithesis, Synthesis.'" In *The Journal of the History of Ideas.* Philadelphia: University of Pennsylvania Press, 1958.

Müller, Max, ed. *Tao Te Ching,* Vol. 39 of *Sacred Books of the East.* Translated by James Legge. Oxford: Oxford University Press, 1891.

Murphy, Francesca Aran. *God is Not a Story: Realism Revisited.* Oxford: Oxford University Press, 2007.

New York University. "Chimpanzee language claims lost in translation, researchers conclude." *ScienceDaily.* Accessed: December 19, 2015. www.sciencedaily.com/releases/2015/11/151102125429.htm.

Nicholas of Cusa. *On Learned Ignorance.* Translated by Jasper Hopkins from *De Docta Ignorantia.* Minneapolis, MN: Arthur J. Banning, 1981.

Niebuhr, H[elmut] Richard. *Christ and Culture.* New York: Harper Colophon Books, 1975.

Nietzsche, Friedrich. *The Antichrist.* Translated by H. L. Mencken. Lexington, KY: Pantianos Classics, 2017.

―――. *Beyond Good and Evil: Prelude to a Philosophy of the Future.* Translated by Judith Norman. Edited by Rolf-Peter Horstmann and Judith Norman. Cambridge: Cambridge University Press, 2002.

―――. *The Birth of Tragedy and Other Writings.* Translated by Ronald Speirs. Edited by Raymond Geuss and Ronald Speirs. Cambridge: Cambridge University Press, 1999.

―――. *The Gay Science.* Translated by Josefine Nauckhoff. Edited by Bernard Williams. Cambridge: Cambridge University Press, 2001.

―――. *The Will to Power.* Translated by Walter Kaufmann and R. J. Hollingdale. New York: Vintage Books, 1968.

―――. *Twilight of the Idols.* Translator unknown. Kindle edition, n. d.

The Noble Qur'an: Interpretation of the Meanings of the Noble Qur'an in the English Language. Summarized by Muhammad Taqi-ud-Dinbin Al-Hilali and Muhammad Muhsin Khan. Riyadh, Saudi Arabia: 1993.

Norman, Richard. *The Moral Philosophers: An Introduction to Ethics.* Oxford: Oxford University Press, 1998. Second edition.

Orwell, George. *1984: A Novel.* New Delhi: Rupa Publications, 2013.

Osborne, Eric Francis. *Irenaeus of Lyons.* Cambridge: Cambridge University Press, 2001.

Otto, Rudolf. *The Idea of the Holy: An Inquiry into the Non-Rational Factor in the Idea of the Divine and Its Relation to the Rational.* Translated by John W. Harvey. Oxford: Oxford University Press, 1923.

Ovid. *Metamorphoses, Vol. 1.* Bks. 1–8. Translated by Frank Justus Miller. Revised by G. P. Goold. *Loeb Classical Library* 42. Cambridge, MA: Harvard University Press, 1916.

Pagels, Elaine. *The Gnostic Gospels.* New York: Vintage Books, 1979.

Parker, Robert. *Miasma: Pollution and Purification in Early Greek Religion.* Oxford: Clarendon, 1983.

Parmenides. "Fragments." In *Early Greek Philosophy.* Translated by John Burnet. London: A & C Black, 1920. Third edition.

Pascal, Blaise. *Pensées.* New York: E. P. Dutton, 1958. Kindle edition.

Pattison, George. *God and Being: An Inquiry.* Oxford: Oxford University Press, 2013.

Peirce, Charles Sanders. "Perceptual Judgments." In *The Philosophical Writings of Peirce.* Edited by Justus Buchler. New York: Dover Publications, 1955. Kindle edition.

Philo of Alexandria. *On the Creation.* Translated by F. H. Colson and G. H. Whitaker. *Loeb Classical Library* 226. Cambridge, MA: Harvard University Press, 1929.

Plato. *Euthyphro. Apology. Crito. Phaedo. Phaedrus.* Translated by Harold North Fowler. *Loeb Classical Library* 36. Cambridge, MA: Harvard University Press, 1914.

―――. *Laches. Protagoras. Meno. Euthydemus.* Translated by W. R. M. Lamb. *Loeb Classical Library* 165. Cambridge, MA: Harvard University Press, 1977.

―――. *Lysis. Symposium. Gorgias.* Translated by W. R. M. Lamb. *Loeb Classical Library* 166. Cambridge, MA: Harvard University Press, 1925.

―――. *Republic.* Vols. 1 and 2. Edited and translated by Christopher Emlyn-Jones, William Preddy. *Loeb Classical Library* 237. Cambridge, MA: Harvard University Press, 2013.

―――. *Timaeus. Critias. Cleitophon. Menexenus. Epistles.* Translated by R. G. Bury. *Loeb Classical Library* 234. Cambridge, MA: Harvard University Press, 1929.

Plotinus. *Enneads.* 7 vols. Translated by A. H. Armstrong. *Loeb Classical Library* 440–45, 468. Cambridge, MA: Harvard University Press, 1966–1988.

Plutarch. *Lives, Vol. 1.* Translated by Bernadotte Perrin. *Loeb Classical Library* 46. Cambridge, MA: Harvard University Press, 1914.

Pokorný, Dušan. "The Failure of the Soviet Experiment." In *Efficiency and Justice in the Industrial World, Vol. 1.* Armonk, NY: Routledge, M. E. Sharpe, 1992.

Polanyi, Michael. *Personal Knowledge: Towards a Post-Critical Philosophy.* Chicago, IL: University of Chicago Press, 1958, 1962.

Puccio, Gerard J. and David W. Gonzáles. "Nurturing Creative Thinking: Western Approaches and Eastern Issues." In *Creativity: When East Meets West*. Edited by Sing Lau, Ann N. N. Hui, and Grace Y. C. Ng. Singapore: World Scientific Publishing, 2004.

Pseudo-Apollodorus. *The Library*. Translated by J. G. Frazer. *Loeb Classical Library* 121. Cambridge, MA: Harvard University Press, 1995.

Rabinowitz, Louis Isaac. "Reward and Punishment." *Jewish Virtual Library*. http://www.jewishvirtuallibrary.org/jsource/judaica/ejud_0002_0017_0_16693.html.

Radhakrishnan, Sarvepalli. *Eastern Philosophy and Western Thought*. London, Oxford, and New York: Oxford University Press, 1969.

———. *The Ethics of the Vedanta and its Metaphysical Presuppositions*. Madras: The Guardian Press, 1908.

Rahner, Karl. *The Trinity*. Translated by Joseph Donceel. New York: Bloomsbury, 2001. Reprint edition.

Rand, Ayn. *The Virtue of Selfishness: A New Concept of Egoism*. New York: Signet, 1961.

Rawls, John. *A Theory of Justice*. Cambridge, MA: Belknap Press of Harvard University Press, 1999.

Reale, Giovanni. *A History of Ancient Philosophy, Vol. 4: The Schools of the Imperial Age*. Translated and edited by John R. Catan. Albany: State University of New York Press, 1990.

Ricoeur, Paul. *Fallible Man*. Translated by Charles A. Kelbley. Introduction by Walter J. Lowe. New York: Fordham University Press, 1986.

———. *Figuring the Sacred: Religion, Narrative, and Imagination*. Translated by David Pellauer. Edited by Mark I. Wallace. Minneapolis, MN: Fortress, 1995.

———. *Interpretation Theory: Discourse and the Surplus of Meaning*. Fort Worth: Texas Christian University Press, 1976.

———. *The Symbolism of Evil*. Translated by Emerson Buchanan. Boston, MA: Beacon, 1967.

———. *Time and Narrative*. Translated by Kathleen McLaughlin and David Pellauer. Chicago, IL and London: University of Chicago Press, 1990.

Ritter, Gerhard. *Frederick the Great*. Translated by Peter Paret. Berkeley, Los Angeles, and London: University of California Press, 1968.

Robinson, James M., ed. *The Nag Hammadi Library*. San Francisco, CA: HarperCollins, 1990.

Rostowski, Jacek. "The Inter-enterprise Debt Explosion in the Former Soviet Union: Causes, Consequences, Cures." *Communist Economics and Economic Transformation* Vol. 5, no. 2 (1993): 131–59.

Rousseau, Jean-Jacques. *The Social Contract, and Emile*. Translated by G. D. H. Cole and Barbara Foxley. E-artnow, 2018. Kindle edition.

Ryle, Gilbert. *The Concept of Mind*. London: Routledge, 2009.

Russell, Bertrand. *Mysticism and Logic and Other Essays*. London: Longman, 1919.

Sailhamer, John H[erbert]. *Genesis*. 2 vols. Grand Rapids, MI: Zondervan, 1990.

Sartre, Jean-Paul. *Being and Nothingness*. Translated by Hazel E. Barnes. New York: Philosophical Library, 1956.

Sauter, Gerhard, and John Barton, editors. *Revelations and Stories: Narrative Theology and the Centrality of Story*. Abingdon: Routledge, 2000.

Sax, William Sturman, ed. *The Gods at Play: Līlā in South Asia*. Oxford: Oxford University Press, 1995.

Schelling, F[riedrich] W[ilhelm] J[oseph] von. *Ideas for a Philosophy of Nature*. Translated by Errol Harris and Peter Heath. Cambridge: Cambridge University Press, 1988. Reprint edition, 1995.

———. *Philosophical Inquiries into the Nature of Human Freedom*. Translated by J. Gutmann. Chicago, IL: Open Court Publishing, 1977.

———. *Philosophy of Art: An Oration on the Relation between the Plastic Arts and Nature*. Translated by A. Johnson. London: John Chapman, 1845.

Schiller, J[ohann] C[hristoph] Friedrich. "Letters on the Aesthetic Education of Man." Translated by Elizabeth M. Wilkinson and L. A. Willoughby. In *Essays*. Edited by Walter Hinderer and Daniel O. Dahlstrom. New York: Continuum, 2001.

———. *On Grace and Dignity*. Translated by George Gregory. New York: New Benjamin Franklin House, 1982. (Schiller Institute)

Schlegel, Friedrich. "Critical Fragment, Number 89." In *Philosophical Fragments*. Translated by Peter Firchow. Minneapolis: University of Minnesota Press, 1991.

———. *Literary Notebooks*. London: Athlone, 1957.

Scholem, Gershom. *On the Kabbalah and Its Symbolism*. Translated by Ralph Manheim. New York: Schocken Books, 1960.

Schopenhauer, Arthur. *The Essential Schopenhauer: Key Selections from The World as Will and Representation and Other Works*. Edited by Wolfgang Schirmacher. HarperCollins e-book. Kindle edition.

———. *Parerga and Paralipomena*. 2 vols. Translated by Christopher Janaway. Cambridge: Cambridge University Press, 2015.

Schweitzer, Albert. *Indian Thought and Its Development*. Translated by Charles E. B. Russell. Redditch, Worcestershire: Read Books. Kindle edition.

Scotus, John Duns. *Philosophical Writings*. Translated by Allan Wolter. Indianapolis, IN and Cambridge, MA: Hackett Publishing, 1987.

Searle, John. "Minds, Brains, and Programs." In *Philosophy of Mind: Contemporary Readings*. Edited by Timothy O'Connor and David Robb. London: Routledge, Taylor & Francis Group, 2003.

Sedley, David. "The Protagonists." In *Doubt and Dogmatism: Studies in Hellenistic Epistemology*. Edited by Malcolm Schofield, Myles Burnyeat, and Jonathan Barnes. Oxford: Oxford University, 1980.

Seymour-Smith, Martin. *The 100 Most Influential Books Ever Written: The History of Thought from Ancient Times to Today*. Secaucus, NJ: Citadel Press/Carol Publishing, 1998.

Shank, J. B. *The Newton Wars and the Beginning of the French Enlightenment*. Chicago, IL: University of Chicago Press, 2008.

Shoham, Shlomo Giora. *The Measure of All Things: Anthropology*. Newcastle upon Tyne: Cambridge Scholars Publishing, 2013.

Silva, Moisés. *Philippians*. Grand Rapids, MI: Baker Book House, 1992.

Simplicius. *On Aristotle's Physics 5*. Translated by J. O. Urmson. Ithaca, NY: Cornell University Press, 1997.

Sire, James. *The Universe Next Door*. Downers Grove, IL: IVP Academic, 2009.

Skinner, Quentin. *The Return of Grand Theory in the Human Sciences*. Cambridge: Cambridge University Press, 1990.

Smith, James K. A. *Who's Afraid of Postmodernism?: Taking Derrida, Lyotard, and Foucault to Church*. Grand Rapids, MI: Baker Academic, 2006.

Sneed, Mark R., ed. "Introduction." In *Was There a Wisdom Tradition? New Prospects in Israelite Wisdom Studies*. Atlanta, GA: SBL Press, 2015.

Solomon, Robert. *Dark Feelings, Grim Thoughts: Experience and Reflection in Camus and Sartre*. Oxford: Oxford University Press, 2006.

Speight, Allen. S. v. "Friedrich Schlegel." In *The Stanford Encyclopedia of Philosophy*. Winter 2015 edition. Edited by Edward N. Zalta. http://plato.stanford.edu/archives/win2015/entries/schlegel/.

Spencer, Herbert. *Principles of Sociology*. 3 vols. New York: D. Appleton, 1898.

Spinoza, Baruch. *The Ethics*. Translated by R. H. M. Elwes. B & R Samizdat Express, 2014.

———. *Theological-Political Treatise*. Translated by Samuel Shirley. Indianapolis, IN and Cambridge MA: Hackett Publishing, 2001. Second edition.

St. John of the Cross. *The Dark Night of the Soul*. Translated and edited by E. Allison Peers. Los Angeles: Image Books, 1959.

Stiver, Dan. *The Philosophy of Religious Language: Sign, Symbol, and Story*. Oxford: Blackwell, 1996.

Stoyanov, Yuri. *The Other God: Dualist Religions from Antiquity to the Cathar Heresy*. New Haven, CT: Yale University Press, 2000.

Stroup, George W. *The Promise of Narrative Theology*. Eugene, OR: Wipf & Stock, 1997.

Swinburne, Richard. *The Coherence of Theism*. Oxford: Oxford University Press, 1993.

———. *The Existence of God*. Oxford: Clarendon, 2004.

———. "The Soul." In *Philosophy of Mind: Contemporary Readings*. Edited by Timothy O'Connor and David Robb. London: Routledge, Taylor & Francis Group, 2003.

Tallon, Philip. *The Poetics of Evil: Toward an Aesthetic Theodicy*. Oxford & New York: Oxford University Press, 2012.

Targum Neofiti 1: Genesis. Translated by Martin McNamara. Collegeville, MN: Liturgical Press, 1994.

Targum Pseudo-Jonathan: Genesis. Translated by Michael Maher. Collegeville, MN: Liturgical Press, 1992.

Taylor, Mark C. *Erring: A Postmodern A/theology*. Chicago, IL and London: University of Chicago Press, 1984.

Tilley, Terrence W. *Talking of God: An Introduction to Philosophical Analysis of Religious Language*. New York: Paulist Press, 1978.

Tillich, Paul. *The Interpretation of History*. Translated by N. A. Rasetzki and Elsa L. Talmey. New York: Charles Scribner's Sons, 1936.

———. *Systematic Theology*. 3 vols. Chicago, IL: University of Chicago Press, 1973.

Torrance, T[homas] F[orsyth]. *Incarnation: The Person and Life of Christ*. Downers Grove, IL: InterVarsity, 2008.

———. *Space, Time and Incarnation*. Edinburgh: T & T Clark, 1997.

Townsend, Dabney. "From Shaftesbury to Kant: The Development of the Concept of Aesthetic Experience." *Journal of the History of Ideas 48*, no. 2 (April–June 1987): 287–305.

Tracy, David. *Blessed Rage for Order: The New Pluralism in Theology*. New York: Seabury Press, 1975.

Trueblood, Elton. *The Predicament of Modern Man*. New York and London: Harper & Brothers, 1944.

Tuggy, Dale. *What Is the Trinity: Thinking about the Father, Son, and Holy Spirit*. N.p., 2017.

Varghese, Roy Abraham. *The Wonder of the World: A Journey from Modern Science to the Mind of God*. Fountain Hills, AZ: Tyr Publishing, 2003.

Vaught, Ashley Underwood. "The Specter of Spinoza in Schelling's '*Freiheitscrift*.'" PhD diss., Villanova University, 2008. ProQuest.

Wahba, Mahmoud A., and Lawrence G. Bridwell. "Maslow Reconsidered: A Review of Research on the Need Hierarchy Theory." *Organizational Behavior and Human Performance 15*, no. 2 (1976): 212–40.

Wainwright, Arthur W. *The Trinity in the New Testament*. Eugene, OR: Wipf & Stock, 2001.

Walls, Jerry L. *Heaven, Hell, and Purgatory: Rethinking the Things That Matter Most*. Grand Rapids, MI: Brazos Press, 2015.

Ward, Keith. *God, Chance and Necessity*. Oxford: One World, 1996.

Warren, J. Benedict. S.v "Quiroga, Vasco de." *Encyclopedia of Mexico: History, Society, and Culture, Vol. 2*. Edited by Michael S. Werner. Chicago, IL: Fitzroy Dearborn, 1997.

Watt, Alan Norman. "Nietzsche and Rhetoric." PhD diss., University of Warwick, 1992. http://wrap.warwick.ac.uk/4327/1/WRAP_THESIS_Watt_1992.pdf.

Whitehead, Alfred North. *The Adventure of Ideas*. New York: Simon & Schuster, 1967.

Whitfield, Charles L. *Co-Dependence: Healing the Human Condition*. Deerfield Beach, FL: Health Communications, Inc., 1991.

Willard, Dallas. *The Disappearance of Moral Knowledge*. Edited and completed by Steven Porter, Aaron Preston, and Gregg A. Tens Elshof. New York: Routledge, 2018.

Williams, Norman Powell. *Ideas of the Fall and Original Sin: A Historical and Critical Study*. London: Longmans, Green & Co., 1927.

Wilson, Edward O. *Consilience: The Unity of Knowledge*. New York: Vintage Books, 1999.

Wittgenstein, Ludwig. *Philosophical Investigations*. Translated by G. E. M. Anscombe. Oxford: Basil Blackwell, 1958.

———. *Tractatus Logico-Philosophicus*. Translated by C. K. Ogden. London: Kegan Paul, Trench, Trubner, 1922.

Wood, Allen W. *Hegel's Ethical Thought*. Cambridge: Cambridge University Press, 1990.

Woodfin, Yandall. *With All Your Mind: A Christian Philosophy*. Nashville, TN: Abingdon, 1980.

Wrede, William. *Das Messiasgeheimnis in den Evangelien*. Göttingen, 1901. Published in English as *The Messianic Secret*. Translated by J. C. G. Greig. London: Clarke, 1971.

Wright, N[icholas] T[homas]. *Surprised by Hope: Rethinking Heaven, the Resurrection, and the Mission of the Church.* New York: HarperOne, 2008.

Wright, Stephen John. *Dogmatic Aesthetics: A Theology of Beauty in Dialogue with Robert W. Jenson.* Minneapolis, MN: Fortress Press, 2014.

Wyschogrod, Edith. *Saints and Postmodernism: Revisioning Moral Philosophy.* Chicago, IL: University of Chicago Press, 1990.

Young, William Paul. *The Shack.* Newbury Park, CA: Windblown Media, 2007.

Zagzebski, Linda Trinkaus. *Exemplarist Moral Theory.* Oxford: Oxford University Press, 2017.

Index

About the Author

Randall B. Bush, university professor of philosophy at Union University in Jackson, Tennessee, holds two earned doctorates: one in theology from Southwestern Baptist Theological Seminary in Fort Worth, Texas, and the other in modern theology from the University of Oxford. For twelve years, he served as director of Union's Interdisciplinary Honors Program. His Oxford doctoral thesis was published under the title, *Recent Ideas of Divine Conflict*. He also is a novelist and a children's book writer whose published creative works include a young-adult fantasy novel, *The Quest for Asdin*; four children's Christmas novels, *Gabriel's Magic Ornament*, *Widgmus World*, *The Mailbox Tree*, and *A Christmas Comedy*; and an illustrated poem, *The Caterbury Tails*. Bush is also an accomplished pianist and vocalist and presently serves as an organist at the First Baptist Church of Jackson, Tennessee.